YOU MAY BE READING THE WRONG WAY!

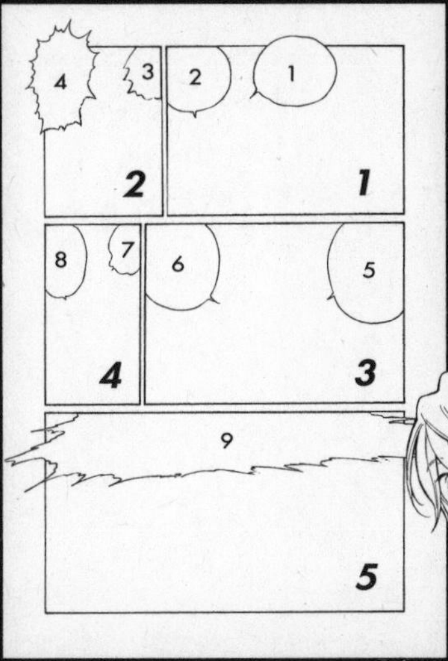
1
2
3
4
1
2
5
6
7
8
3
4
9
5

This book reads from right to left to maintain the original presentation and art of the Japanese edition, so action, sound effects and word balloons are reversed. This diagram shows how to follow the panels. Turn to the other side of the book to begin.

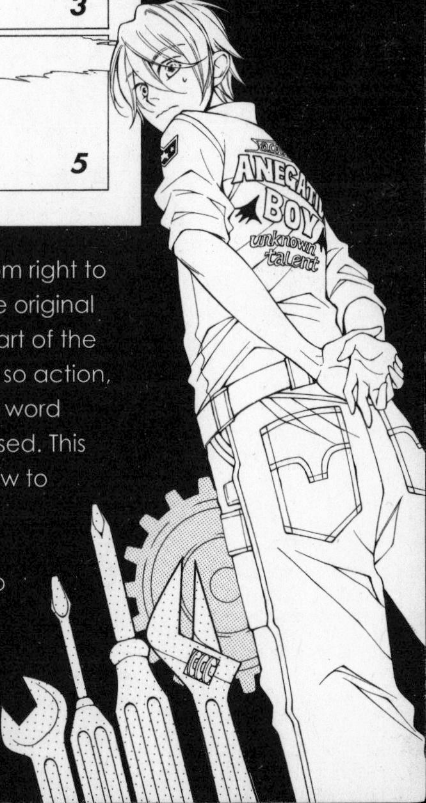
ANEGATI
BOY
unknown talent

IDOL *dreams*

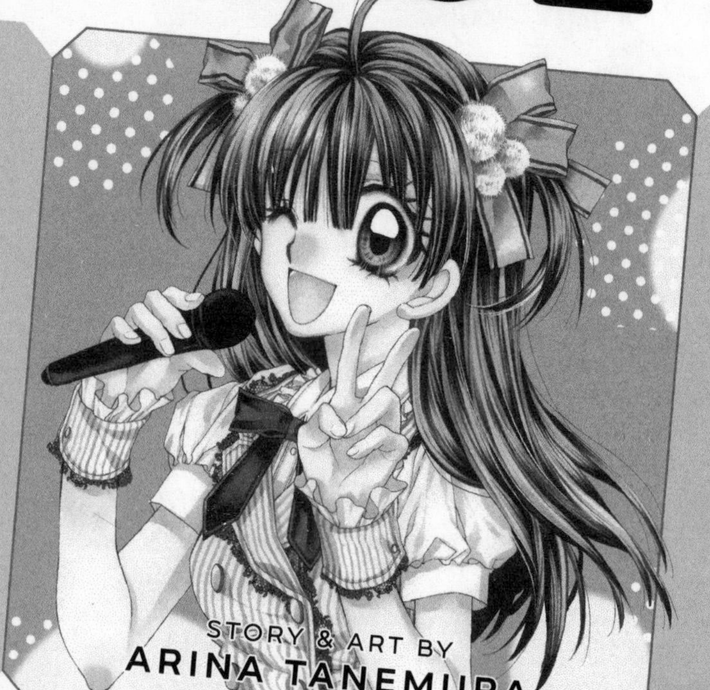

STORY & ART BY
ARINA TANEMURA

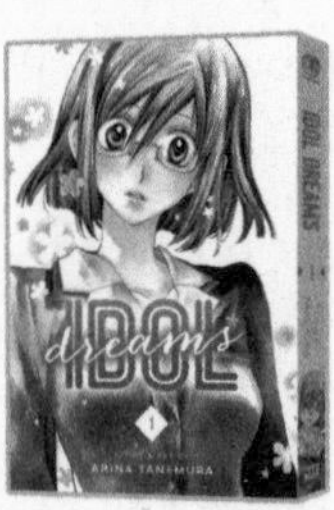
IDOL DREAMS
IDOL dreams
1
ARINA TANEMURA

At age 31, office worker Chikage Deguchi feels she missed her chances at love and success. When word gets out that she's a virgin, Chikage is humiliated and wishes she could turn back time to when she was still young and popular. She takes an experimental drug that changes her appearance back to when she was 15. Now Chikage is determined to pursue everything she missed out on all those years ago—including becoming a star!

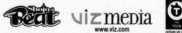

Shojo Beat VIZ media www.viz.com RATED T FOR TEEN ratings.viz.com

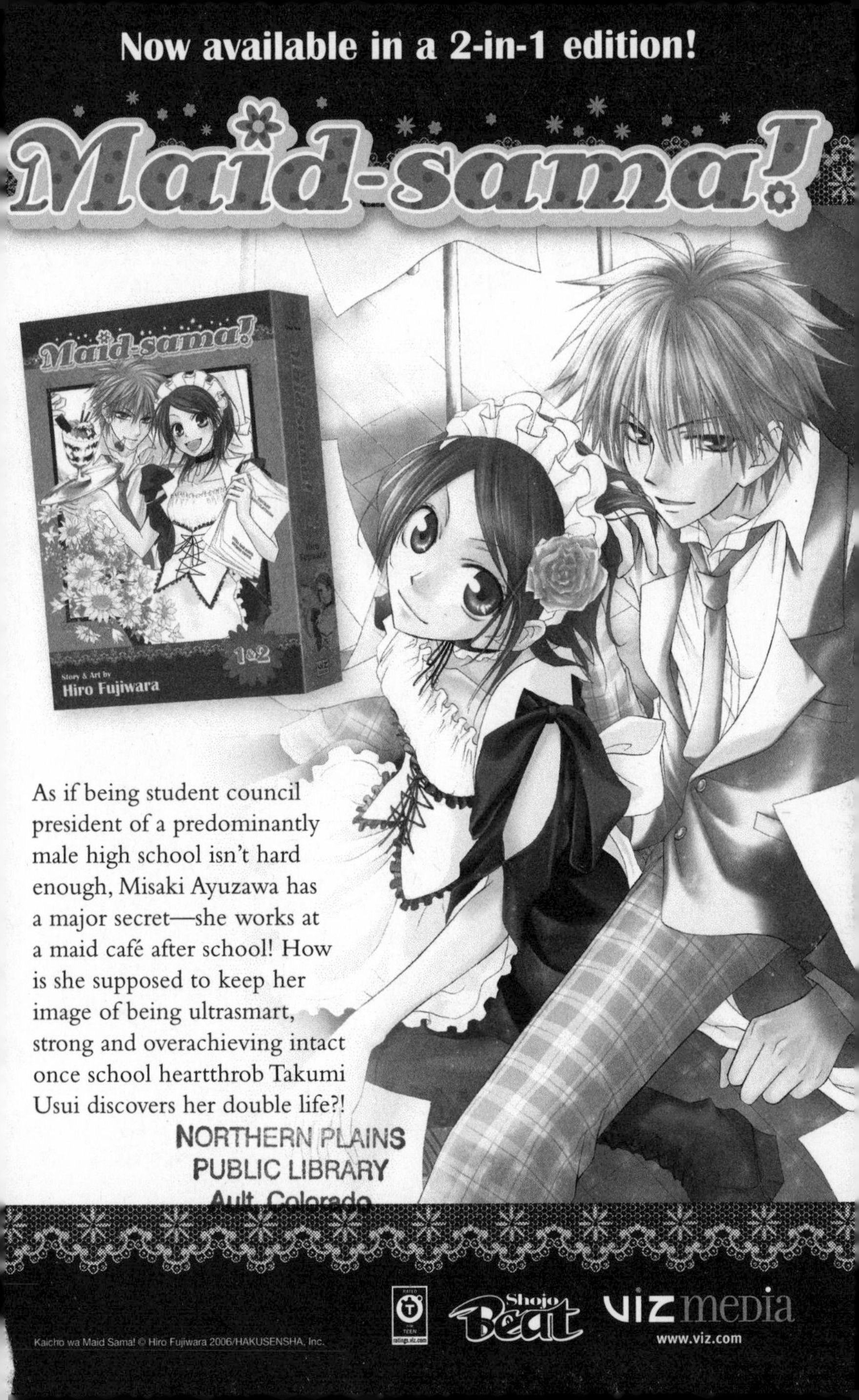
Now available in a 2-in-1 edition!
Maid-sama!
Maid-sama!
1&2
Story & Art by
Hiro Fujiwara
As if being student council president of a predominantly male high school isn't hard enough, Misaki Ayuzawa has a major secret—she works at a maid café after school! How is she supposed to keep her image of being ultrasmart, strong and overachieving intact once school heartthrob Takumi Usui discovers her double life?!
NORTHERN PLAINS
PUBLIC LIBRARY
Ault, Colorado
Shojo Beat
VIZ media
www.viz.com
Kaicho wa Maid Sama! © Hiro Fujiwara 2006/HAKUSENSHA, Inc.

Ouran High School
Host Club BOX SET

Story and Art by
Bisco Hatori

Escape to the world of the young, rich and sexy

All 18 volumes in a collector's box with an Ouran High School stationery notepad!

In this screwball romantic comedy, Haruhi, a poor girl at a rich kids' school, is forced to repay an $80,000 debt by working for the school's swankiest, all-male club—as a boy! There she discovers just how wealthy the six members are and how different the rich are from everybody else...

www.viz.com

Behind the Scenes!!

VOLUME 4

Shojo Beat Edition

STORY AND ART BY Bisco Hatori

English Translation & Adaptation/John Werry
Touch-Up Art & Lettering/Sabrina Heep
Design/ Izumi Evers
Editor/Pancha Diaz

Urakata!! by Bisco Hatori
© Bisco Hatori 2016
All rights reserved.
First published in Japan in 2016 by HAKUSENSHA, Inc., Tokyo.
English language translation rights arranged with HAKUSENSHA, Inc.,
Tokyo.

Printed in the U.S.A.

Published by VIZ Media, LLC
P.O. Box 77010
San Francisco, CA 94107

10 9 8 7 6 5 4 3 2 1
First printing, August 2017

www.viz.com

www.shojobeat.com

AUTHOR BIO

Since I'm doing *Behind the Scenes!!*, I thought I should try some DIY...so I made a caster base (just a board with casters). My work was rougher than I expected, so I'm shocked. How can this be?

-Bisco Hatori

Bisco Hatori made her manga debut with *Isshun kan no Romance* (A Moment of Romance) in *LaLa DX* magazine. The comedy *Ouran High School Host Club* was her breakout hit and was published in English by VIZ Media. Her other works include *Detarame Mousouryoku Opera* (Sloppy Vaporous Opera), *Petite Pêche!* and the vampire romance *Millennium Snow*, which was also published in English by VIZ Media.

Behind the Scenes!!

04

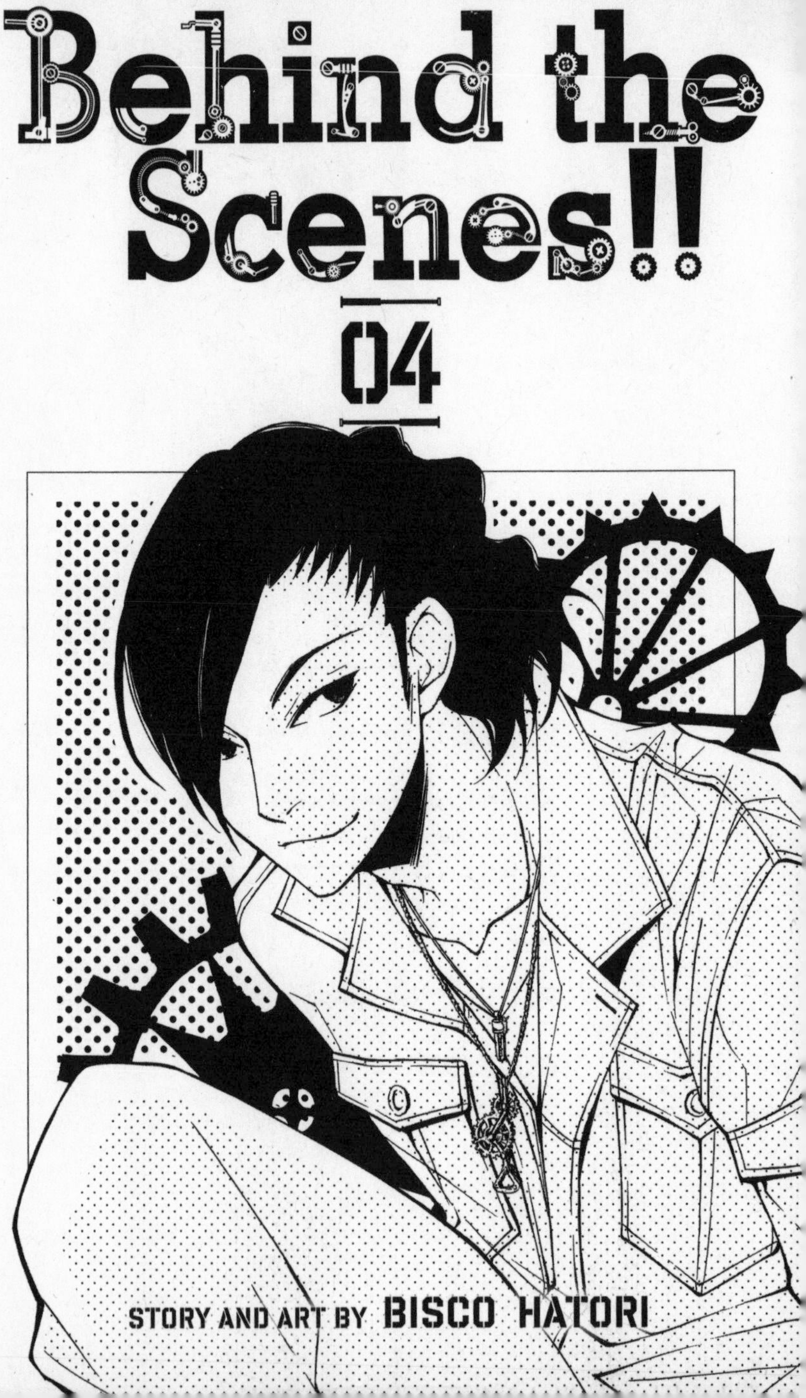

STORY AND ART BY BISCO HATORI

Behind the Scenes!!

04

CONTENTS

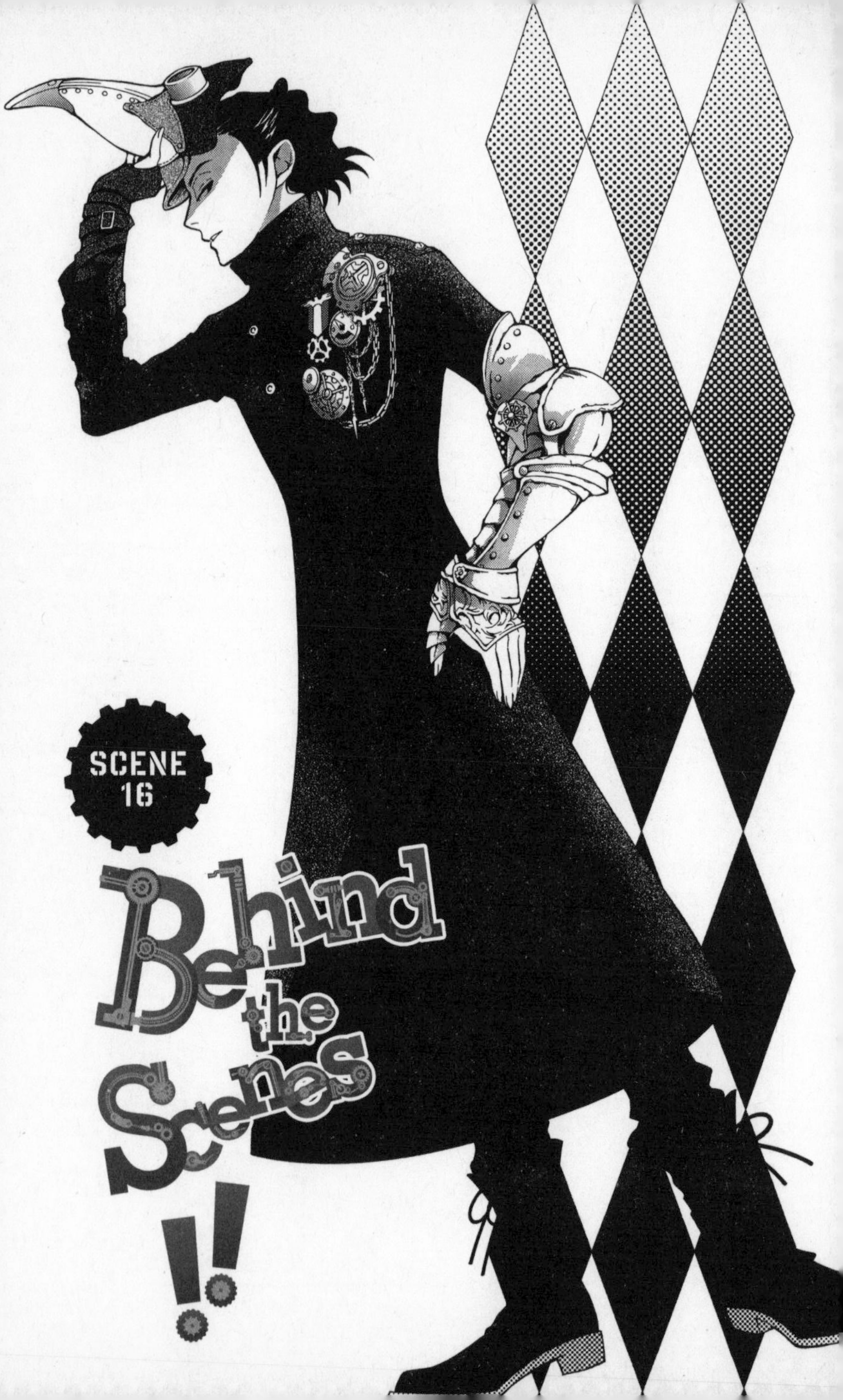
SCENE
16
Behind the Scenes!!

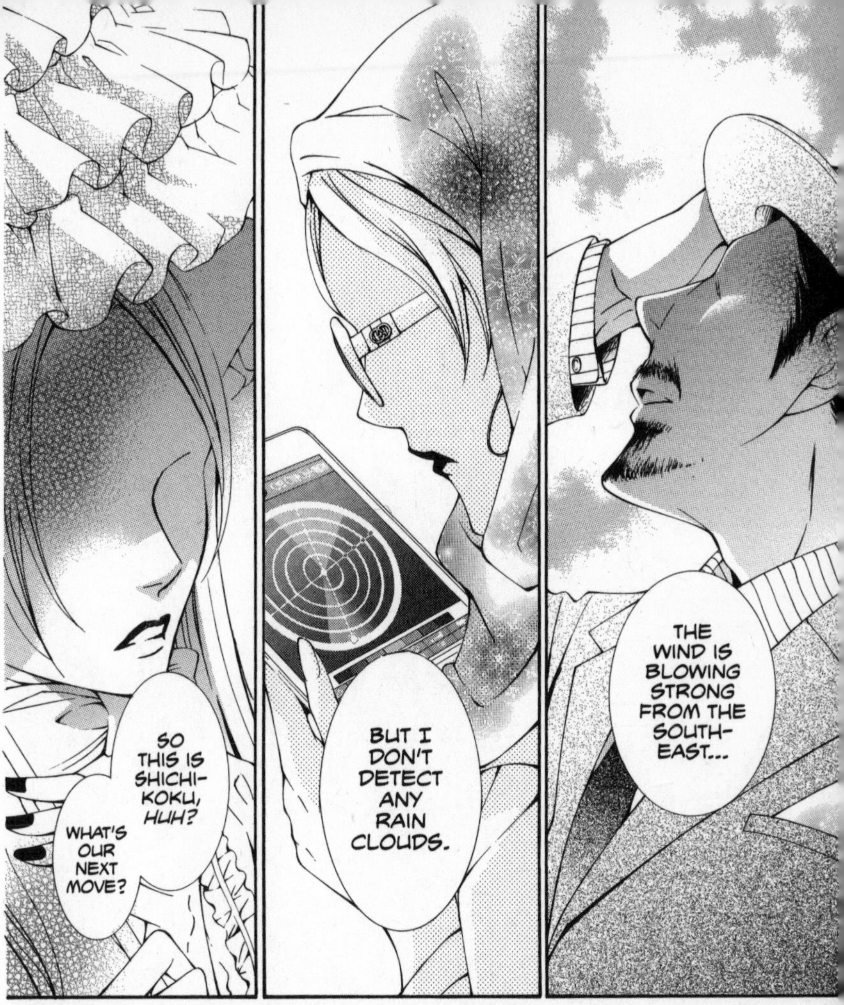
THE WIND IS BLOWING STRONG FROM THE SOUTH-EAST...
BUT I DON'T DETECT ANY RAIN CLOUDS.
SO THIS IS SHICHI-KOKU, HUH?
WHAT'S OUR NEXT MOVE?

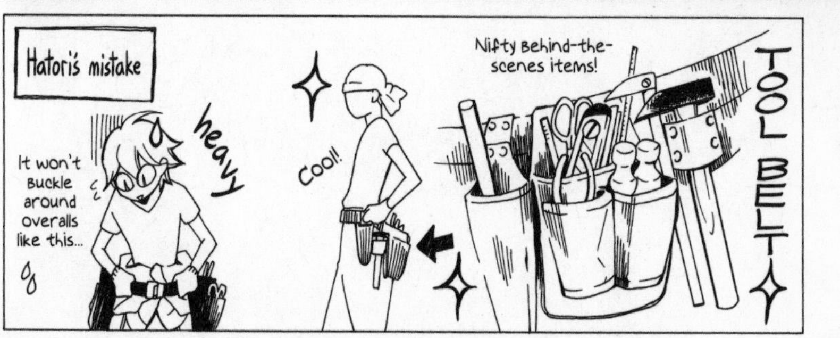
Hatori's mistake
TOOL BELT
Nifty Behind-the-scenes items!
Cool!
heavy
It won't buckle around overalls like this...

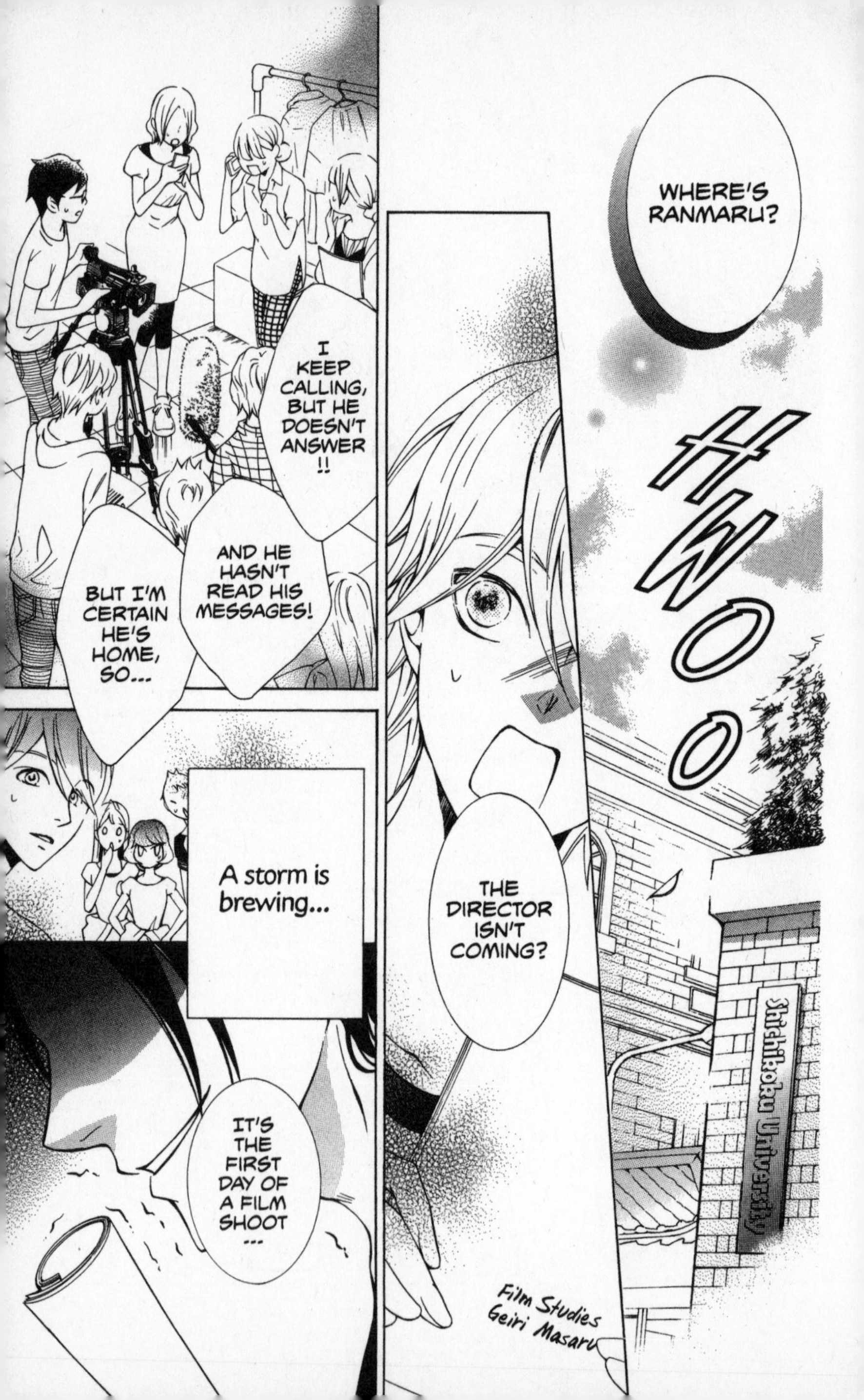
WHERE'S RANMARU?
HWOO
THE DIRECTOR ISN'T COMING?
Shichikoku University
Film Studies Geiri Masaru
I KEEP CALLING, BUT HE DOESN'T ANSWER!!
AND HE HASN'T READ HIS MESSAGES!
BUT I'M CERTAIN HE'S HOME, SO...
A storm is brewing...
IT'S THE FIRST DAY OF A FILM SHOOT...

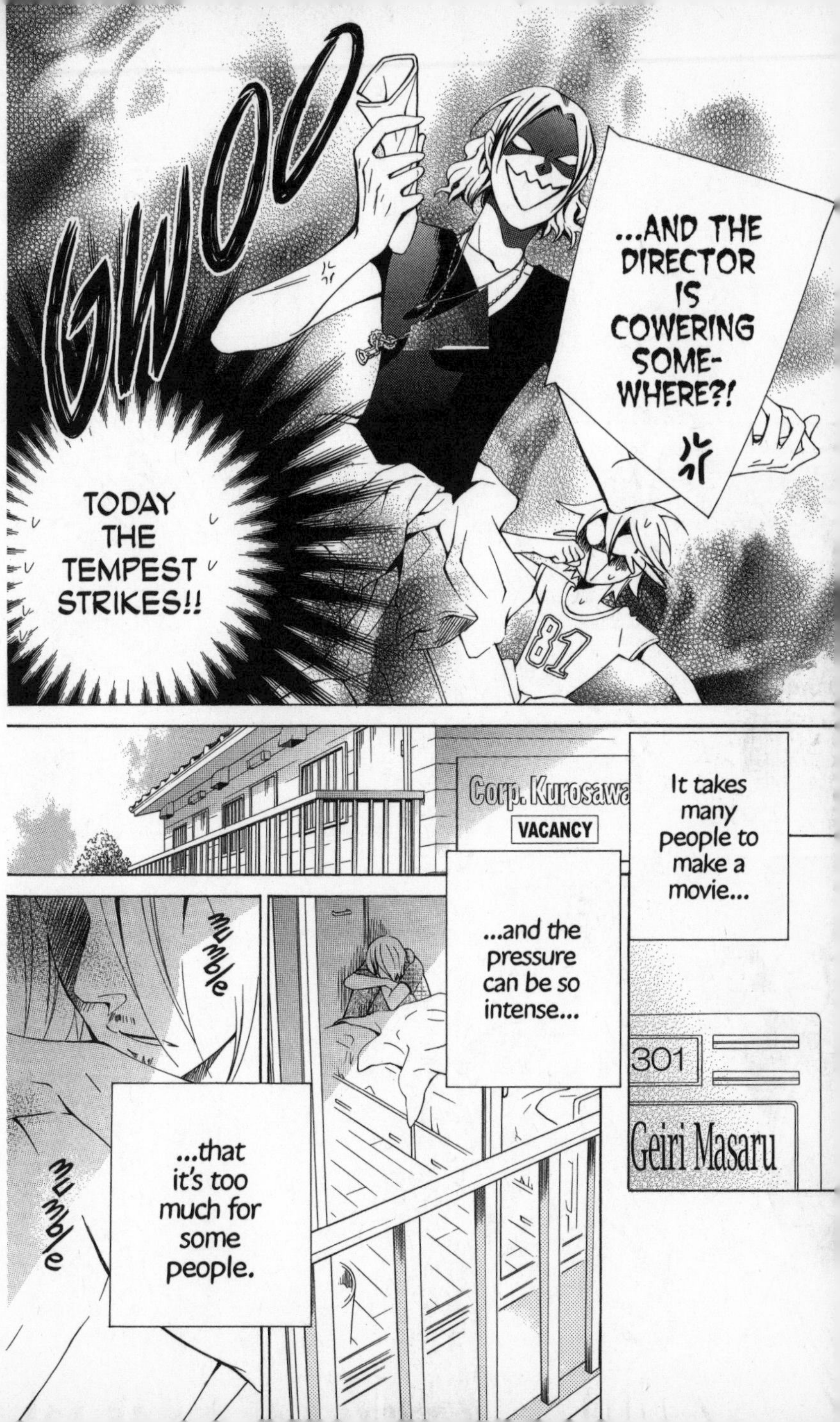
...AND THE DIRECTOR IS COWERING SOME-WHERE?!
GWOO
TODAY THE TEMPEST STRIKES!!
81
It takes many people to make a movie...
Corp. Kurosawa
VACANCY
...and the pressure can be so intense...
301
Geiri Masaru
...that it's too much for some people.
mumble
mumble

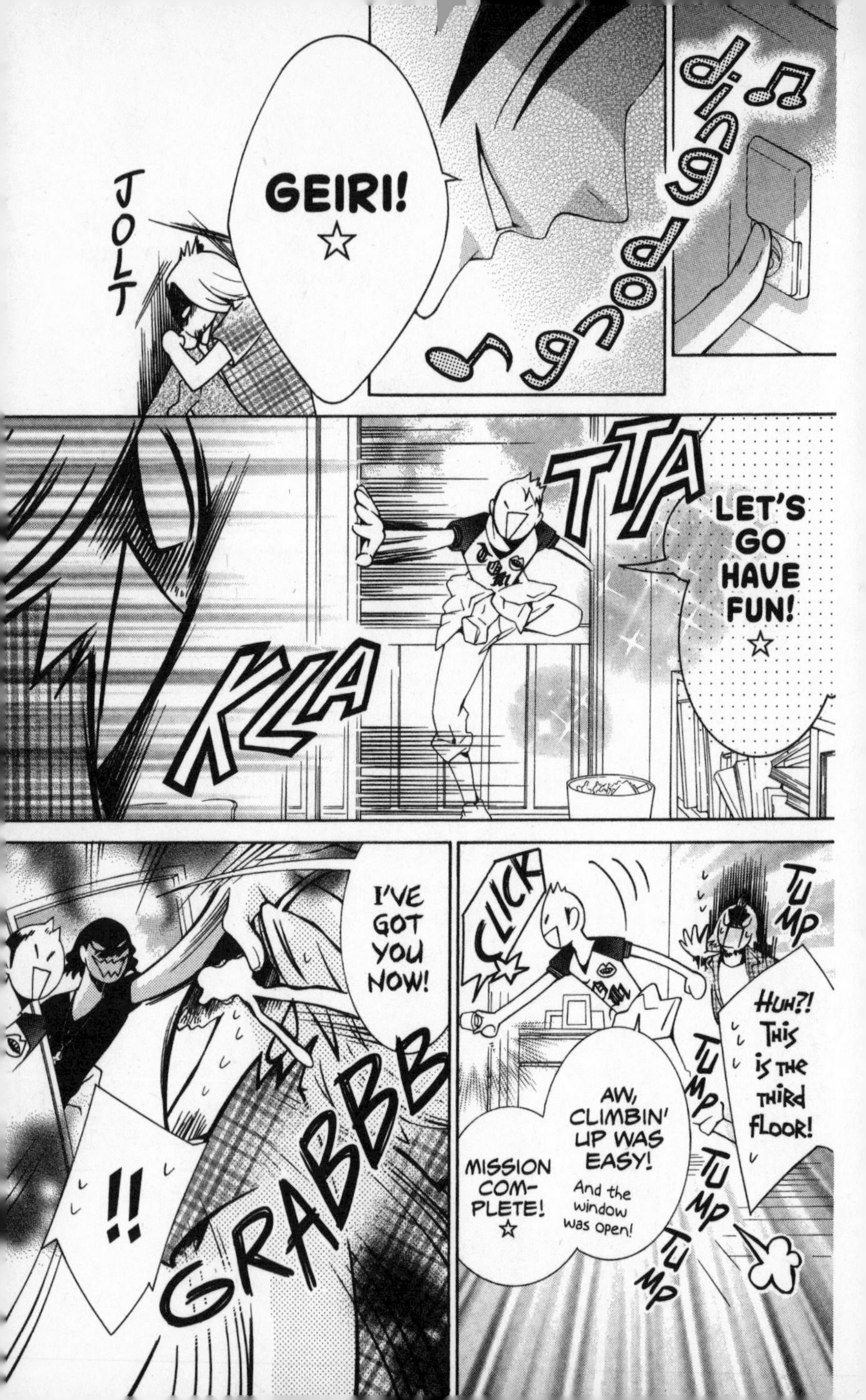

dingdong ♪♪
GEIRI! ☆
JOLT
LET'S GO HAVE FUN! ☆
TTA
KLLA
TUMP
HUH?! THIS IS THE THIRD FLOOR!
TUMP TUMP TUMP TUMP
CLICK ☆
AW, CLIMBIN' UP WAS EASY!
And the window was open!
MISSION COMPLETE! ☆
I'VE GOT YOU NOW!
GRABBB
!!

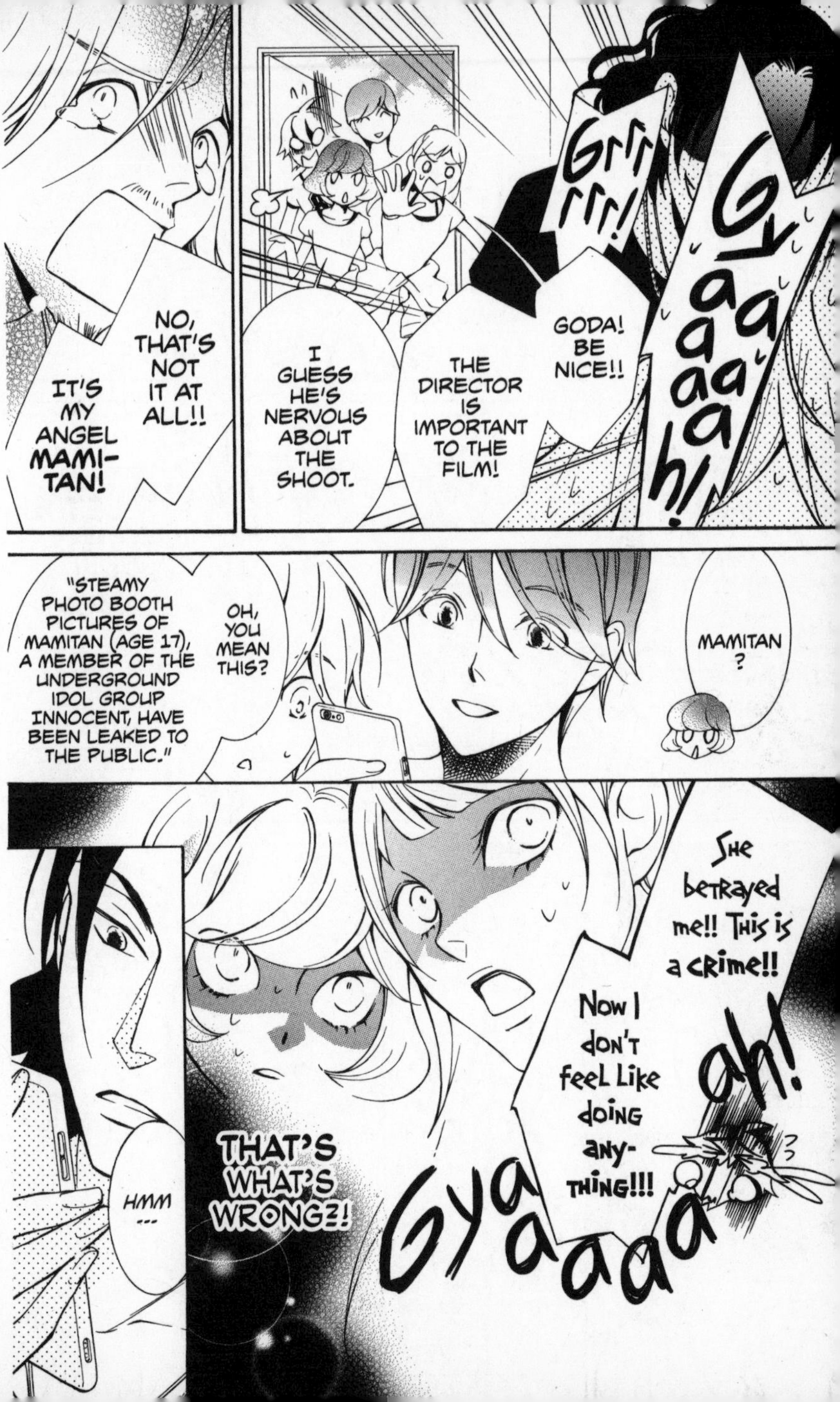
Grrr rrr!
Gyaaaaaah!!
GODA! BE NICE!!
THE DIRECTOR IS IMPORTANT TO THE FILM!
I GUESS HE'S NERVOUS ABOUT THE SHOOT.
NO, THAT'S NOT IT AT ALL!!
IT'S MY ANGEL MAMI-TAN!
MAMITAN?
OH, YOU MEAN THIS?
"STEAMY PHOTO BOOTH PICTURES OF MAMITAN (AGE 17), A MEMBER OF THE UNDERGROUND IDOL GROUP INNOCENT, HAVE BEEN LEAKED TO THE PUBLIC."
She betrayed me!! This is a crime!!
Now I don't feel like doing any-thing!!!
Gyaaaaaah!
THAT'S WHAT'S WRONG?!
HMM...

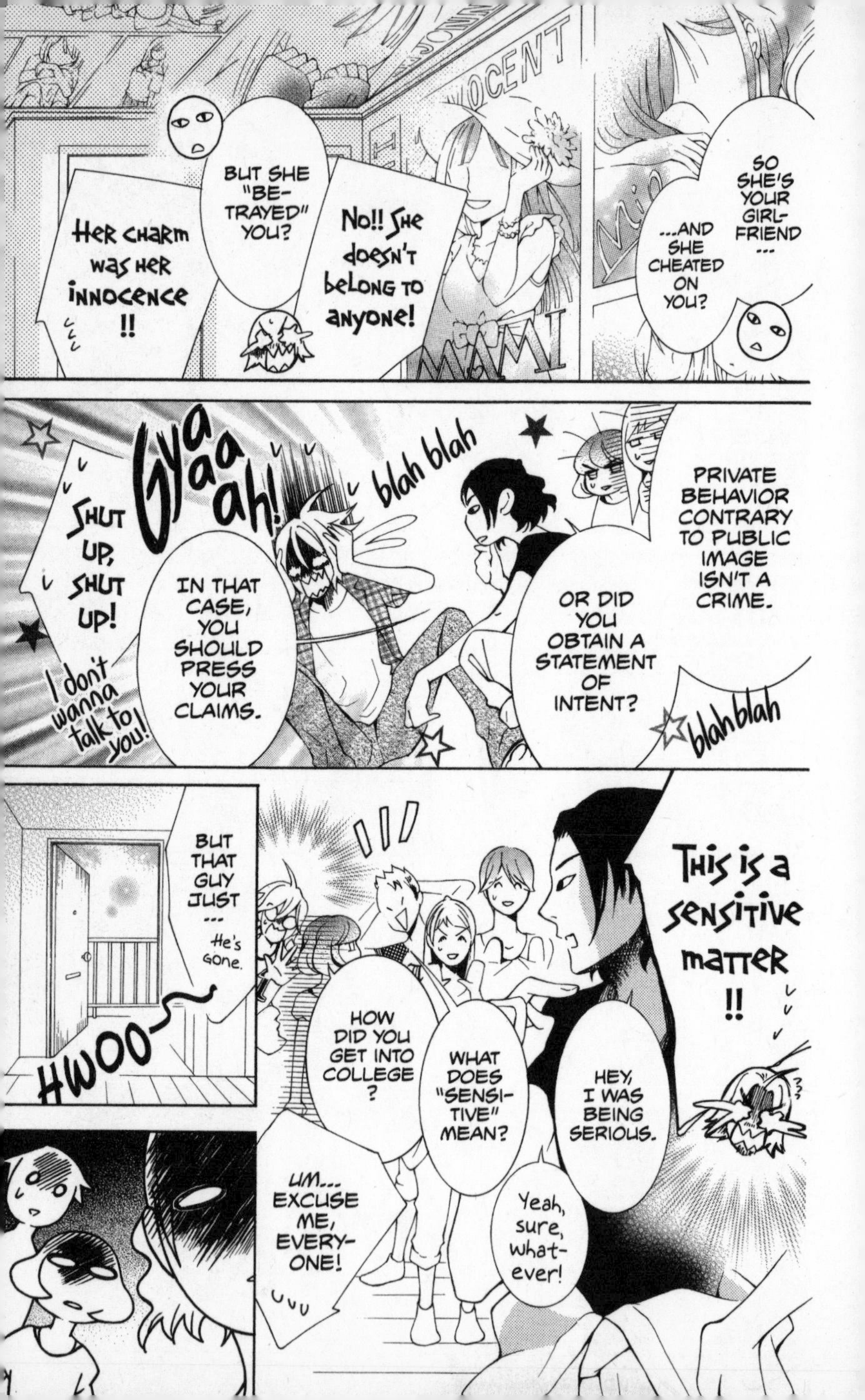
SO SHE'S YOUR GIRL-FRIEND...
...AND SHE CHEATED ON YOU?
No!! She doesn't belong to anyone!
BUT SHE "BE-TRAYED" YOU?
Her charm was her innocence!!
PRIVATE BEHAVIOR CONTRARY TO PUBLIC IMAGE ISN'T A CRIME.
blah blah
OR DID YOU OBTAIN A STATEMENT OF INTENT?
blah blah
Gyaaah!
IN THAT CASE, YOU SHOULD PRESS YOUR CLAIMS.
SHUT UP, SHUT UP!
I don't wanna talk to you!
This is a sensitive matter!!
HEY, I WAS BEING SERIOUS.
Yeah, sure, what-ever!
WHAT DOES "SENSI-TIVE" MEAN?
HOW DID YOU GET INTO COLLEGE?
BUT THAT GUY JUST...
He's gone.
HWOO~
UM... EXCUSE ME, EVERY-ONE!

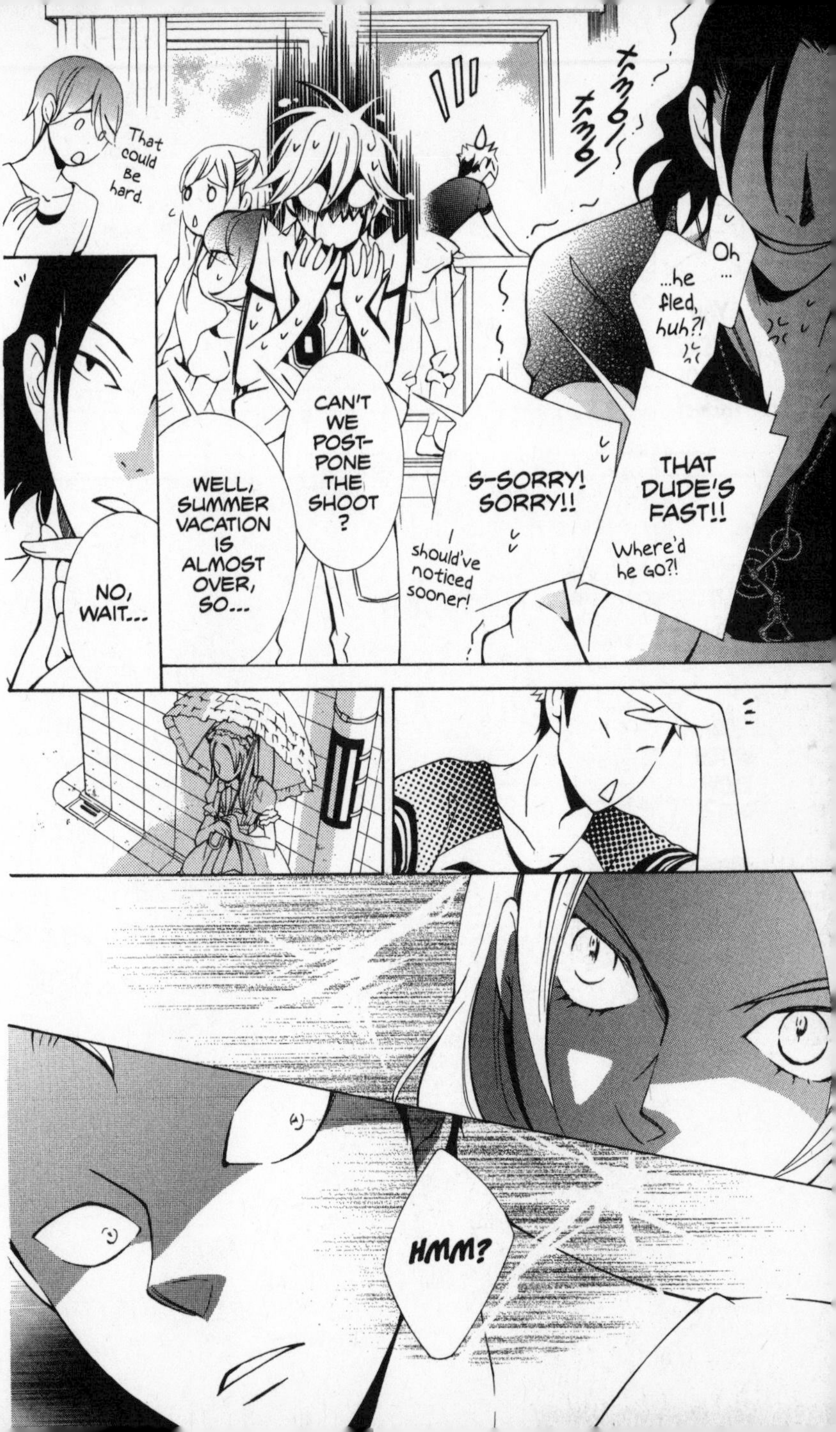
Oh ... ...he fled, huh?!
THAT DUDE'S FAST!!
Where'd he GO?!
S-SORRY! SORRY!!
I should've noticed sooner!
CAN'T WE POST-PONE THE SHOOT?
That could be hard.
WELL, SUMMER VACATION IS ALMOST OVER, SO...
NO, WAIT...
HMM?

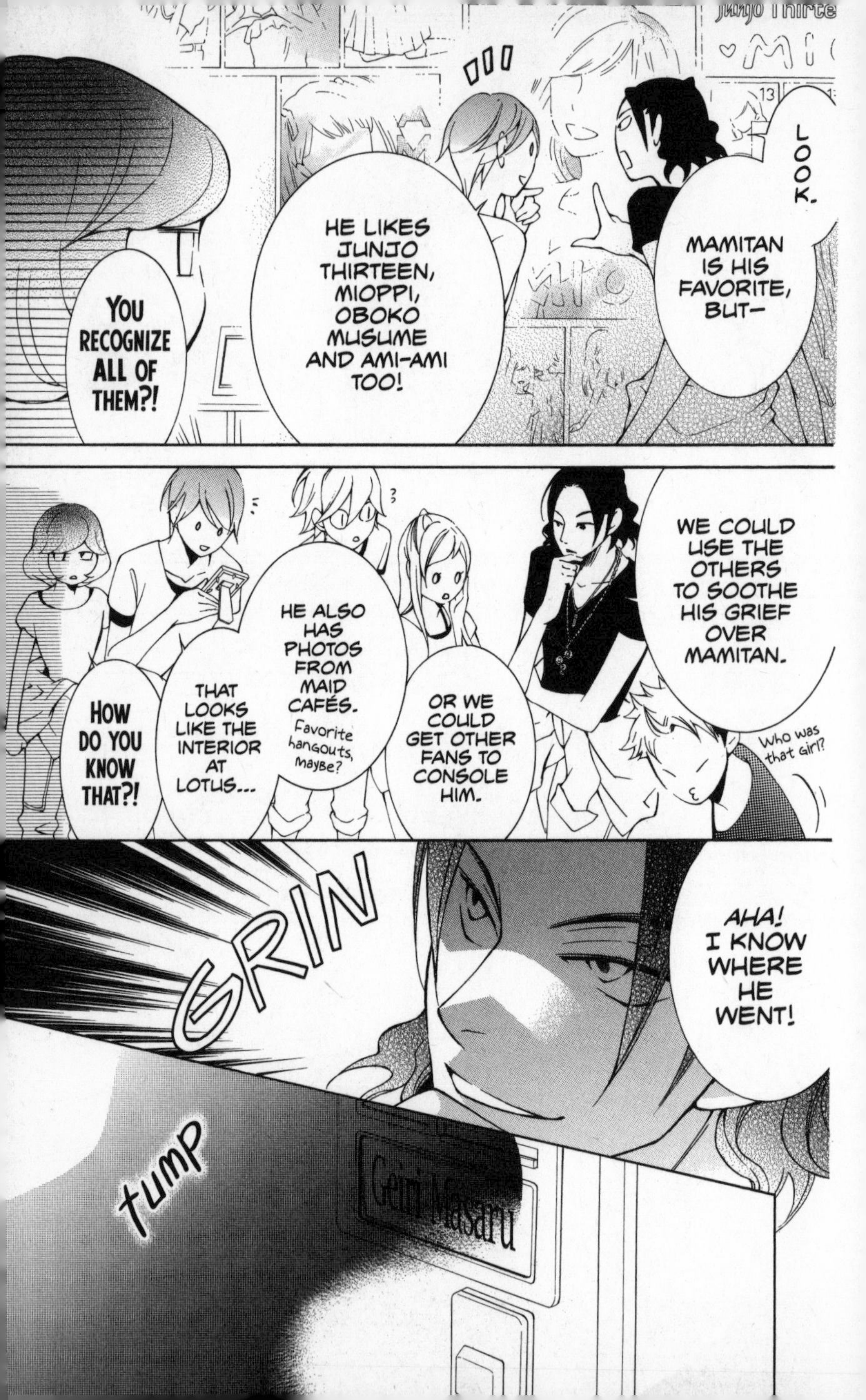
LOOK.
MAMITAN IS HIS FAVORITE, BUT—
HE LIKES JUNJO THIRTEEN, MIOPPI, OBOKO MUSUME AND AMI-AMI TOO!
YOU RECOGNIZE ALL OF THEM?!
WE COULD USE THE OTHERS TO SOOTHE HIS GRIEF OVER MAMITAN.
Who was that Girl?
OR WE COULD GET OTHER FANS TO CONSOLE HIM.
HE ALSO HAS PHOTOS FROM MAID CAFÉS.
Favorite hangouts, maybe?
THAT LOOKS LIKE THE INTERIOR AT LOTUS...
HOW DO YOU KNOW THAT?!
AHA! I KNOW WHERE HE WENT!
GRIN
Geiri Masaru
tump

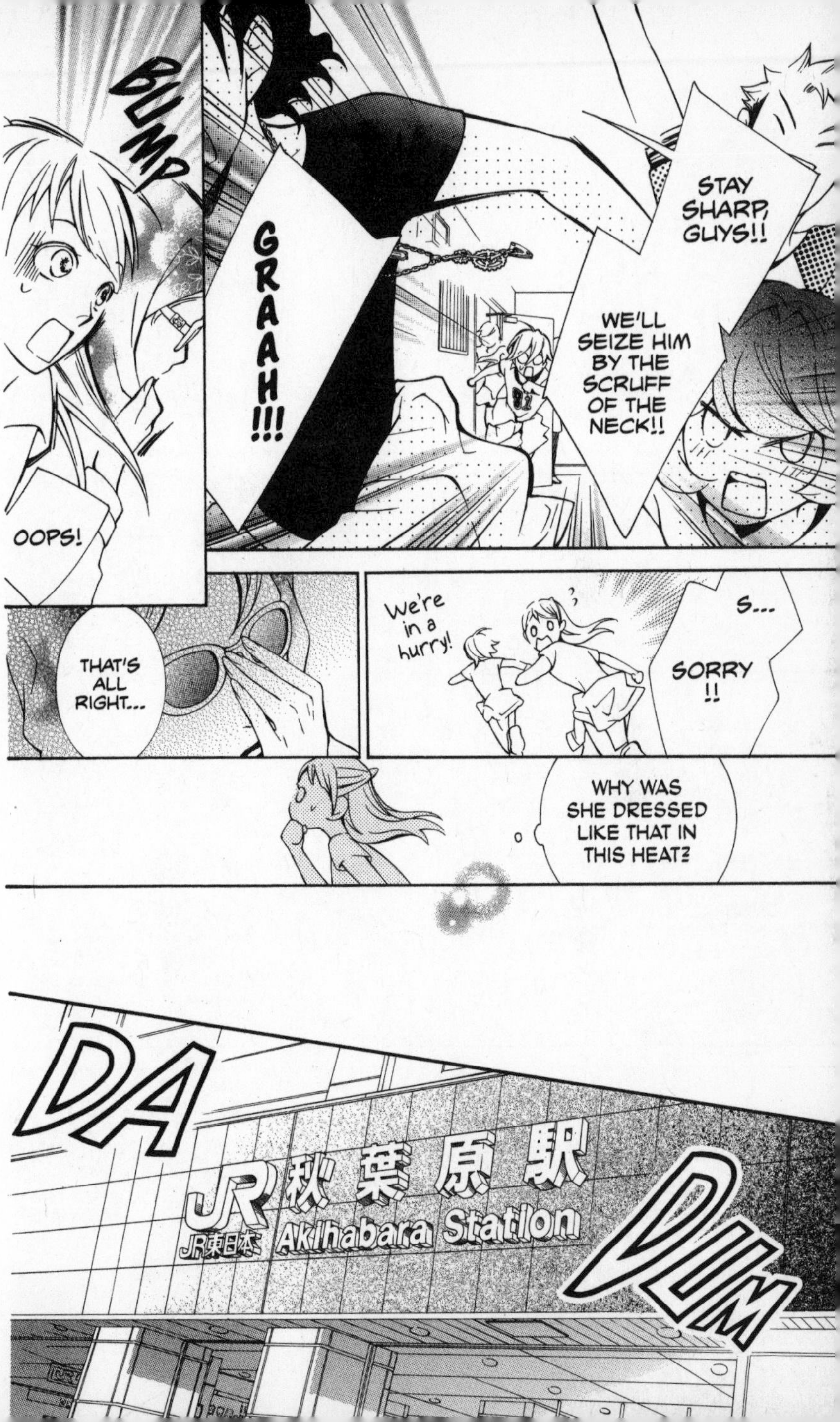
STAY SHARP, GUYS!!
WE'LL SEIZE HIM BY THE SCRUFF OF THE NECK!!
GRAAH!!!
BUMP
OOPS!
S...
SORRY!!
We're in a hurry!
THAT'S ALL RIGHT...
WHY WAS SHE DRESSED LIKE THAT IN THIS HEAT?
DA
JR 秋葉原駅
JR東日本 Akihabara Station
DUM

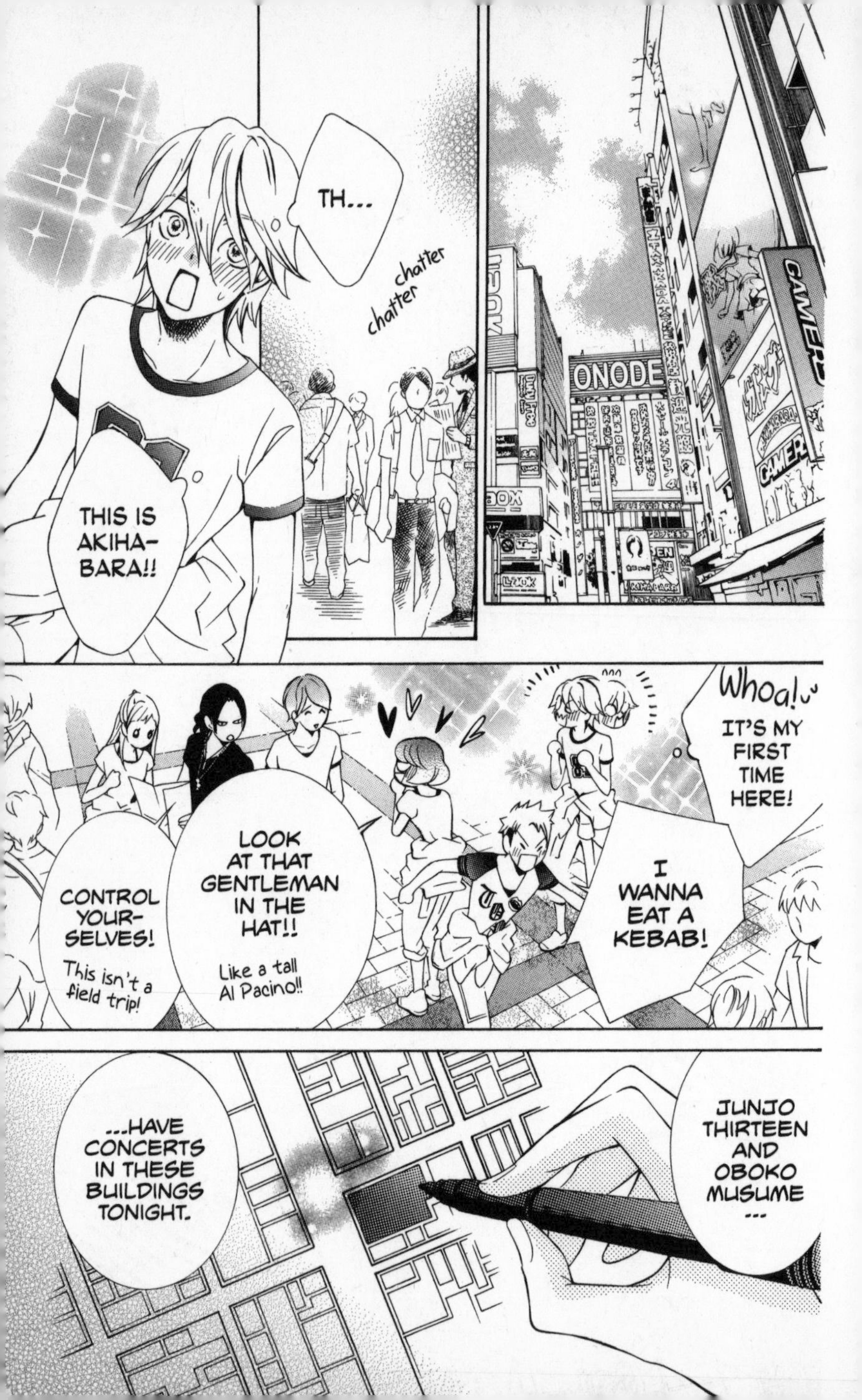
ONODE
TH...
chatter
chatter
THIS IS AKIHA-BARA!!
Whoa!
IT'S MY FIRST TIME HERE!
I WANNA EAT A KEBAB!
LOOK AT THAT GENTLEMAN IN THE HAT!!
Like a tall Al Pacino!!
CONTROL YOUR-SELVES!
This isn't a field trip!
JUNJO THIRTEEN AND OBOKO MUSUME ...
...HAVE CONCERTS IN THESE BUILDINGS TONIGHT.

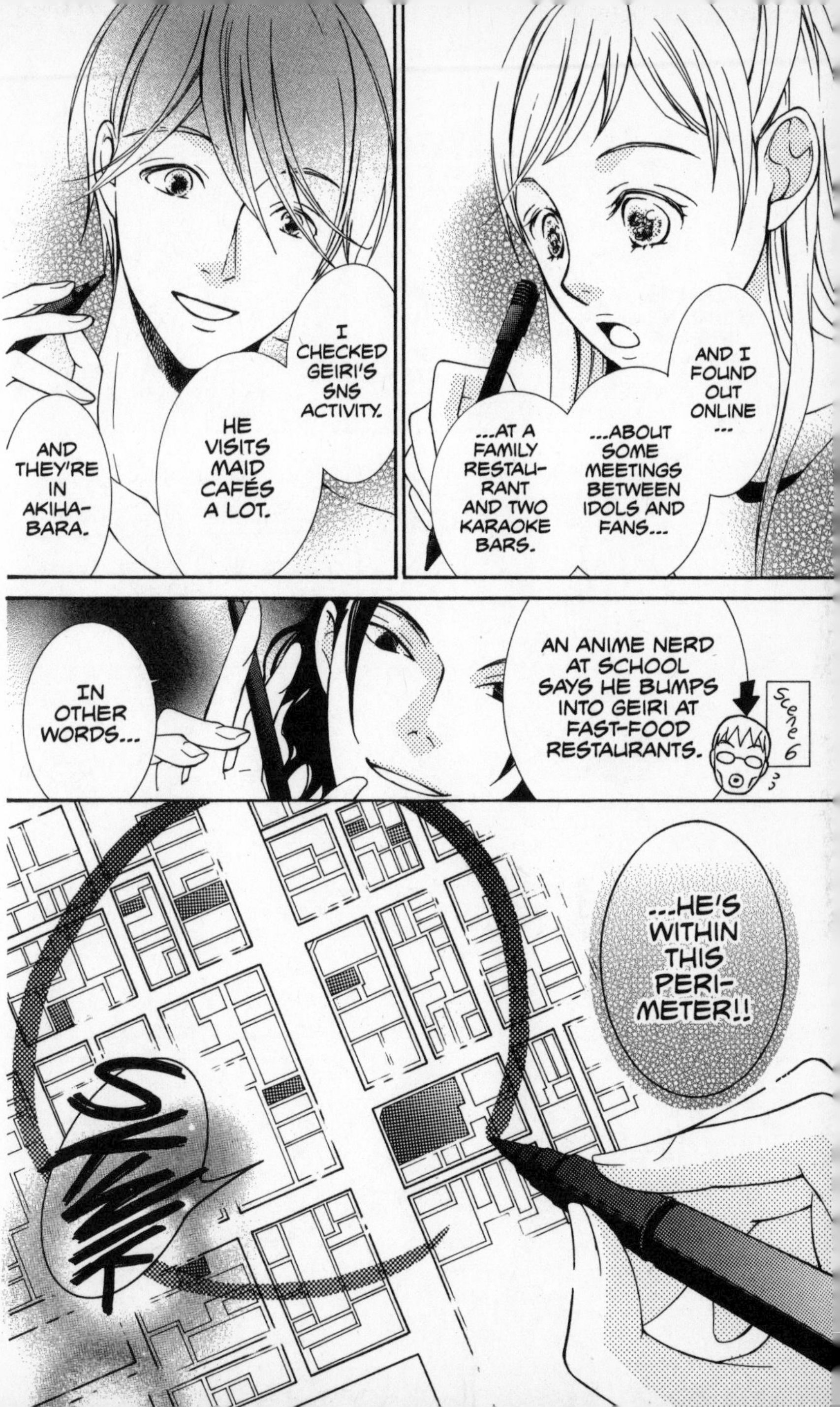
AND I FOUND OUT ONLINE...
...ABOUT SOME MEETINGS BETWEEN IDOLS AND FANS...
...AT A FAMILY RESTAURANT AND TWO KARAOKE BARS.
I CHECKED GEIRI'S SNS ACTIVITY.
HE VISITS MAID CAFÉS A LOT.
AND THEY'RE IN AKIHABARA.
AN ANIME NERD AT SCHOOL SAYS HE BUMPS INTO GEIRI AT FAST-FOOD RESTAURANTS.
Scene 6
IN OTHER WORDS...
...HE'S WITHIN THIS PERIMETER!!
SKWIK

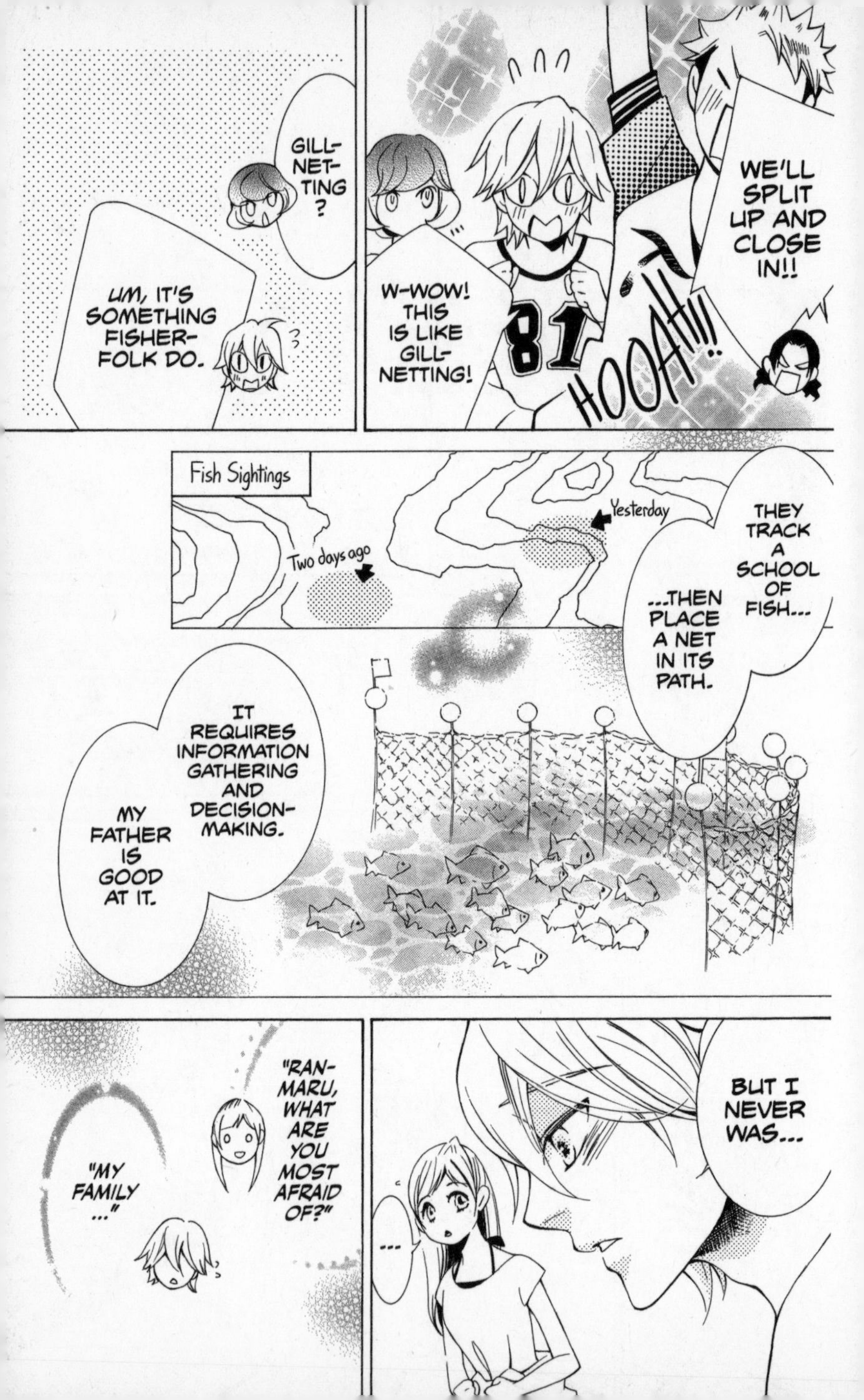
WE'LL SPLIT UP AND CLOSE IN!!
HOOAH!!!
W-WOW! THIS IS LIKE GILL-NETTING!
GILL-NETTING?
UM, IT'S SOMETHING FISHER-FOLK DO.
Fish Sightings
Yesterday
Two days ago
THEY TRACK A SCHOOL OF FISH...
...THEN PLACE A NET IN ITS PATH.
IT REQUIRES INFORMATION GATHERING AND DECISION-MAKING.
MY FATHER IS GOOD AT IT.
BUT I NEVER WAS...
...
"RANMARU, WHAT ARE YOU MOST AFRAID OF?"
"MY FAMILY..."

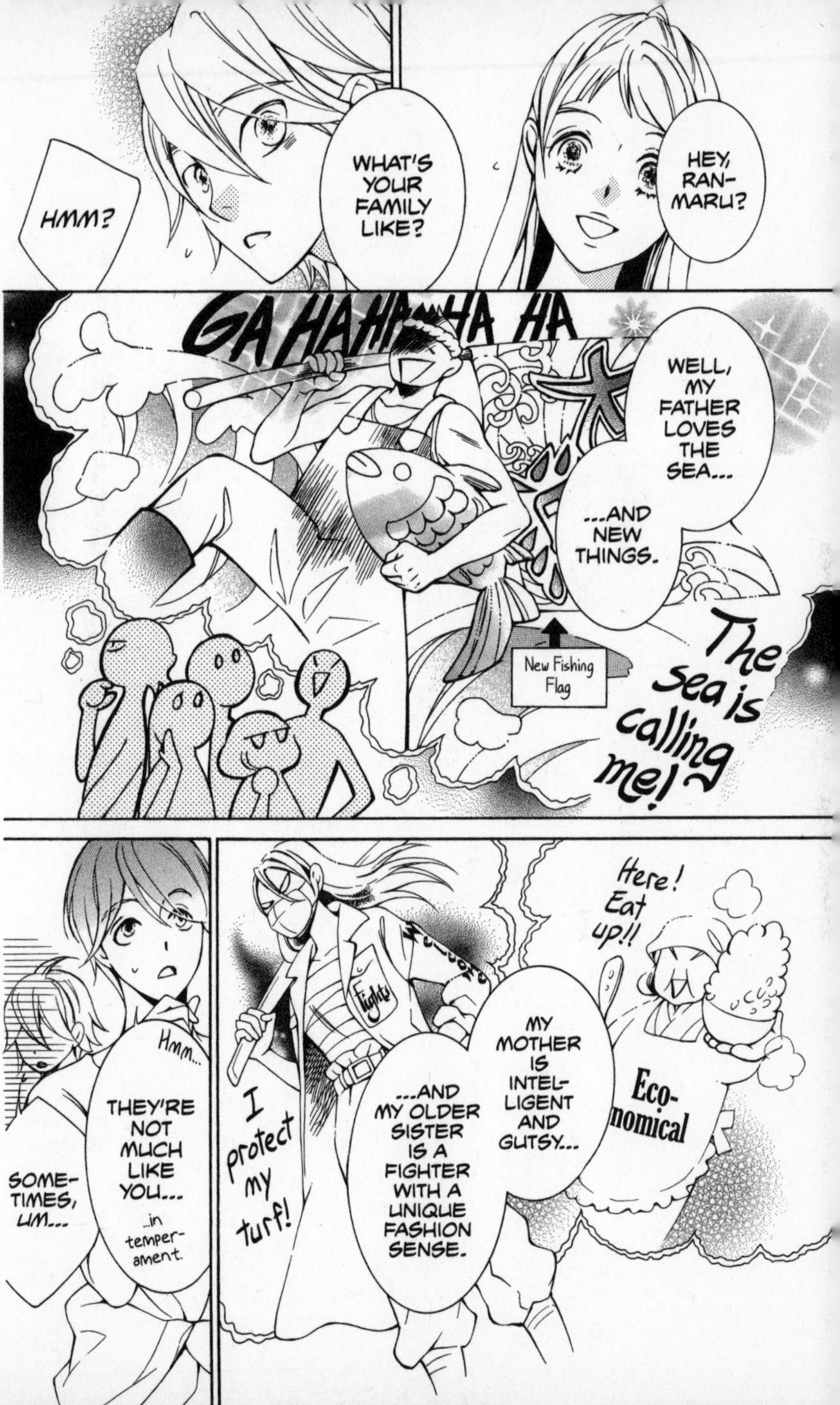
HEY, RAN-MARU?
WHAT'S YOUR FAMILY LIKE?
HMM?
GA HAHA HA HA
WELL, MY FATHER LOVES THE SEA...
...AND NEW THINGS.
New Fishing Flag
The sea is calling me!
Here! Eat up!!
Eco-nomical
MY MOTHER IS INTEL-LIGENT AND GUTSY...
...AND MY OLDER SISTER IS A FIGHTER WITH A UNIQUE FASHION SENSE.
Fights
I protect my turf!
Hmm...
THEY'RE NOT MUCH LIKE YOU...
...in temper-ament.
SOME-TIMES, UM...

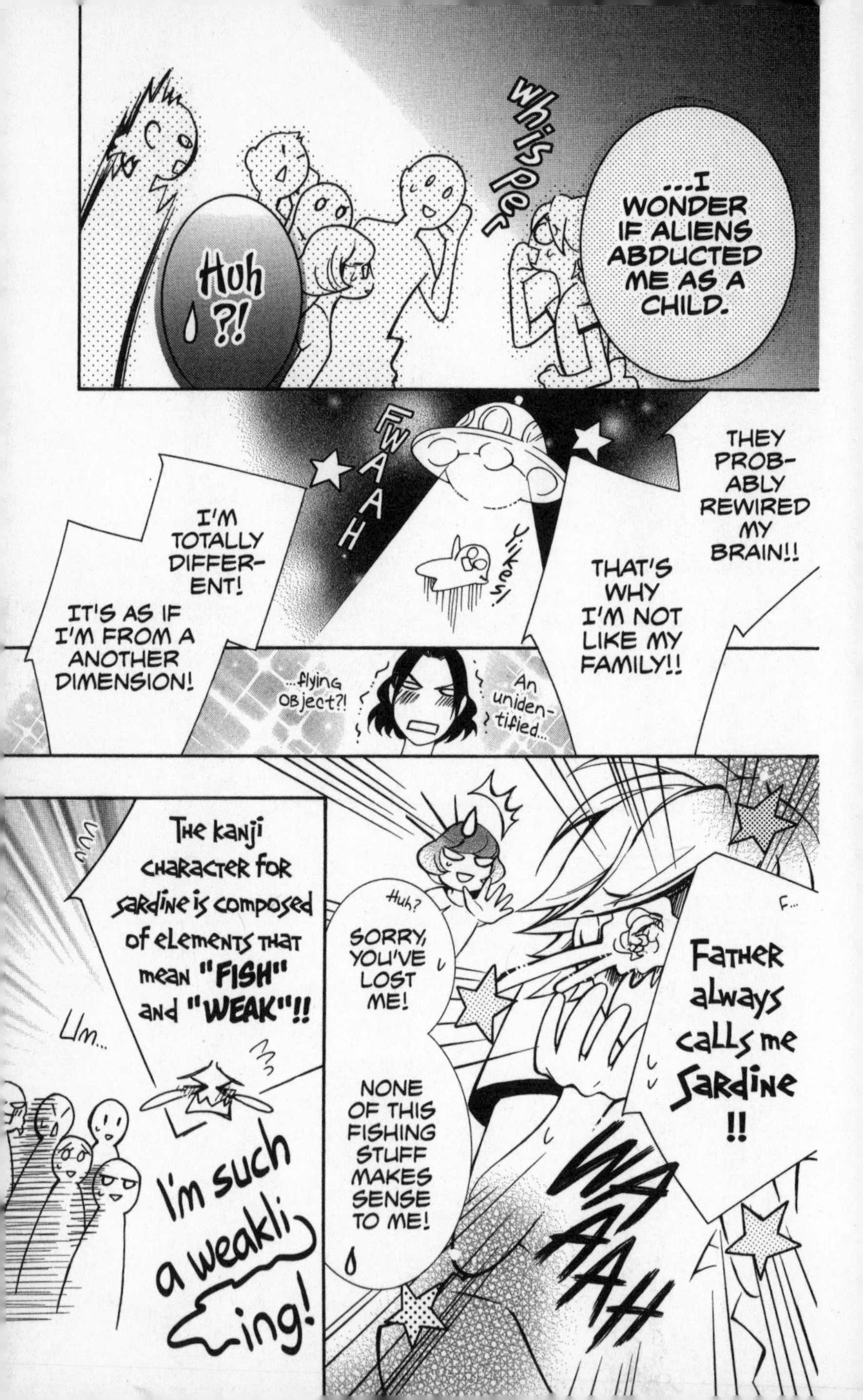
...I WONDER IF ALIENS ABDUCTED ME AS A CHILD.
whisper
Huh ?!
THEY PROBABLY REWIRED MY BRAIN!!
THAT'S WHY I'M NOT LIKE MY FAMILY!!
FWAAAH
Yikes!
I'M TOTALLY DIFFERENT!
IT'S AS IF I'M FROM A ANOTHER DIMENSION!
An unidentified...
...flying object?!
F...
Father always calls me Sardine!!
WAAAH
Huh?
SORRY, YOU'VE LOST ME!
NONE OF THIS FISHING STUFF MAKES SENSE TO ME!
Uuu
The kanji character for sardine is composed of elements that mean "FISH" and "WEAK"!!
Um...
I'm such a weakling!

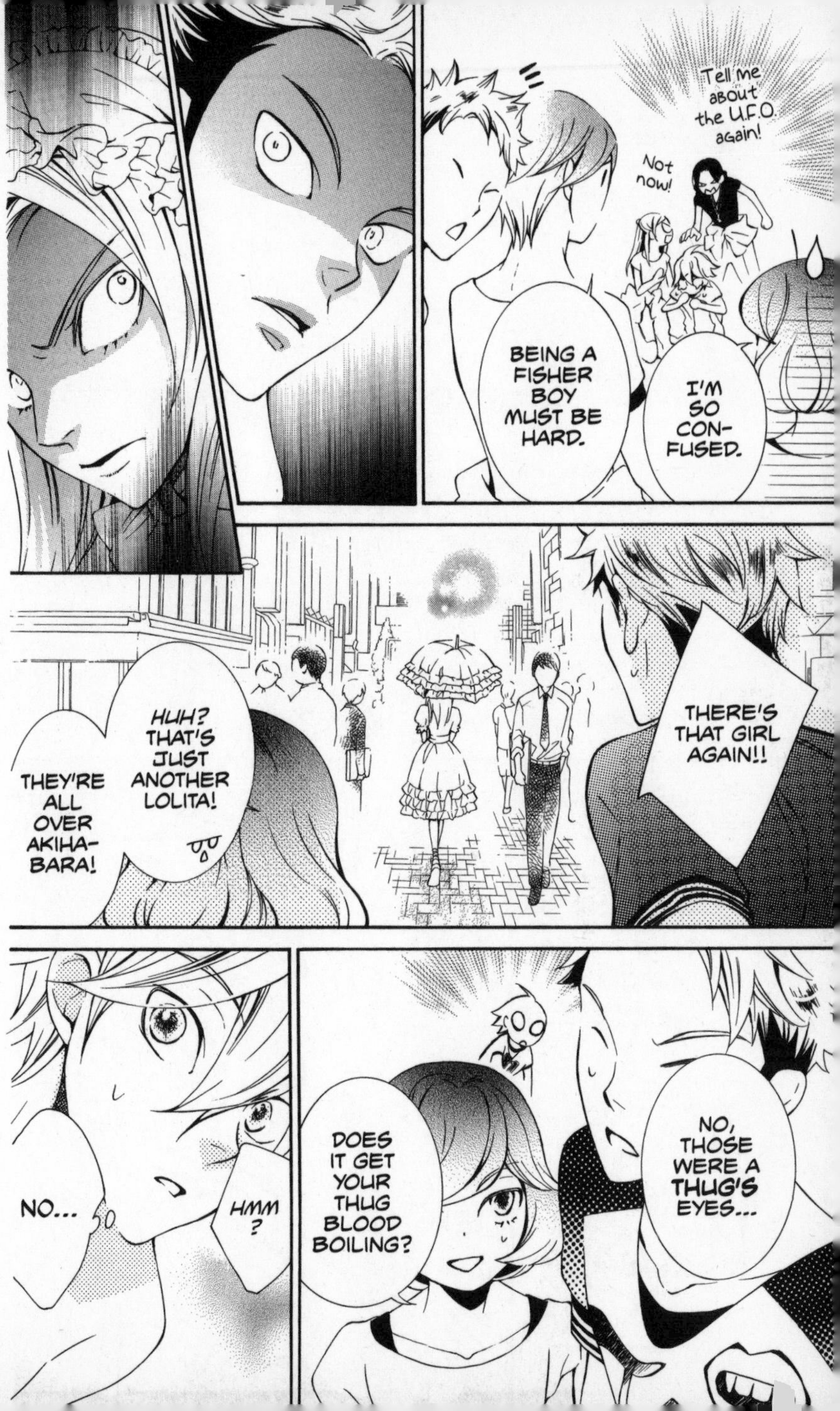

Tell me about the U.F.O. again!
Not now!
I'M SO CON-FUSED.
BEING A FISHER BOY MUST BE HARD.
THERE'S THAT GIRL AGAIN!!
HUH? THAT'S JUST ANOTHER LOLITA!
THEY'RE ALL OVER AKIHA-BARA!
NO, THOSE WERE A THUG'S EYES...
DOES IT GET YOUR THUG BLOOD BOILING?
HMM?
NO...

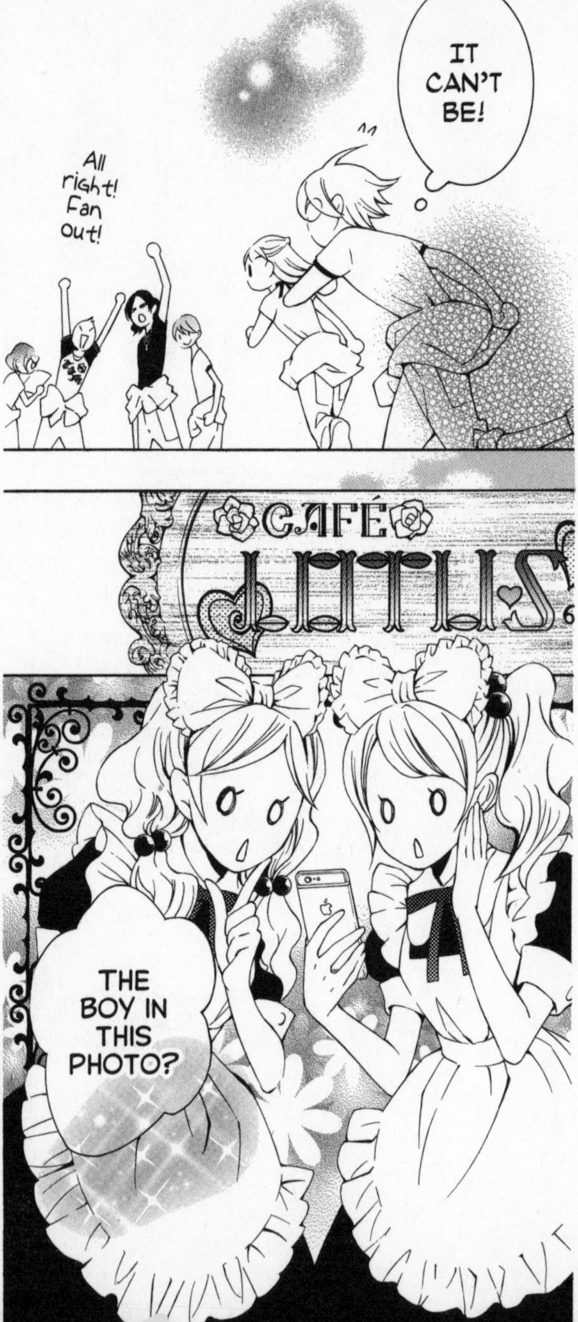
IT CAN'T BE!
All right! Fan out!
CAFÉ LOTUS
THE BOY IN THIS PHOTO?

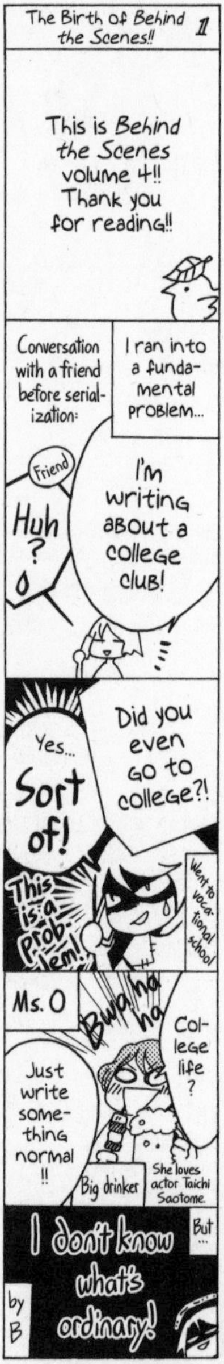
The Birth of Behind the Scenes!! 1
This is Behind the Scenes volume 4!! Thank you for reading!!
I ran into a fundamental problem...
Conversation with a friend before serialization:
I'm writing about a college club!
Friend
Huh?
Did you even go to college?!
Yes... Sort of!
This is a problem!
Went to vocational school
Ms. O
Bwa ha ha
College life?
Just write something normal!!
She loves actor Taichi Saotome.
Big drinker
But...
I don't know what's ordinary!
by B

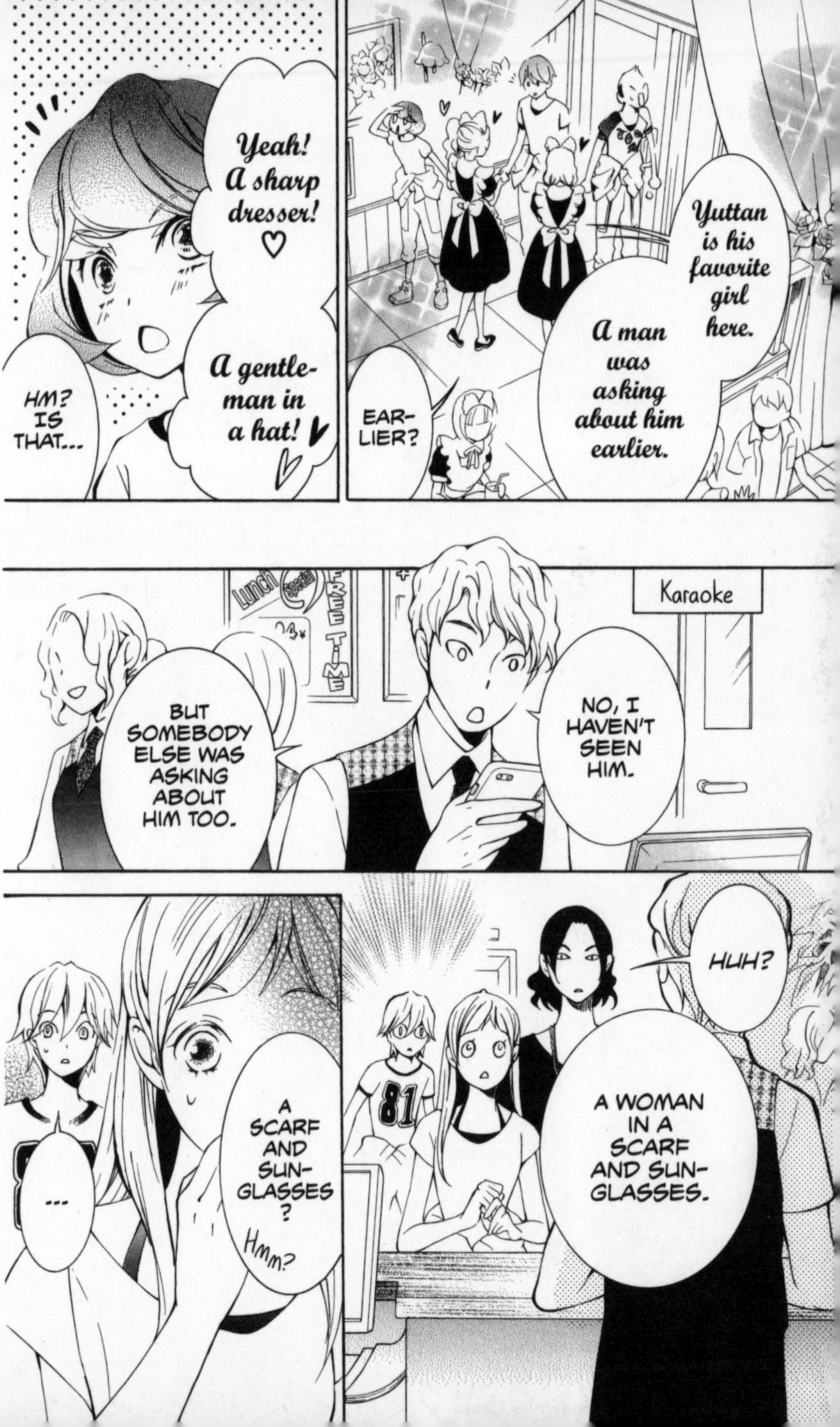
Yuttan is his favorite girl here.
A man was asking about him earlier.
EAR-LIER?
Yeah! A sharp dresser! ♡
A gentle-man in a hat! ♥
HM? IS THAT...
Karaoke
NO, I HAVEN'T SEEN HIM.
Lunch special
FREE TIME
BUT SOMEBODY ELSE WAS ASKING ABOUT HIM TOO.
HUH?
A WOMAN IN A SCARF AND SUN-GLASSES.
A SCARF AND SUN-GLASSES?
Hmm?
...

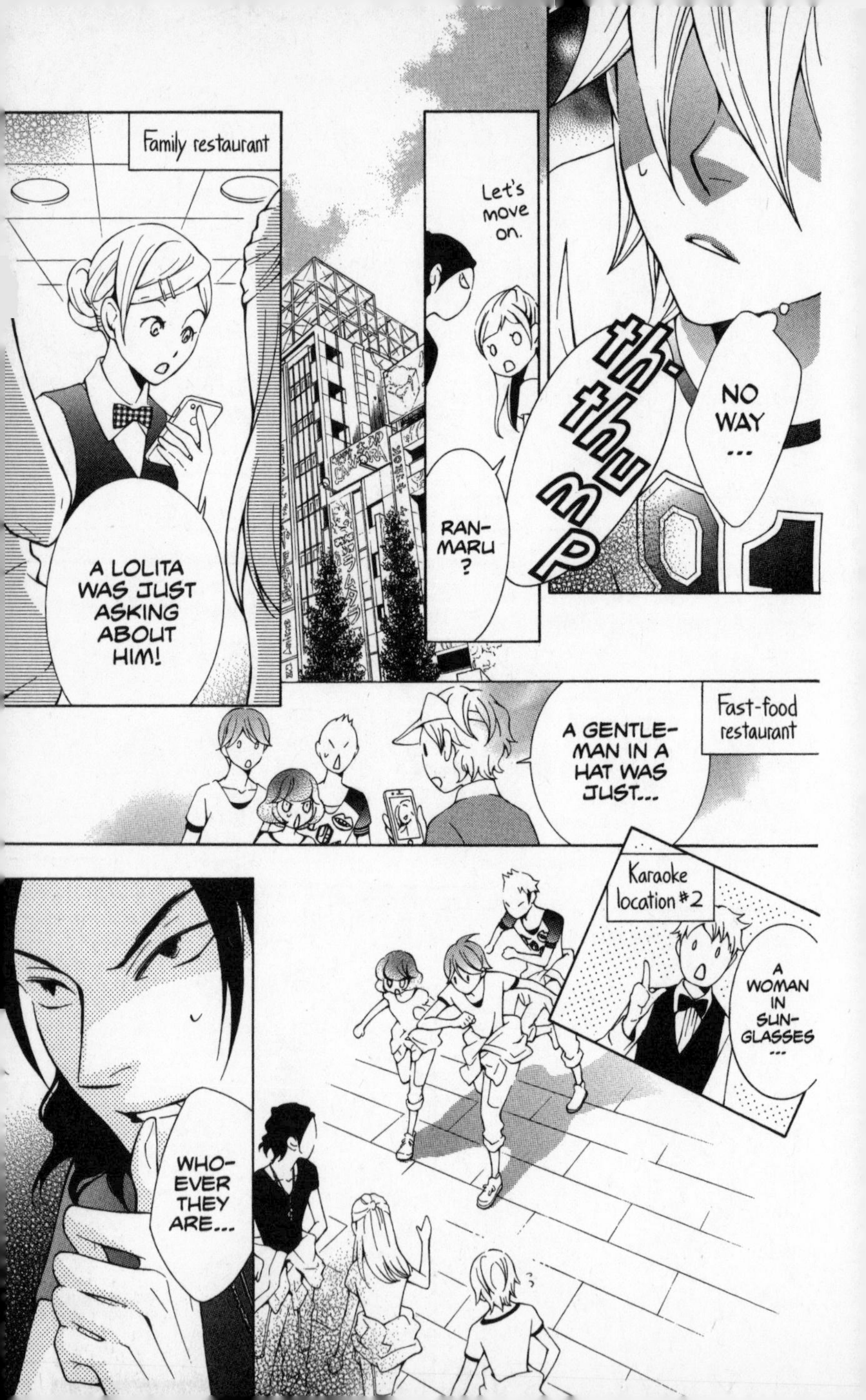
NO WAY...
th-thump
Let's move on.
RAN-MARU?
Family restaurant
A LOLITA WAS JUST ASKING ABOUT HIM!
Fast-food restaurant
A GENTLE-MAN IN A HAT WAS JUST...
Karaoke location #2
A WOMAN IN SUN-GLASSES...
WHO-EVER THEY ARE...

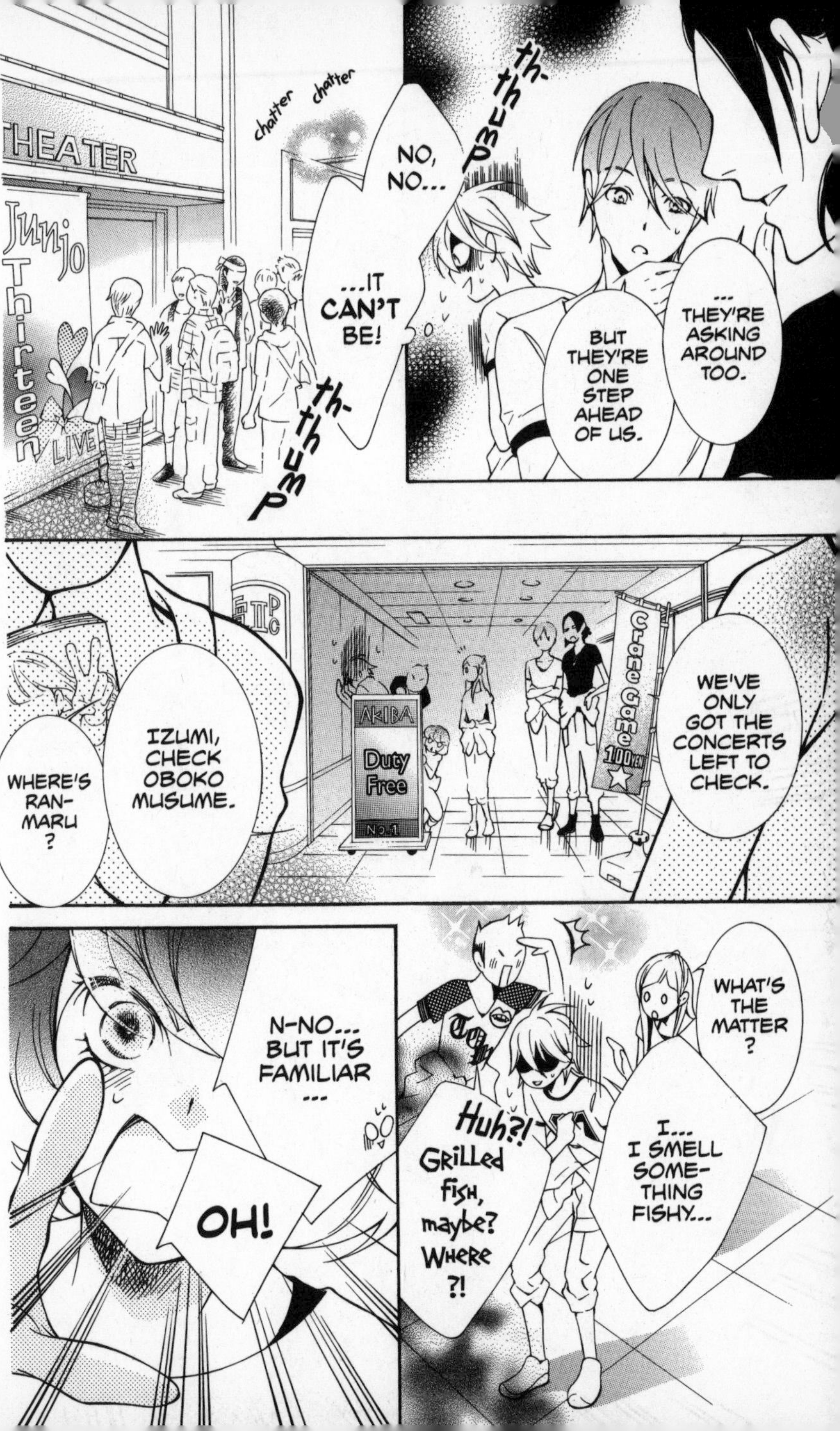
...THEY'RE ASKING AROUND TOO.
BUT THEY'RE ONE STEP AHEAD OF US.
th-thump
NO, NO...
...IT CAN'T BE!
th-thump
chatter chatter
THEATER
Junjo Thirteen LIVE
WE'VE ONLY GOT THE CONCERTS LEFT TO CHECK.
Crane Game 100YEN
AKIBA Duty Free No.1
IZUMI, CHECK OBOKO MUSUME.
WHERE'S RAN-MARU?
WHAT'S THE MATTER?
I... I SMELL SOME-THING FISHY...
Huh?! Grilled fish, maybe? Where?!
N-NO... BUT IT'S FAMILIAR...
OH!

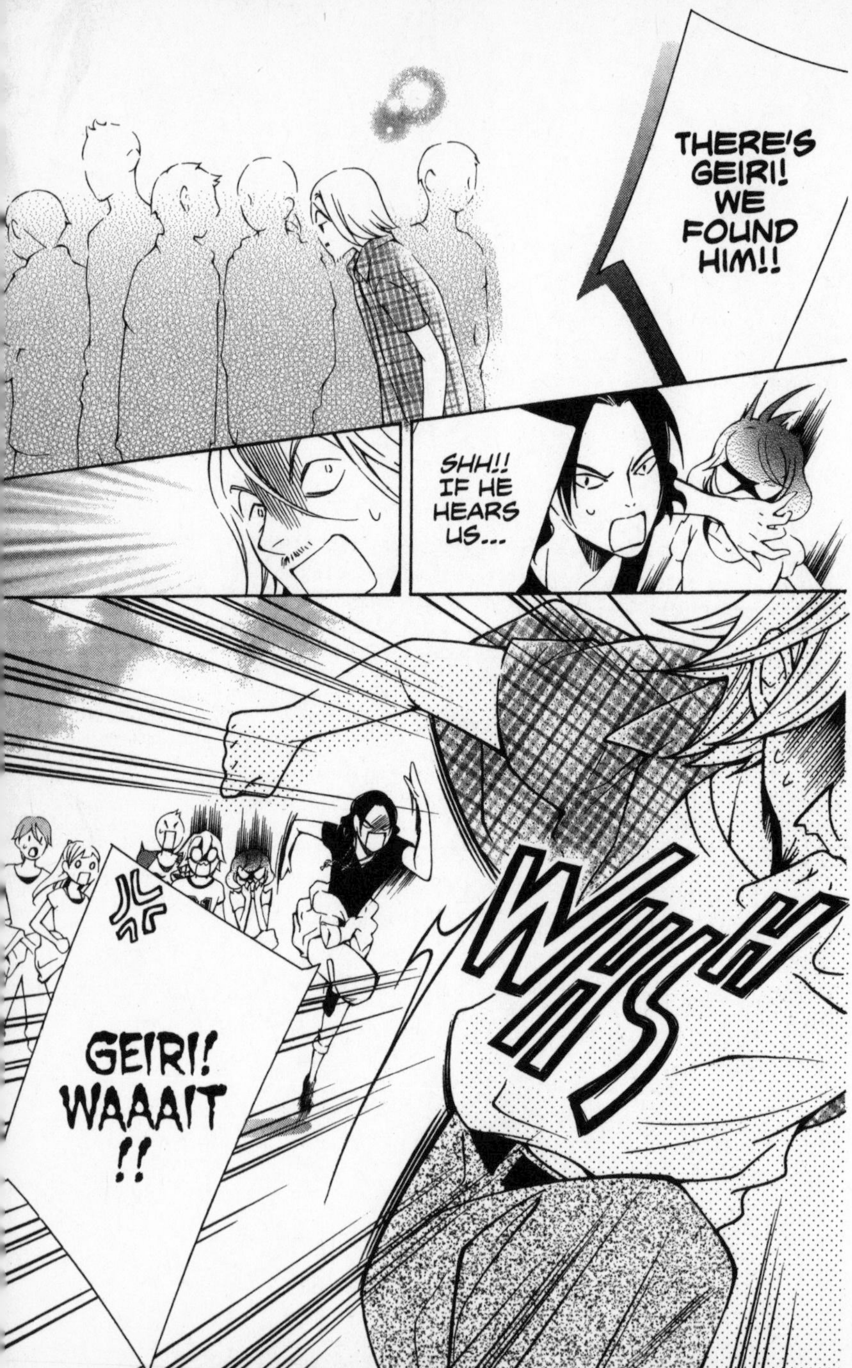
THERE'S GEIRI! WE FOUND HIM!!
SHH!! IF HE HEARS US...
WHSH
GEIRI! WAAAIT !!

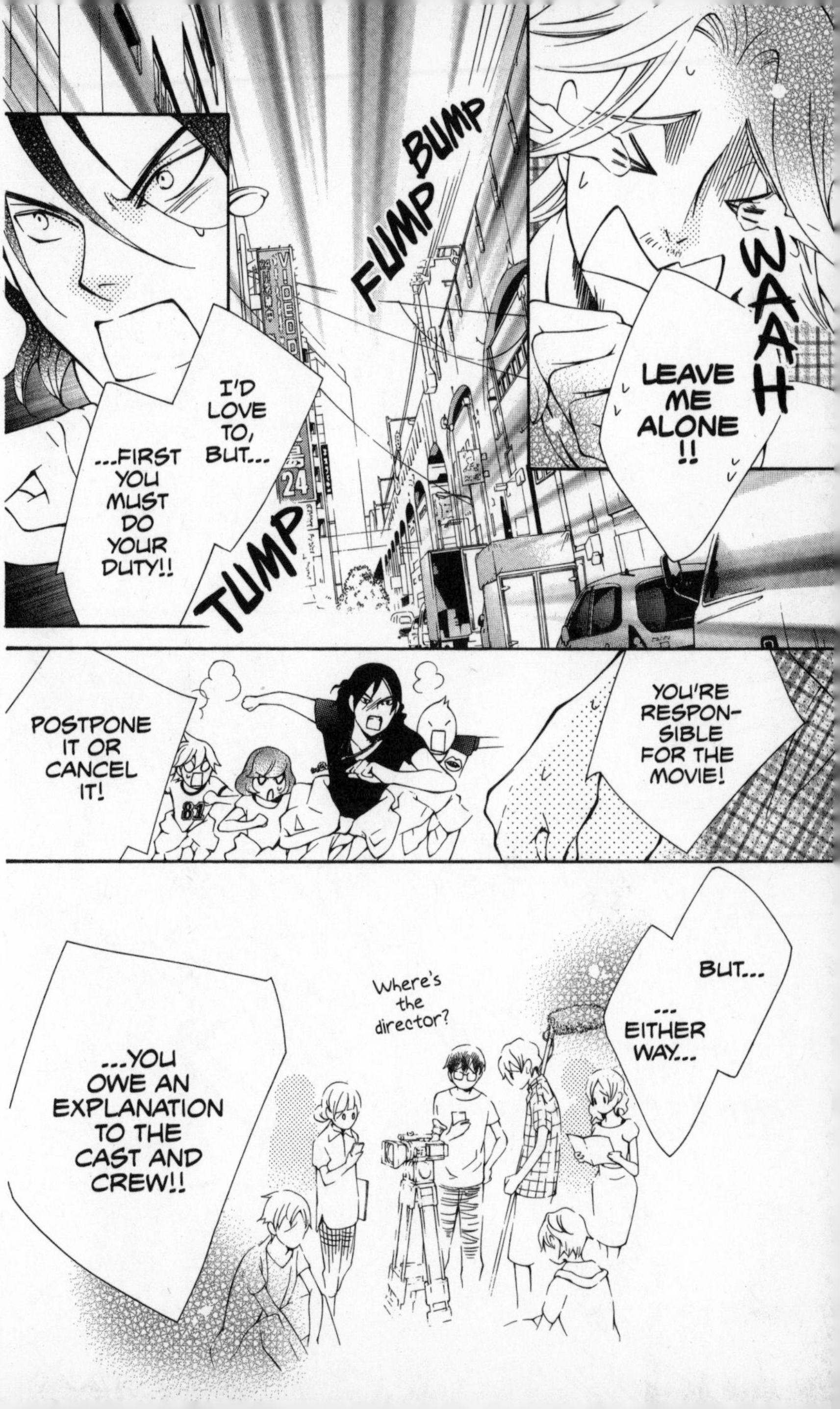
WAAH
LEAVE ME ALONE!!
BUMP
FUMP
TUMP
I'D LOVE TO, BUT...
...FIRST YOU MUST DO YOUR DUTY!!
YOU'RE RESPONSIBLE FOR THE MOVIE!
POSTPONE IT OR CANCEL IT!
BUT...
...EITHER WAY...
Where's the director?
...YOU OWE AN EXPLANATION TO THE CAST AND CREW!!

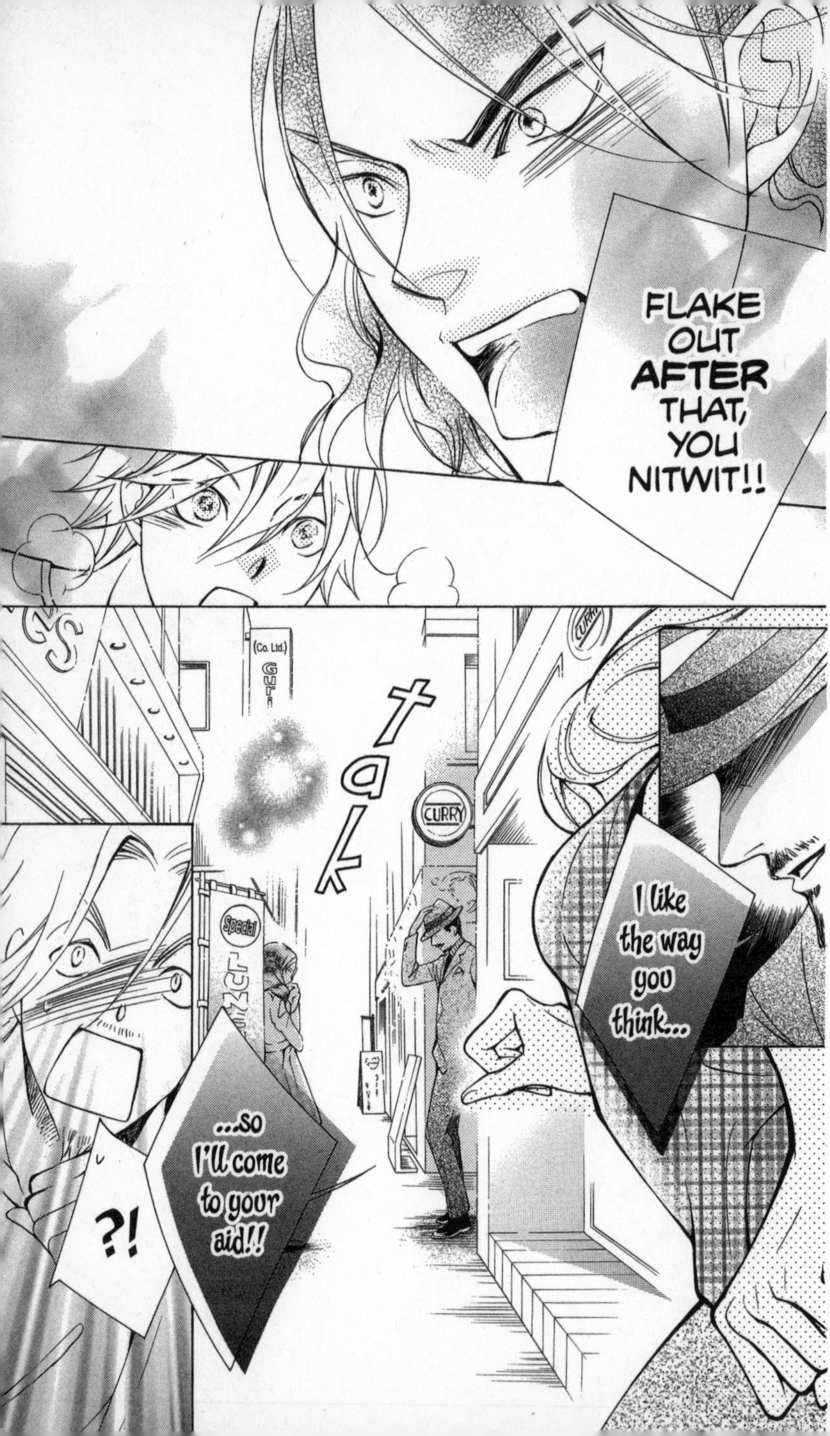
FLAKE OUT AFTER THAT, YOU NITWIT!!
I like the way you think...
tak
CURRY
(Co. Ltd.) Guri
Special
...so I'll come to your aid!!
?!

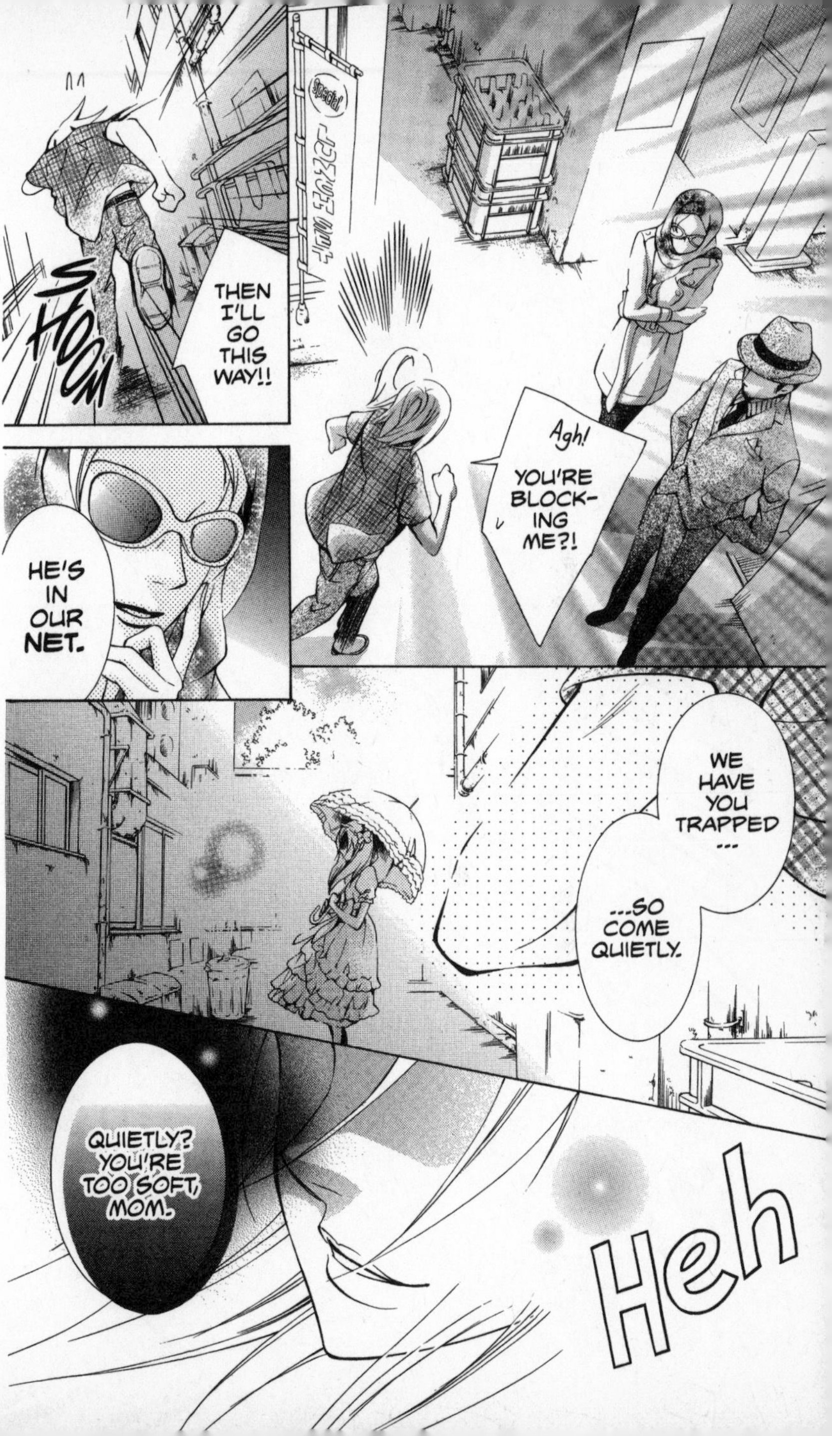
Agh!
YOU'RE BLOCKING ME?!
THEN I'LL GO THIS WAY!!
SHOOM
HE'S IN OUR NET.
WE HAVE YOU TRAPPED...
...SO COME QUIETLY.
Heh
QUIETLY? YOU'RE TOO SOFT, MOM.

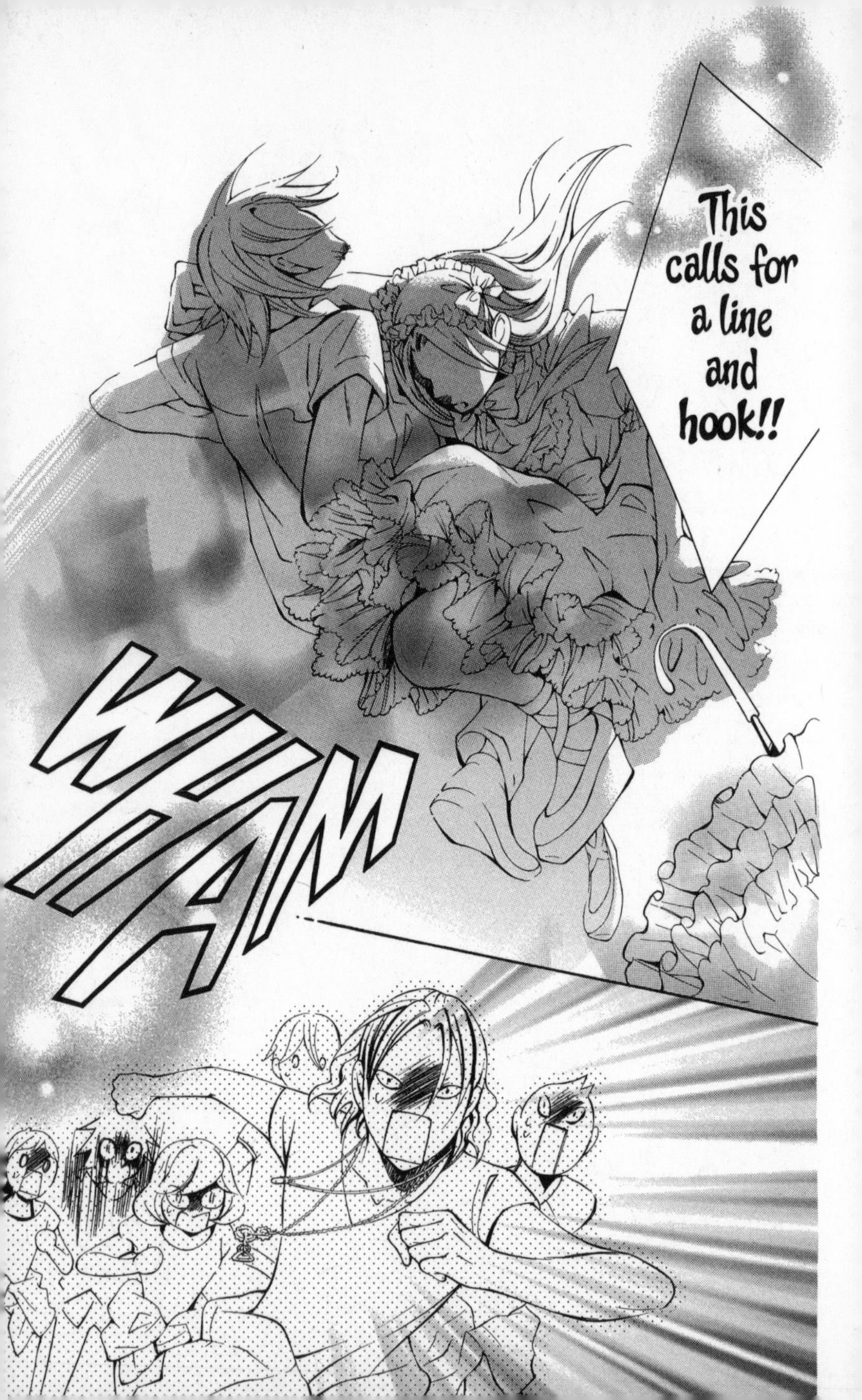
This calls for a line and hook!!
WHAM

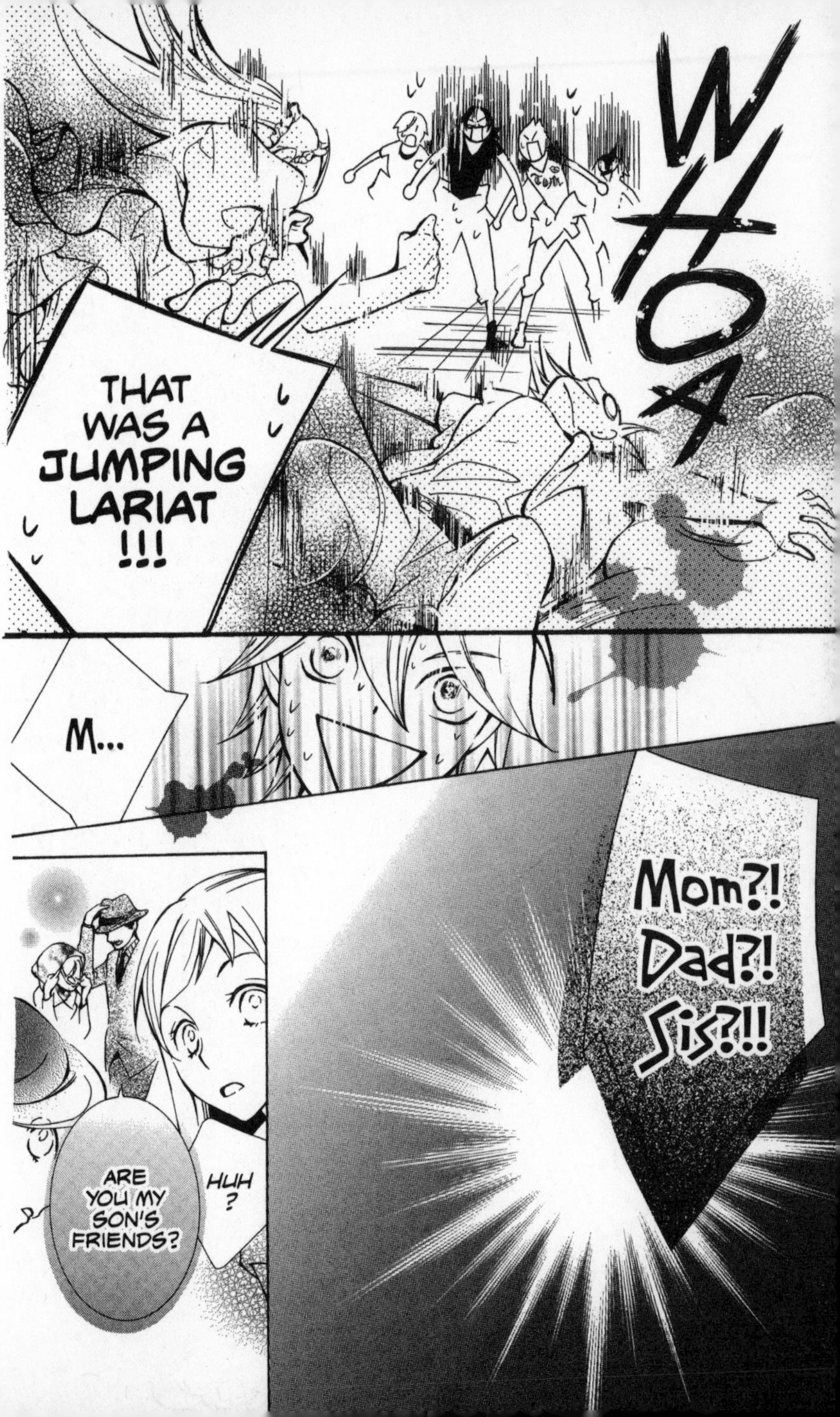
WHOA
THAT WAS A JUMPING LARIAT !!!
M...
Mom?! Dad?! Sis?!!
HUH?
ARE YOU MY SON'S FRIENDS?

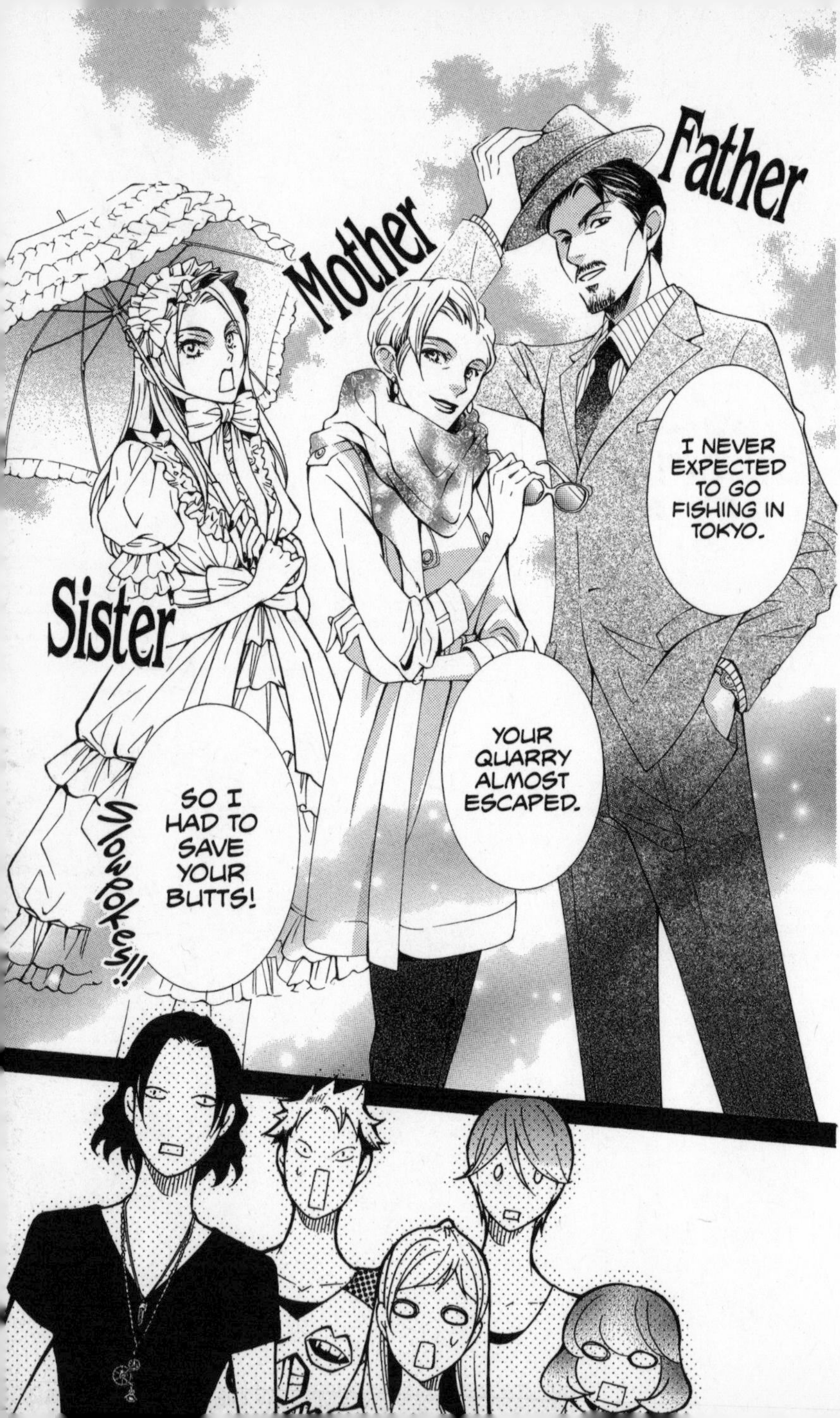
Father
I NEVER EXPECTED TO GO FISHING IN TOKYO.
Mother
YOUR QUARRY ALMOST ESCAPED.
Sister
SO I HAD TO SAVE YOUR BUTTS!
Slowpokes!!

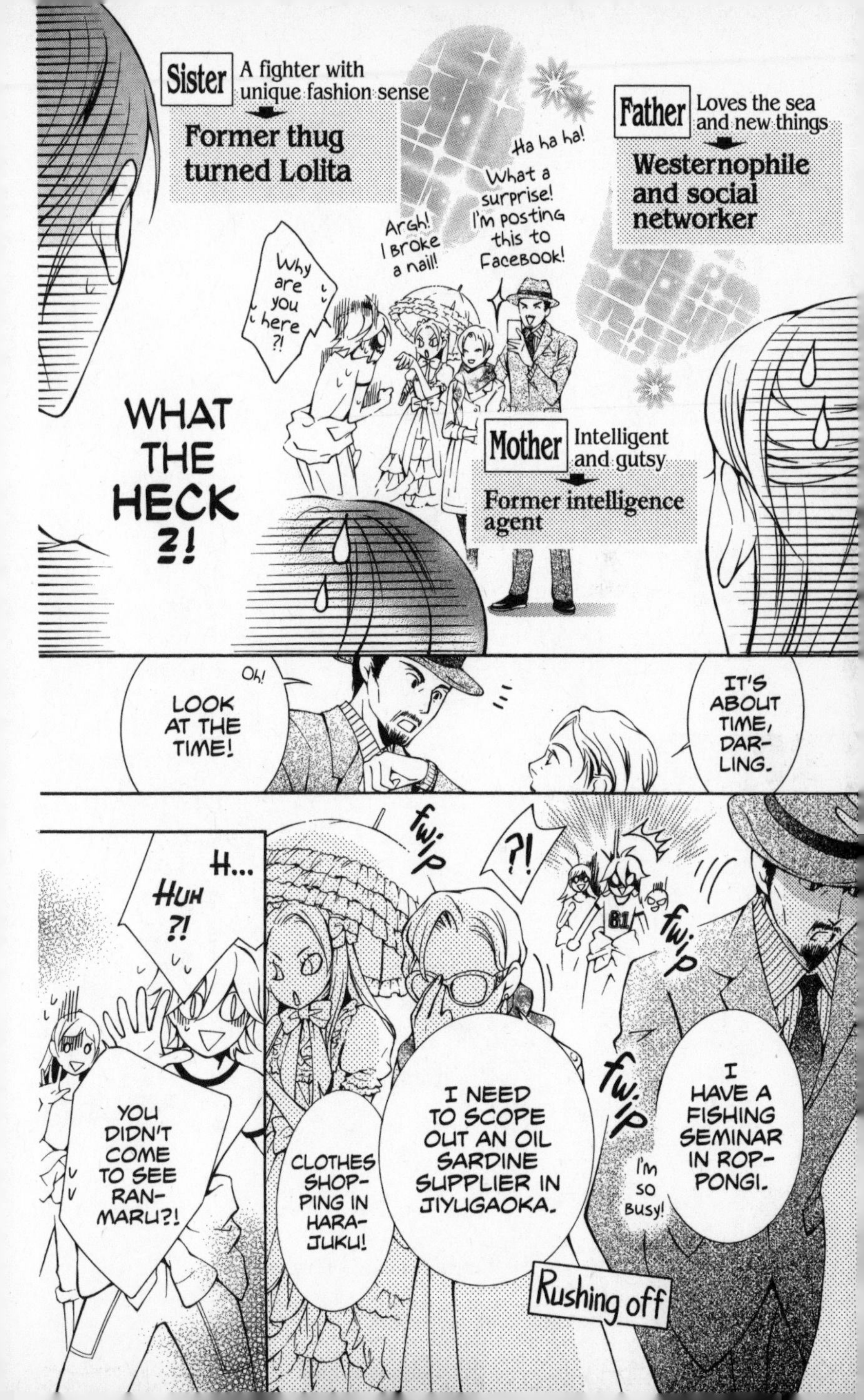
Father Loves the sea and new things
Westernophile and social networker
Ha ha ha!
What a surprise! I'm posting this to Facebook!
Argh! I broke a nail!
Sister A fighter with unique fashion sense
Former thug turned Lolita
Why are you here?!
Mother Intelligent and gutsy
Former intelligence agent
WHAT THE HECK?!
Oh!
LOOK AT THE TIME!
IT'S ABOUT TIME, DAR-LING.
fwip
I HAVE A FISHING SEMINAR IN ROP-PONGI.
I'm so busy!
fwip
?!
fwip
I NEED TO SCOPE OUT AN OIL SARDINE SUPPLIER IN JIYUGAOKA.
CLOTHES SHOP-PING IN HARA-JUKU!
Rushing off
H...
HUH?!
YOU DIDN'T COME TO SEE RAN-MARU?!

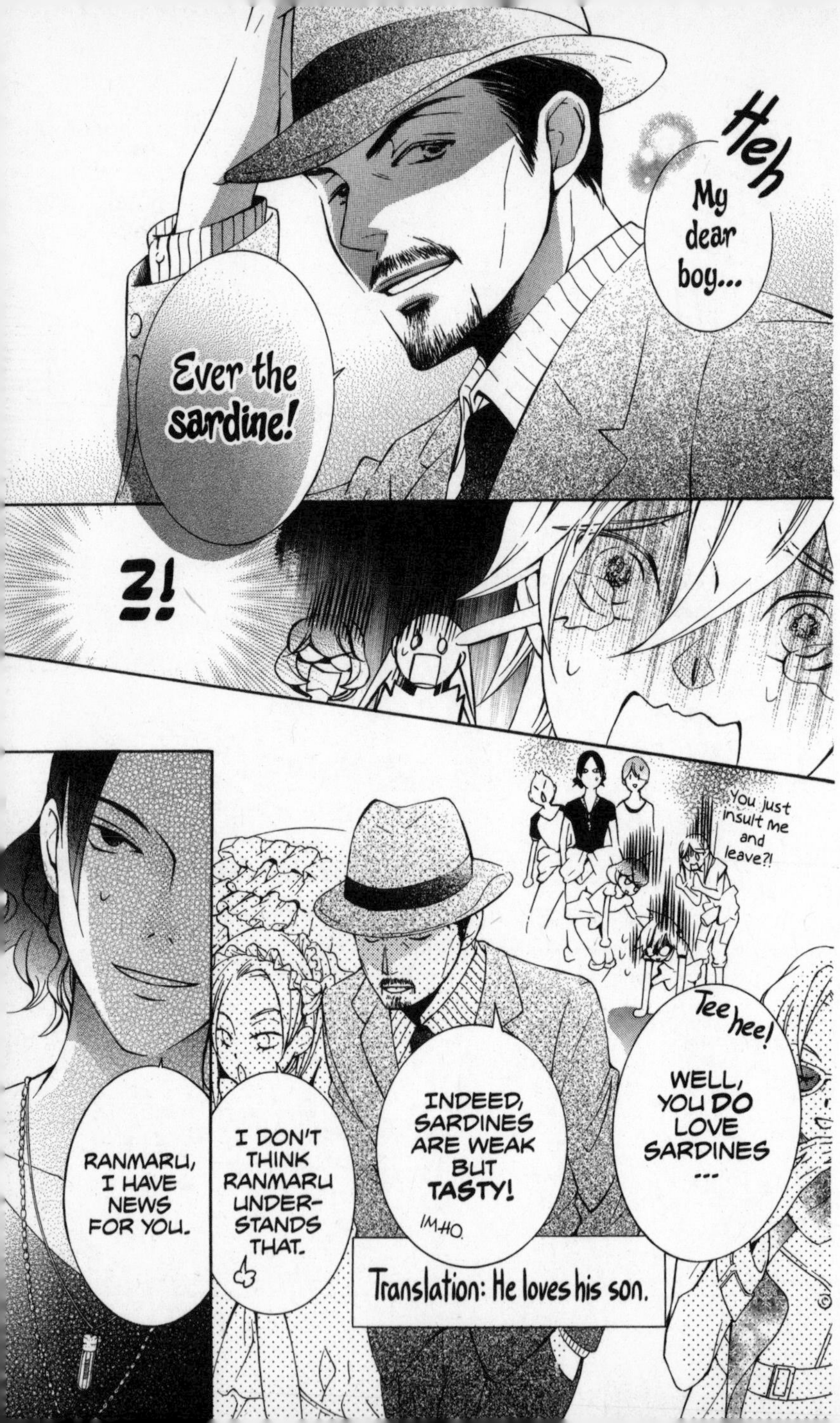
Heh
My dear boy...
Ever the sardine!
Z!
You just insult me and leave?!
Tee hee!
WELL, YOU DO LOVE SARDINES ...
INDEED, SARDINES ARE WEAK BUT TASTY!
IMHO.
Translation: He loves his son.
I DON'T THINK RANMARU UNDERSTANDS THAT.
RANMARU, I HAVE NEWS FOR YOU.

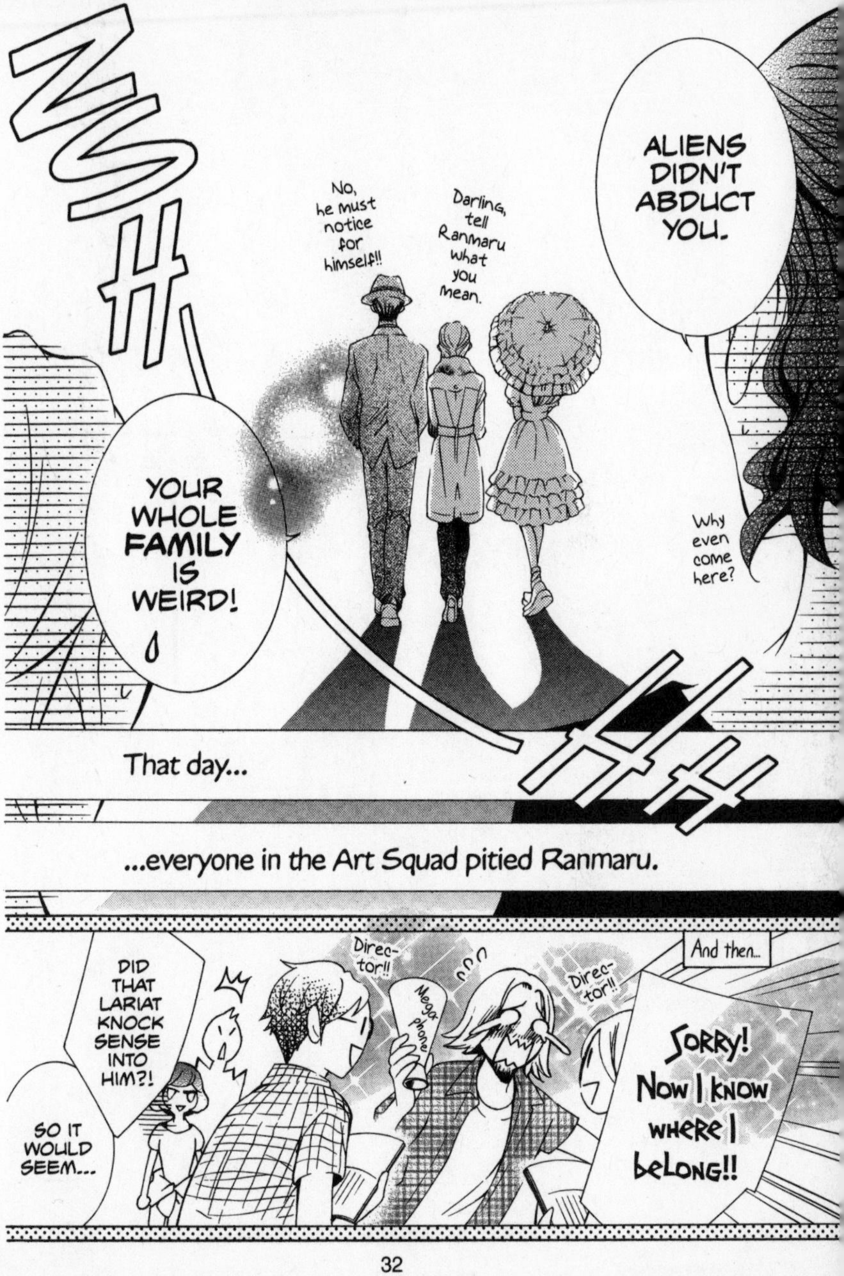
ALIENS DIDN'T ABDUCT YOU.
Why even come here?
Darling, tell Ranmaru what you mean.
No, he must notice for himself!!
YOUR WHOLE FAMILY IS WEIRD!
That day...
...everyone in the Art Squad pitied Ranmaru.
And then...
SORRY! Now I know where I belong!!
Direc-tor!!
Mega phone
Direc-tor!!
DID THAT LARIAT KNOCK SENSE INTO HIM?!
SO IT WOULD SEEM...

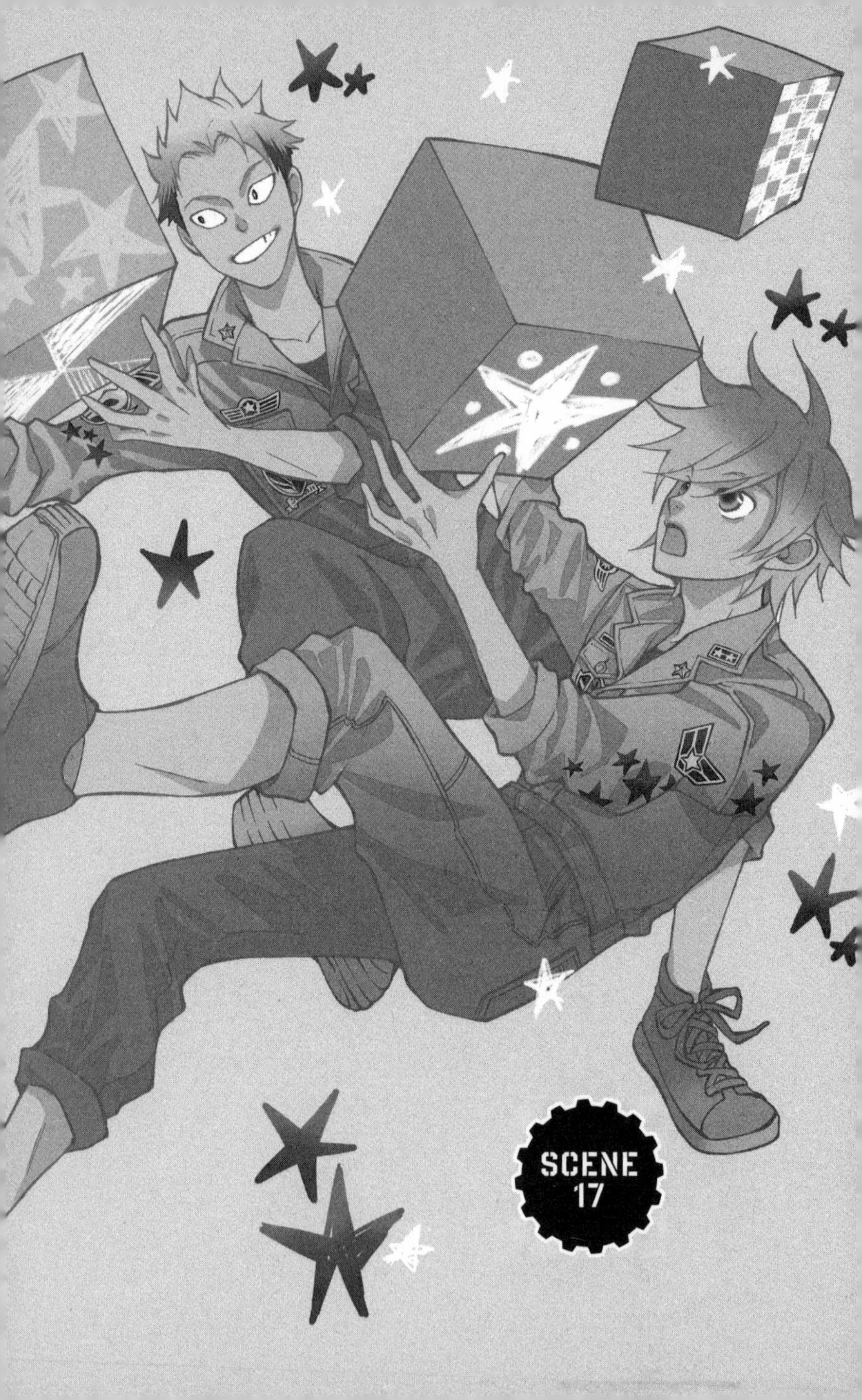
SCENE
17

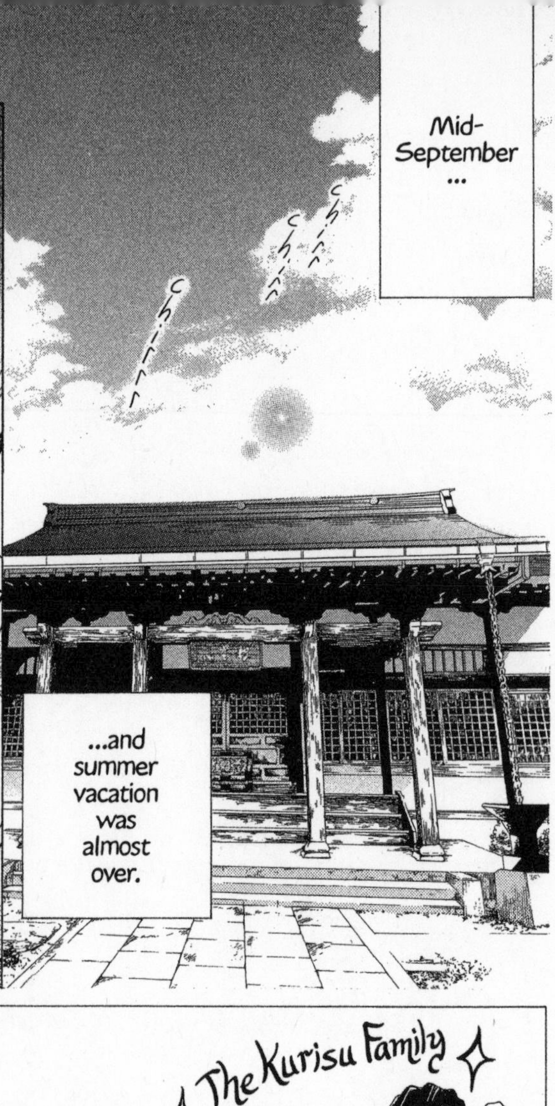
Mid-September ...
...and summer vacation was almost over.
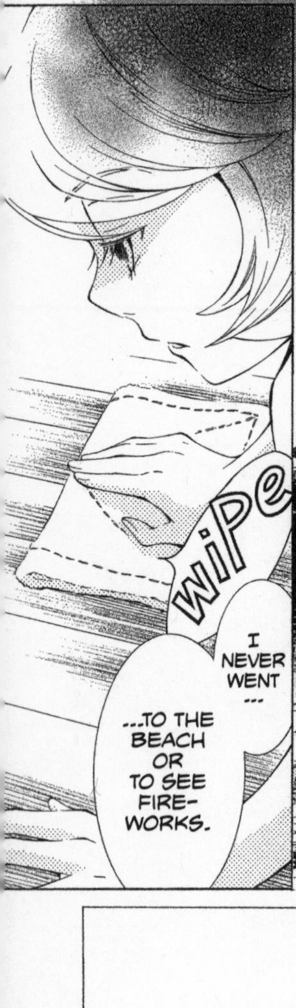
wipe
I NEVER WENT ...
...TO THE BEACH OR TO SEE FIRE-WORKS.
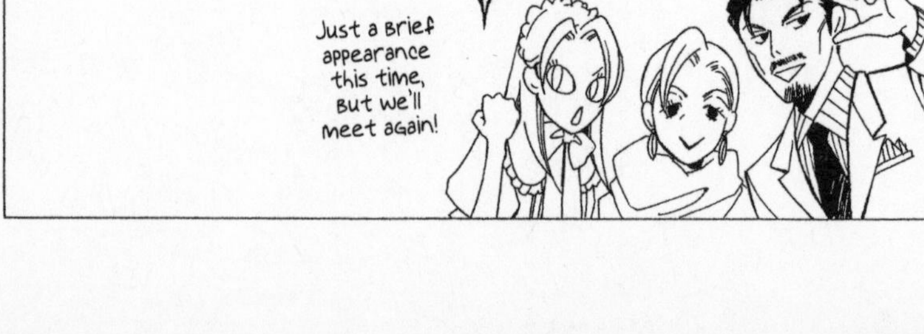
The Kurisu Family
Just a brief appearance this time, but we'll meet again!

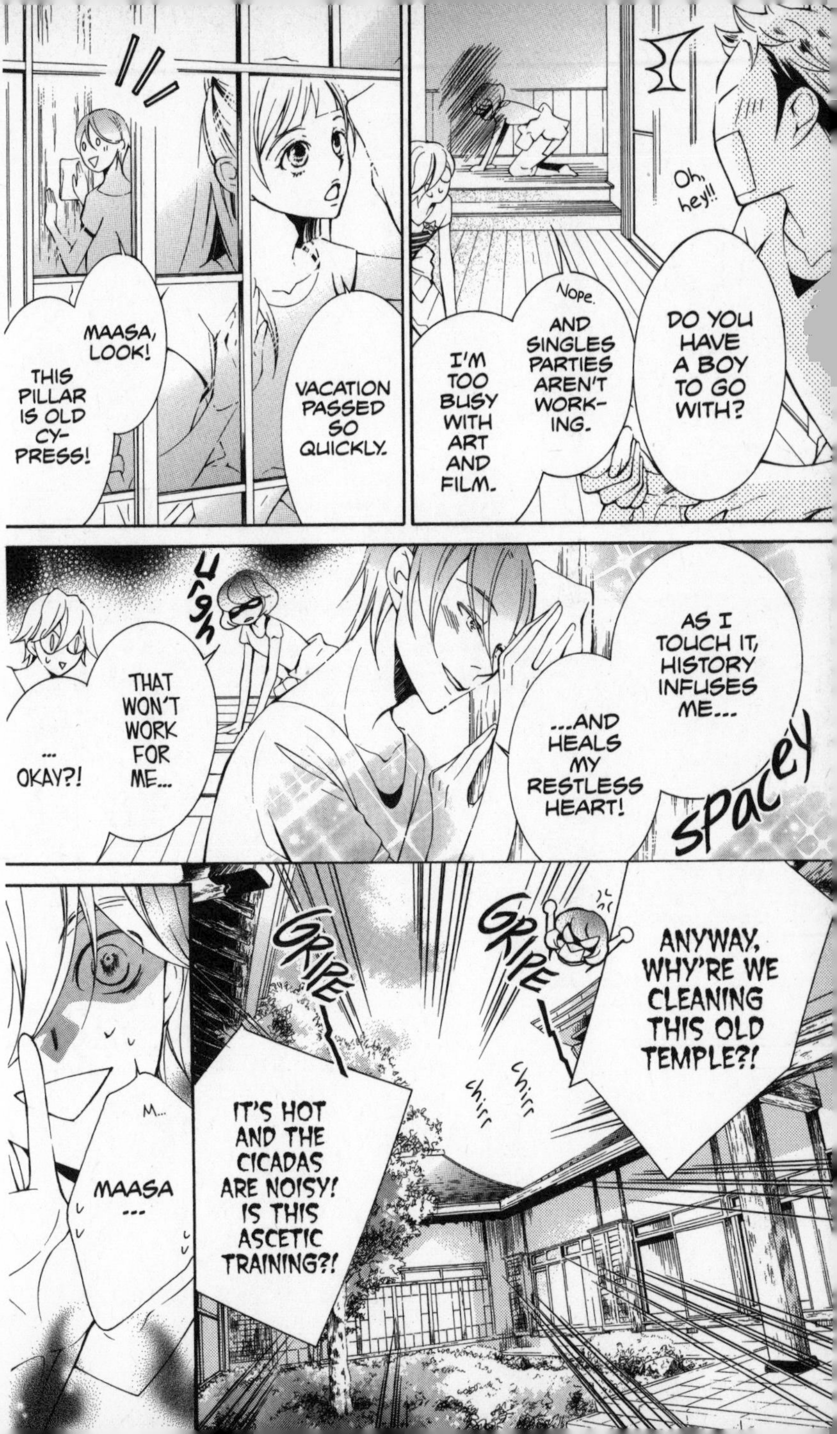
Oh, hey!!
DO YOU HAVE A BOY TO GO WITH?
Nope.
AND SINGLES PARTIES AREN'T WORKING.
I'M TOO BUSY WITH ART AND FILM.
VACATION PASSED SO QUICKLY.
MAASA, LOOK!
THIS PILLAR IS OLD CYPRESS!
AS I TOUCH IT, HISTORY INFUSES ME...
...AND HEALS MY RESTLESS HEART!
spacey
Urgh
THAT WON'T WORK FOR ME...
...OKAY?!
ANYWAY, WHY'RE WE CLEANING THIS OLD TEMPLE?!
GRIPE
GRIPE
chirr
chirr
IT'S HOT AND THE CICADAS ARE NOISY! IS THIS ASCETIC TRAINING?!
M... MAASA...

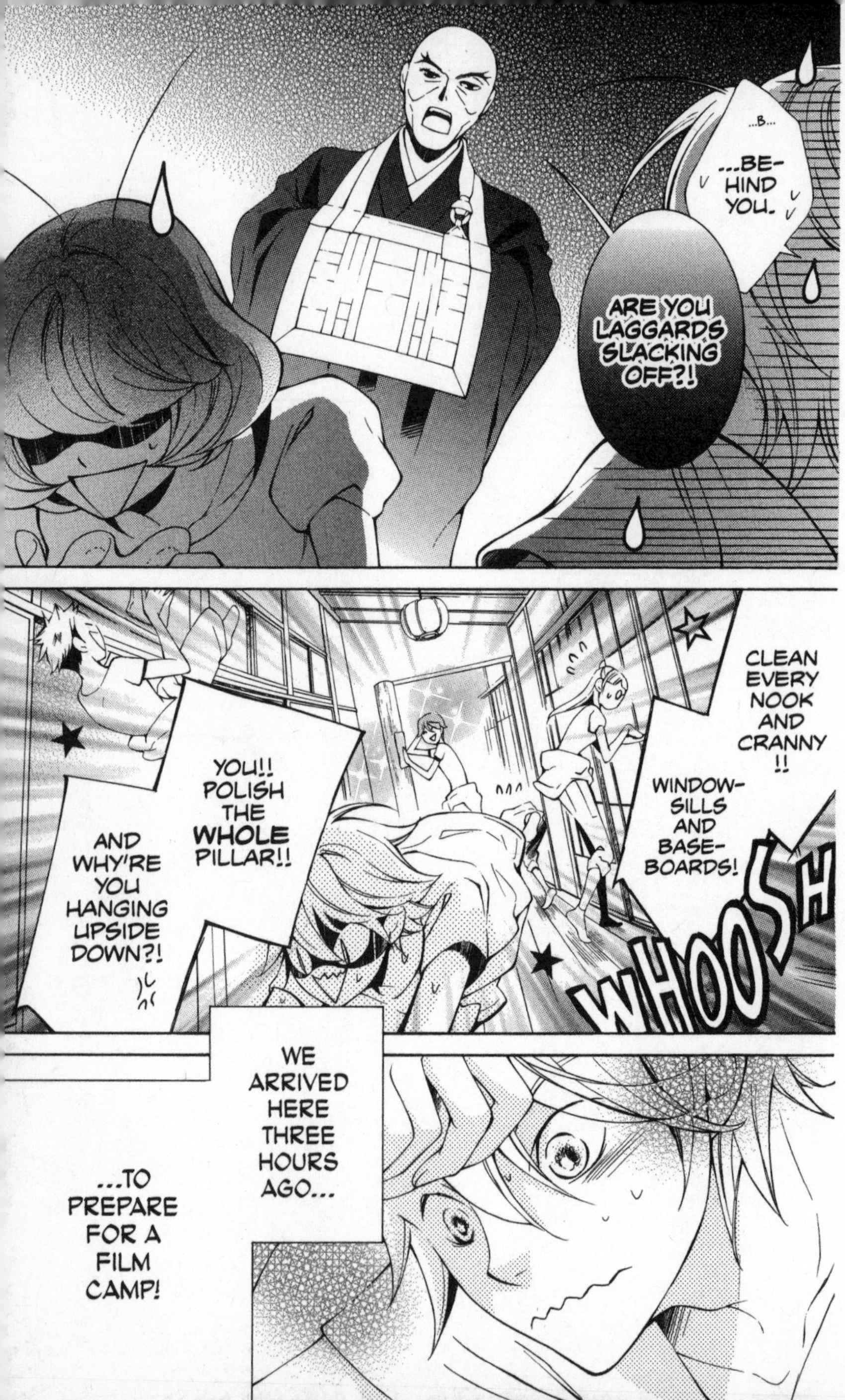
...B...
...BE-HIND YOU.
ARE YOU LAGGARDS SLACKING OFF?!
CLEAN EVERY NOOK AND CRANNY!!
WINDOW-SILLS AND BASE-BOARDS!
WHOOSH
YOU!! POLISH THE WHOLE PILLAR!!
AND WHY'RE YOU HANGING UPSIDE DOWN?!
WE ARRIVED HERE THREE HOURS AGO...
...TO PREPARE FOR A FILM CAMP!

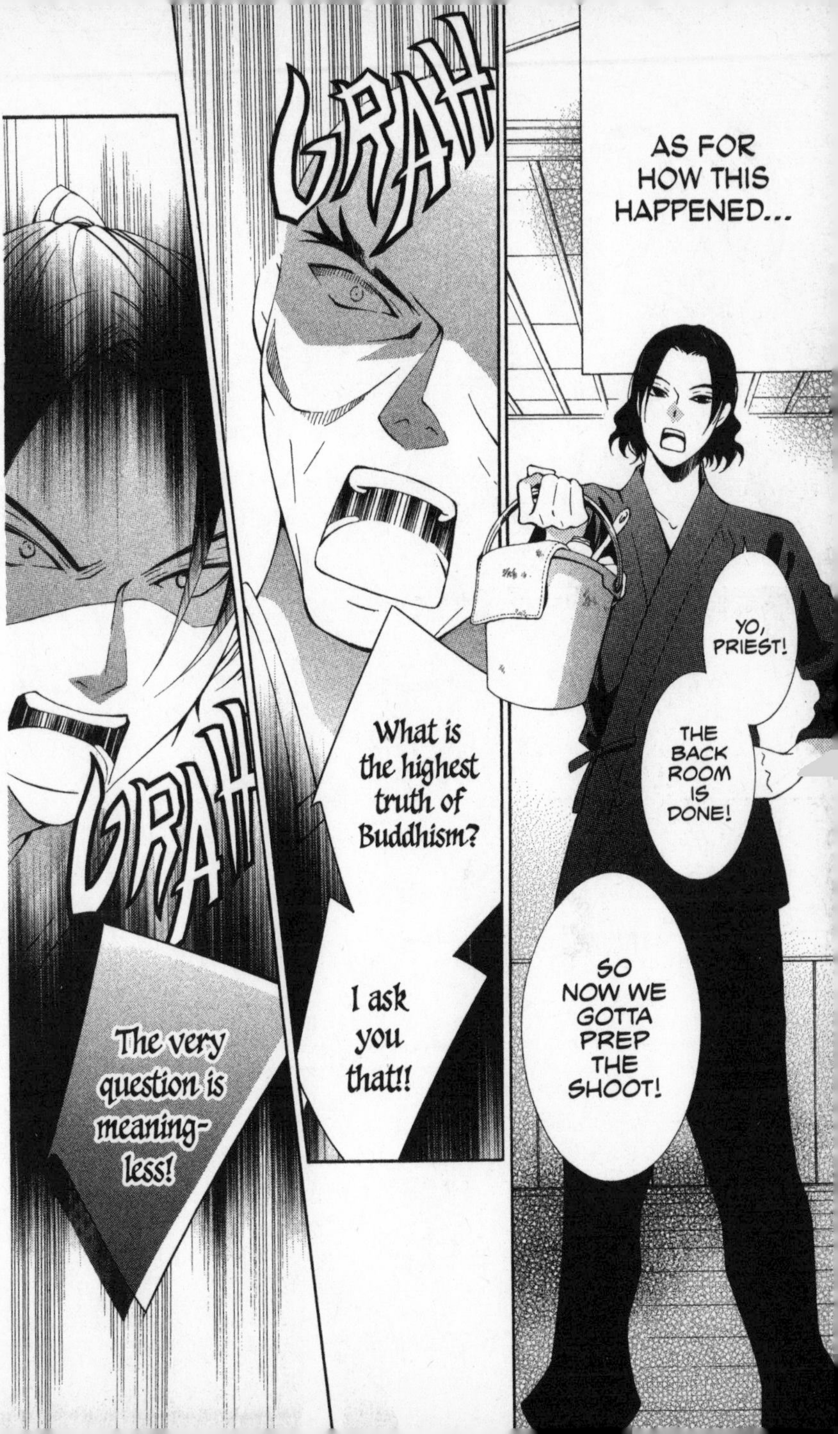
AS FOR HOW THIS HAPPENED...
YO, PRIEST!
THE BACK ROOM IS DONE!
SO NOW WE GOTTA PREP THE SHOOT!
GRAH
What is the highest truth of Buddhism?
I ask you that!!
GRAH
The very question is meaning-less!

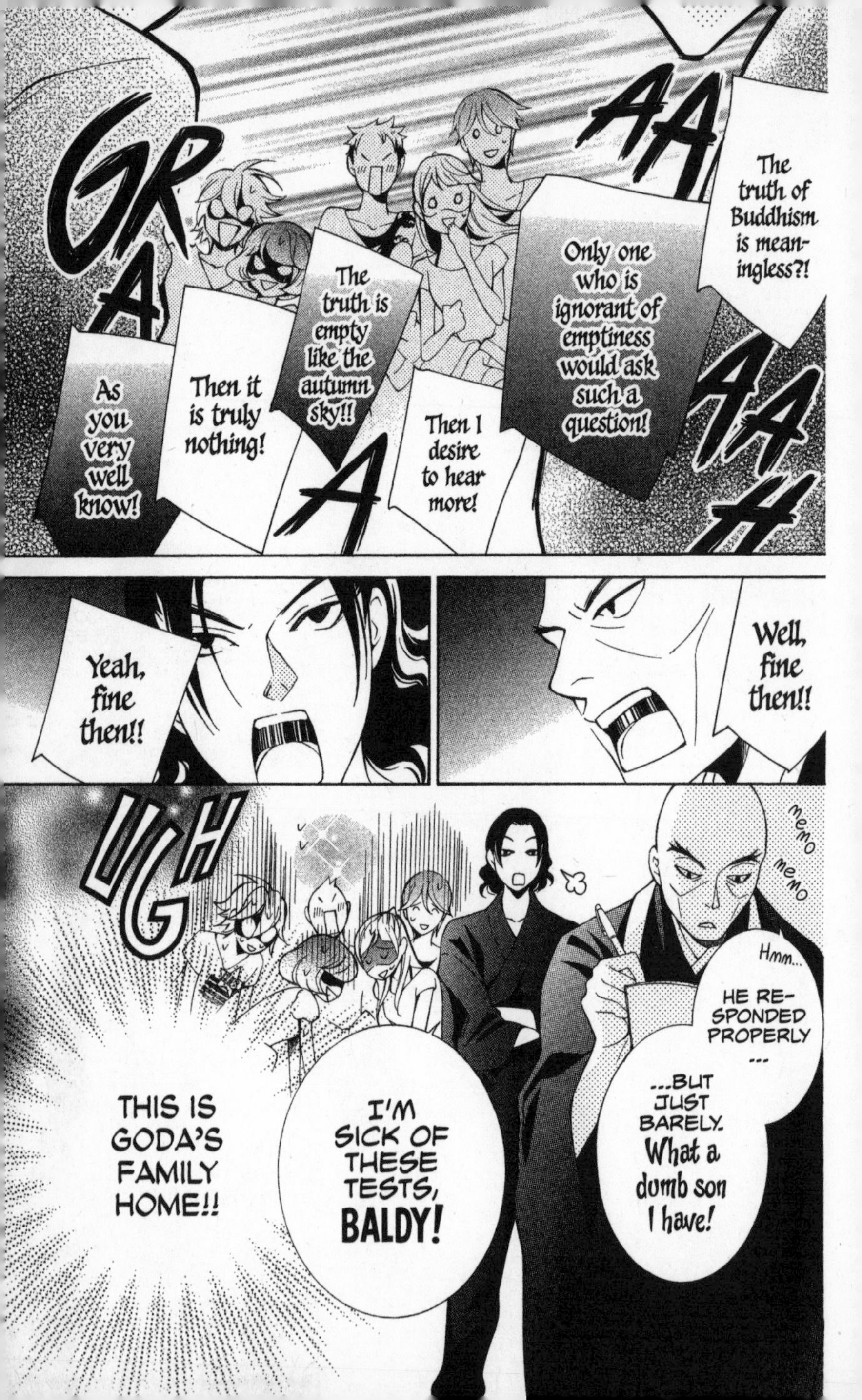
AA
The truth of Buddhism is meaningless?!
AAH
Only one who is ignorant of emptiness would ask such a question!
Then I desire to hear more!
The truth is empty like the autumn sky!!
A
Then it is truly nothing!
As you very well know!
GRA
Well, fine then!!
Yeah, fine then!!
memo memo
Hmm...
HE RESPONDED PROPERLY...
...BUT JUST BARELY. What a dumb son I have!
I'M SICK OF THESE TESTS, BALDY!
UGH
THIS IS GODA'S FAMILY HOME!!

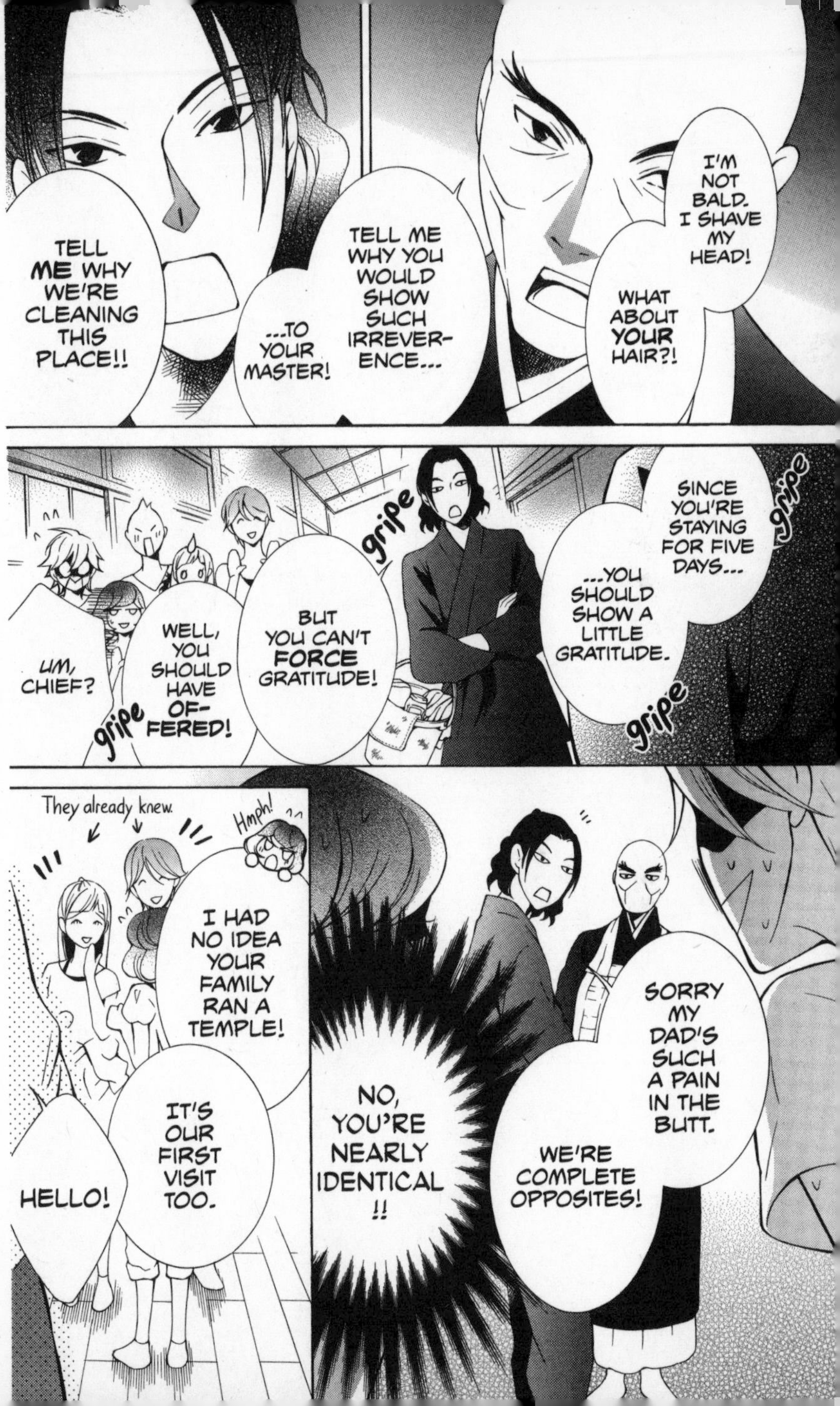
I'M NOT BALD. I SHAVE MY HEAD!
WHAT ABOUT YOUR HAIR?!
TELL ME WHY YOU WOULD SHOW SUCH IRREVERENCE...
...TO YOUR MASTER!
TELL ME WHY WE'RE CLEANING THIS PLACE!!
SINCE YOU'RE STAYING FOR FIVE DAYS...
gripe
...YOU SHOULD SHOW A LITTLE GRATITUDE.
gripe
gripe
BUT YOU CAN'T FORCE GRATITUDE!
WELL, YOU SHOULD HAVE OF-FERED!
gripe
UM, CHIEF?
SORRY MY DAD'S SUCH A PAIN IN THE BUTT.
WE'RE COMPLETE OPPOSITES!
NO, YOU'RE NEARLY IDENTICAL!!
Hmph!
They already knew.
I HAD NO IDEA YOUR FAMILY RAN A TEMPLE!
IT'S OUR FIRST VISIT TOO.
HELLO!

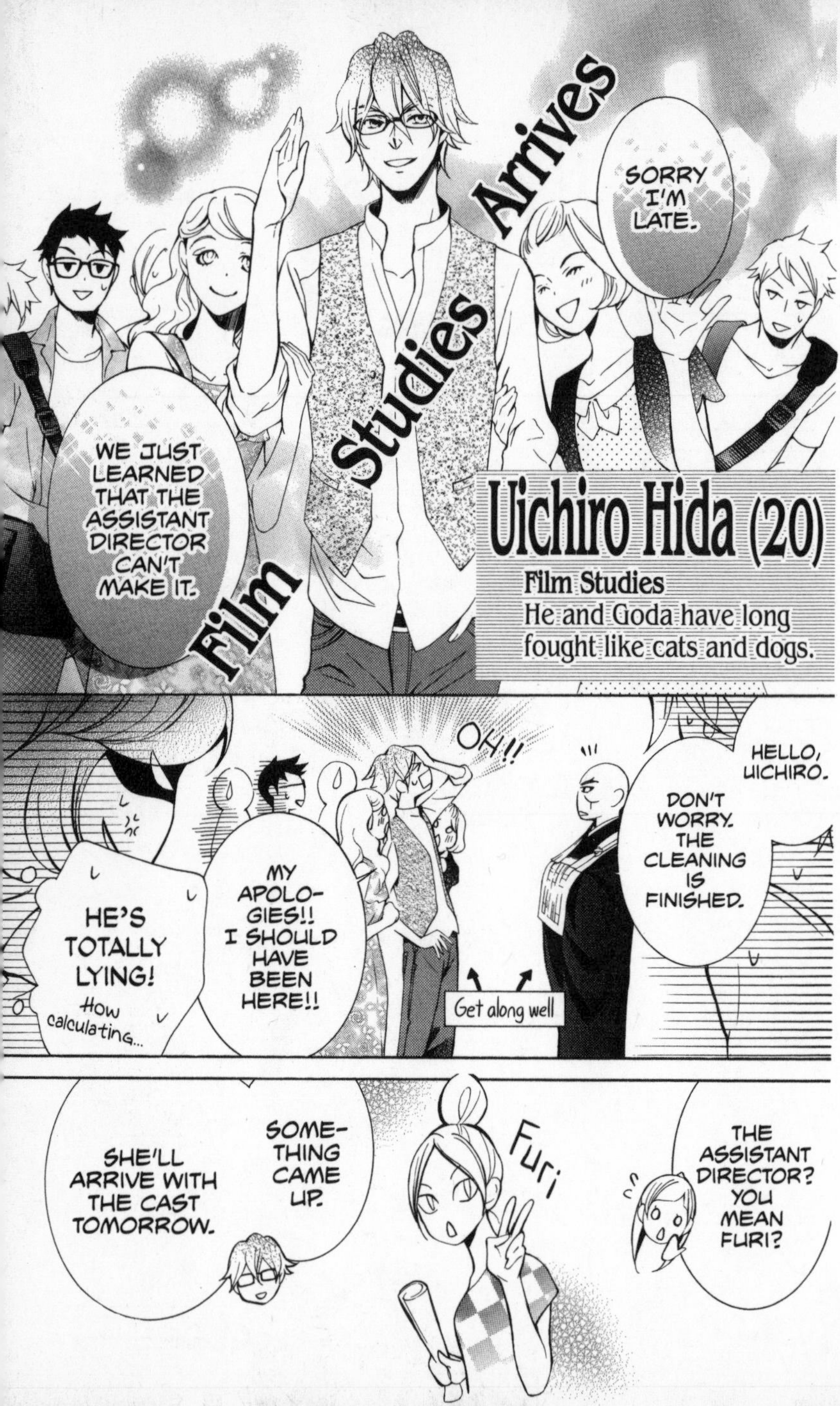
SORRY I'M LATE.
Film Studies Arrives
Uichiro Hida (20)
Film Studies
He and Goda have long fought like cats and dogs.
WE JUST LEARNED THAT THE ASSISTANT DIRECTOR CAN'T MAKE IT.
HELLO, UICHIRO.
DON'T WORRY. THE CLEANING IS FINISHED.
OH!!
Get along well
MY APOLOGIES!! I SHOULD HAVE BEEN HERE!!
HE'S TOTALLY LYING!
How calculating...
THE ASSISTANT DIRECTOR? YOU MEAN FURI?
Furi
SOMETHING CAME UP.
SHE'LL ARRIVE WITH THE CAST TOMORROW.

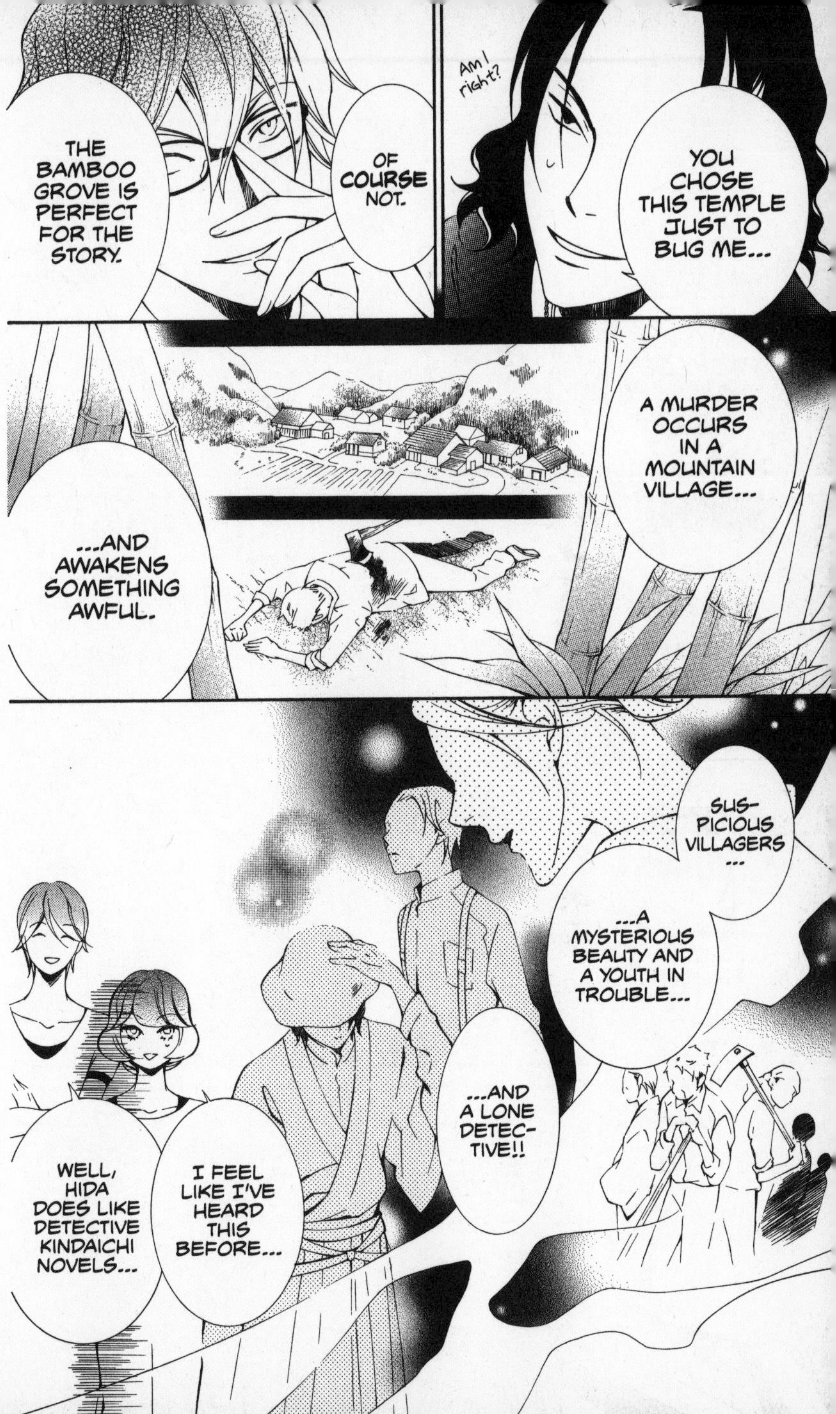
YOU CHOSE THIS TEMPLE JUST TO BUG ME...
Am I right?
OF COURSE NOT.
THE BAMBOO GROVE IS PERFECT FOR THE STORY.
A MURDER OCCURS IN A MOUNTAIN VILLAGE...
...AND AWAKENS SOMETHING AWFUL.
SUS-PICIOUS VILLAGERS...
...A MYSTERIOUS BEAUTY AND A YOUTH IN TROUBLE...
...AND A LONE DETEC-TIVE!!
I FEEL LIKE I'VE HEARD THIS BEFORE...
WELL, HIDA DOES LIKE DETECTIVE KINDAICHI NOVELS...

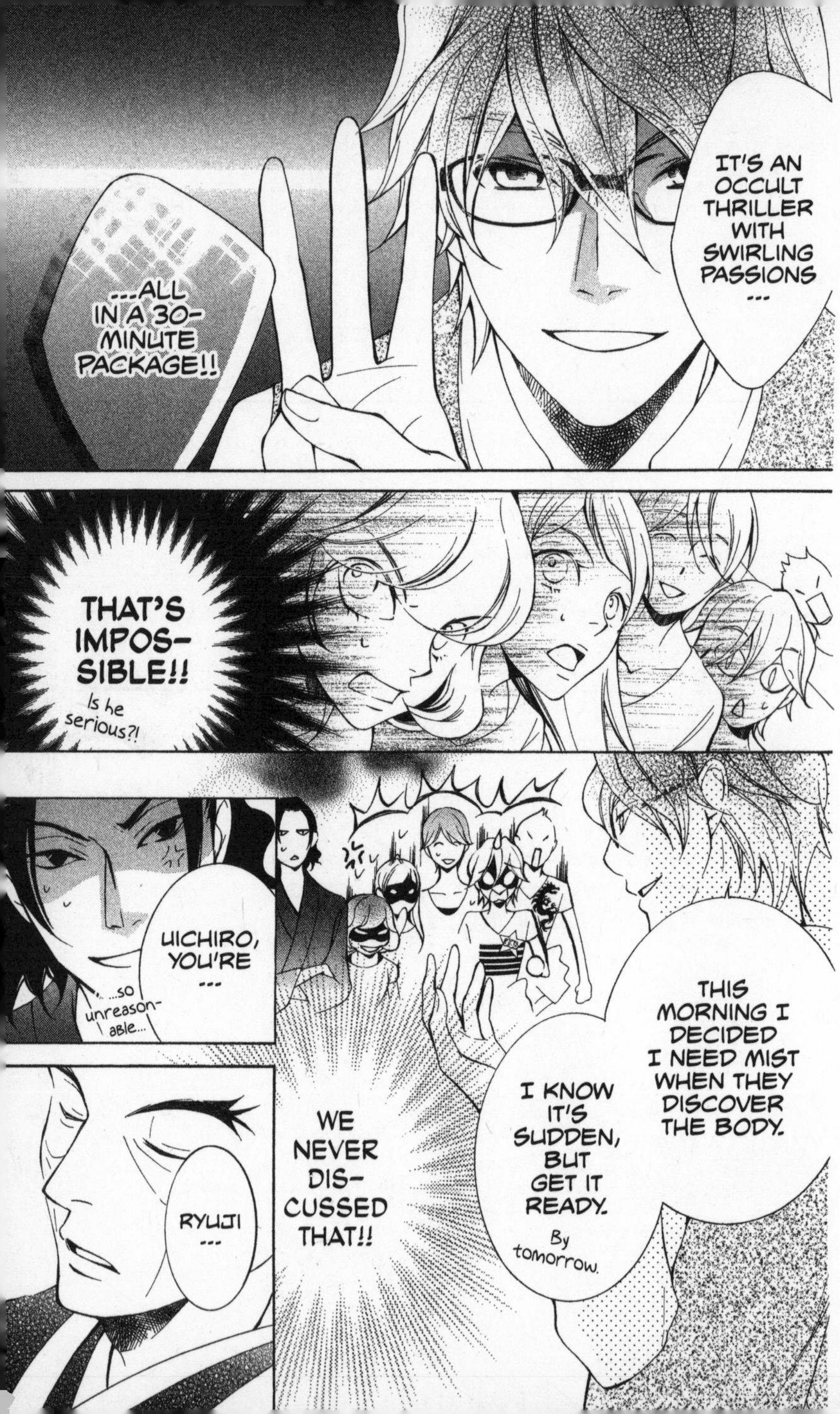
IT'S AN OCCULT THRILLER WITH SWIRLING PASSIONS...
...ALL IN A 30-MINUTE PACKAGE!!
THAT'S IMPOSSIBLE!!
Is he serious?!
THIS MORNING I DECIDED I NEED MIST WHEN THEY DISCOVER THE BODY.
I KNOW IT'S SUDDEN, BUT GET IT READY.
By tomorrow.
WE NEVER DIS-CUSSED THAT!!
UICHIRO, YOU'RE...
...so unreason-able...
RYUJI...

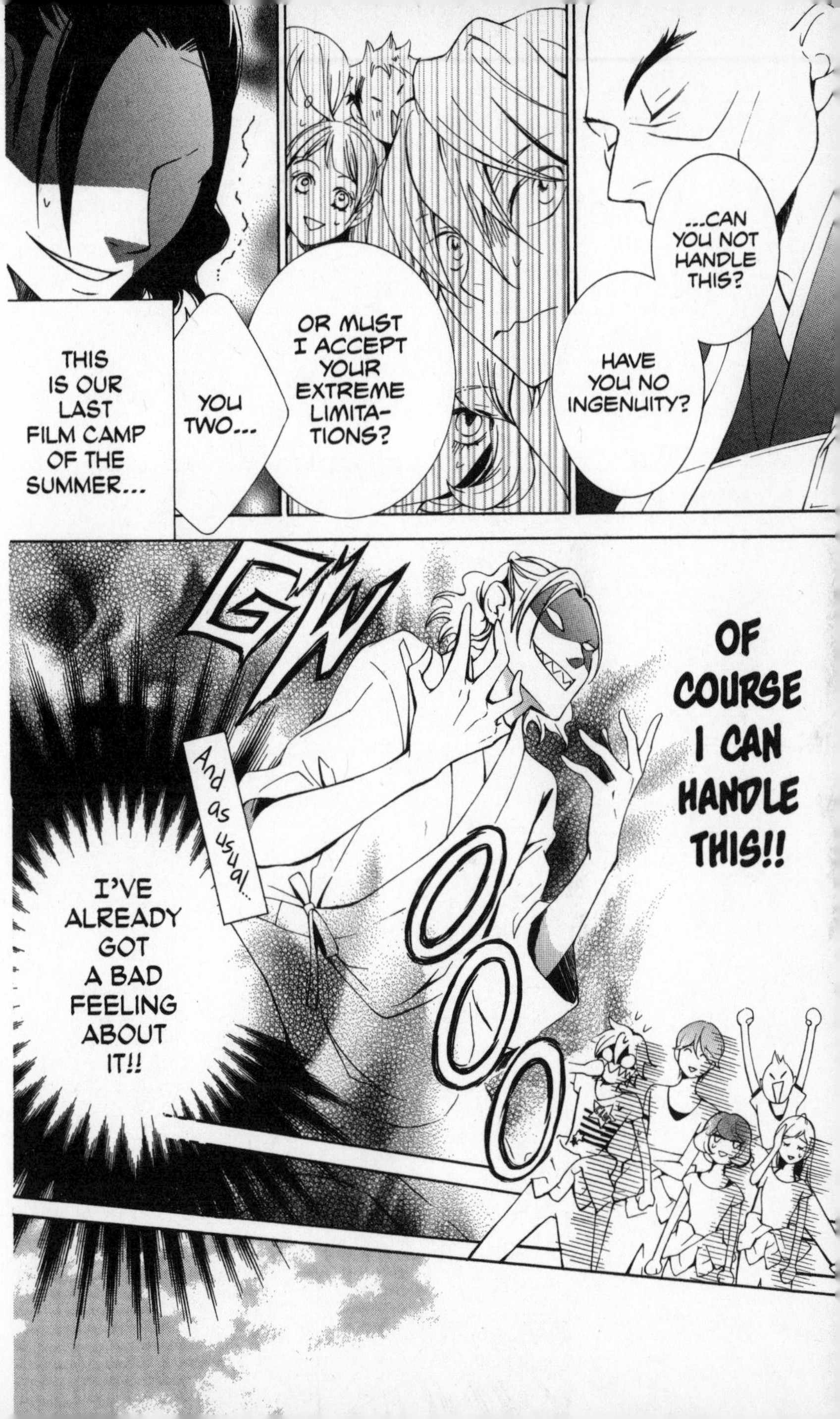
...CAN YOU NOT HANDLE THIS?
HAVE YOU NO INGENUITY?
OR MUST I ACCEPT YOUR EXTREME LIMITATIONS?
YOU TWO...
THIS IS OUR LAST FILM CAMP OF THE SUMMER...
OF COURSE I CAN HANDLE THIS!!
GW
OOO
And as usual...
I'VE ALREADY GOT A BAD FEELING ABOUT IT!!

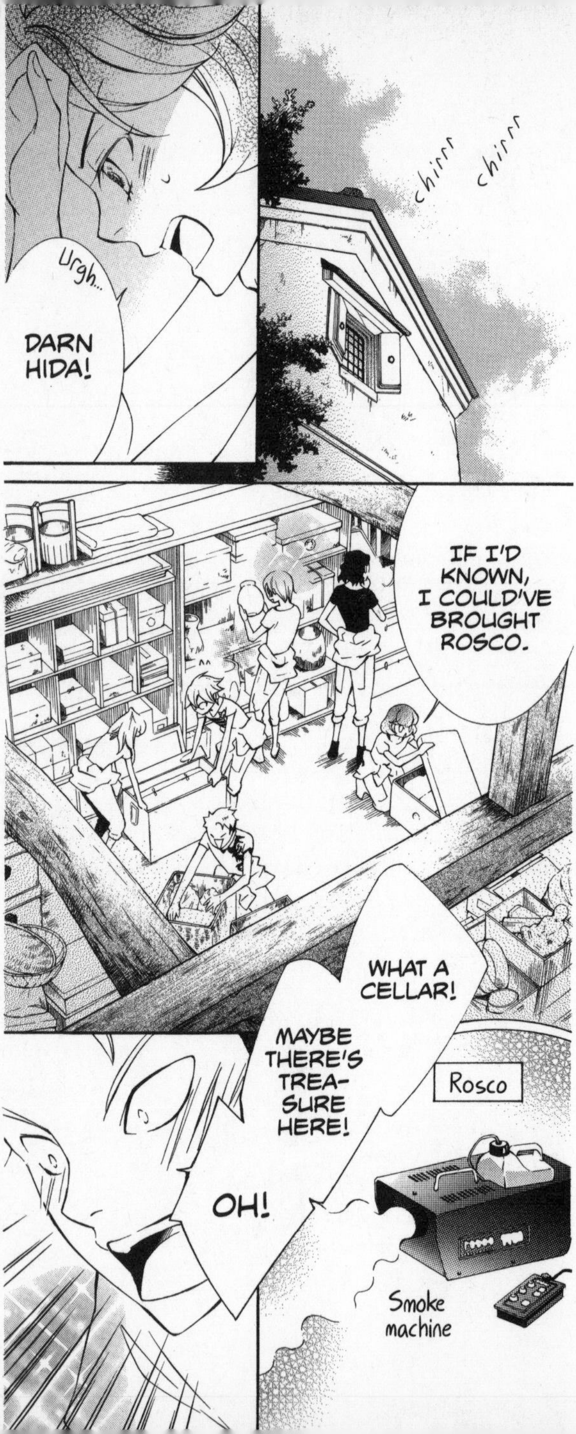
chirrr
chirrr
Urgh...
DARN HIDA!
IF I'D KNOWN, I COULD'VE BROUGHT ROSCO.
WHAT A CELLAR!
MAYBE THERE'S TREA-SURE HERE!
Rosco
Smoke machine
OH!

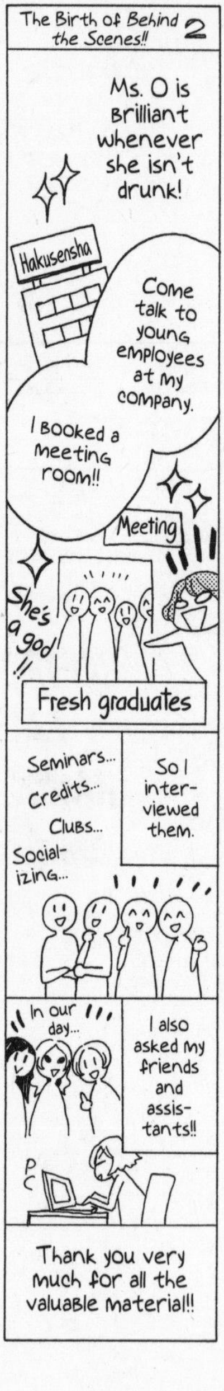
The Birth of Behind the Scenes!! 2
Ms. O is brilliant whenever she isn't drunk!
Hakusensha
Come talk to young employees at my company.
I booked a meeting room!!
Meeting
She's a god!!
Fresh graduates
So I interviewed them.
Seminars...
Credits...
Clubs...
Social-izing...
I also asked my friends and assis-tants!!
In our day...
PC
Thank you very much for all the valuable material!!

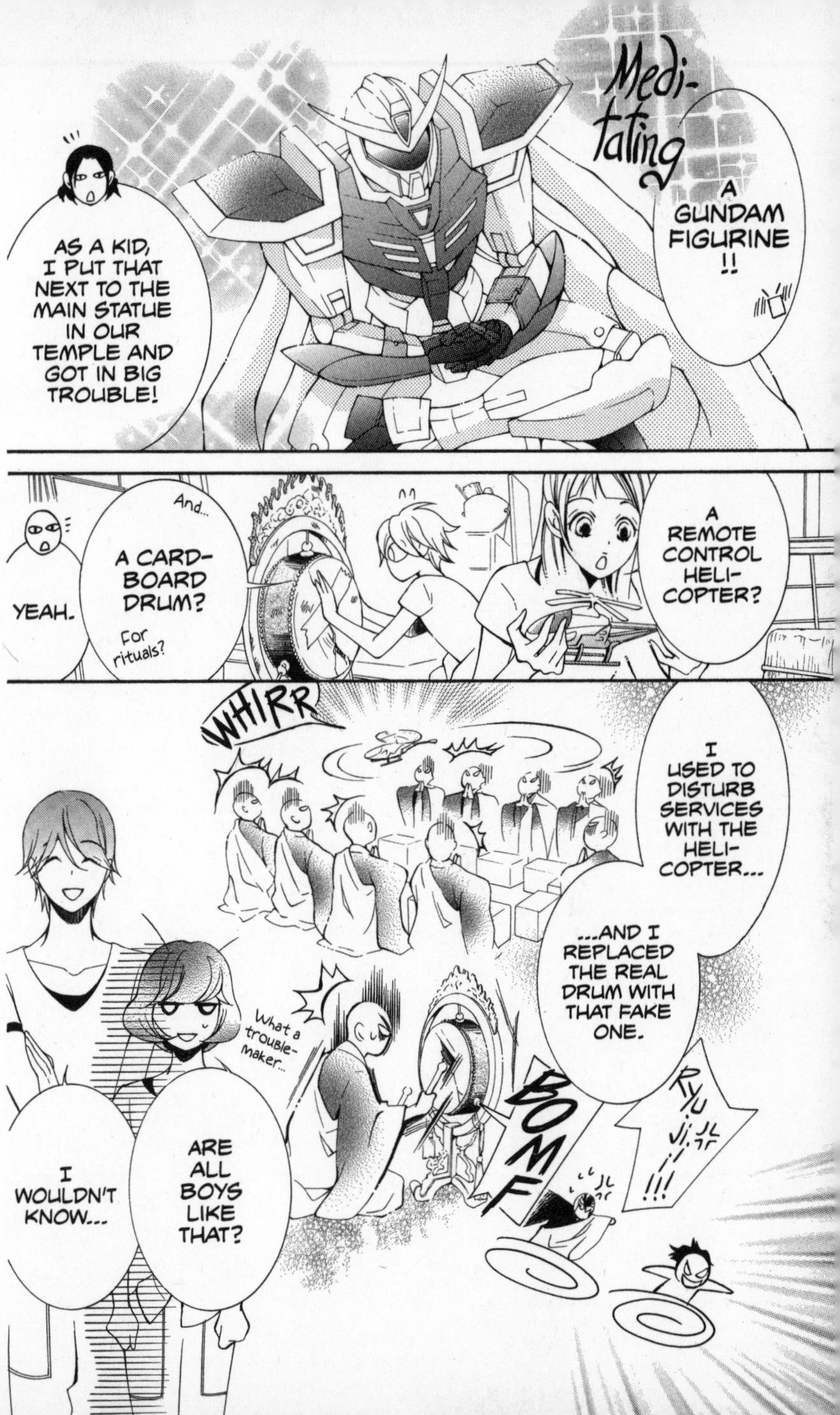
Medi-tating
A GUNDAM FIGURINE !!
AS A KID, I PUT THAT NEXT TO THE MAIN STATUE IN OUR TEMPLE AND GOT IN BIG TROUBLE!
A REMOTE CONTROL HELI-COPTER?
And...
A CARD-BOARD DRUM?
For rituals?
YEAH.
WHIRR
I USED TO DISTURB SERVICES WITH THE HELI-COPTER...
...AND I REPLACED THE REAL DRUM WITH THAT FAKE ONE.
RYUJI...!!!
BOMF
What a trouble-maker...
ARE ALL BOYS LIKE THAT?
I WOULDN'T KNOW...

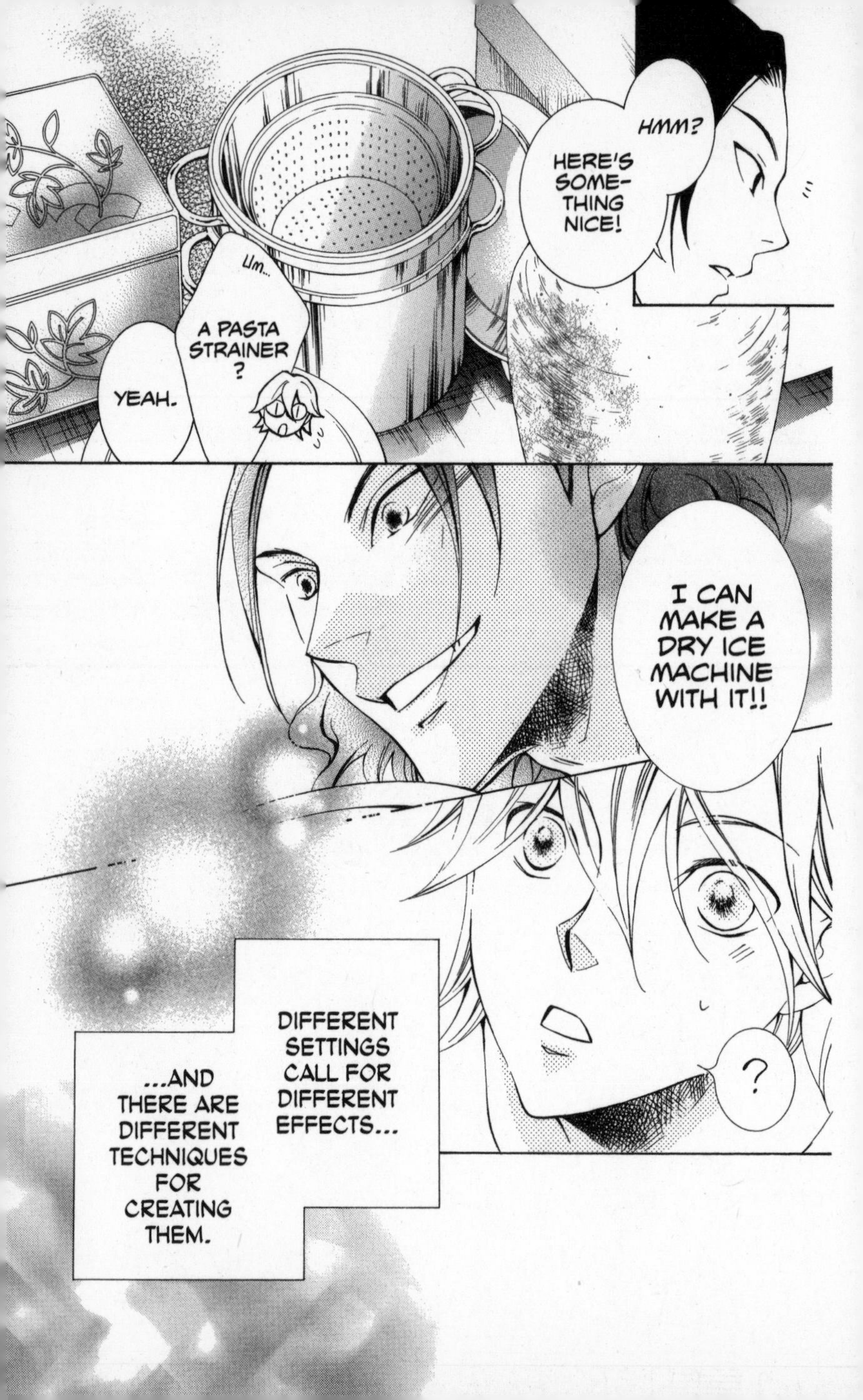
HMM?
HERE'S SOME-THING NICE!
Um...
A PASTA STRAINER?
YEAH.
I CAN MAKE A DRY ICE MACHINE WITH IT!!
?
DIFFERENT SETTINGS CALL FOR DIFFERENT EFFECTS...
...AND THERE ARE DIFFERENT TECHNIQUES FOR CREATING THEM.

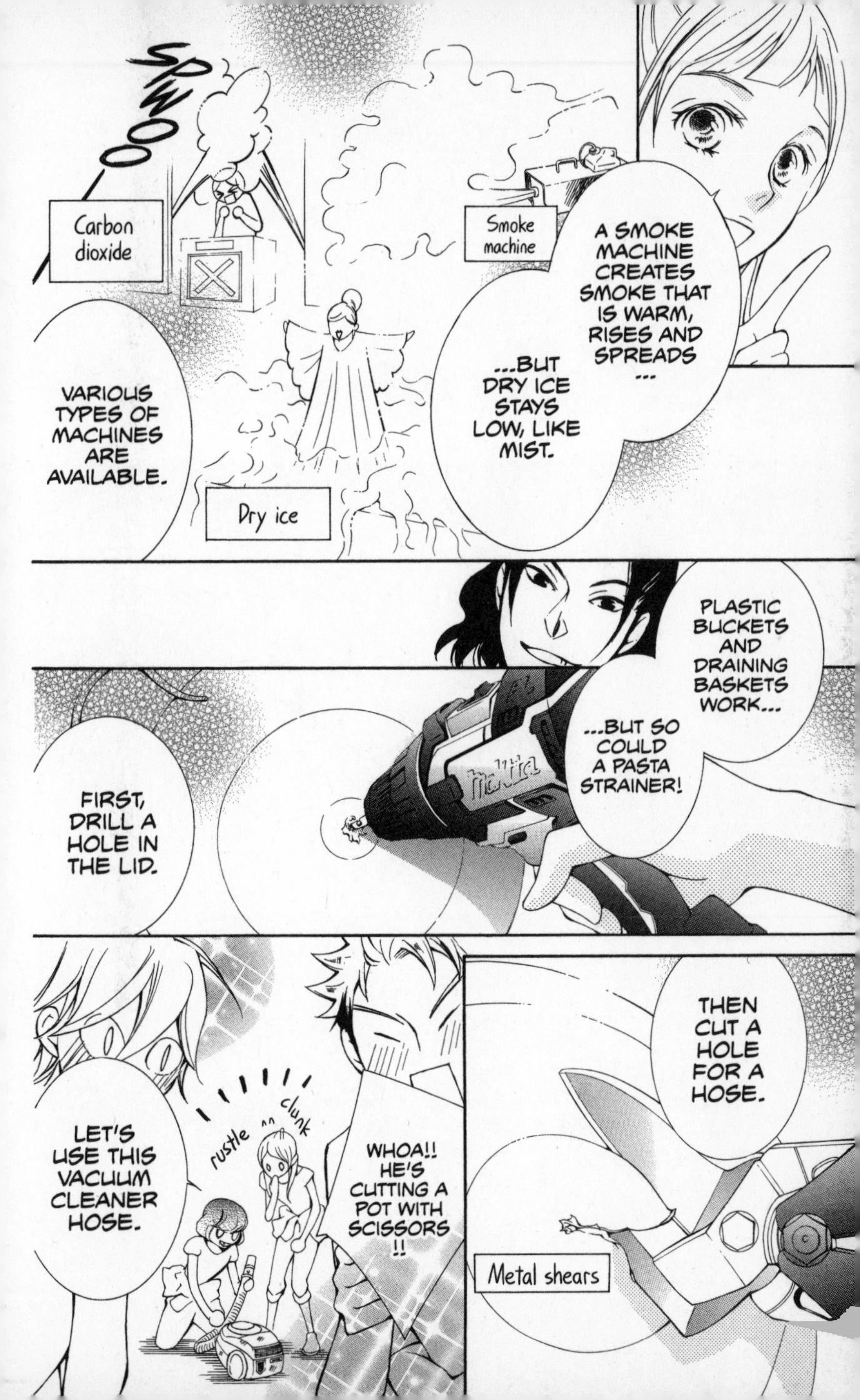
A SMOKE MACHINE CREATES SMOKE THAT IS WARM, RISES AND SPREADS ...
Smoke machine
...BUT DRY ICE STAYS LOW, LIKE MIST.
SPWOO
Carbon dioxide
VARIOUS TYPES OF MACHINES ARE AVAILABLE.
Dry ice
PLASTIC BUCKETS AND DRAINING BASKETS WORK...
...BUT SO COULD A PASTA STRAINER!
FIRST, DRILL A HOLE IN THE LID.
THEN CUT A HOLE FOR A HOSE.
Metal shears
WHOA!! HE'S CUTTING A POT WITH SCISSORS!!
clunk
rustle
LET'S USE THIS VACUUM CLEANER HOSE.

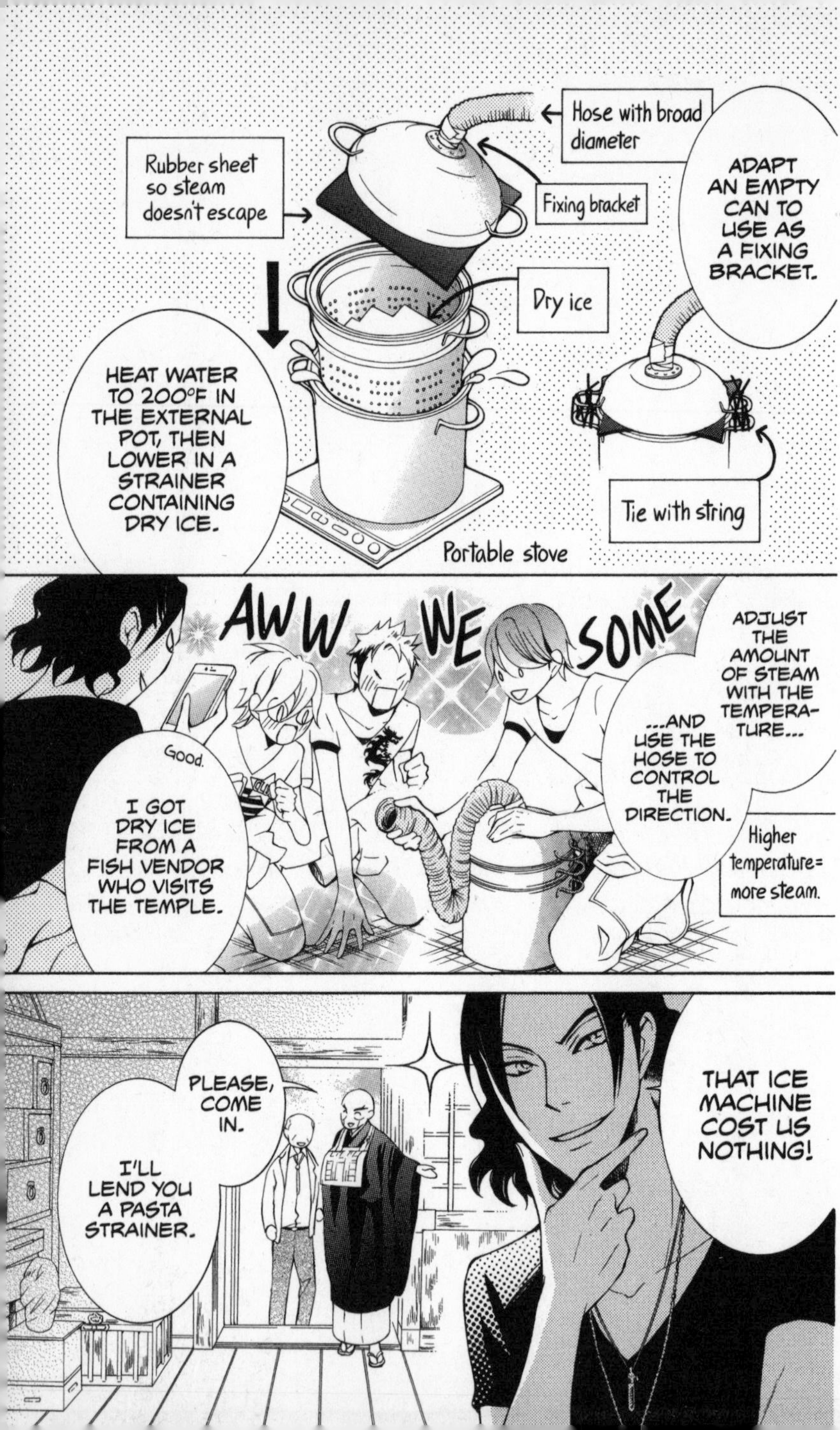
Hose with broad diameter
ADAPT AN EMPTY CAN TO USE AS A FIXING BRACKET.
Fixing bracket
Rubber sheet so steam doesn't escape
Dry ice
Tie with string
HEAT WATER TO 200°F IN THE EXTERNAL POT, THEN LOWER IN A STRAINER CONTAINING DRY ICE.
Portable stove
AWWWESOME
ADJUST THE AMOUNT OF STEAM WITH THE TEMPERATURE...
...AND USE THE HOSE TO CONTROL THE DIRECTION.
Higher temperature= more steam.
Good.
I GOT DRY ICE FROM A FISH VENDOR WHO VISITS THE TEMPLE.
THAT ICE MACHINE COST US NOTHING!
PLEASE, COME IN.
I'LL LEND YOU A PASTA STRAINER.

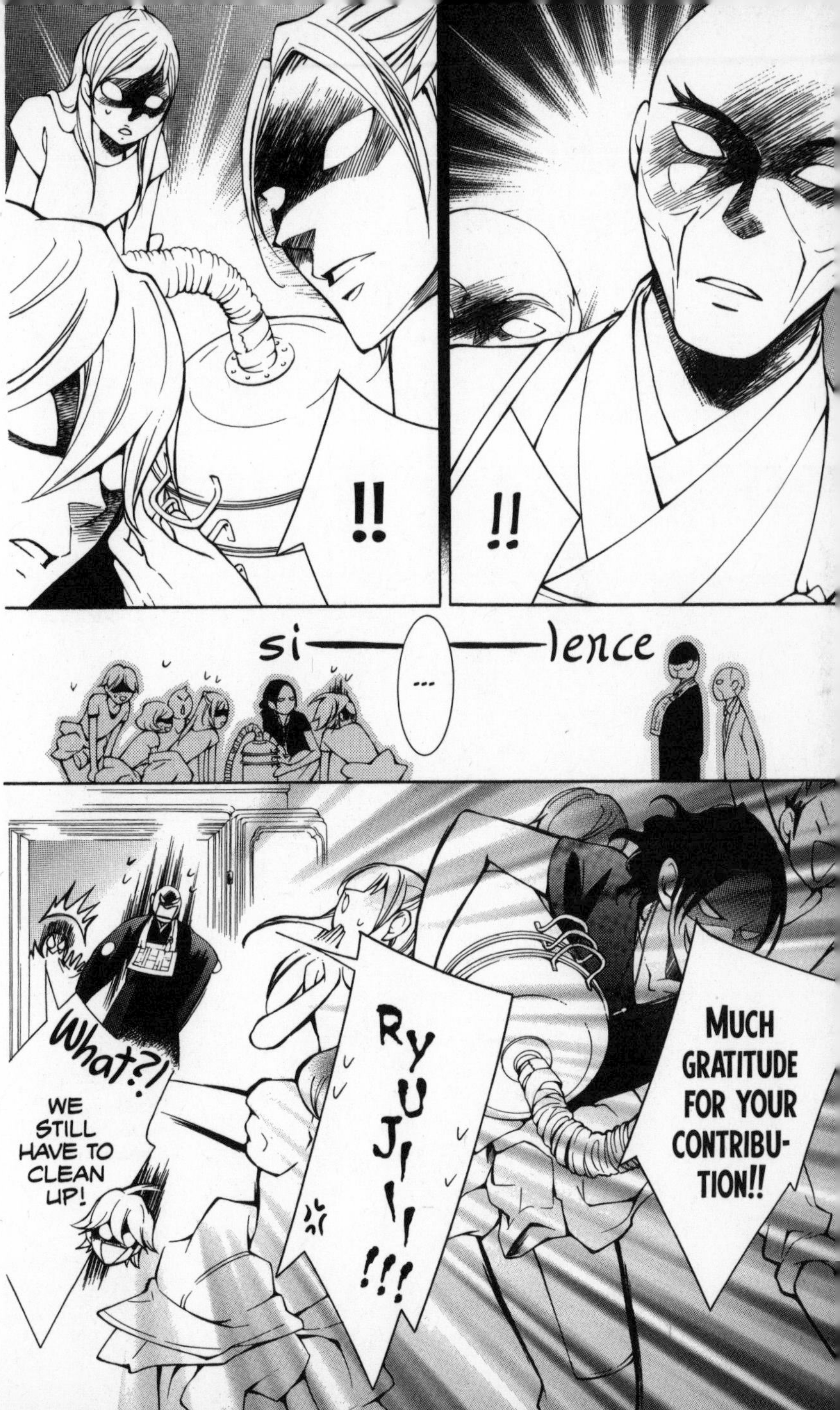
!!
!!
si—…—lence
MUCH GRATITUDE FOR YOUR CONTRIBU-TION!!
RYUJI!!!!!
What?!
WE STILL HAVE TO CLEAN UP!

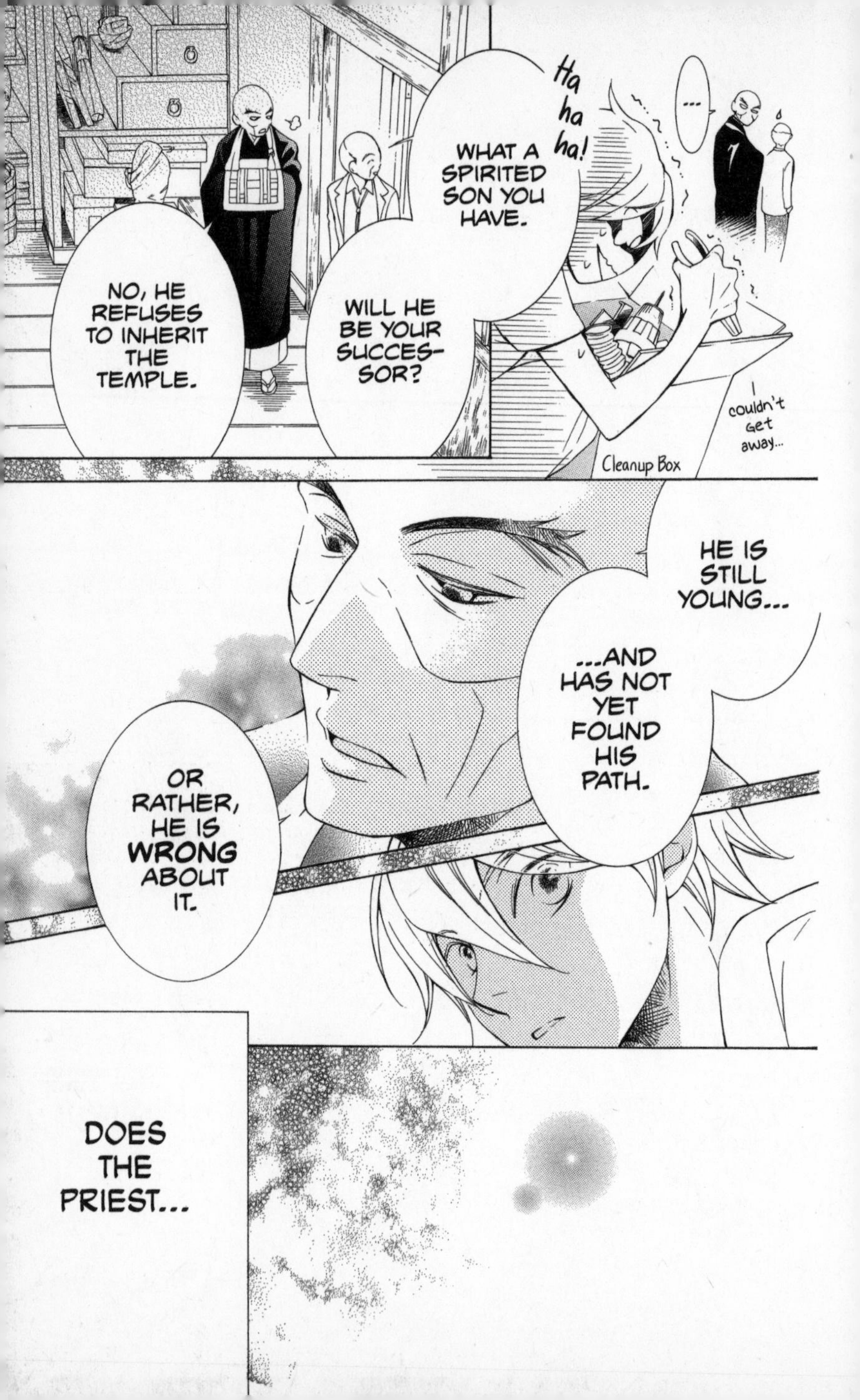
...
Ha ha ha!
WHAT A SPIRITED SON YOU HAVE.
I couldn't get away...
Cleanup Box
WILL HE BE YOUR SUCCES-SOR?
NO, HE REFUSES TO INHERIT THE TEMPLE.
HE IS STILL YOUNG...
...AND HAS NOT YET FOUND HIS PATH.
OR RATHER, HE IS **WRONG** ABOUT IT.
DOES THE PRIEST...

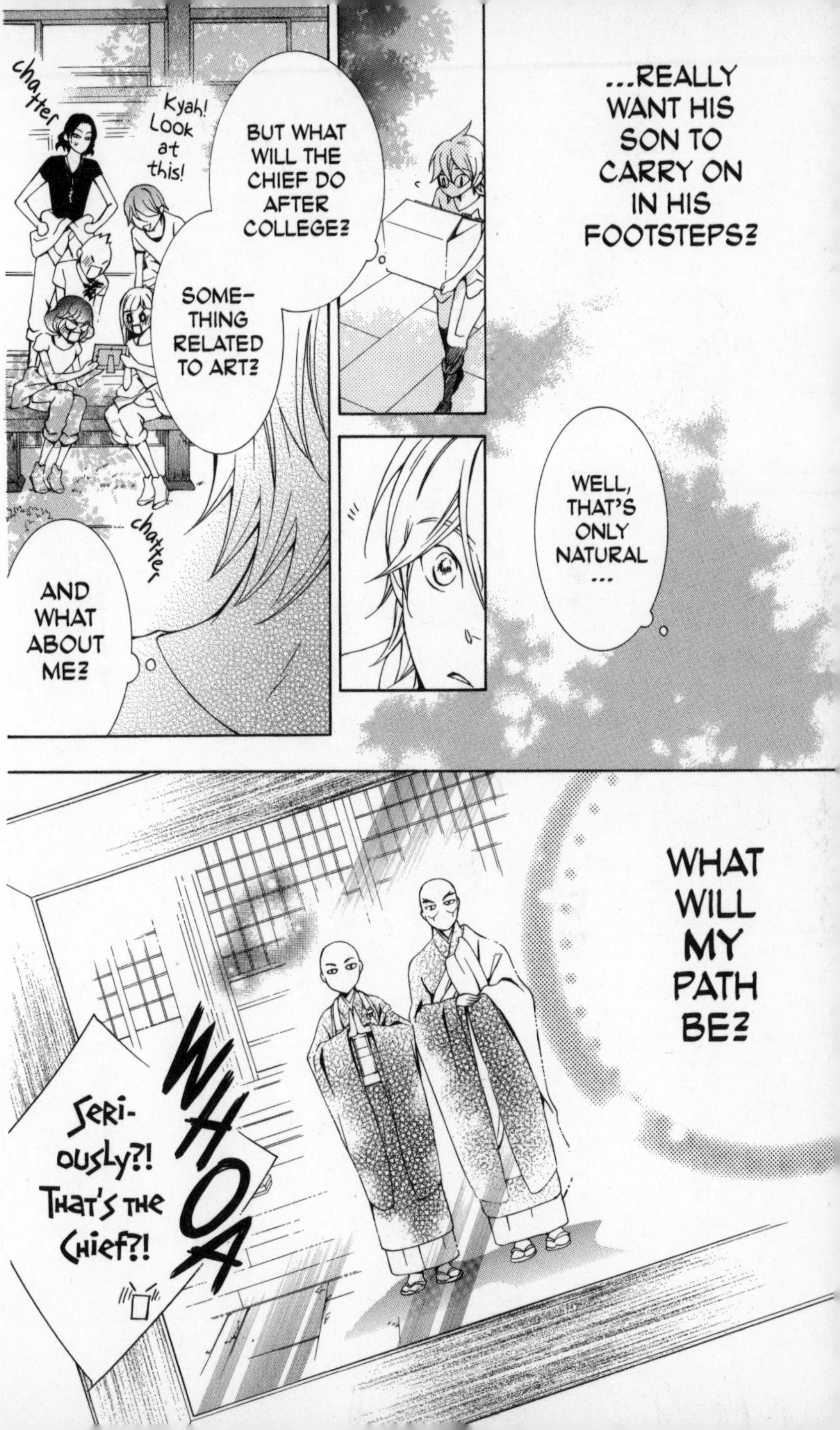
...REALLY WANT HIS SON TO CARRY ON IN HIS FOOTSTEPS?
WELL, THAT'S ONLY NATURAL...
BUT WHAT WILL THE CHIEF DO AFTER COLLEGE?
SOME-THING RELATED TO ART?
Kyah! Look at this!
chatter
chatter
AND WHAT ABOUT ME?
WHAT WILL MY PATH BE?
WHOA
Seri-ously?! That's the Chief?!

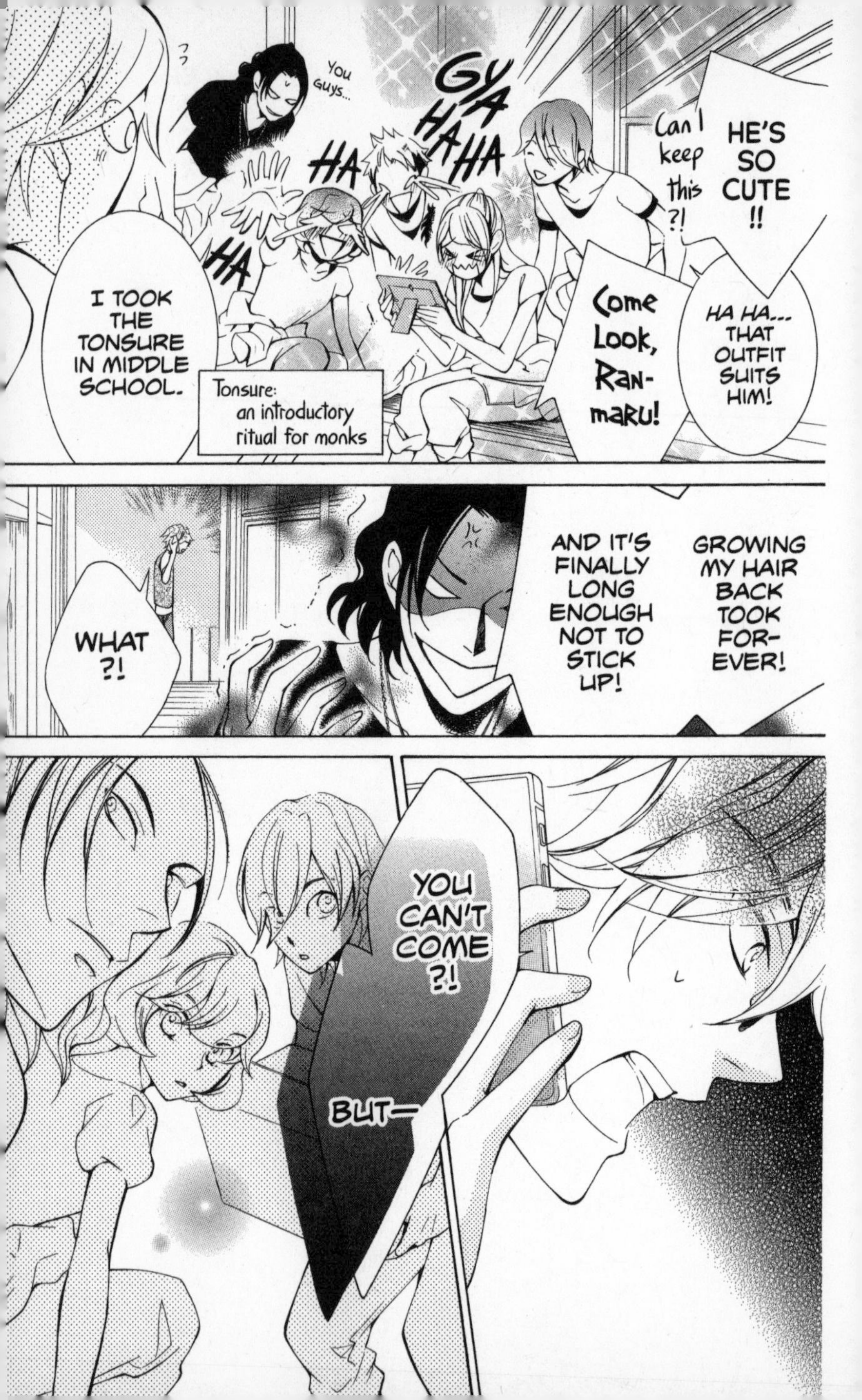
HE'S SO CUTE !!
Can I keep this ?!
HA HA... THAT OUTFIT SUITS HIM!
Come Look, Ran-maru!
GYA HA HA HA HA HA
You guys...
I TOOK THE TONSURE IN MIDDLE SCHOOL.
Tonsure: an introductory ritual for monks
GROWING MY HAIR BACK TOOK FOREVER!
AND IT'S FINALLY LONG ENOUGH NOT TO STICK UP!
WHAT ?!
YOU CAN'T COME ?!
BUT—

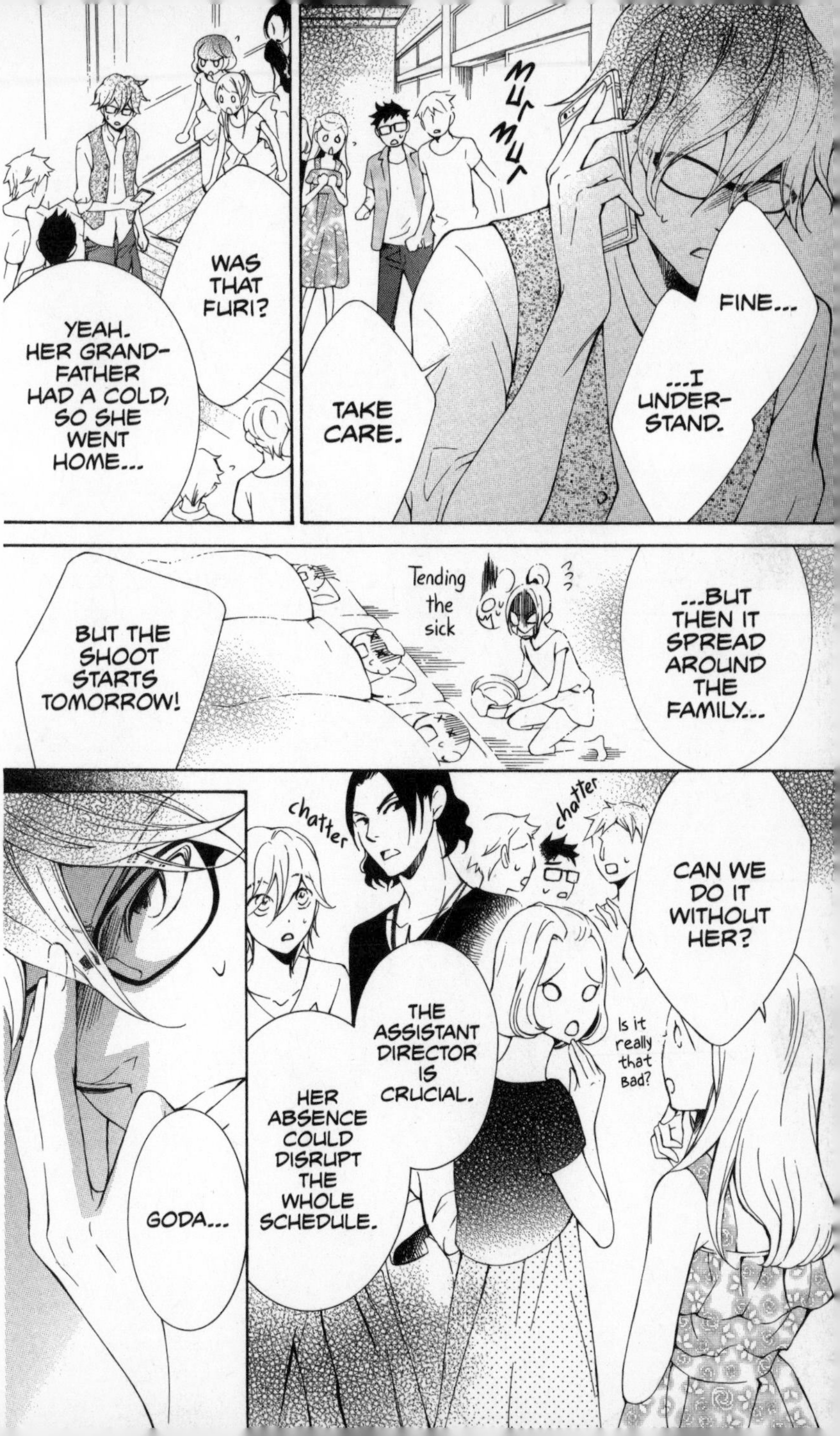
MUMUT
FINE...
...I UNDERSTAND.
TAKE CARE.
WAS THAT FURI?
YEAH. HER GRANDFATHER HAD A COLD, SO SHE WENT HOME...
...BUT THEN IT SPREAD AROUND THE FAMILY...
Tending the sick
BUT THE SHOOT STARTS TOMORROW!
CAN WE DO IT WITHOUT HER?
chatter
chatter
Is it really that bad?
THE ASSISTANT DIRECTOR IS CRUCIAL.
HER ABSENCE COULD DISRUPT THE WHOLE SCHEDULE.
GODA...

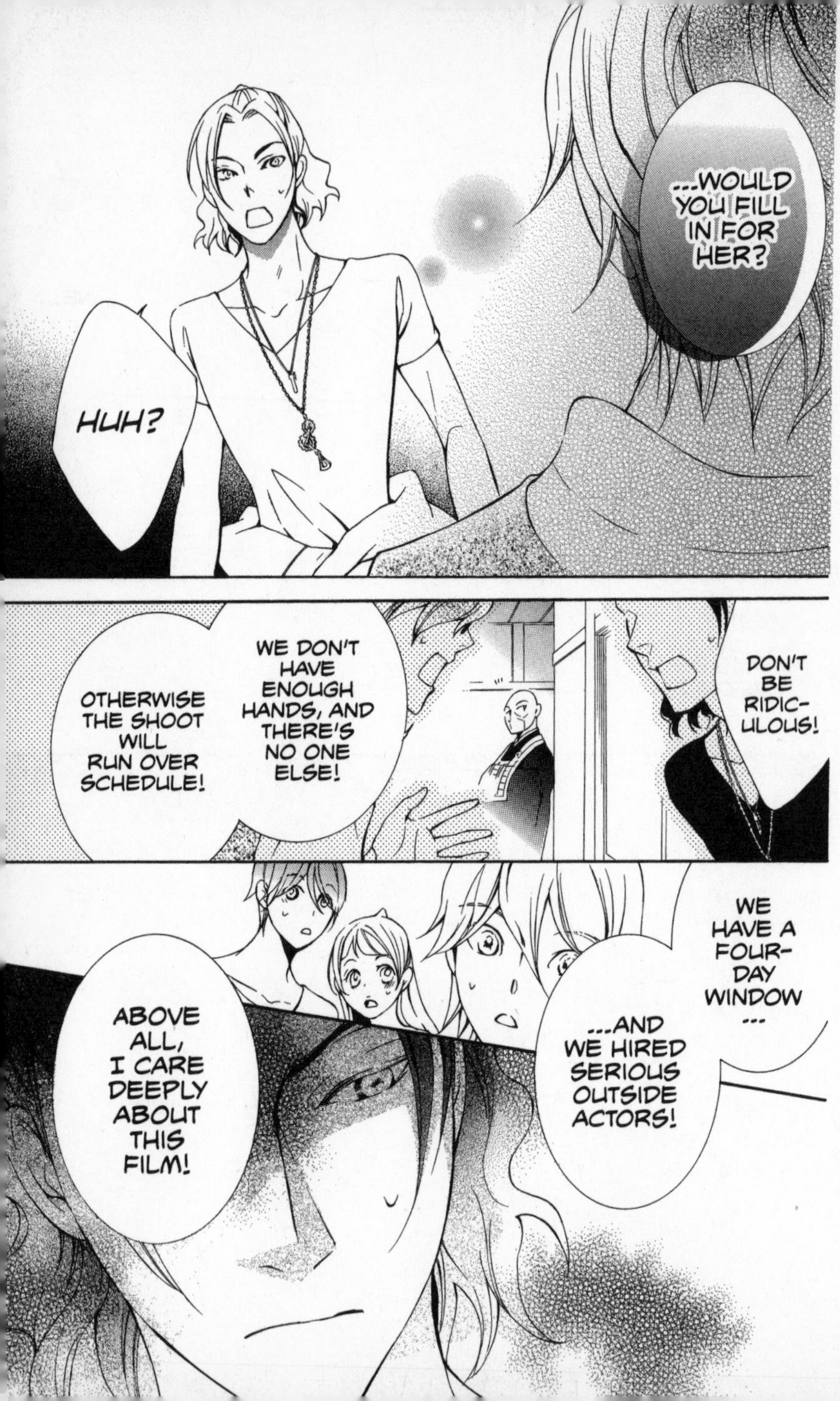
...WOULD YOU FILL IN FOR HER?
HUH?
DON'T BE RIDIC-ULOUS!
WE DON'T HAVE ENOUGH HANDS, AND THERE'S NO ONE ELSE!
OTHERWISE THE SHOOT WILL RUN OVER SCHEDULE!
WE HAVE A FOUR-DAY WINDOW...
...AND WE HIRED SERIOUS OUTSIDE ACTORS!
ABOVE ALL, I CARE DEEPLY ABOUT THIS FILM!

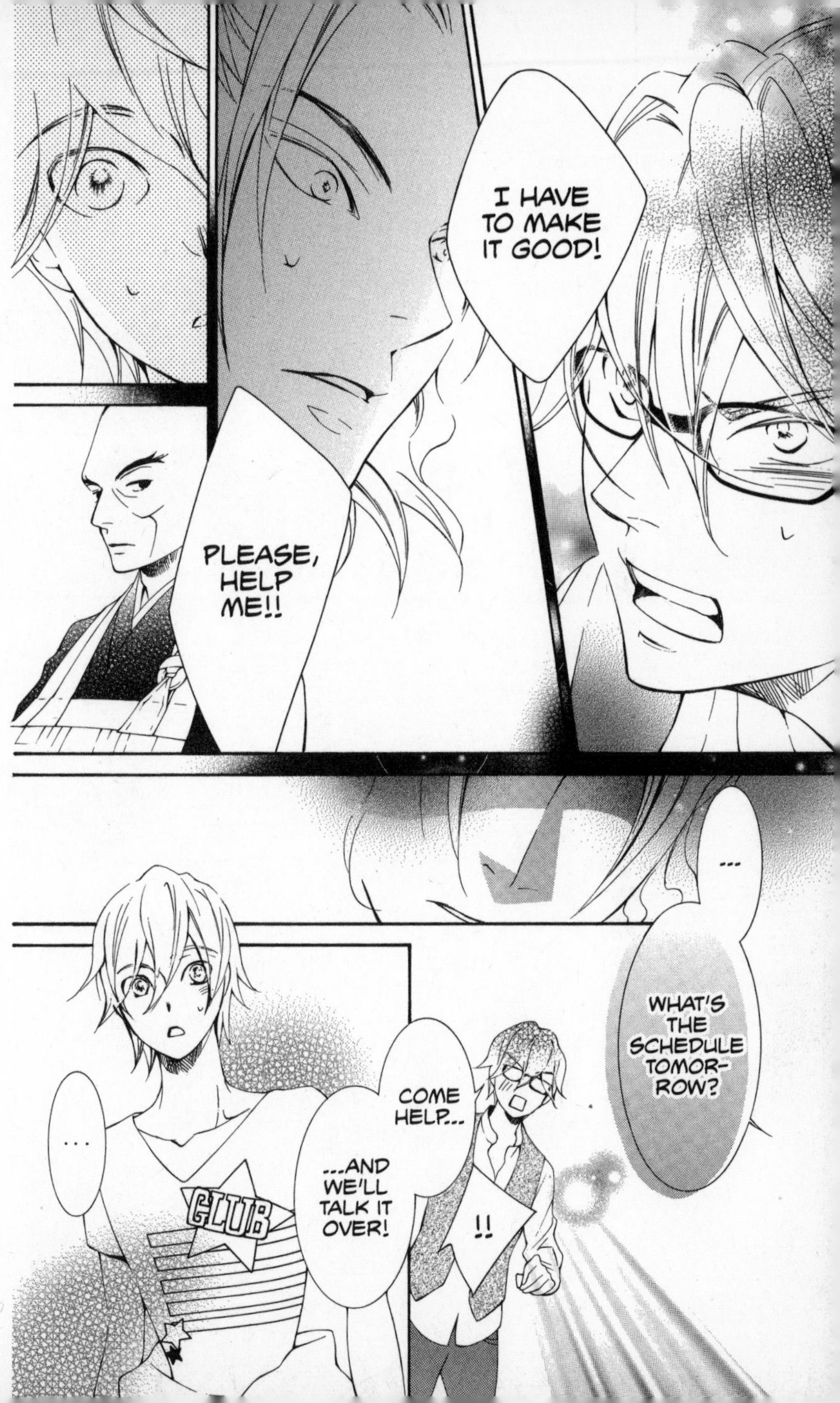
I HAVE TO MAKE IT GOOD!
PLEASE, HELP ME!!
...
WHAT'S THE SCHEDULE TOMOR-ROW?
!!
COME HELP...
...AND WE'LL TALK IT OVER!
. . .

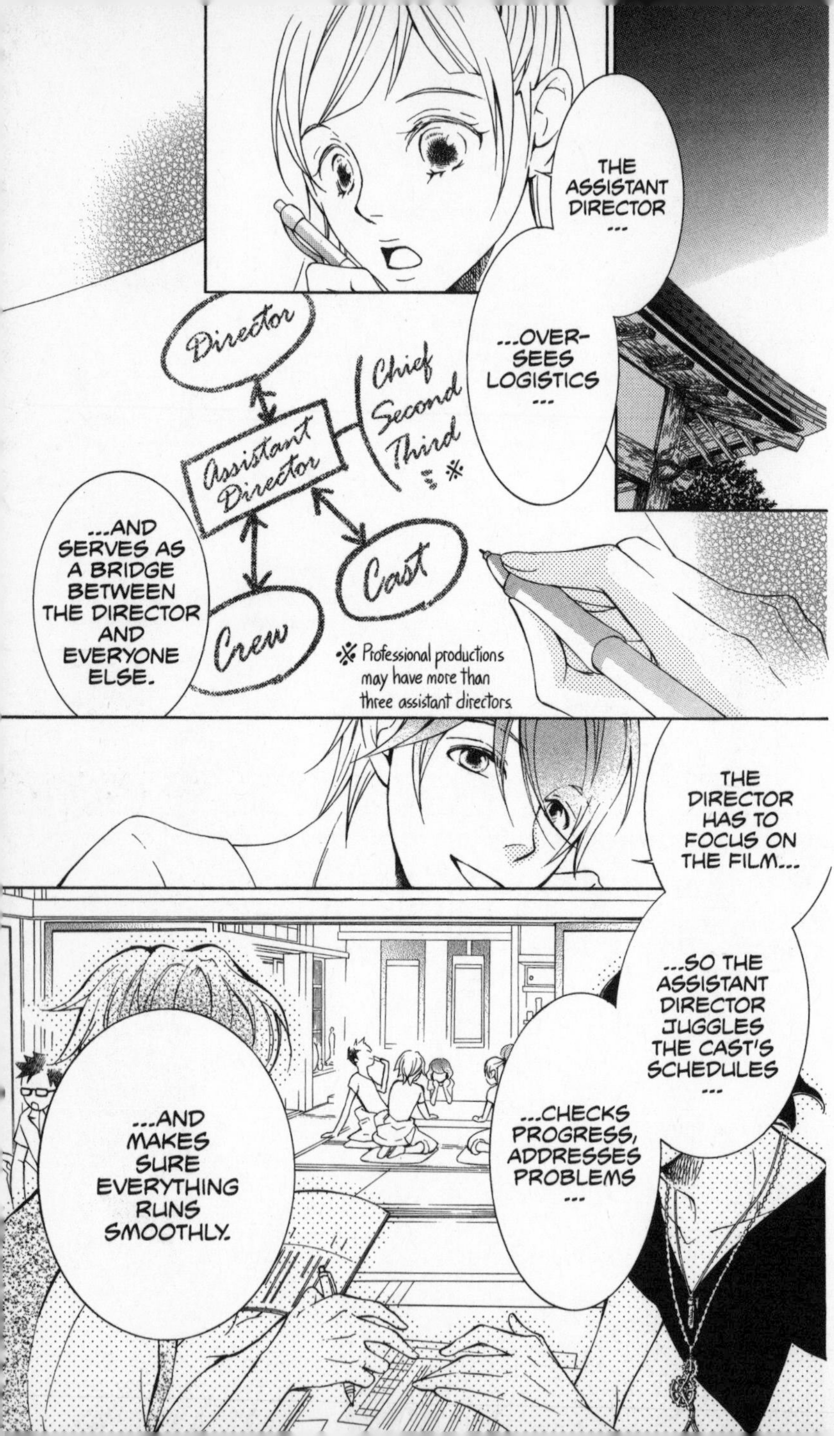
THE ASSISTANT DIRECTOR ...
...OVER-SEES LOGISTICS ...
Director
Assistant Director
Chief
Second
Third
※
Cast
Crew
...AND SERVES AS A BRIDGE BETWEEN THE DIRECTOR AND EVERYONE ELSE.
※ Professional productions may have more than three assistant directors.
THE DIRECTOR HAS TO FOCUS ON THE FILM...
...SO THE ASSISTANT DIRECTOR JUGGLES THE CAST'S SCHEDULES ...
...CHECKS PROGRESS, ADDRESSES PROBLEMS ...
...AND MAKES SURE EVERYTHING RUNS SMOOTHLY.

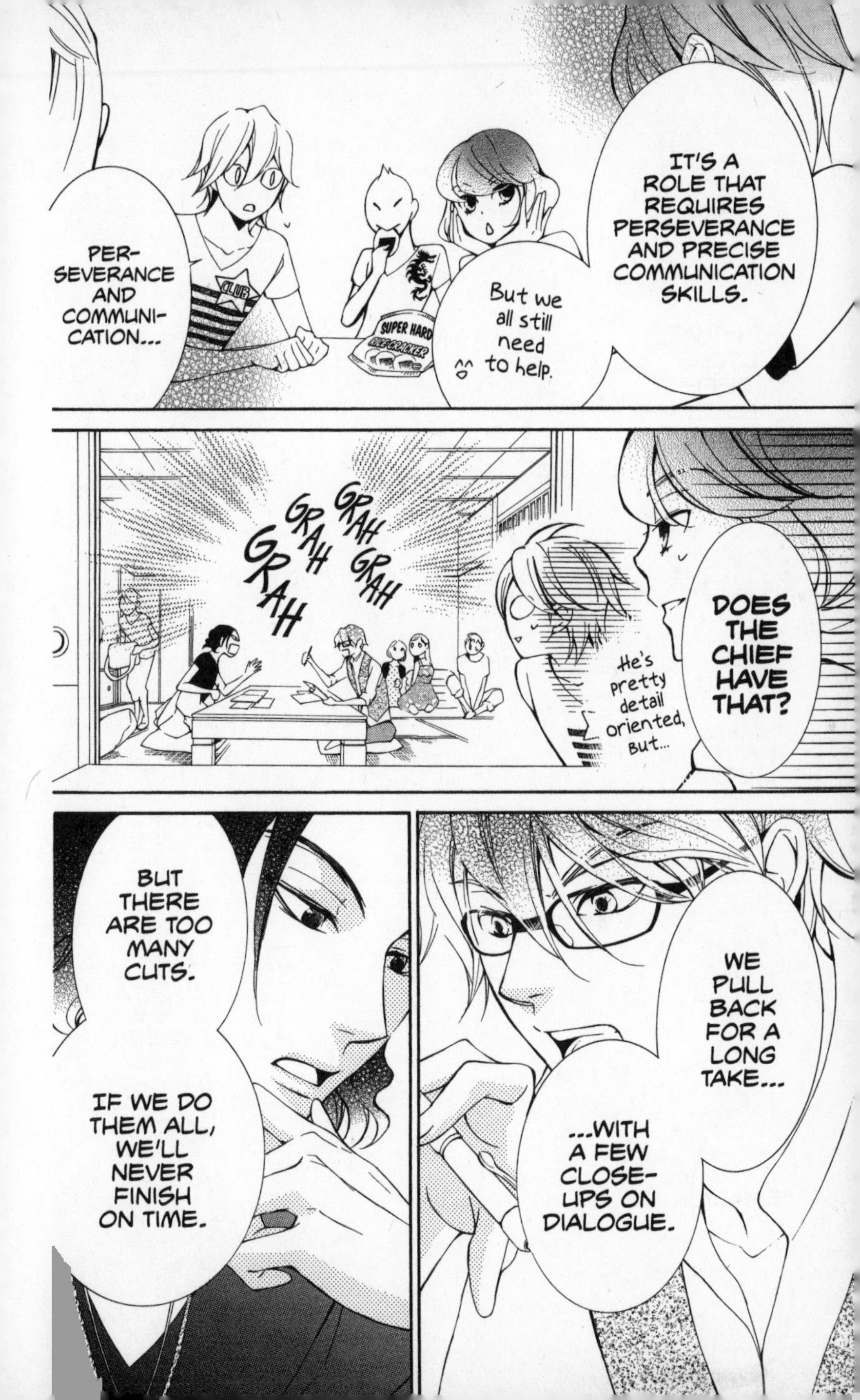
IT'S A ROLE THAT REQUIRES PERSEVERANCE AND PRECISE COMMUNICATION SKILLS.
But we all still need to help.
SUPER HARD
CLUB
PER-SEVERANCE AND COMMUNI-CATION...
DOES THE CHIEF HAVE THAT?
He's pretty detail oriented, But...
GRAH GRAH GRAH GRAH
WE PULL BACK FOR A LONG TAKE...
...WITH A FEW CLOSE-UPS ON DIALOGUE.
BUT THERE ARE TOO MANY CUTS.
IF WE DO THEM ALL, WE'LL NEVER FINISH ON TIME.

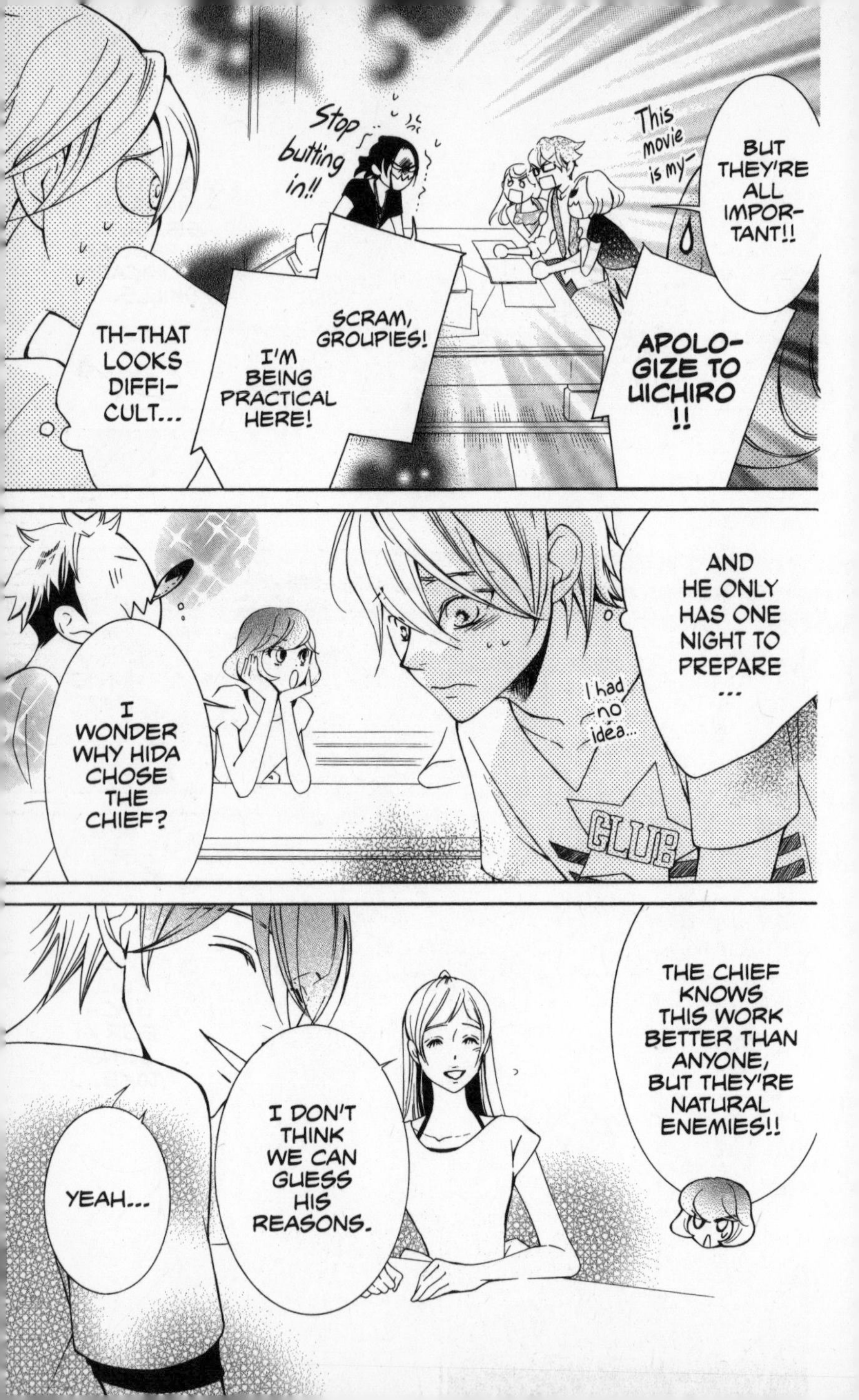
BUT THEY'RE ALL IMPORTANT!!
This movie is my—
APOLOGIZE TO UICHIRO!!
Stop butting in!!
SCRAM, GROUPIES!
I'M BEING PRACTICAL HERE!
TH-THAT LOOKS DIFFI-CULT...
AND HE ONLY HAS ONE NIGHT TO PREPARE...
I had no idea...
CLUB
I WONDER WHY HIDA CHOSE THE CHIEF?
THE CHIEF KNOWS THIS WORK BETTER THAN ANYONE, BUT THEY'RE NATURAL ENEMIES!!
I DON'T THINK WE CAN GUESS HIS REASONS.
YEAH...

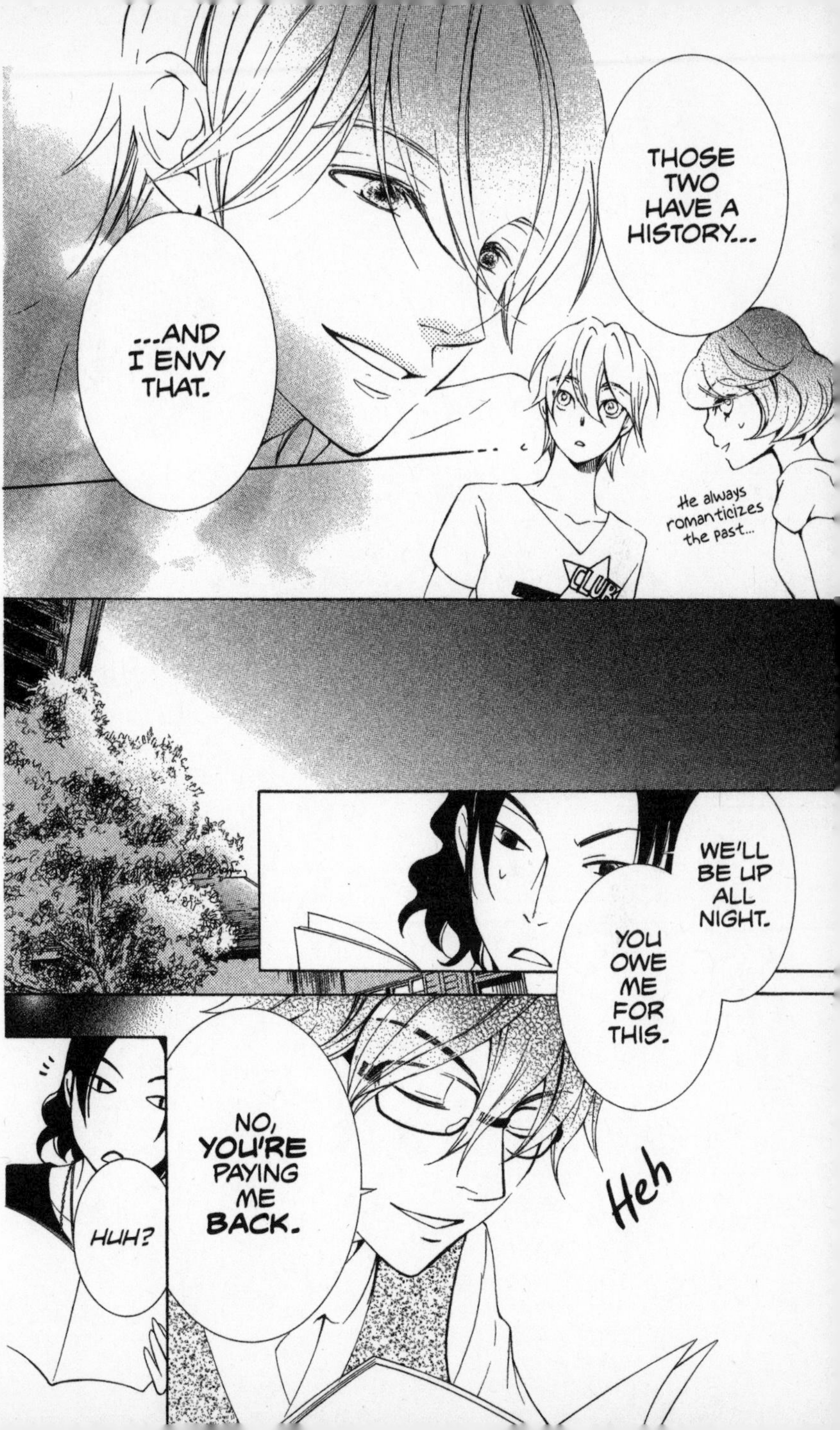
THOSE TWO HAVE A HISTORY...
...AND I ENVY THAT.
He always romanticizes the past...
WE'LL BE UP ALL NIGHT.
YOU OWE ME FOR THIS.
Heh
NO, YOU'RE PAYING ME BACK.
HUH?

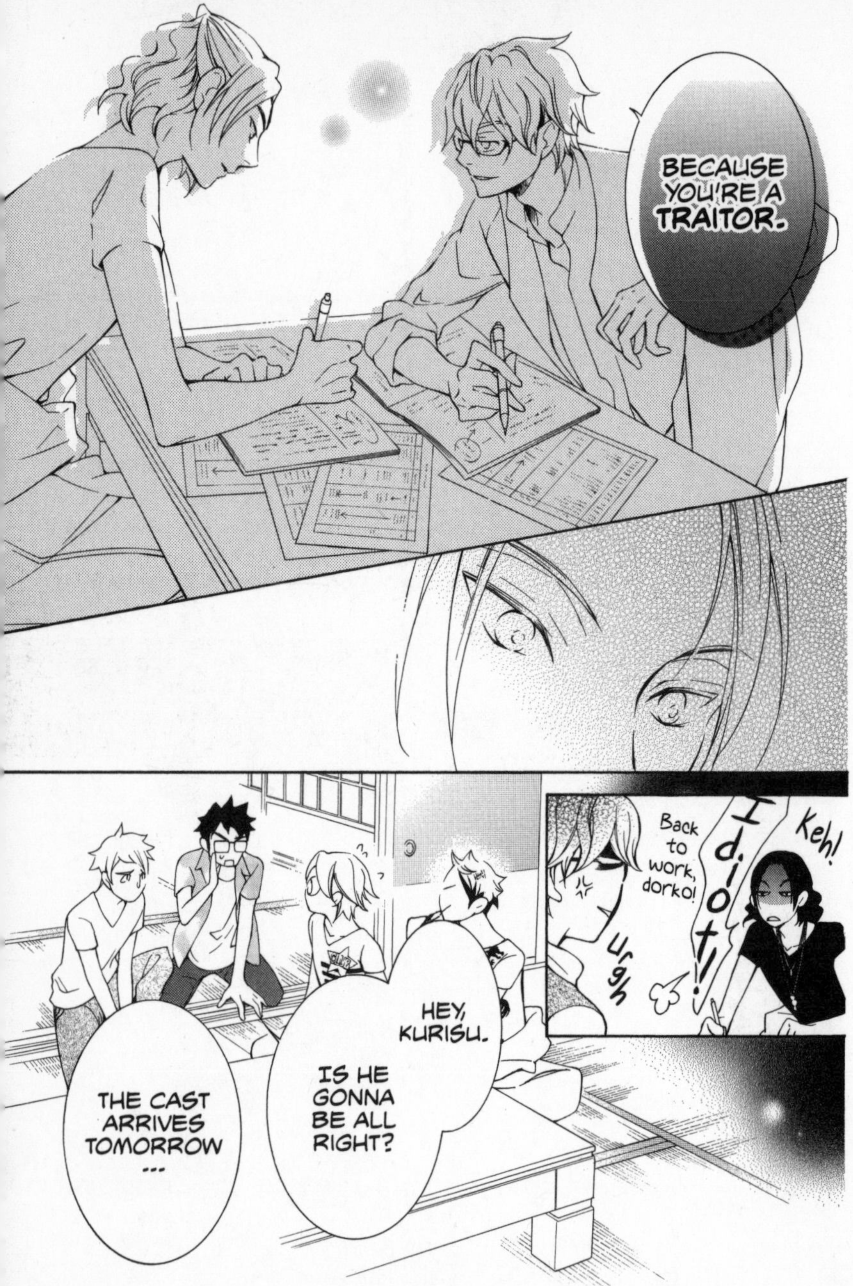
BECAUSE YOU'RE A TRAITOR.
Keh!
Back to work, dorko!
Idiot!!
Urgh
HEY, KURISU.
IS HE GONNA BE ALL RIGHT?
THE CAST ARRIVES TOMORROW ...

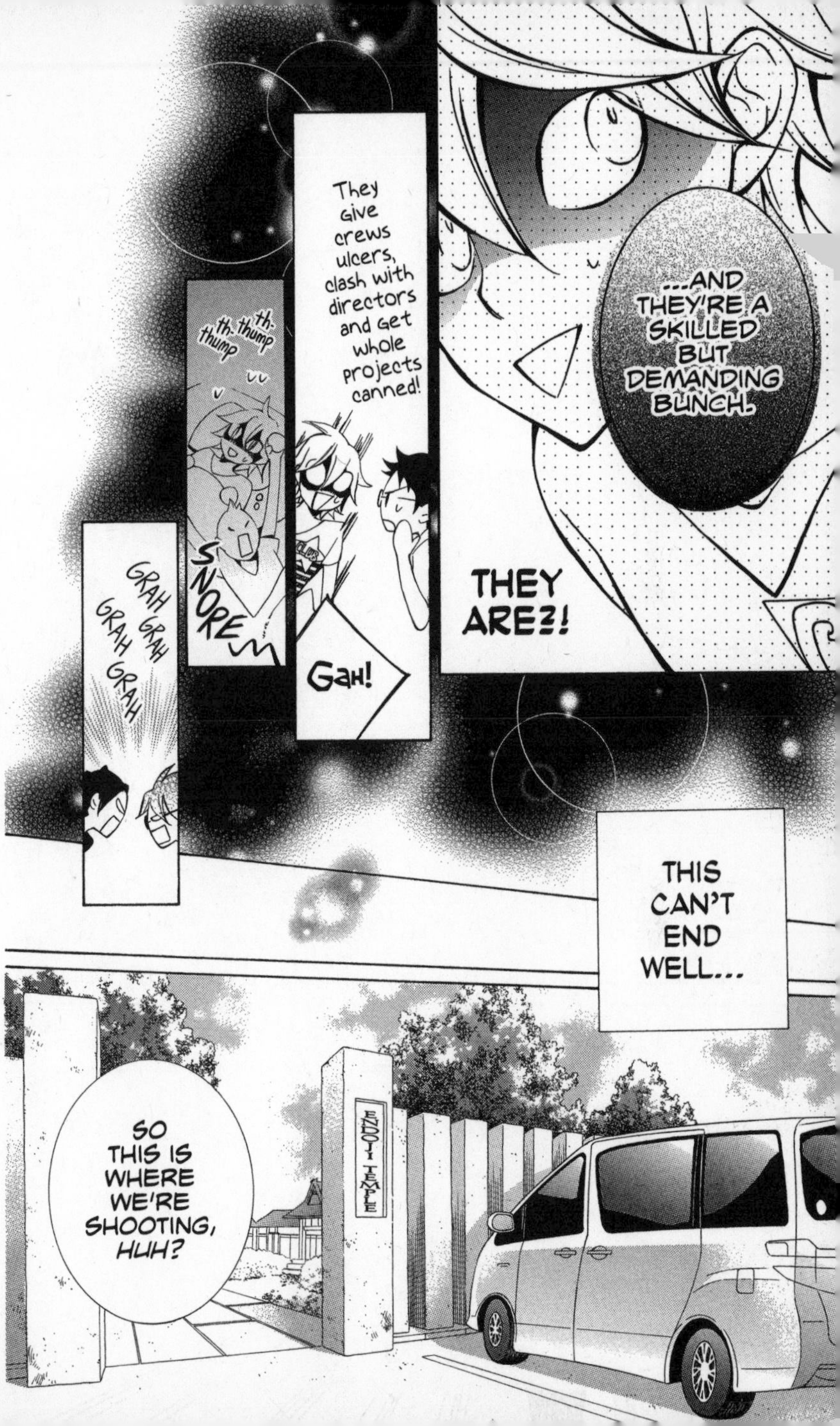
...AND THEY'RE A SKILLED BUT DEMANDING BUNCH.
THEY ARE?!
They give crews ulcers, clash with directors and get whole projects canned!
GAH!
th-thump th-thump
SNORE
GRAH GRAH GRAH GRAH
THIS CAN'T END WELL...
ENDOJI TEMPLE
SO THIS IS WHERE WE'RE SHOOTING, HUH?

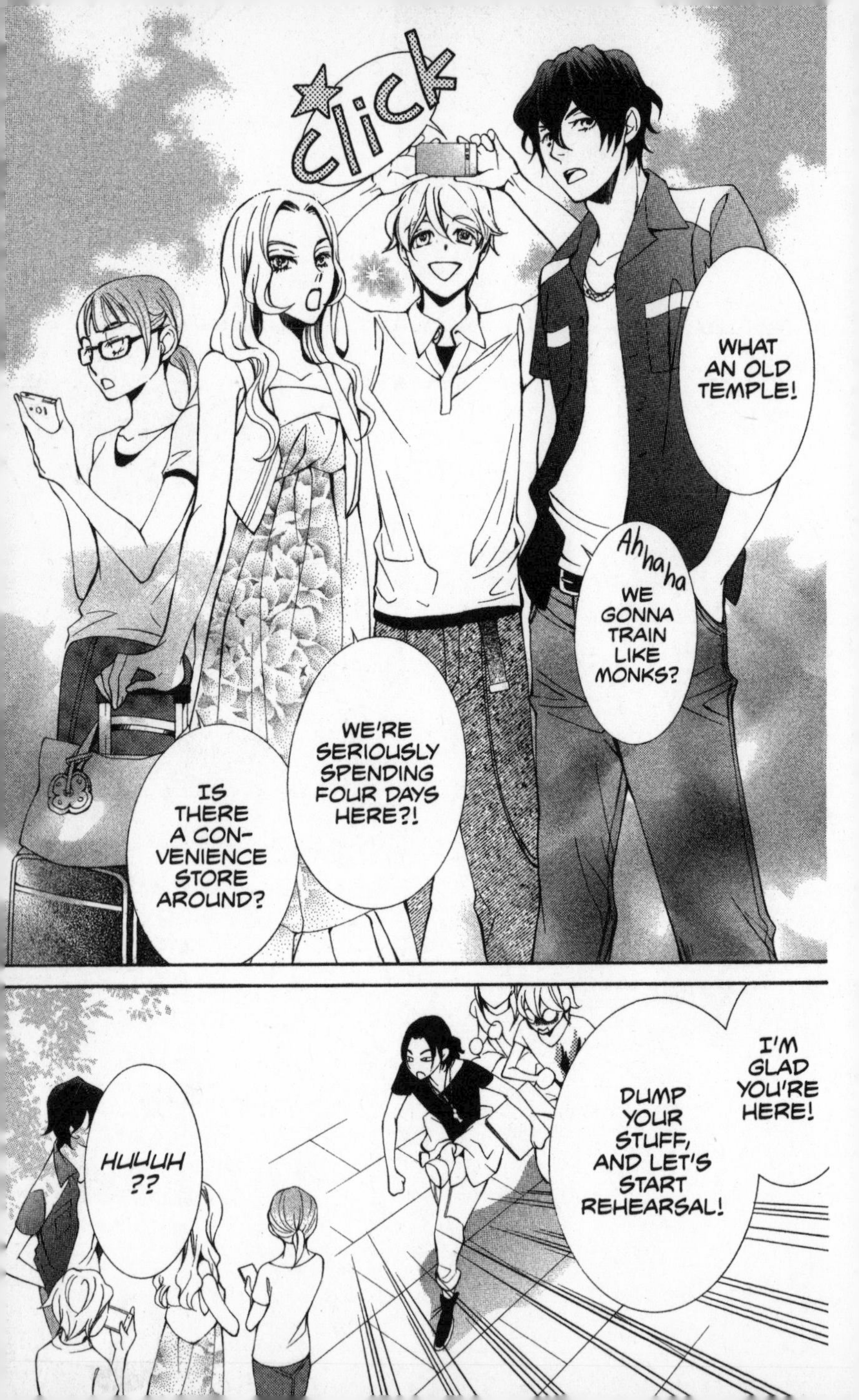
Click
WHAT AN OLD TEMPLE!
Ahhaha
WE GONNA TRAIN LIKE MONKS?
WE'RE SERIOUSLY SPENDING FOUR DAYS HERE?!
IS THERE A CON-VENIENCE STORE AROUND?
I'M GLAD YOU'RE HERE!
DUMP YOUR STUFF, AND LET'S START REHEARSAL!
HUUUH ??

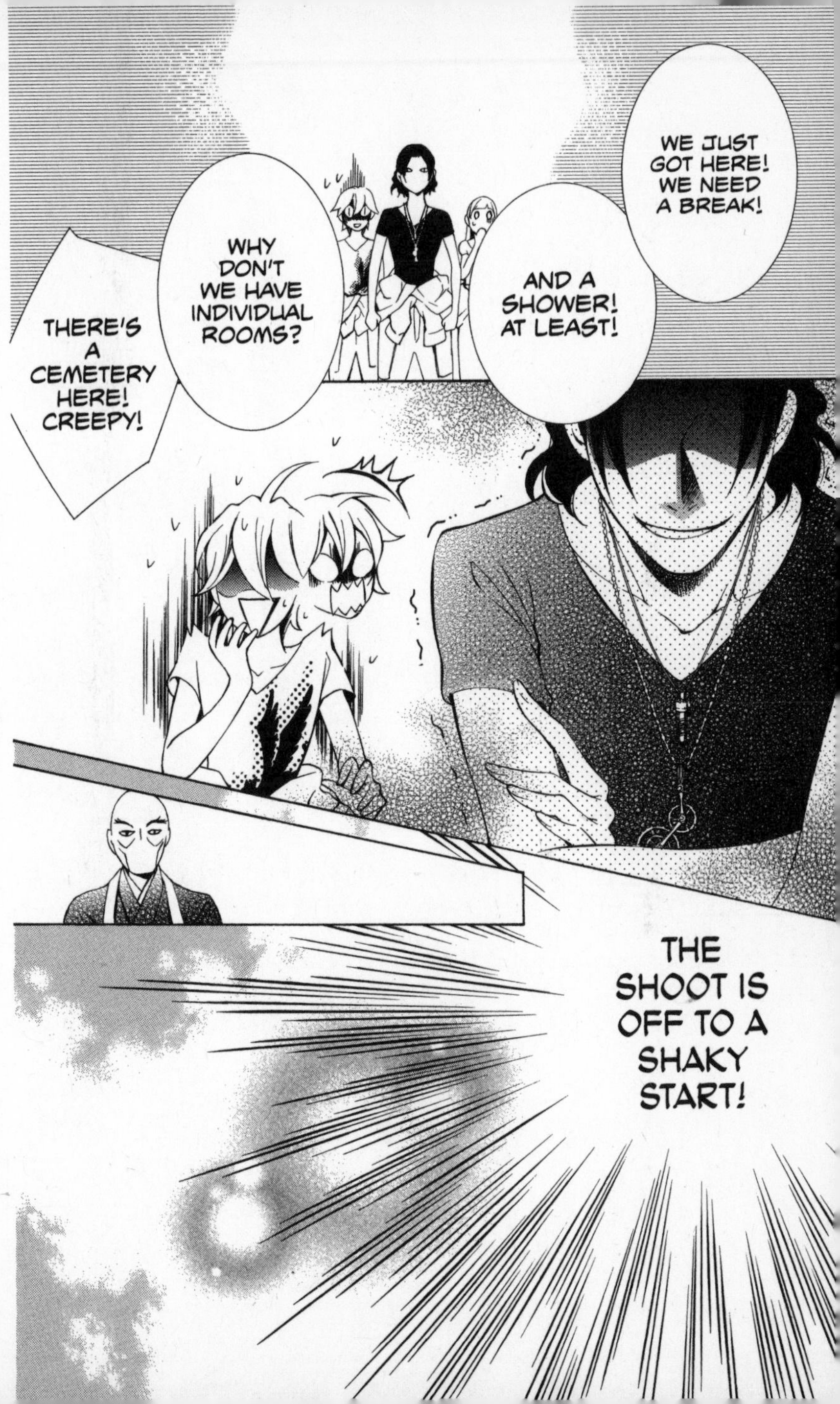
WE JUST GOT HERE! WE NEED A BREAK!
AND A SHOWER! AT LEAST!
WHY DON'T WE HAVE INDIVIDUAL ROOMS?
THERE'S A CEMETERY HERE! CREEPY!
THE SHOOT IS OFF TO A SHAKY START!

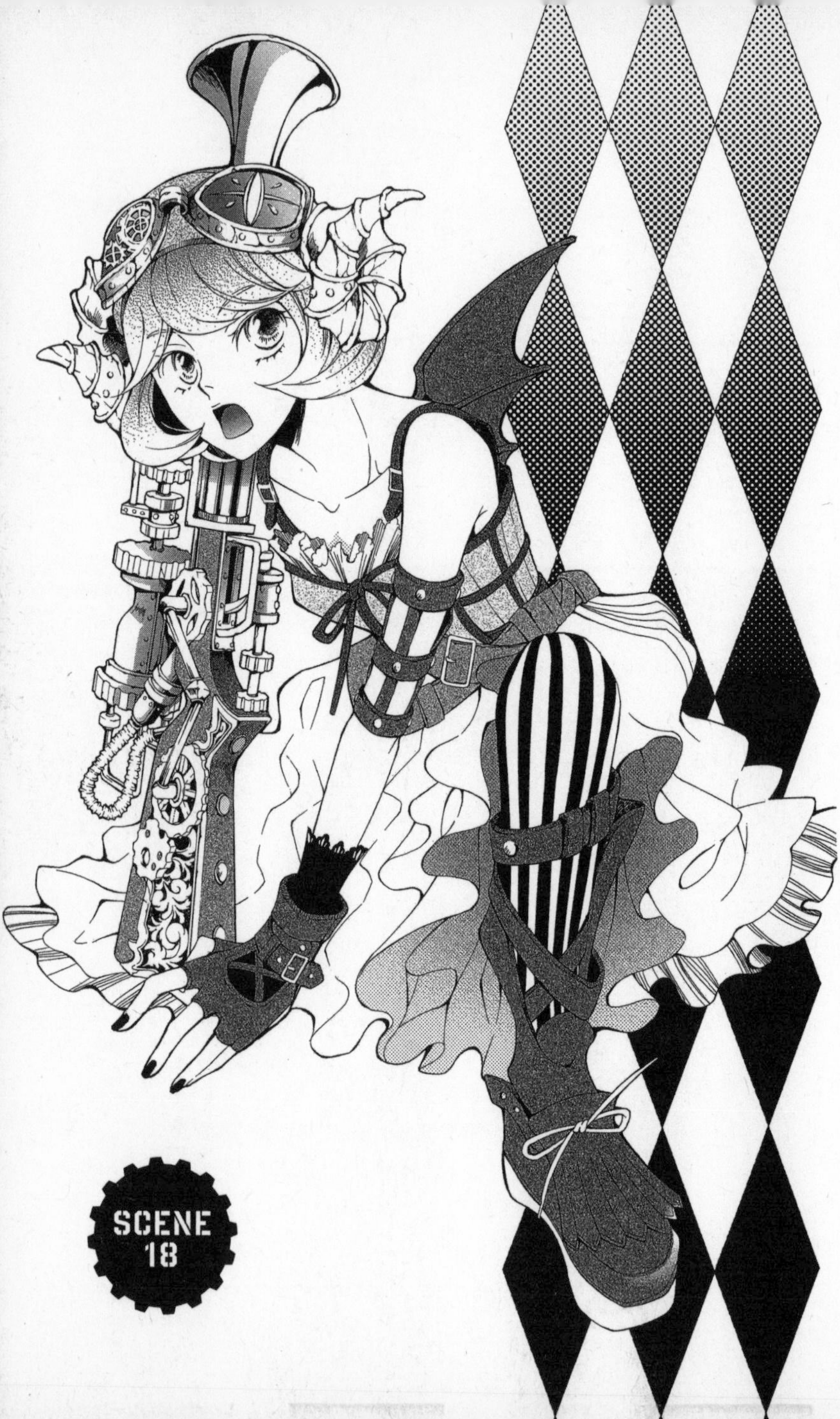
SCENE
18

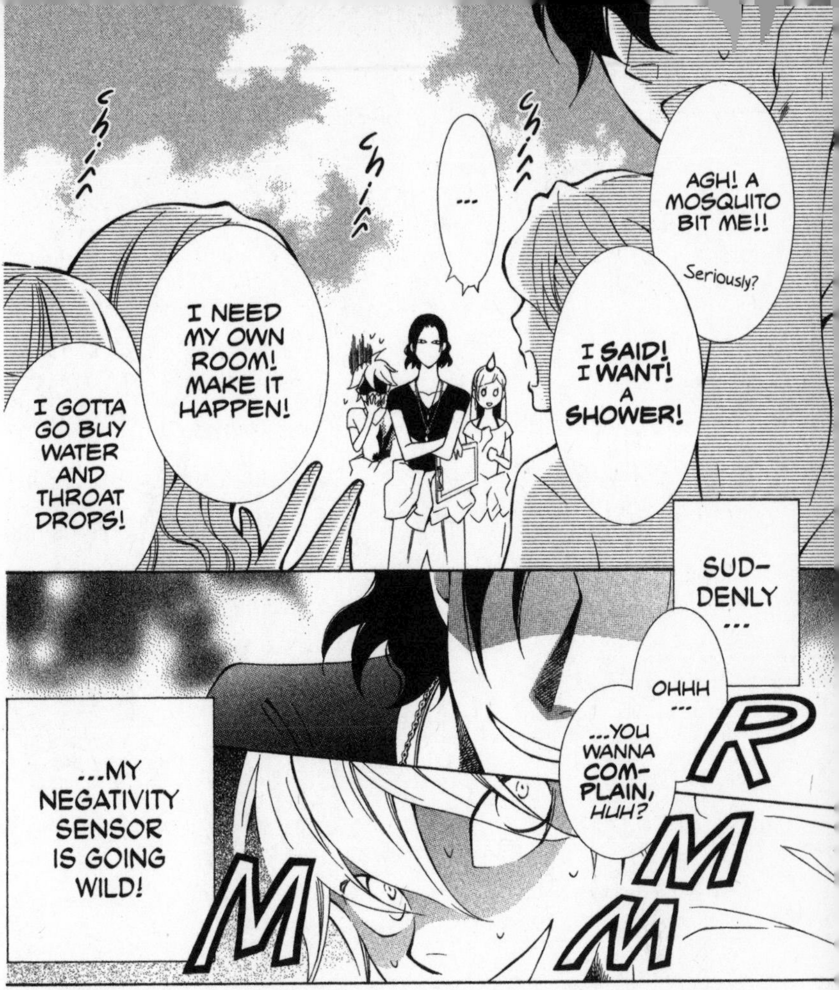
AGH! A MOSQUITO BIT ME!!
Seriously?
I SAID! I WANT! A SHOWER!
...
I NEED MY OWN ROOM! MAKE IT HAPPEN!
I GOTTA GO BUY WATER AND THROAT DROPS!
SUD-DENLY...
OHHH...
...YOU WANNA COM-PLAIN, HUH?
...MY NEGATIVITY SENSOR IS GOING WILD!

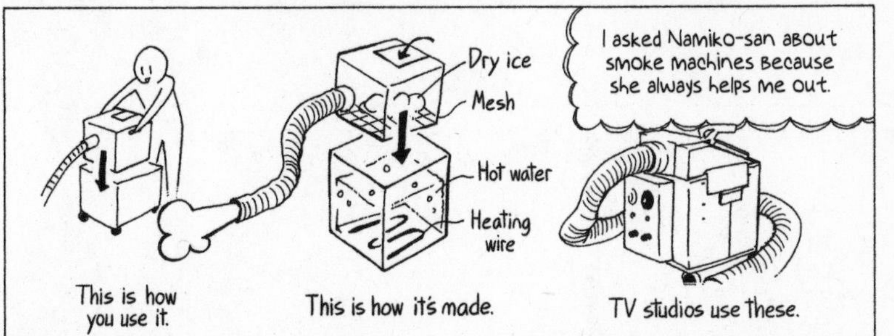
I asked Namiko-san about smoke machines because she always helps me out.
TV studios use these.
Dry ice
Mesh
Hot water
Heating wire
This is how it's made.
This is how you use it.

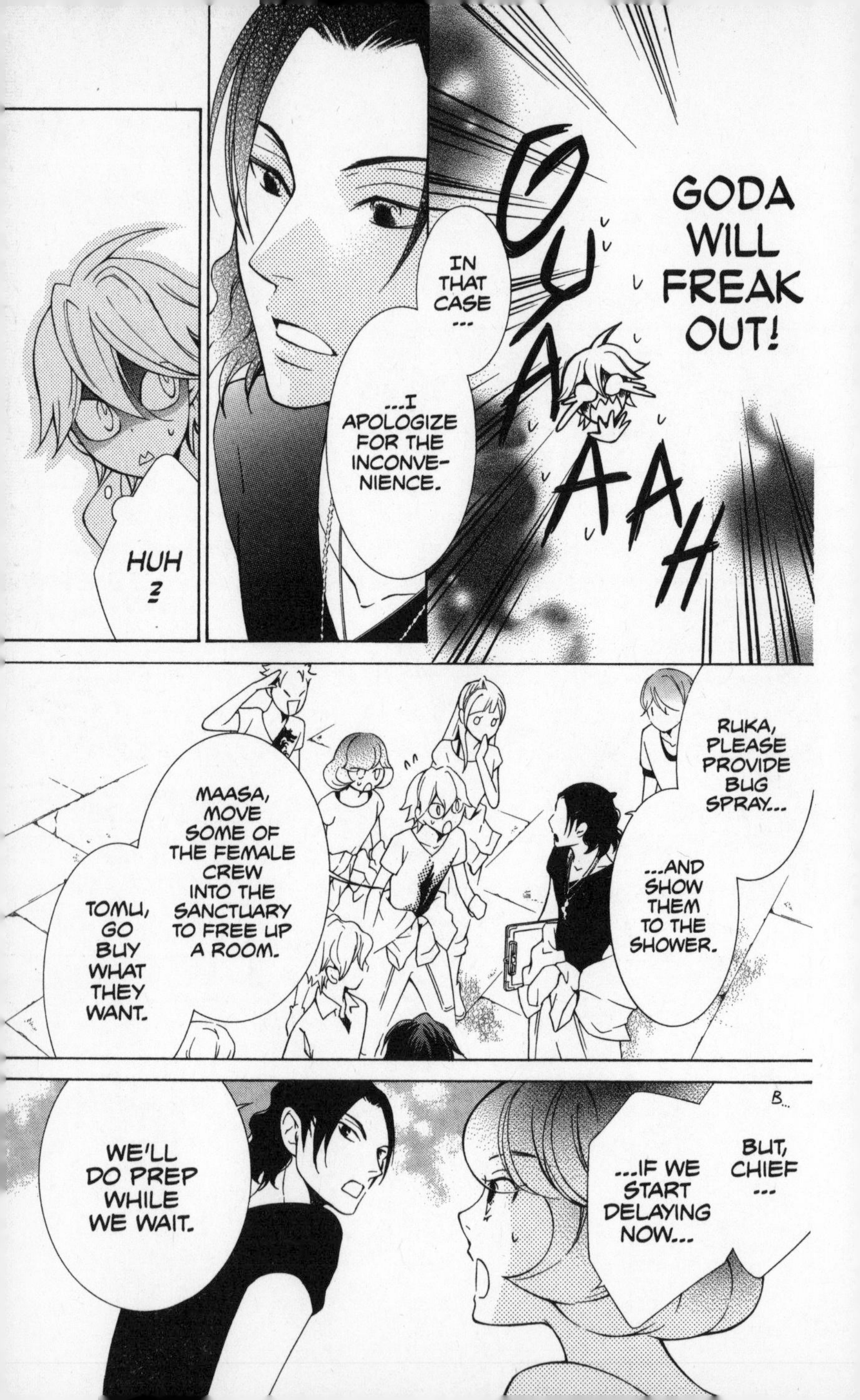
GODA WILL FREAK OUT!
OUYAAAH
IN THAT CASE...
...I APOLOGIZE FOR THE INCONVENIENCE.
HUH?
RUKA, PLEASE PROVIDE BUG SPRAY...
...AND SHOW THEM TO THE SHOWER.
MAASA, MOVE SOME OF THE FEMALE CREW INTO THE SANCTUARY TO FREE UP A ROOM.
TOMU, GO BUY WHAT THEY WANT.
B...
BUT, CHIEF...
...IF WE START DELAYING NOW...
WE'LL DO PREP WHILE WE WAIT.

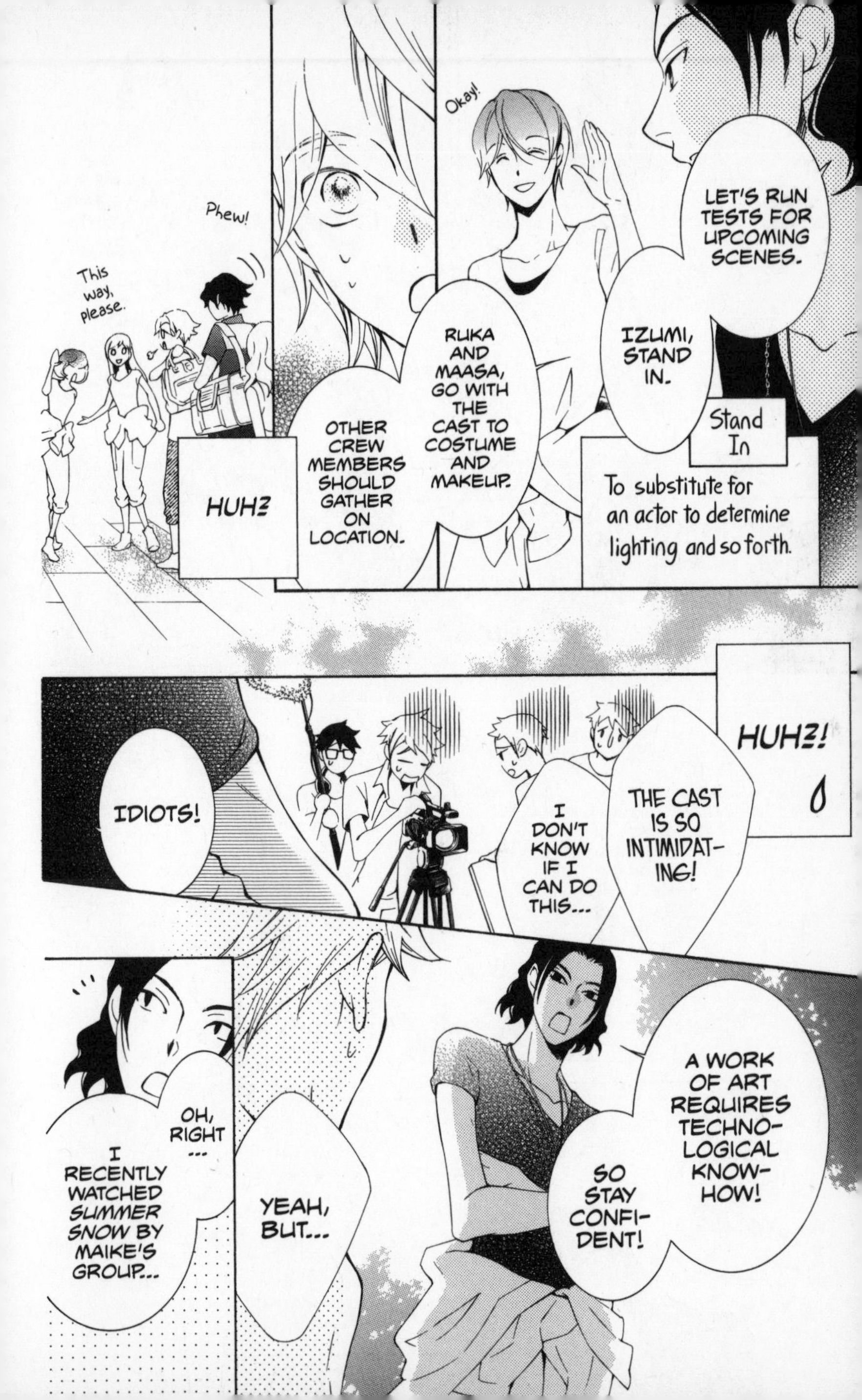
LET'S RUN TESTS FOR UPCOMING SCENES.
IZUMI, STAND IN.
Stand In
To substitute for an actor to determine lighting and so forth.
Okay!
RUKA AND MAASA, GO WITH THE CAST TO COSTUME AND MAKEUP.
OTHER CREW MEMBERS SHOULD GATHER ON LOCATION.
HUH?
Phew!
This way, please.
HUH?!
THE CAST IS SO INTIMIDATING!
I DON'T KNOW IF I CAN DO THIS...
IDIOTS!
A WORK OF ART REQUIRES TECHNOLOGICAL KNOW-HOW!
SO STAY CONFIDENT!
YEAH, BUT...
OH, RIGHT...
I RECENTLY WATCHED SUMMER SNOW BY MAIKE'S GROUP...

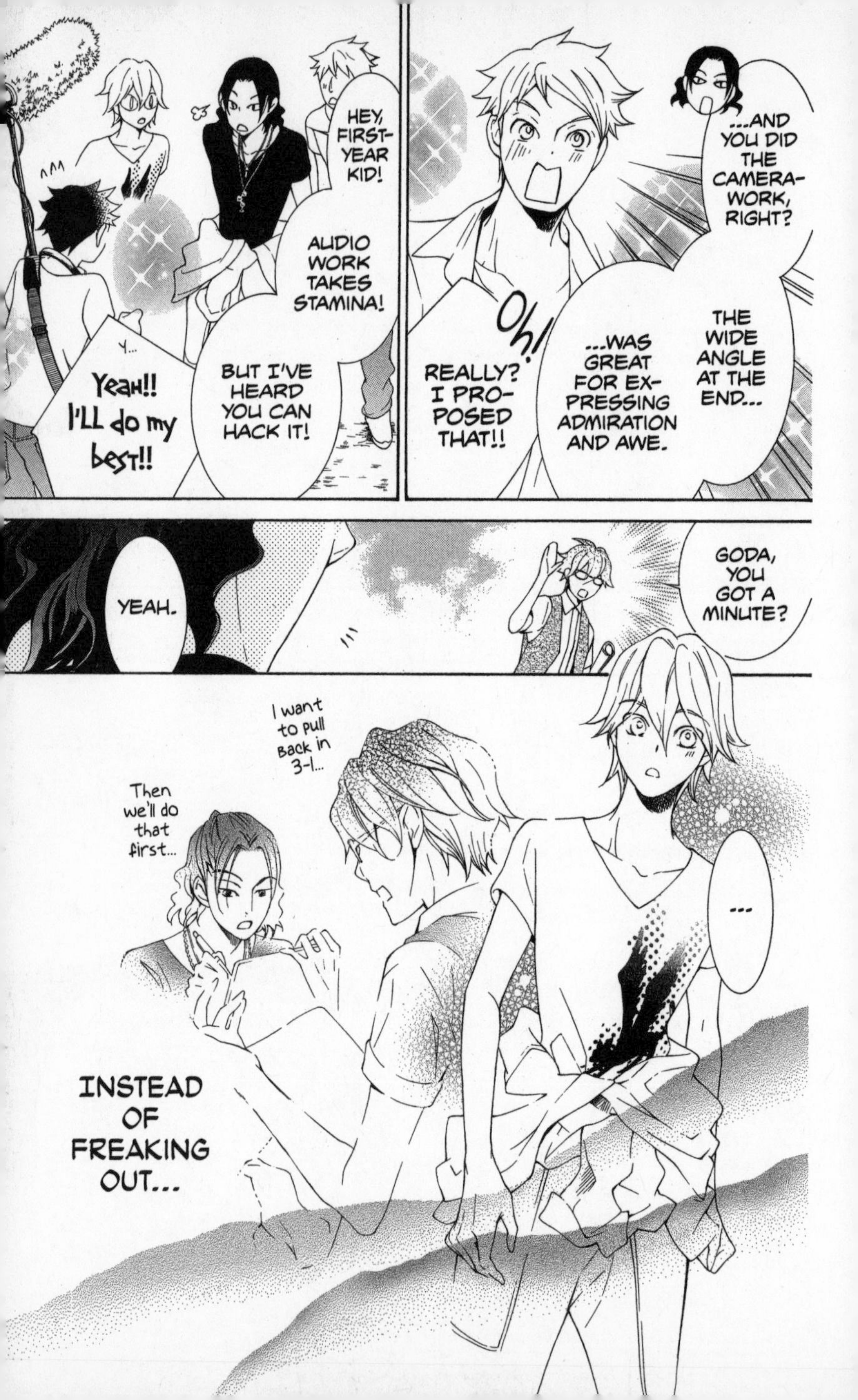
...AND YOU DID THE CAMERA-WORK, RIGHT?
THE WIDE ANGLE AT THE END...
...WAS GREAT FOR EXPRESSING ADMIRATION AND AWE.
Oh!
REALLY? I PROPOSED THAT!!
HEY, FIRST-YEAR KID!
AUDIO WORK TAKES STAMINA!
BUT I'VE HEARD YOU CAN HACK IT!
Y...
Yeah!! I'll do my best!!
GODA, YOU GOT A MINUTE?
YEAH.
...
I want to pull back in 3-1...
Then we'll do that first...
INSTEAD OF FREAKING OUT...

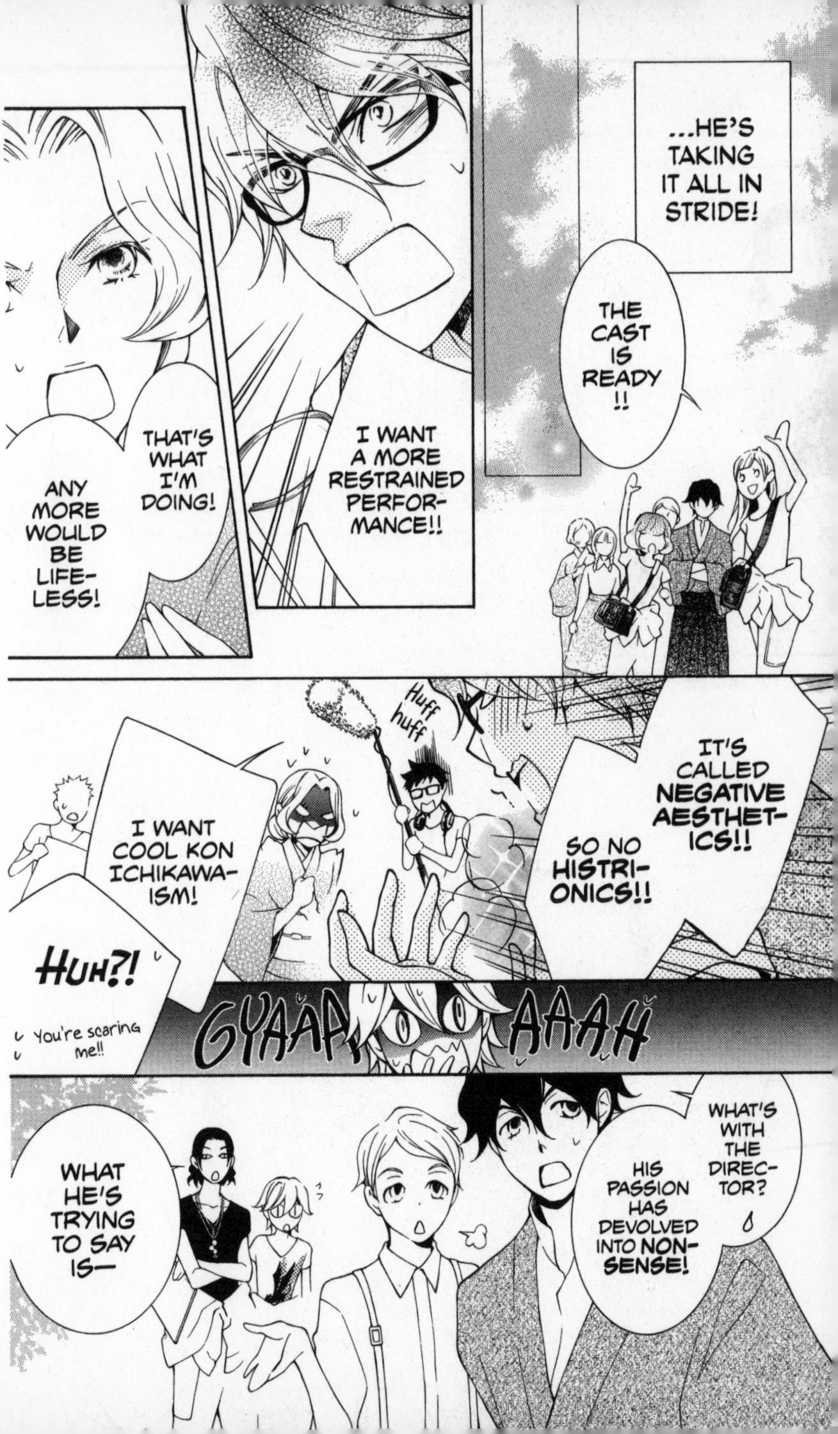
...HE'S TAKING IT ALL IN STRIDE!
THE CAST IS READY!!
I WANT A MORE RESTRAINED PERFORMANCE!!
THAT'S WHAT I'M DOING!
ANY MORE WOULD BE LIFELESS!
Huff huff
IT'S CALLED NEGATIVE AESTHETICS!!
SO NO HISTRIONICS!!
I WANT COOL KON ICHIKAWA-ISM!
HUH?!
GYAAAAAH
You're scaring me!!
WHAT'S WITH THE DIRECTOR?
HIS PASSION HAS DEVOLVED INTO NONSENSE!
WHAT HE'S TRYING TO SAY IS—

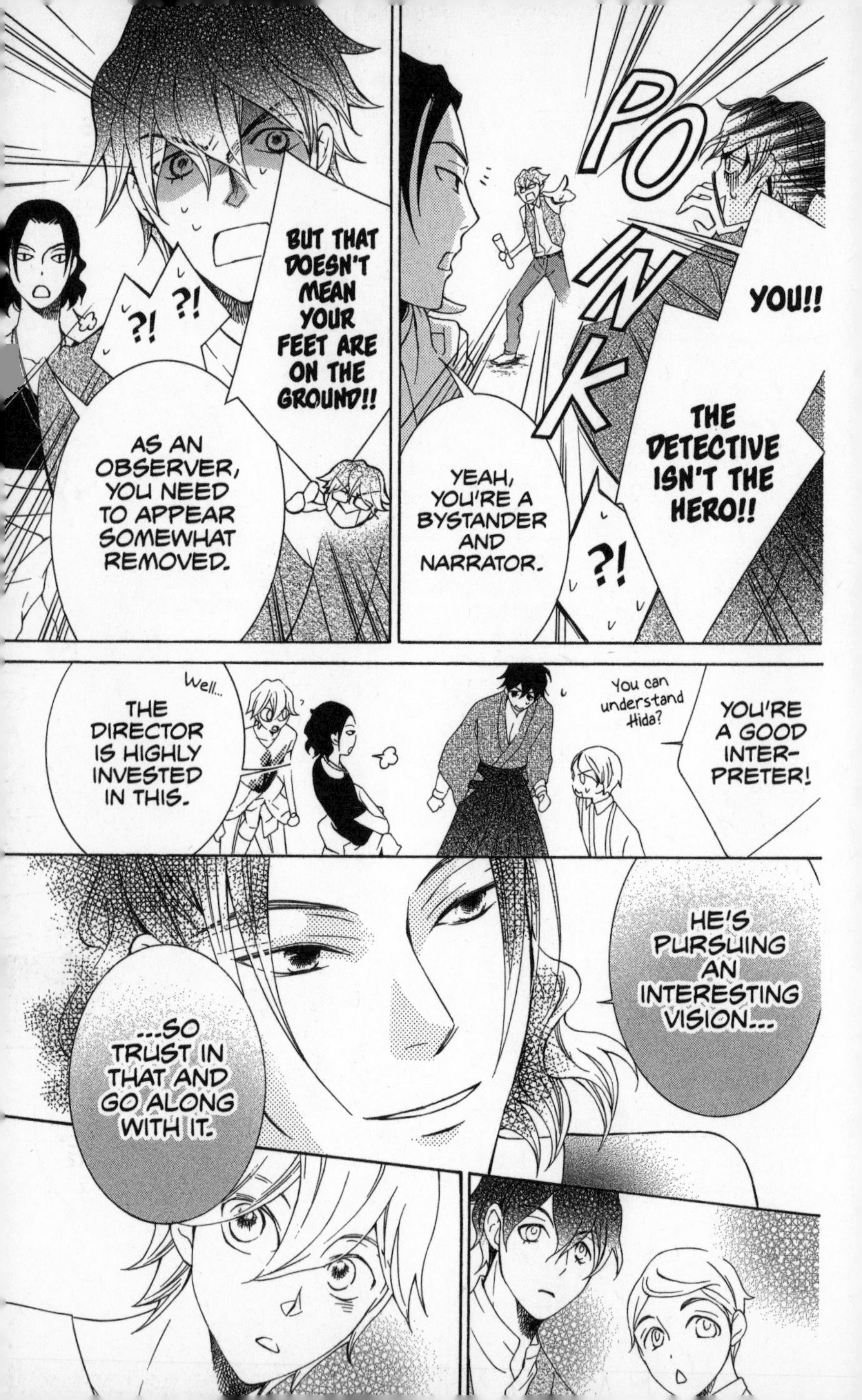
POINK
YOU!!
THE DETECTIVE ISN'T THE HERO!!
?!
YEAH, YOU'RE A BYSTANDER AND NARRATOR.
BUT THAT DOESN'T MEAN YOUR FEET ARE ON THE GROUND!!
?! ?!
AS AN OBSERVER, YOU NEED TO APPEAR SOMEWHAT REMOVED.
YOU'RE A GOOD INTER-PRETER!
You can understand Hida?
Well...
THE DIRECTOR IS HIGHLY INVESTED IN THIS.
HE'S PURSUING AN INTERESTING VISION...
...SO TRUST IN THAT AND GO ALONG WITH IT.

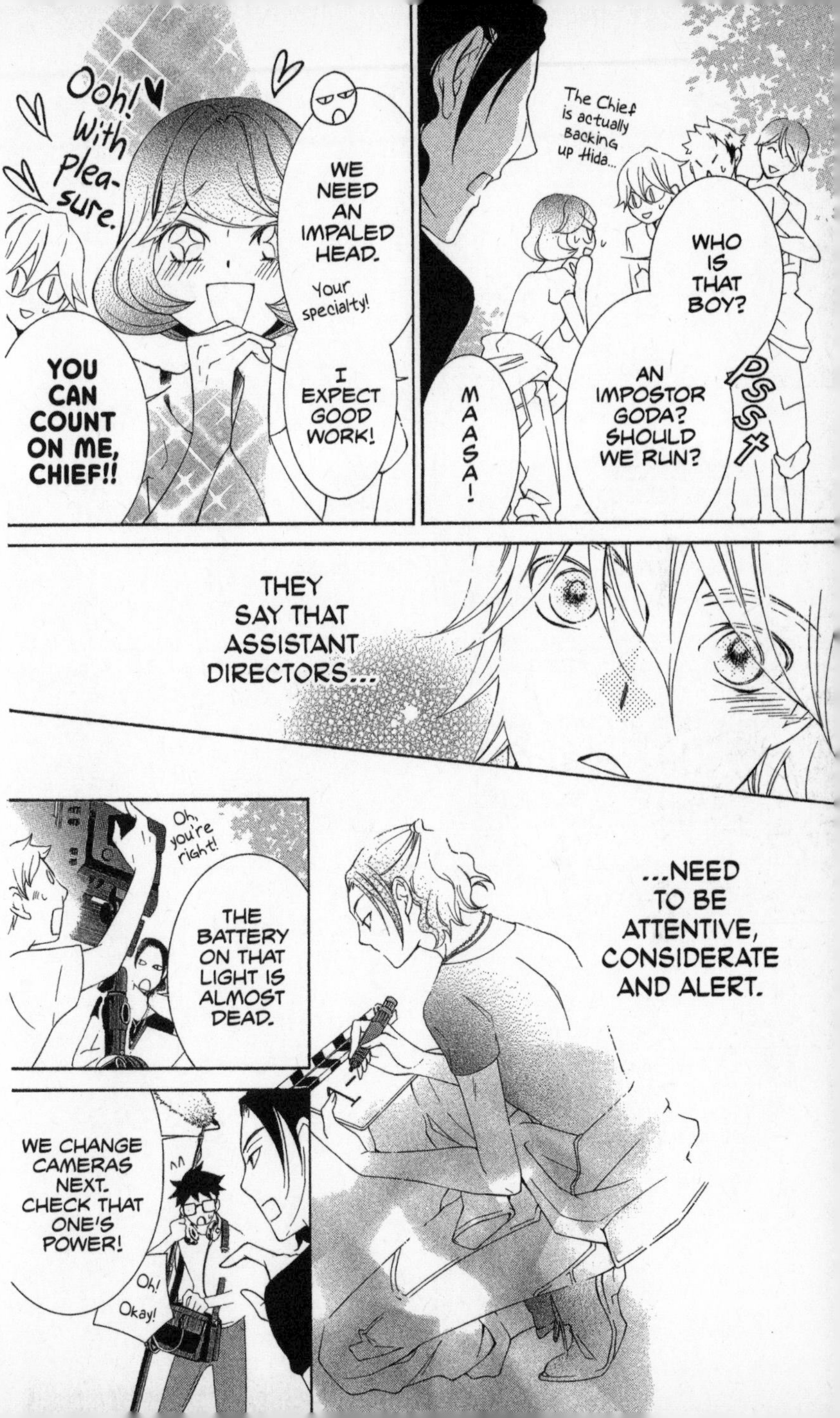
The Chief is actually Backing up Hida...
WHO IS THAT BOY?
AN IMPOSTOR GODA? SHOULD WE RUN?
PSST
MAASA!
WE NEED AN IMPALED HEAD.
Your specialty!
I EXPECT GOOD WORK!
Ooh! With Plea-sure.
YOU CAN COUNT ON ME, CHIEF!!
THEY SAY THAT ASSISTANT DIRECTORS...
...NEED TO BE ATTENTIVE, CONSIDERATE AND ALERT.
THE BATTERY ON THAT LIGHT IS ALMOST DEAD.
Oh, you're right!
WE CHANGE CAMERAS NEXT. CHECK THAT ONE'S POWER!
Oh!
Okay!

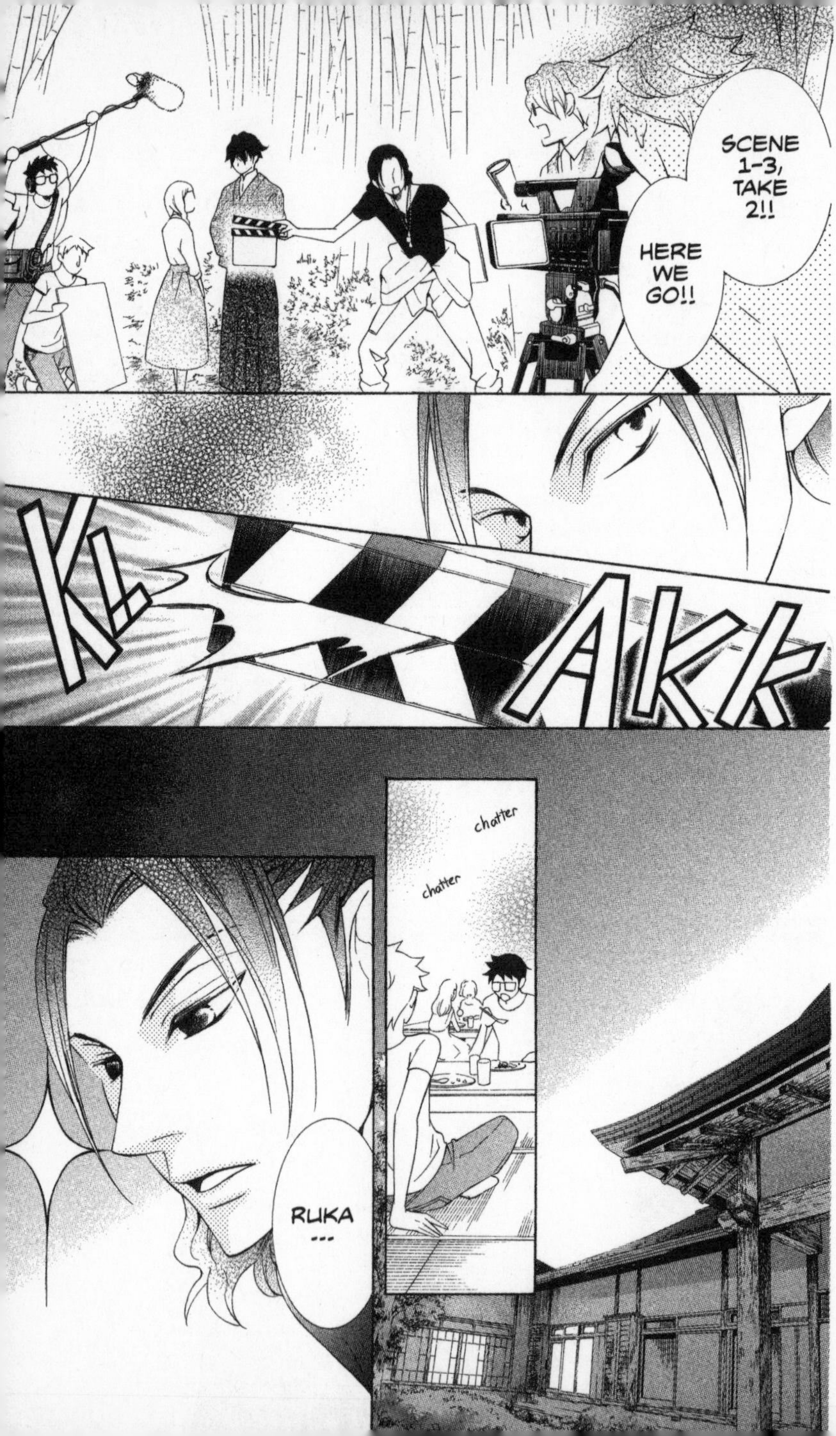
SCENE 1-3, TAKE 2!!
HERE WE GO!!
KLAKK
chatter
chatter
RUKA...

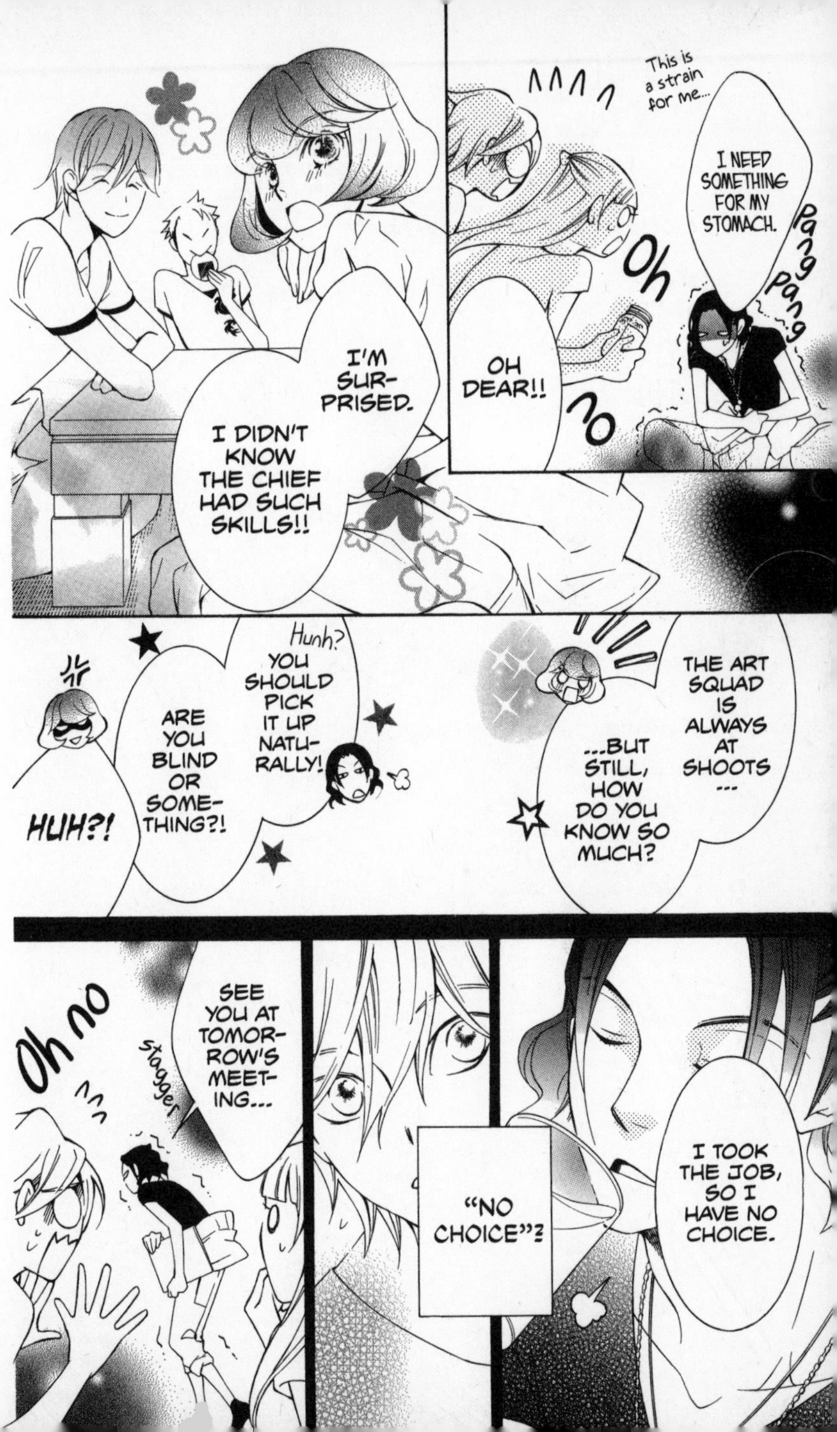

This is a strain for me...
I NEED SOMETHING FOR MY STOMACH.
Pang Pang
Oh no
OH DEAR!!
I'M SUR-PRISED.
I DIDN'T KNOW THE CHIEF HAD SUCH SKILLS!!
THE ART SQUAD IS ALWAYS AT SHOOTS...
...BUT STILL, HOW DO YOU KNOW SO MUCH?
Hunh?
YOU SHOULD PICK IT UP NATU-RALLY!
ARE YOU BLIND OR SOME-THING?!
HUH?!
I TOOK THE JOB, SO I HAVE NO CHOICE.
"NO CHOICE"?
SEE YOU AT TOMOR-ROW'S MEET-ING...
stagger
Oh no

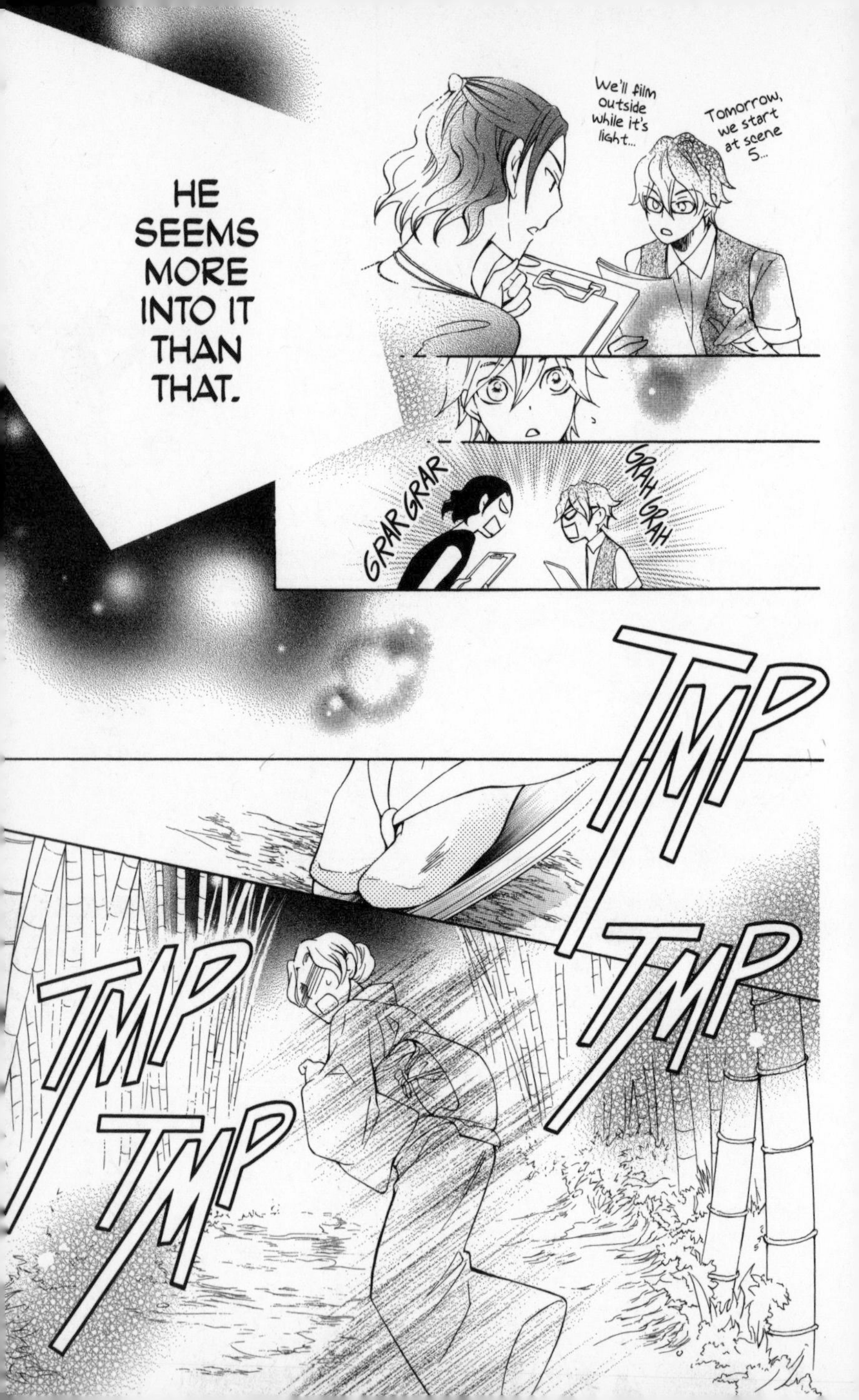
Tomorrow, we start at scene 5...
We'll film outside while it's light...
HE SEEMS MORE INTO IT THAN THAT.
GRAH GRAH
GRAR GRAR
TMP
TMP
TMP
TMP

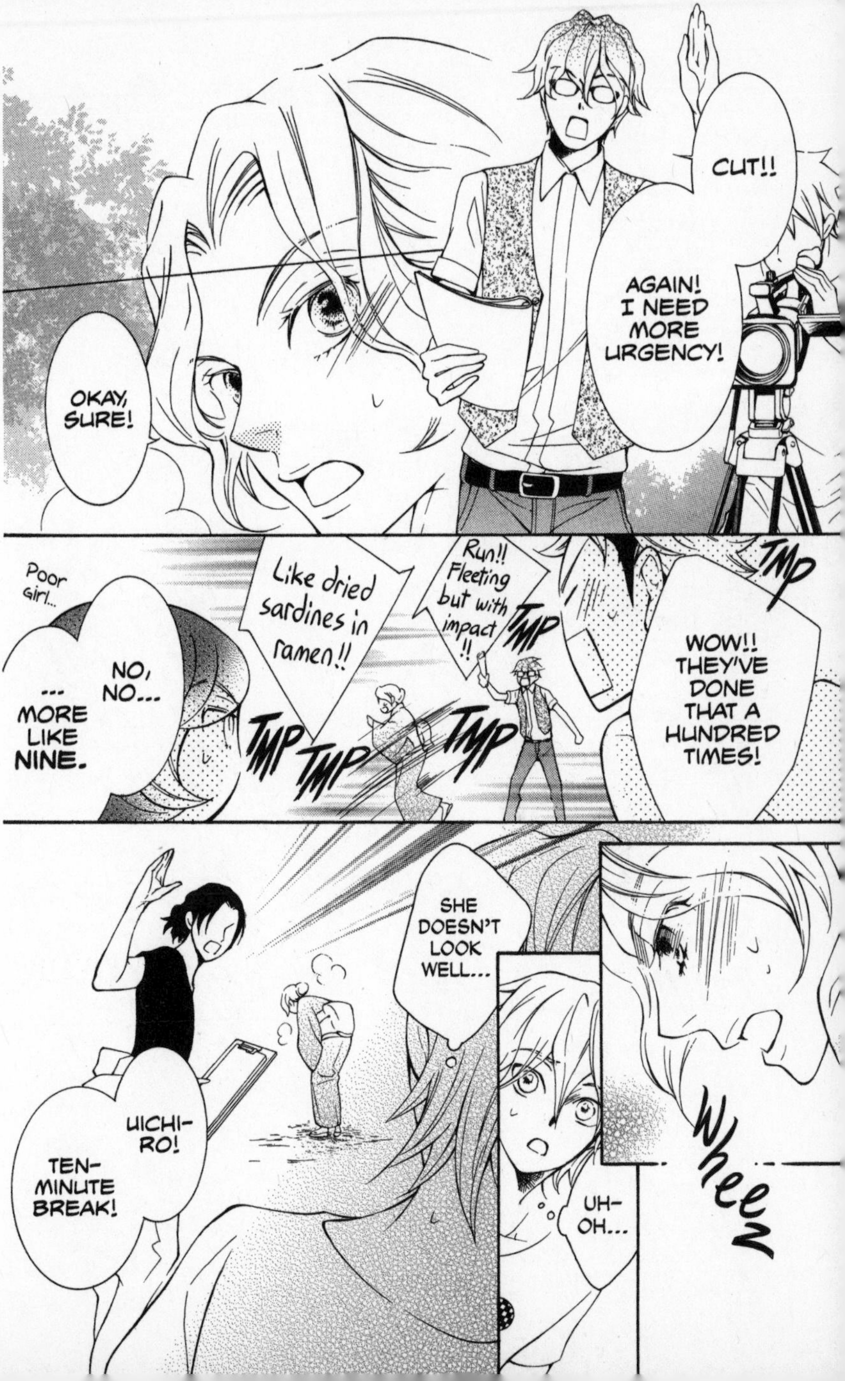
CUT!!
AGAIN! I NEED MORE URGENCY!
OKAY, SURE!
TMP
WOW!! THEY'VE DONE THAT A HUNDRED TIMES!
Run!! Fleeting but with impact!!
TMP
Like dried sardines in ramen!!
TMP
TMP
TMP
NO, NO...
...MORE LIKE NINE.
Poor Girl...
Wheez
SHE DOESN'T LOOK WELL...
UH-OH...
UICHI-RO!
TEN-MINUTE BREAK!

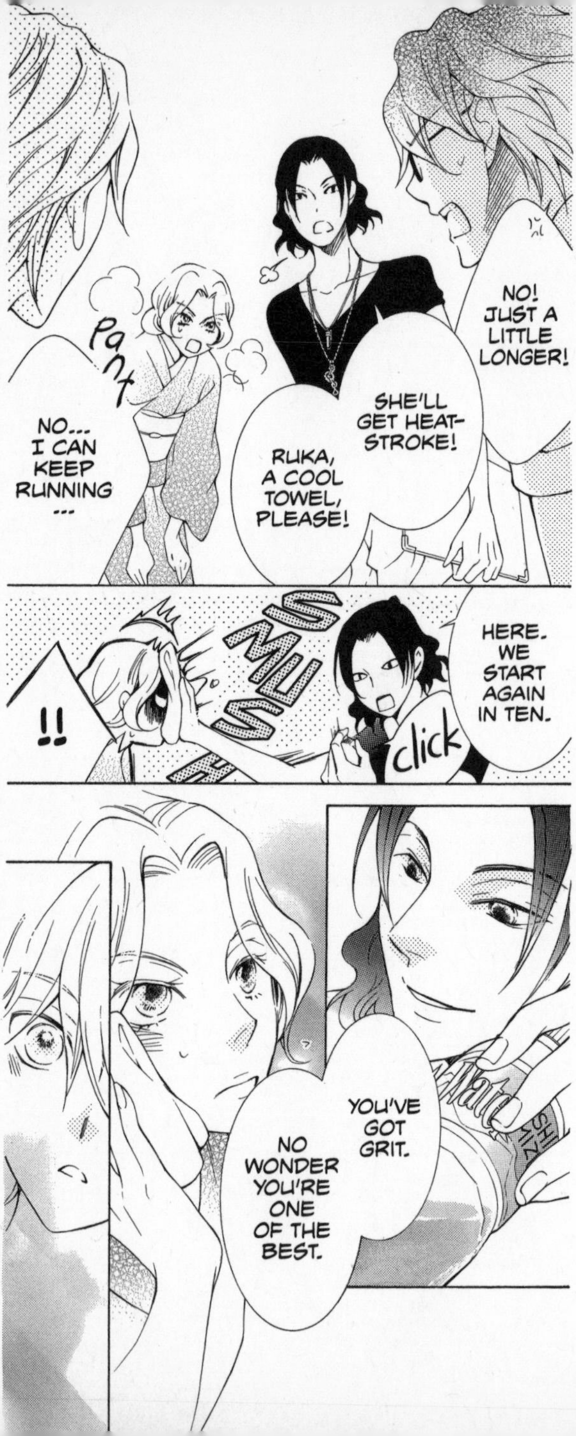
NO! JUST A LITTLE LONGER!
SHE'LL GET HEAT-STROKE!
RUKA, A COOL TOWEL, PLEASE!
NO... I CAN KEEP RUNNING ...
Pant
HERE. WE START AGAIN IN TEN.
click
SMUSH
!!
YOU'VE GOT GRIT.
NO WONDER YOU'RE ONE OF THE BEST.

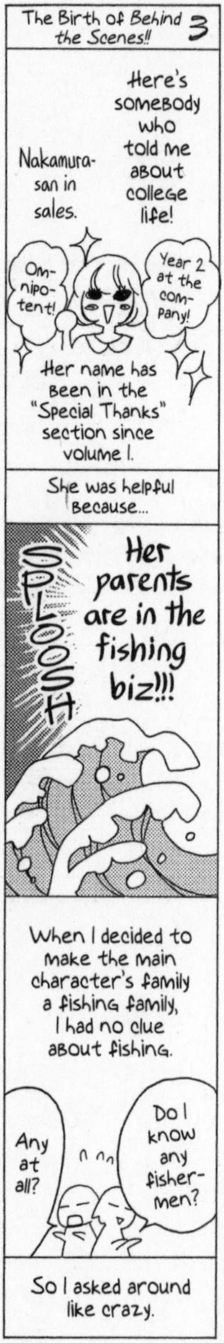
The Birth of Behind the Scenes!! 3
Here's somebody who told me about college life!
Nakamura-san in sales.
Omnipotent!
Year 2 at the company!
Her name has been in the "Special Thanks" section since volume 1.
She was helpful because...
Her parents are in the fishing biz!!!
SPLOOSH
When I decided to make the main character's family a fishing family, I had no clue about fishing.
Do I know any fishermen?
Any at all?
So I asked around like crazy.

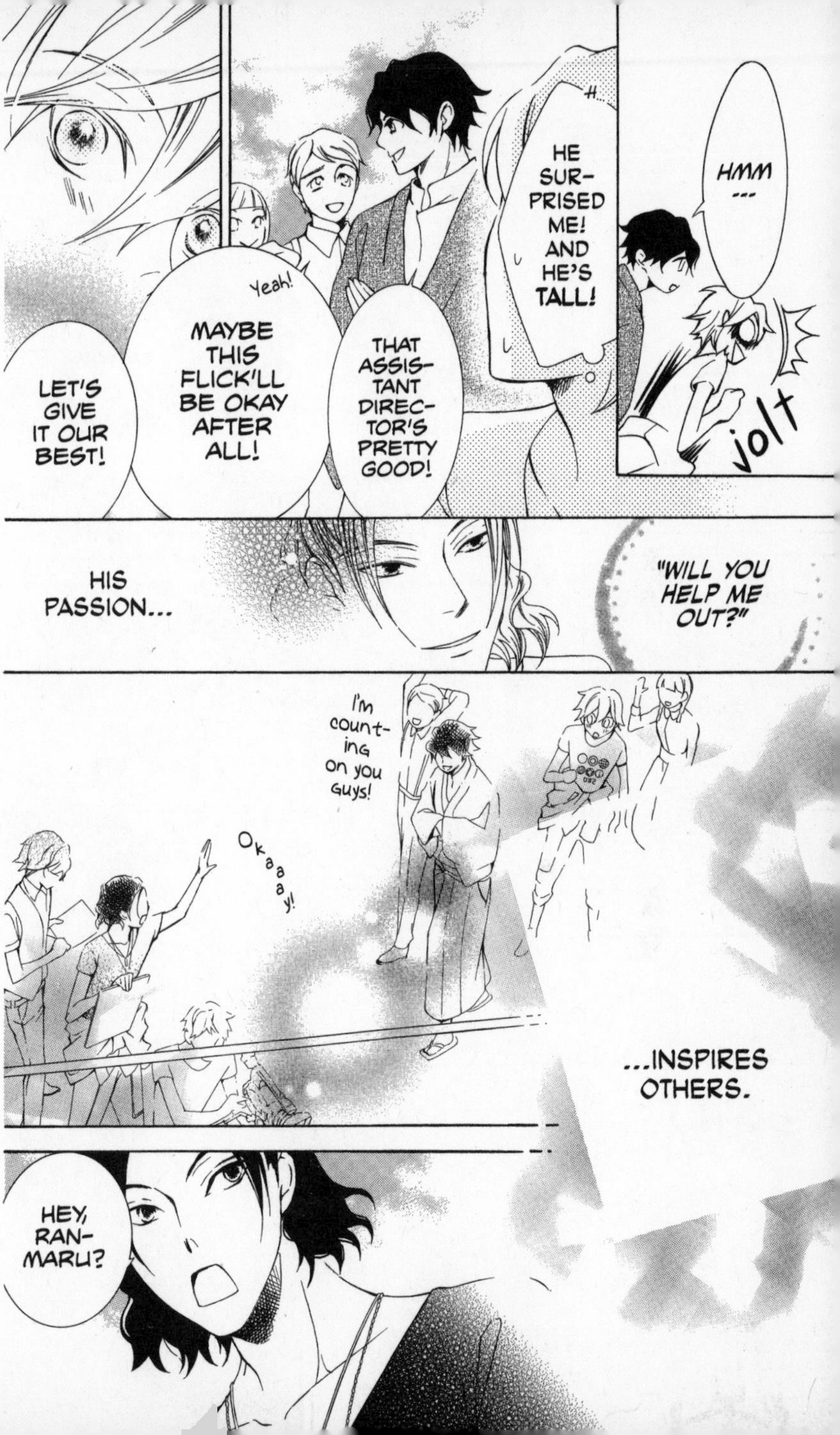
HMM ---
jolt
HE SURPRISED ME! AND HE'S TALL!
THAT ASSISTANT DIRECTOR'S PRETTY GOOD!
Yeah!
MAYBE THIS FLICK'LL BE OKAY AFTER ALL!
LET'S GIVE IT OUR BEST!
"WILL YOU HELP ME OUT?"
HIS PASSION...
...INSPIRES OTHERS.
I'm counting on you guys!
Okaaaay!
HEY, RANMARU?

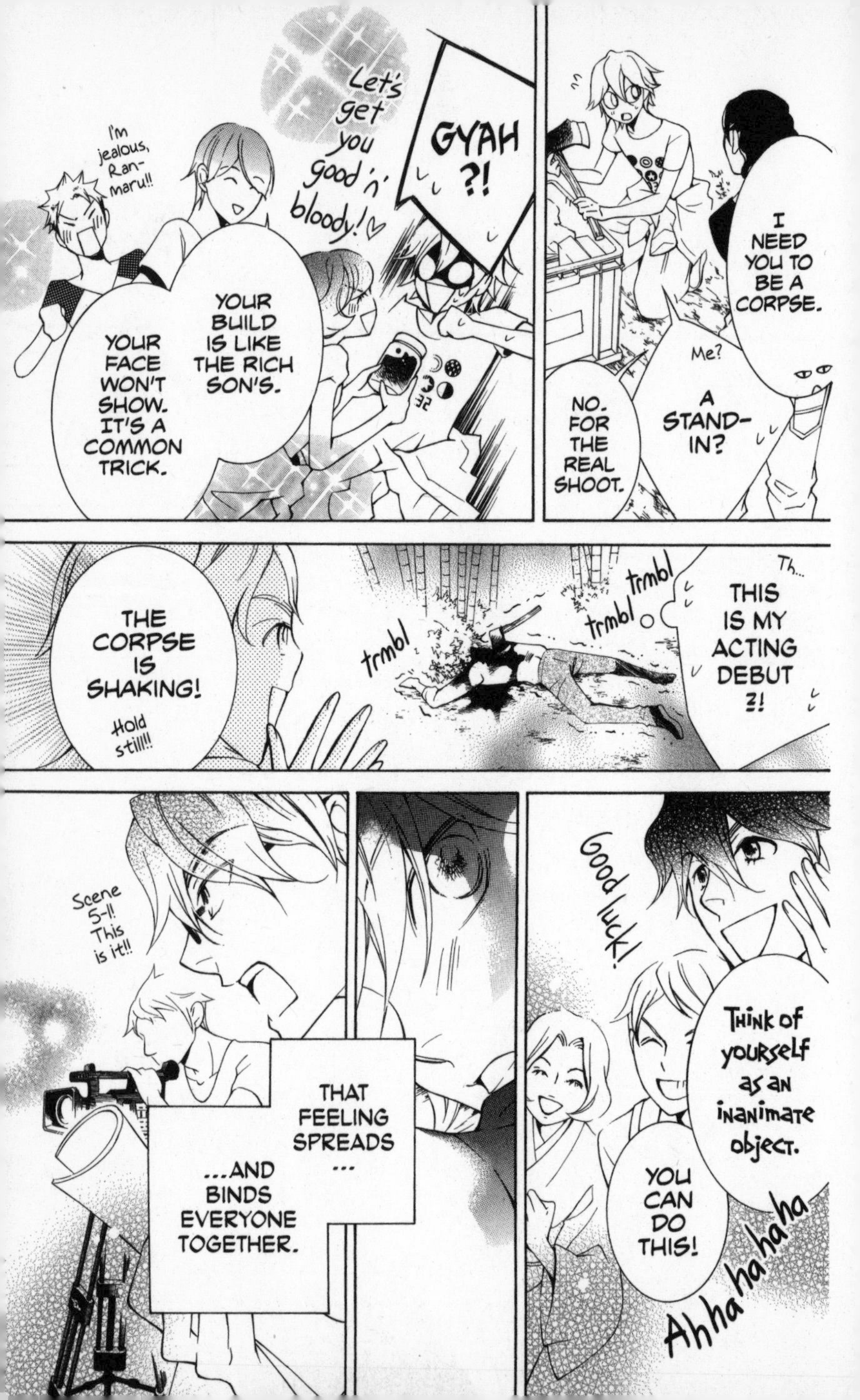
I NEED YOU TO BE A CORPSE.
Me?
A STAND-IN?
NO. FOR THE REAL SHOOT.
GYAH?!
Let's get you good 'n' bloody! ♥
YOUR BUILD IS LIKE THE RICH SON'S.
YOUR FACE WON'T SHOW. IT'S A COMMON TRICK.
I'm jealous, Ran-maru!!
Th...
THIS IS MY ACTING DEBUT?!
trmbl trmbl
trmbl
THE CORPSE IS SHAKING!
Hold still!!
Good luck!
Think of yourself as an inanimate object.
YOU CAN DO THIS!
Ahhahahaha
THAT FEELING SPREADS...
...AND BINDS EVERYONE TOGETHER.
Scene 5-1! This is it!!

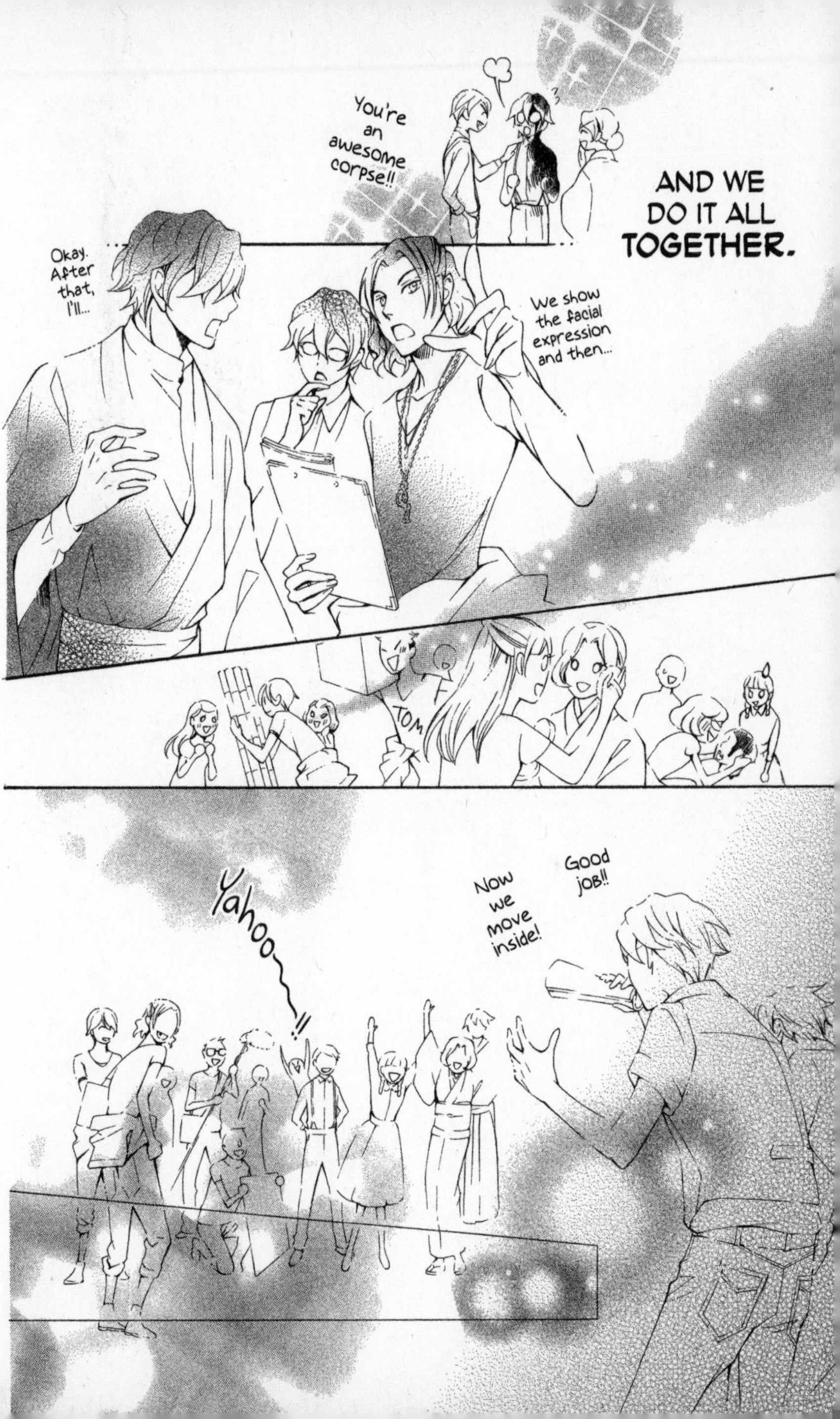
AND WE DO IT ALL TOGETHER.
You're an awesome corpse!!
We show the facial expression and then...
Okay. After that, I'll...
TOM
Good job!!
Now we move inside!
Yahoo~~!!

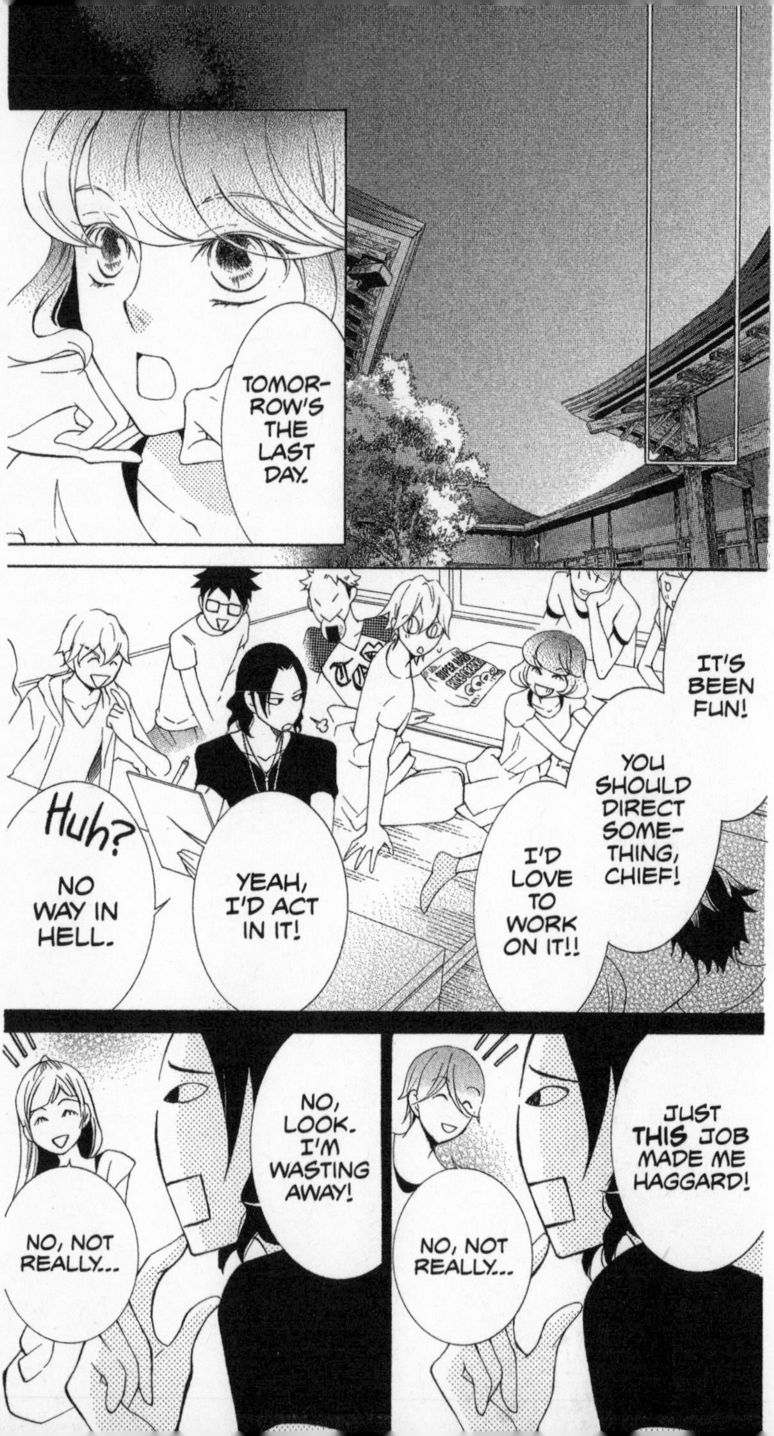
TOMORROW'S THE LAST DAY.
IT'S BEEN FUN!
YOU SHOULD DIRECT SOMETHING, CHIEF!
I'D LOVE TO WORK ON IT!!
YEAH, I'D ACT IN IT!
Huh?
NO WAY IN HELL.
JUST THIS JOB MADE ME HAGGARD!
NO, NOT REALLY...
NO, LOOK. I'M WASTING AWAY!
NO, NOT REALLY...

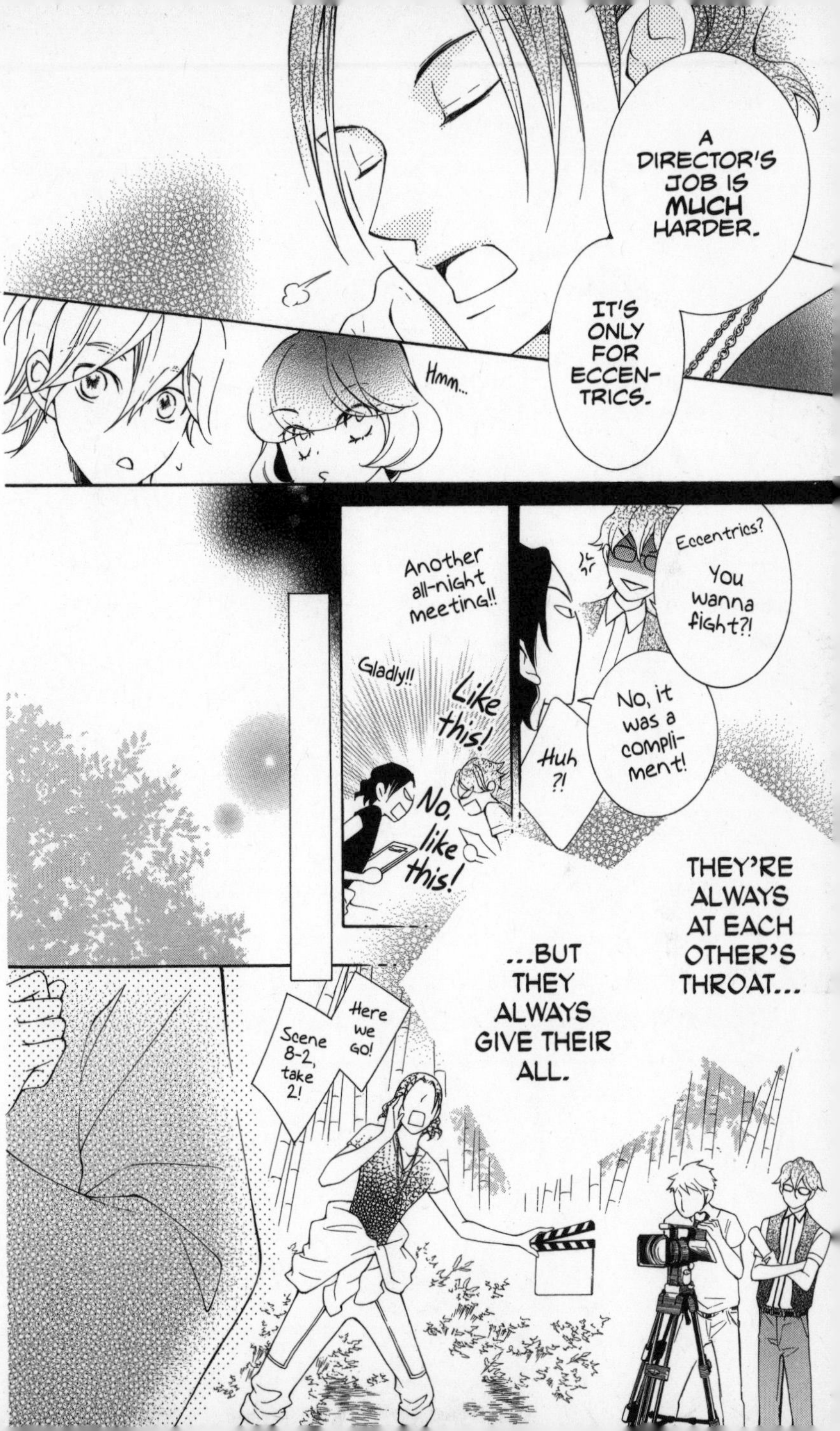
A DIRECTOR'S JOB IS MUCH HARDER.
IT'S ONLY FOR ECCENTRICS.
Hmm...
Eccentrics? You wanna fight?!
No, it was a compliment!
Huh?!
Another all-night meeting!!
Gladly!!
Like this!
No, like this!
THEY'RE ALWAYS AT EACH OTHER'S THROAT...
...BUT THEY ALWAYS GIVE THEIR ALL.
Here we go!
Scene 8-2, take 2!

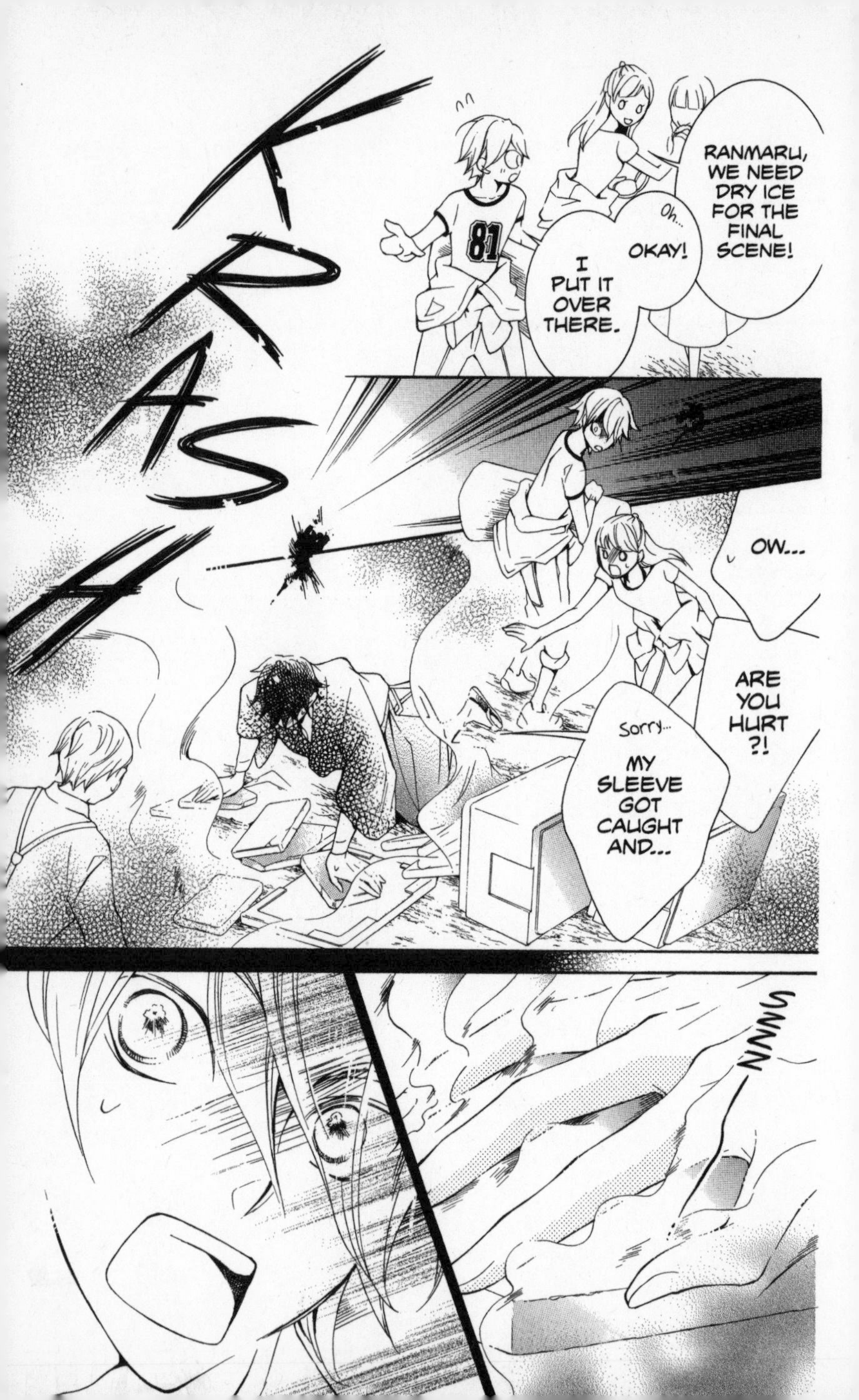

RANMARU, WE NEED DRY ICE FOR THE FINAL SCENE!
Oh... OKAY!
I PUT IT OVER THERE.
KRASH
OW...
ARE YOU HURT?!
Sorry...
MY SLEEVE GOT CAUGHT AND...
SNNNN

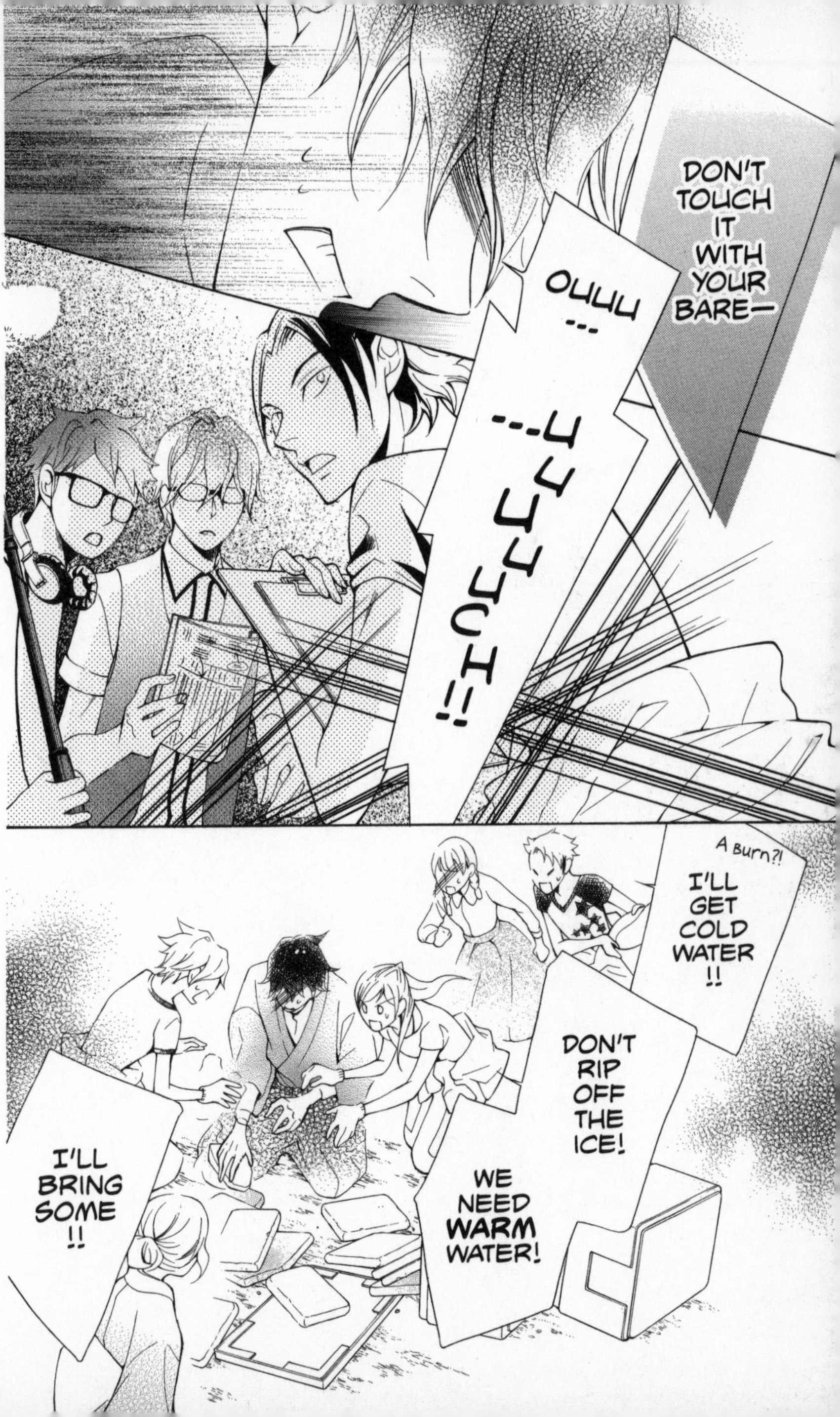
DON'T TOUCH IT WITH YOUR BARE—
OUUU---
---UUUUUCH!!
A Burn?!
I'LL GET COLD WATER!!
DON'T RIP OFF THE ICE!
WE NEED WARM WATER!
I'LL BRING SOME!!

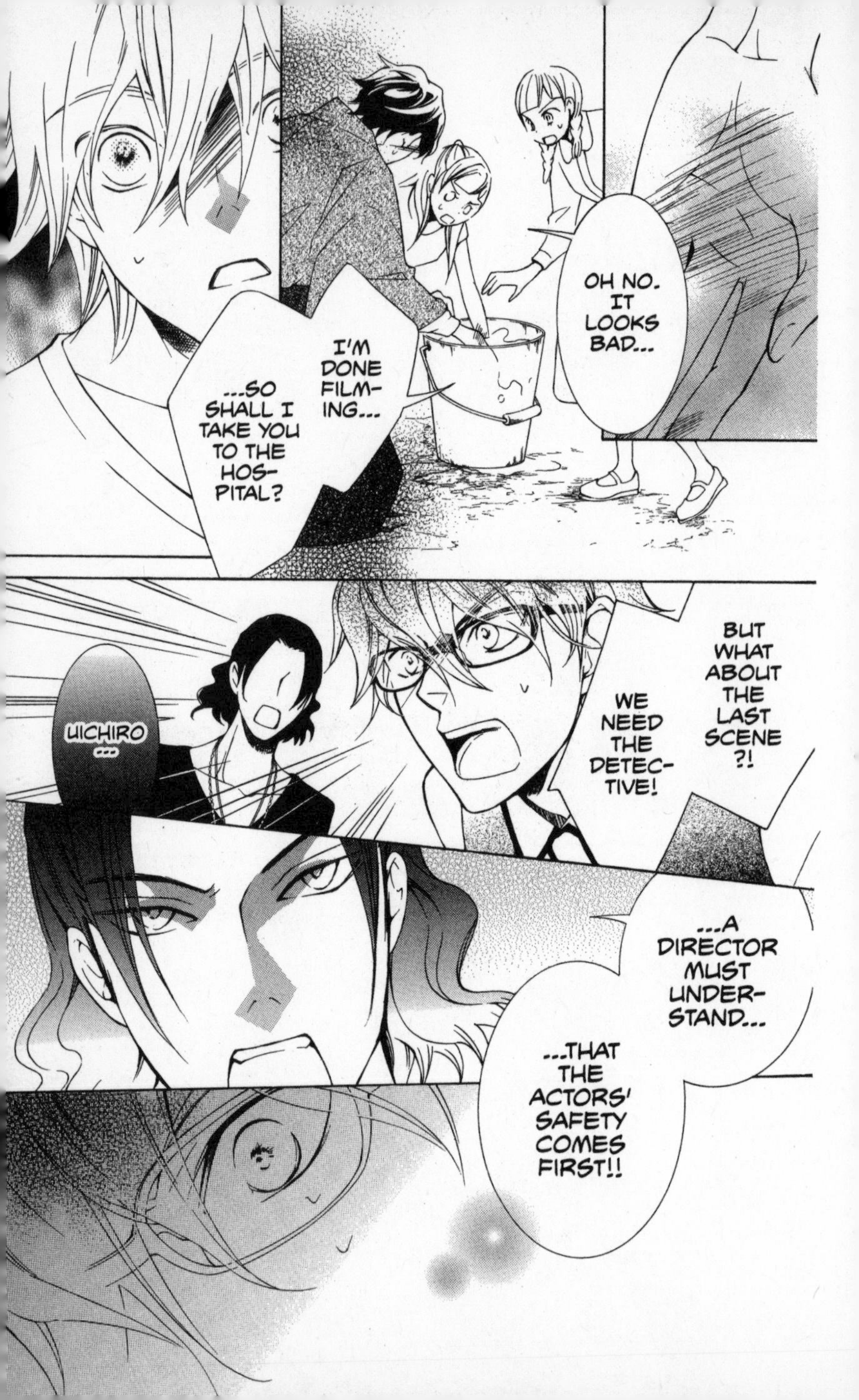
OH NO. IT LOOKS BAD...
I'M DONE FILMING...
...SO SHALL I TAKE YOU TO THE HOSPITAL?
BUT WHAT ABOUT THE LAST SCENE?!
WE NEED THE DETECTIVE!
UICHIRO...
...A DIRECTOR MUST UNDERSTAND...
...THAT THE ACTORS' SAFETY COMES FIRST!!

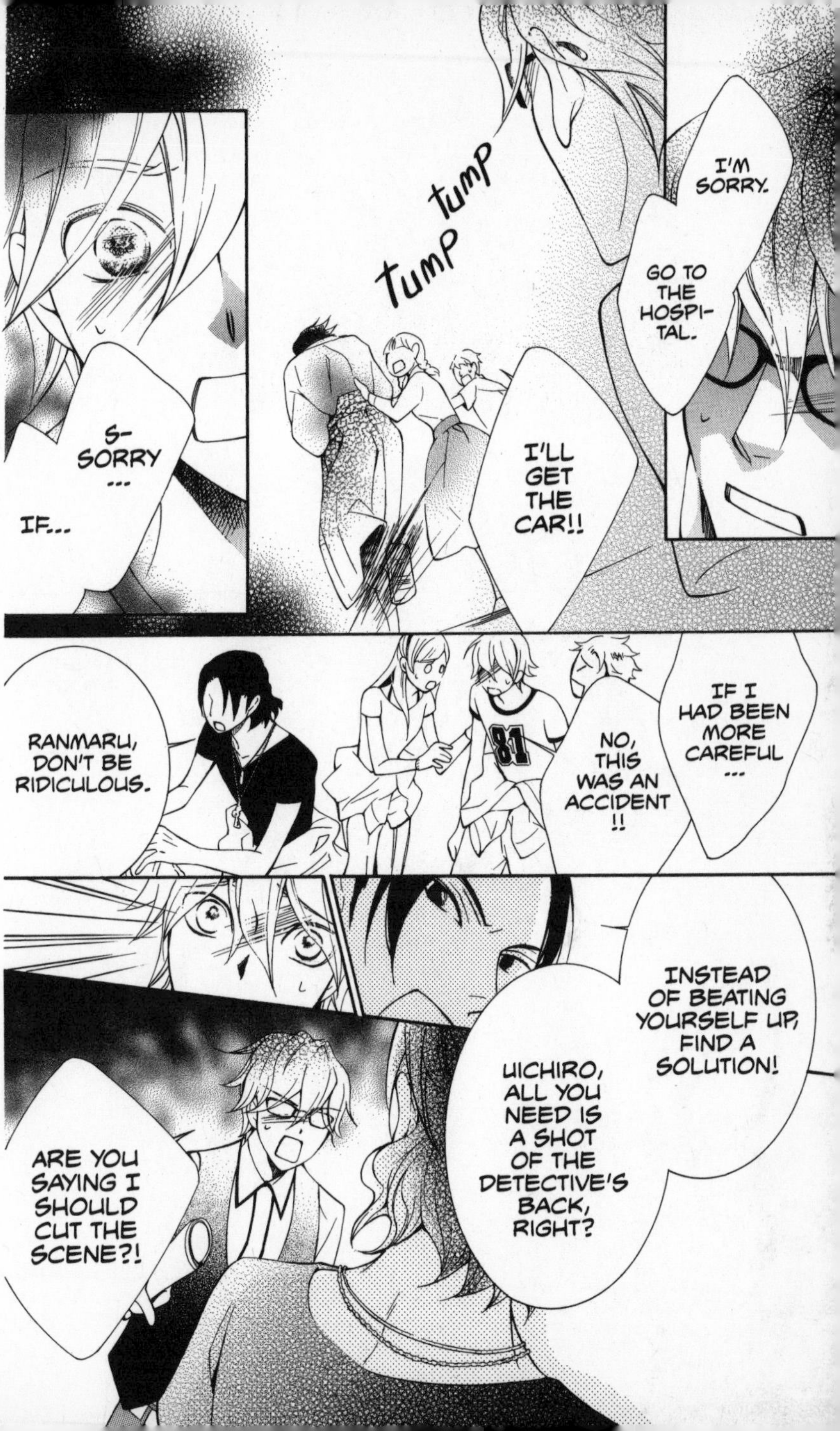
I'M SORRY.
GO TO THE HOSPITAL.
tump tump
I'LL GET THE CAR!!
S-SORRY...
IF...
IF I HAD BEEN MORE CAREFUL...
NO, THIS WAS AN ACCIDENT!!
RANMARU, DON'T BE RIDICULOUS.
INSTEAD OF BEATING YOURSELF UP, FIND A SOLUTION!
UICHIRO, ALL YOU NEED IS A SHOT OF THE DETECTIVE'S BACK, RIGHT?
ARE YOU SAYING I SHOULD CUT THE SCENE?!

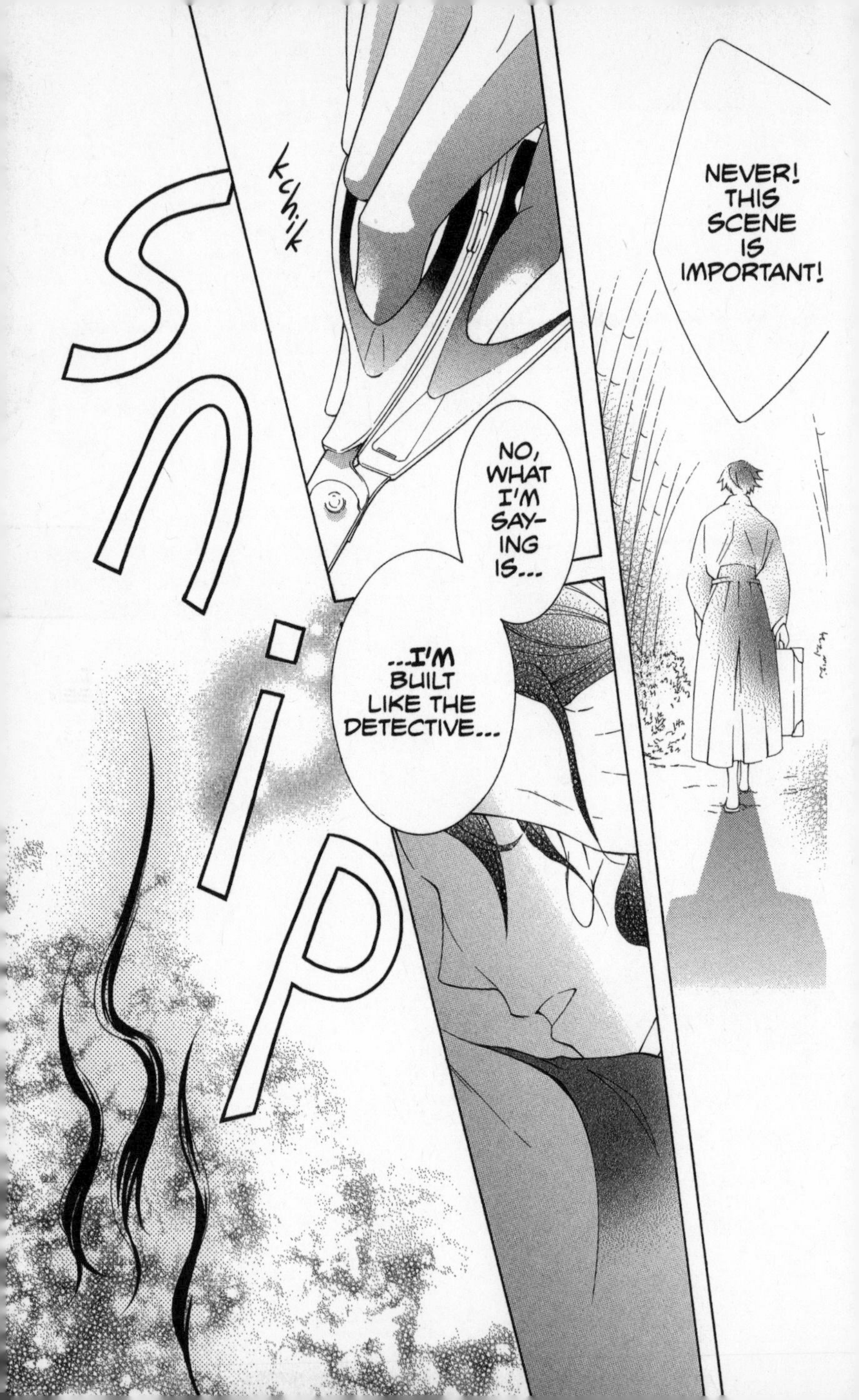
NEVER! THIS SCENE IS IMPORTANT!
kchik
NO, WHAT I'M SAY-ING IS...
...I'M BUILT LIKE THE DETECTIVE...
snip

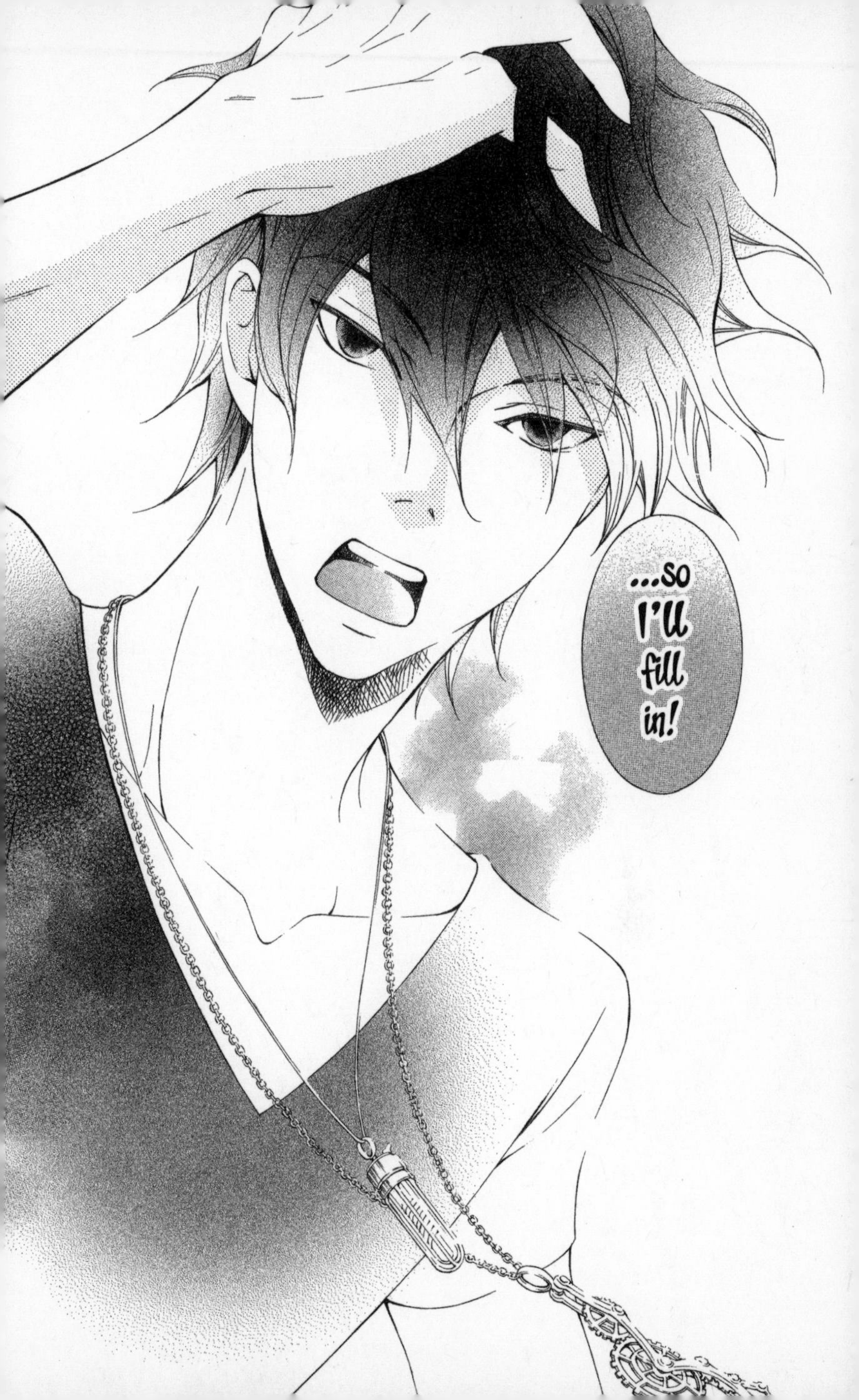
...so I'll fill in!

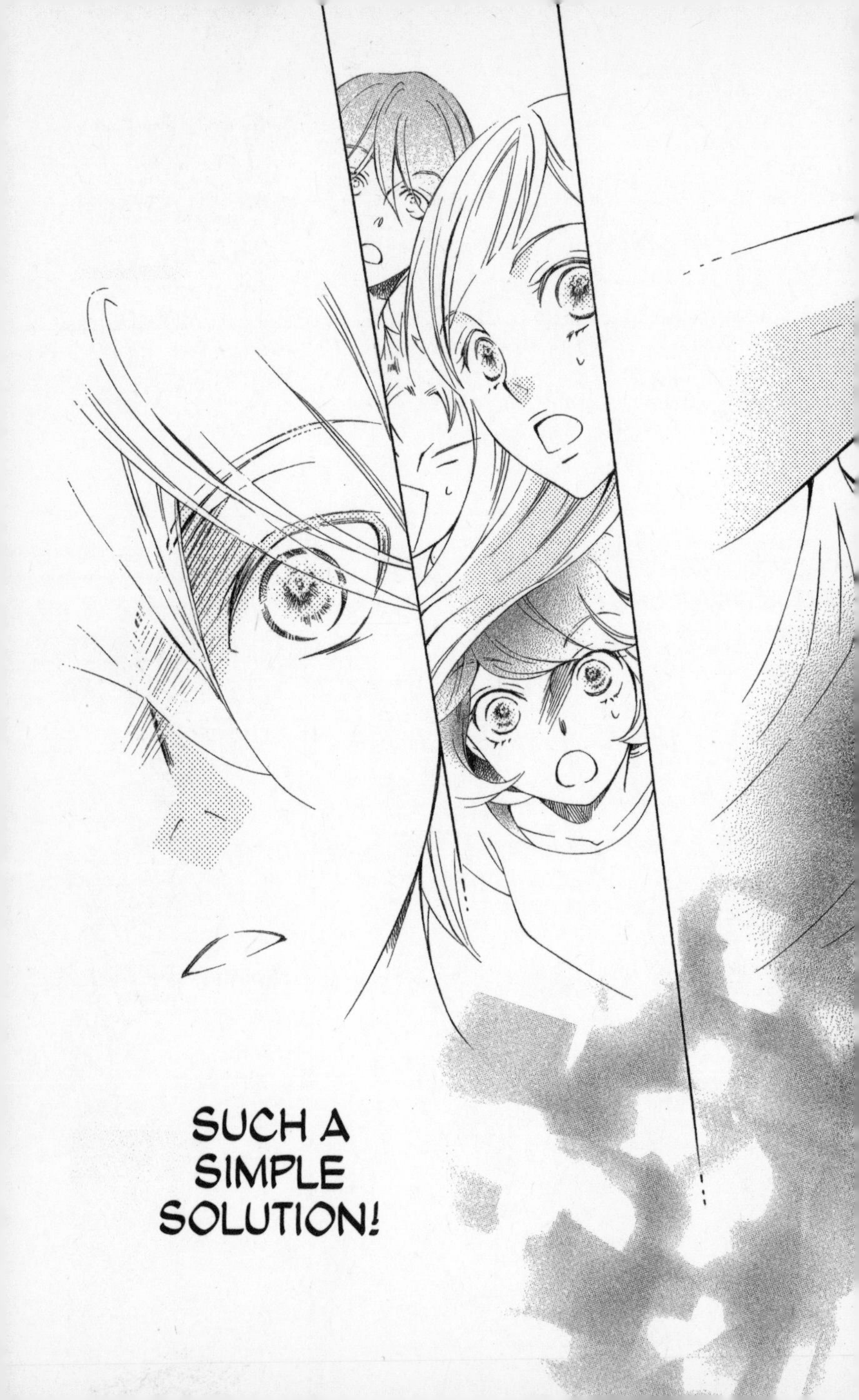
SUCH A SIMPLE SOLUTION!

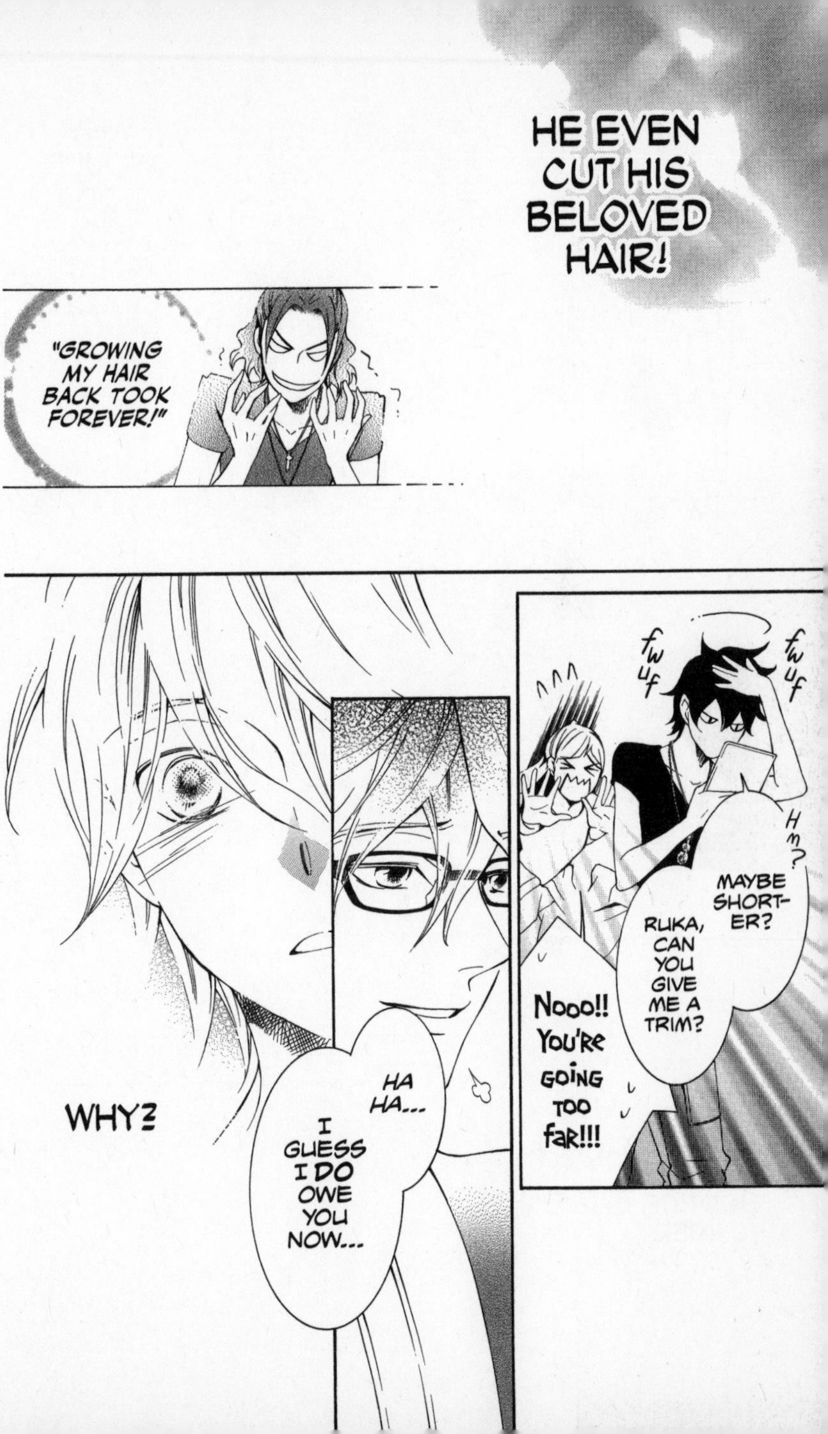
HE EVEN CUT HIS BELOVED HAIR!
"GROWING MY HAIR BACK TOOK FOREVER!"
fwuf
fwuf
Hm?
MAYBE SHORTER?
RUKA, CAN YOU GIVE ME A TRIM?
Nooo!! You're going too far!!!
HA HA...
I GUESS I DO OWE YOU NOW...
WHY?

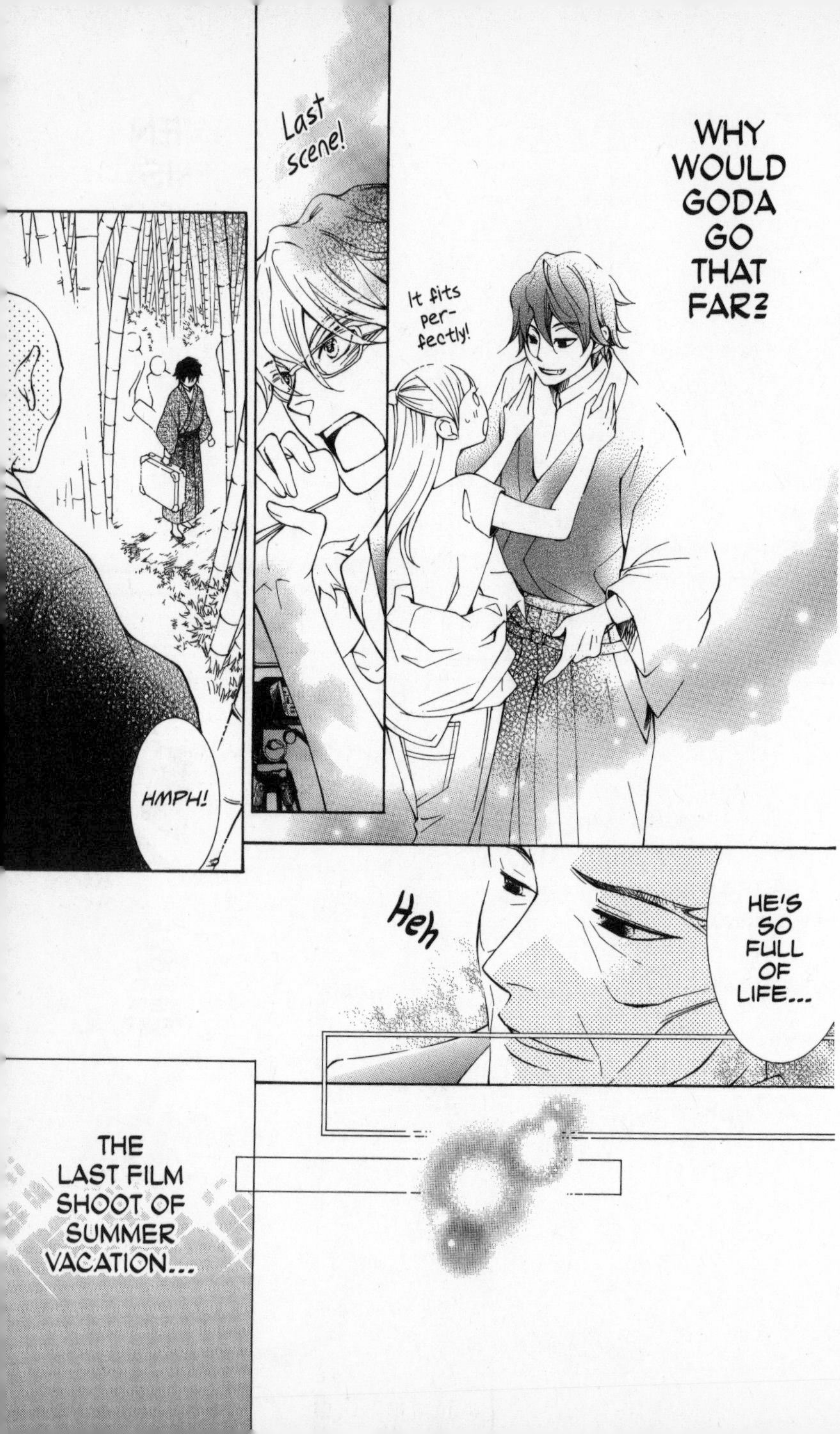
WHY WOULD GODA GO THAT FAR?
It fits per-fectly!
Last scene!
HMPH!
HE'S SO FULL OF LIFE...
Heh
THE LAST FILM SHOOT OF SUMMER VACATION...

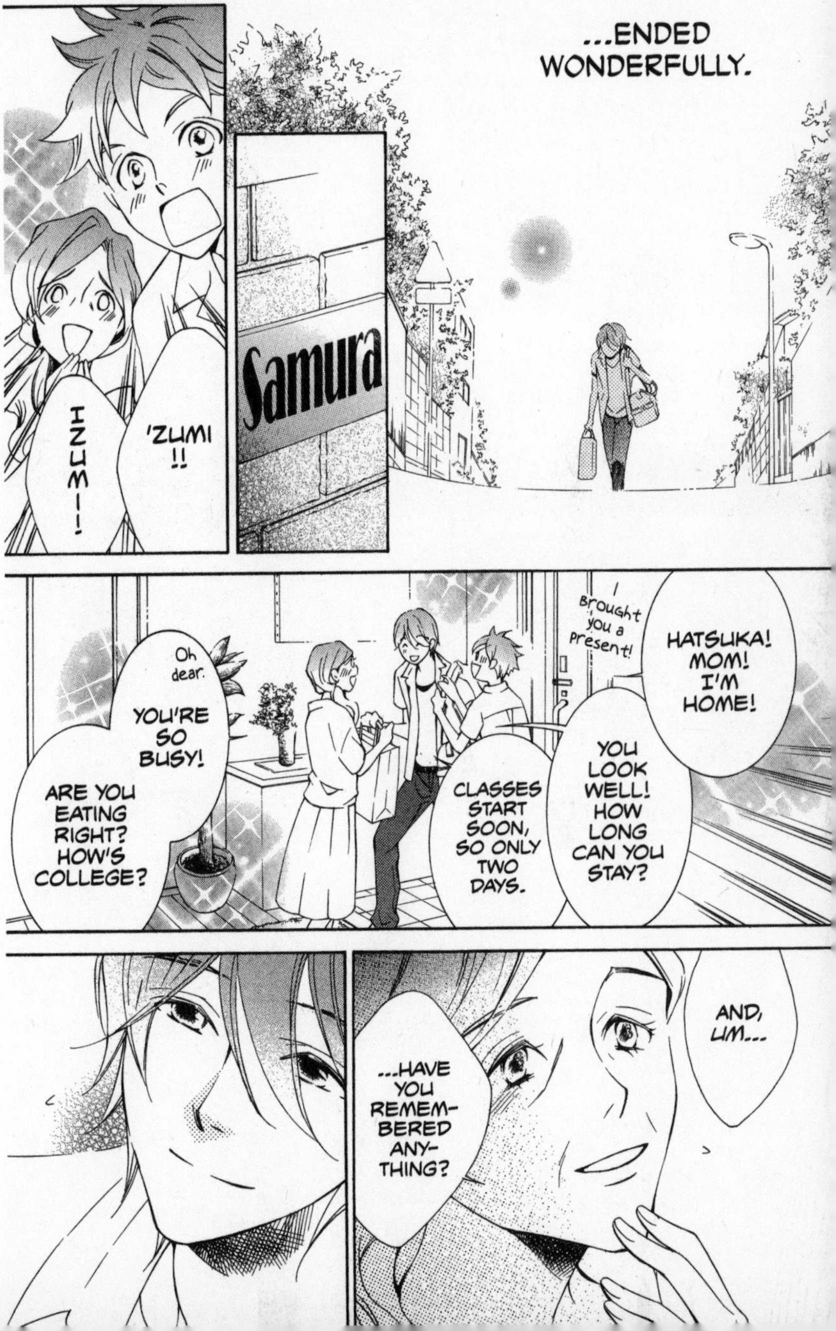
...ENDED WONDERFULLY.
Samura
'ZUMI!!
IZUMI!
HATSUKA! MOM! I'M HOME!
I brought you a present!
YOU LOOK WELL! HOW LONG CAN YOU STAY?
CLASSES START SOON, SO ONLY TWO DAYS.
Oh dear. YOU'RE SO BUSY!
ARE YOU EATING RIGHT? HOW'S COLLEGE?
AND, UM...
...HAVE YOU REMEMBERED ANYTHING?

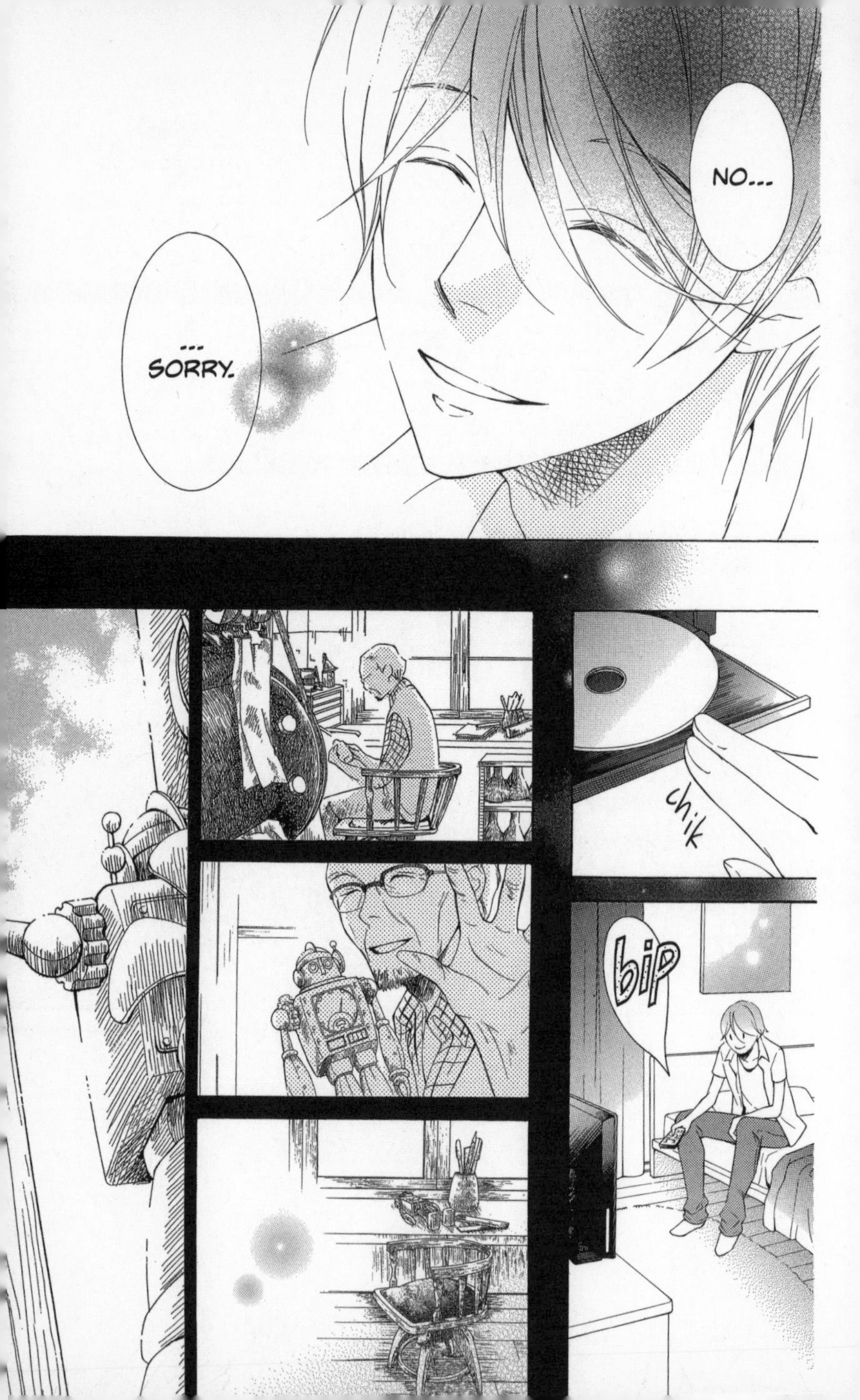
NO...
...SORRY.
chik
bip

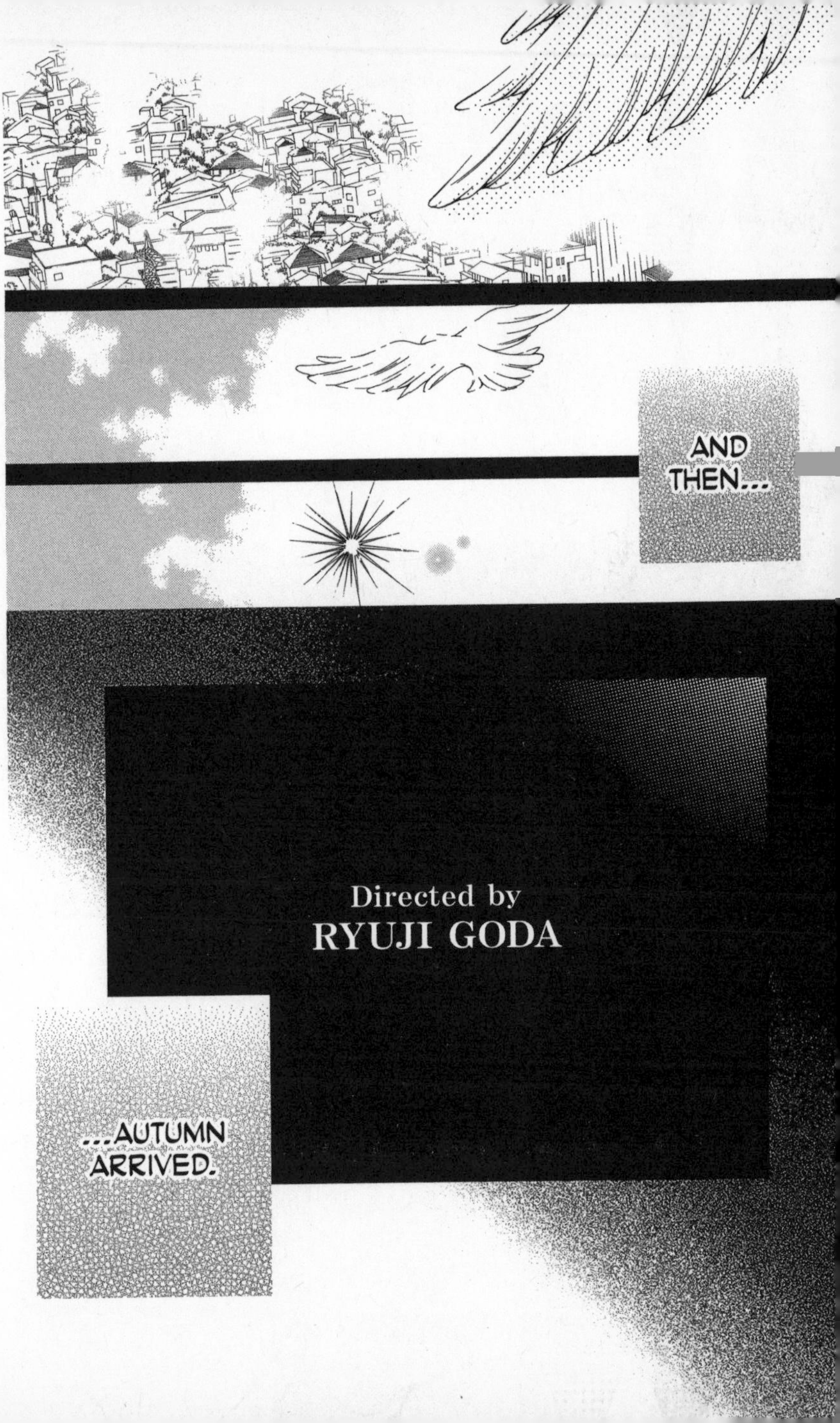
AND THEN...
Directed by
RYUJI GODA
...AUTUMN ARRIVED.

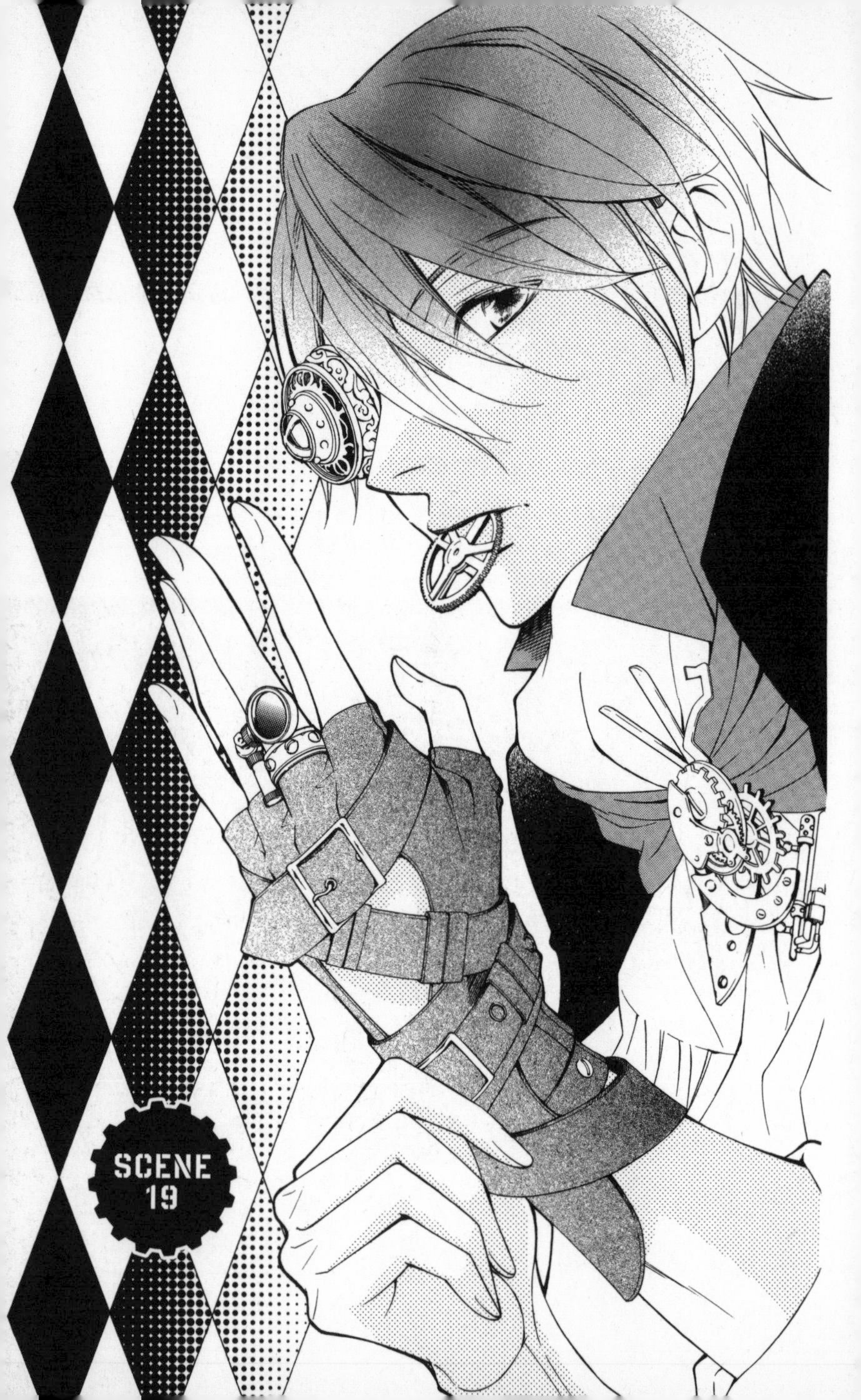
SCENE
19

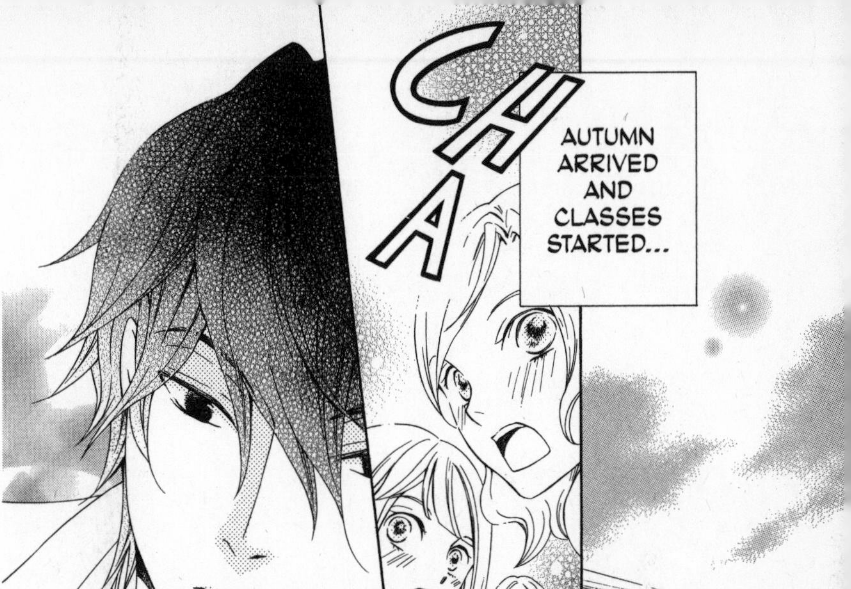
AUTUMN ARRIVED AND CLASSES STARTED...
CHAPTER
Shichikoku University

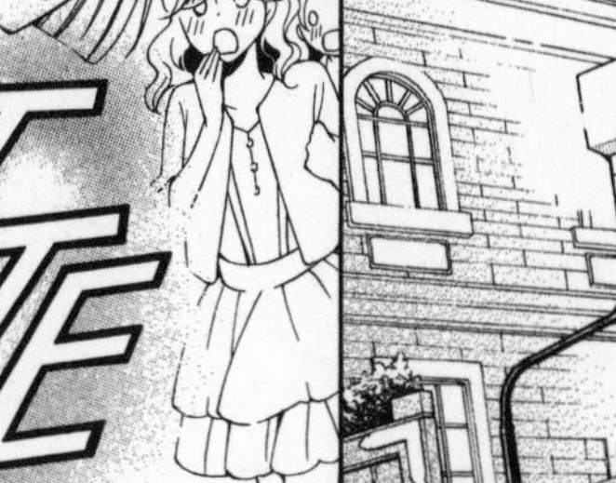

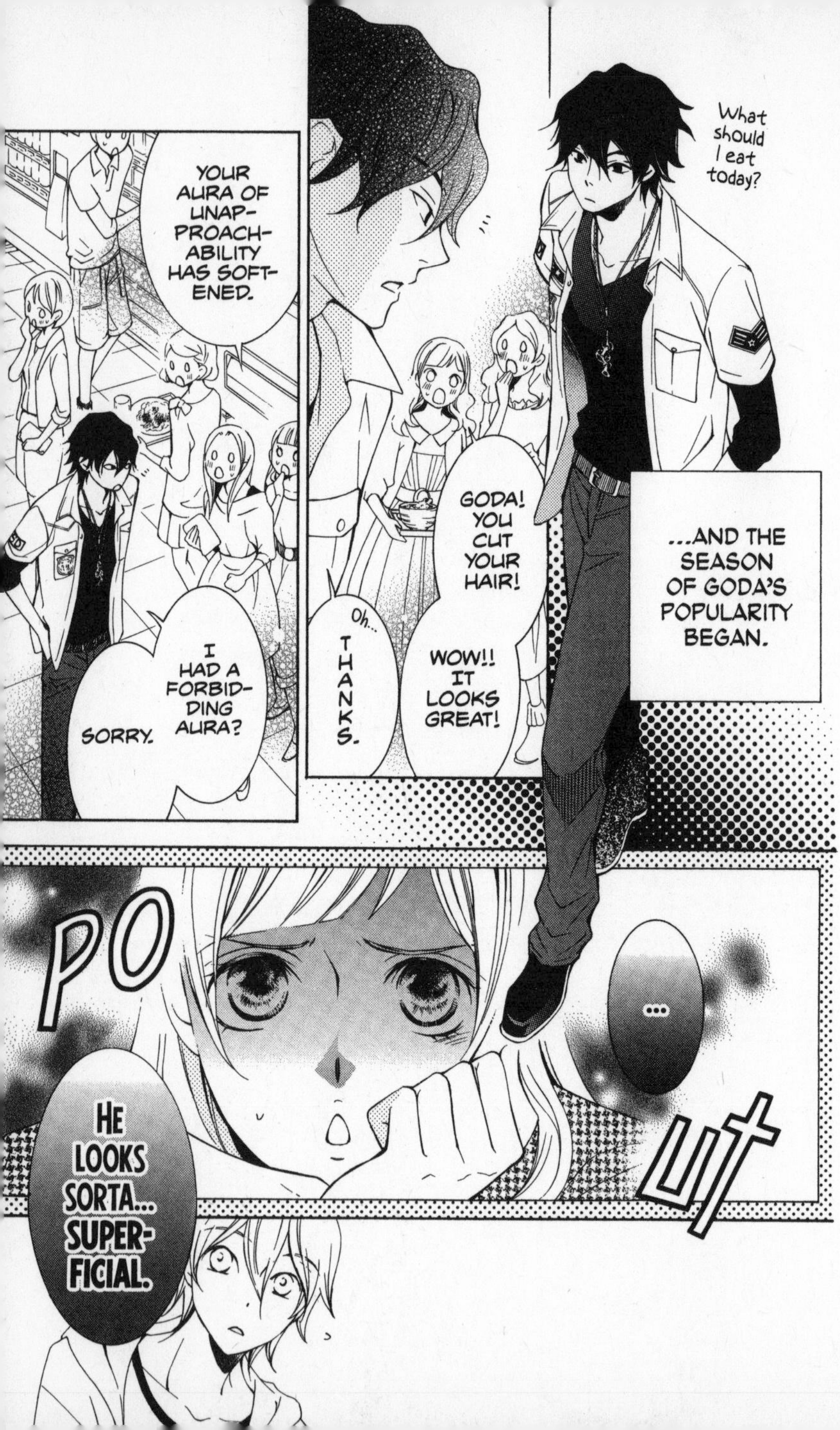
What should I eat today?
...AND THE SEASON OF GODA'S POPULARITY BEGAN.
GODA! YOU CUT YOUR HAIR!
WOW!! IT LOOKS GREAT!
Oh... THANKS.
YOUR AURA OF UNAPPROACHABILITY HAS SOFTENED.
I HAD A FORBIDDING AURA?
SORRY.
POUT
...
HE LOOKS SORTA... SUPERFICIAL.

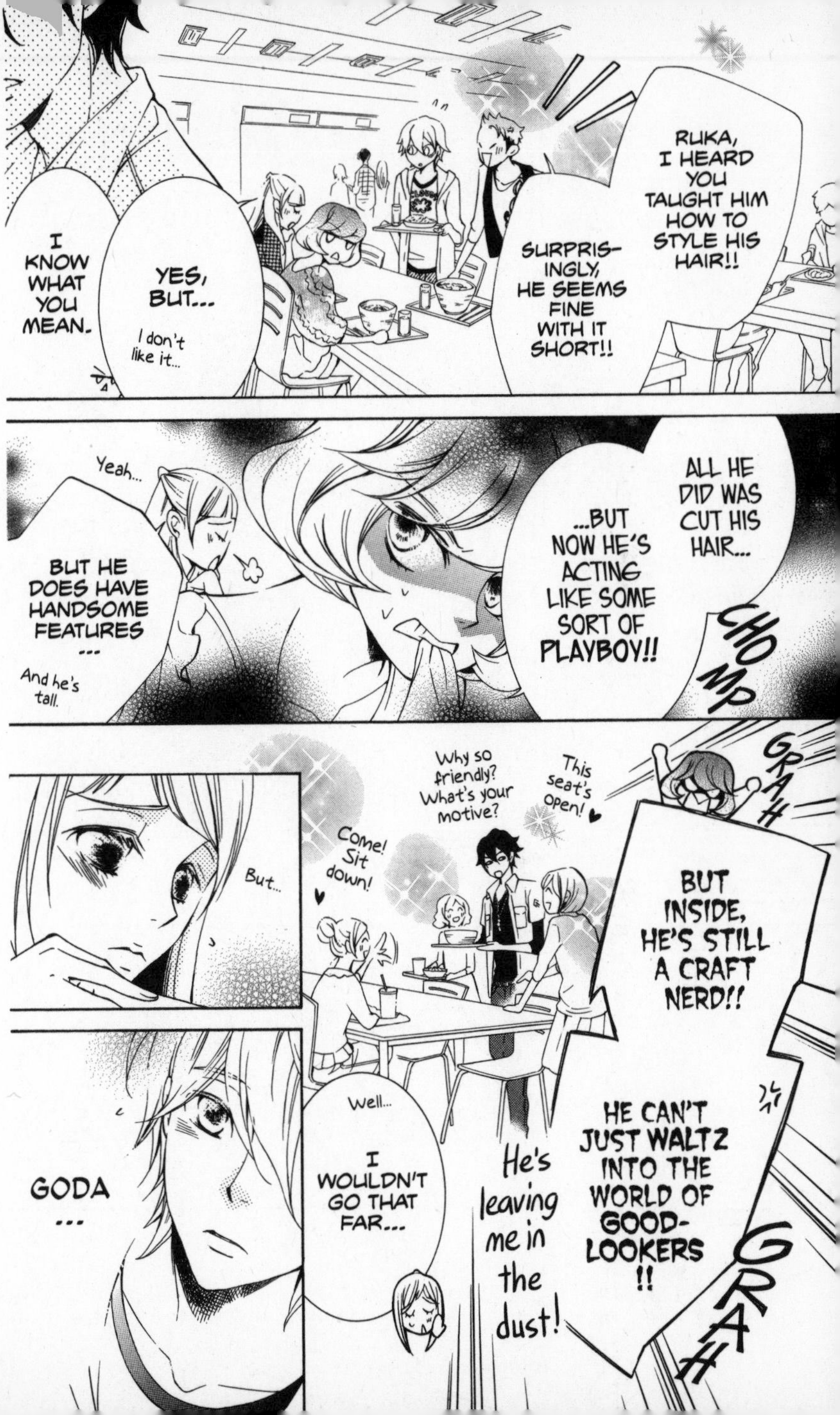
RUKA, I HEARD YOU TAUGHT HIM HOW TO STYLE HIS HAIR!!
SURPRIS-INGLY, HE SEEMS FINE WITH IT SHORT!!
YES, BUT...
I don't like it...
I KNOW WHAT YOU MEAN.
ALL HE DID WAS CUT HIS HAIR...
...BUT NOW HE'S ACTING LIKE SOME SORT OF PLAYBOY!!
CHOMP
Yeah...
BUT HE DOES HAVE HANDSOME FEATURES...
And he's tall.
GRAH
This seat's open!
Why so friendly? What's your motive?
Come! Sit down!
BUT INSIDE, HE'S STILL A CRAFT NERD!!
HE CAN'T JUST WALTZ INTO THE WORLD OF GOOD-LOOKERS!!
GRAH
He's leaving me in the dust!
Well...
I WOULDN'T GO THAT FAR...
But...
GODA...

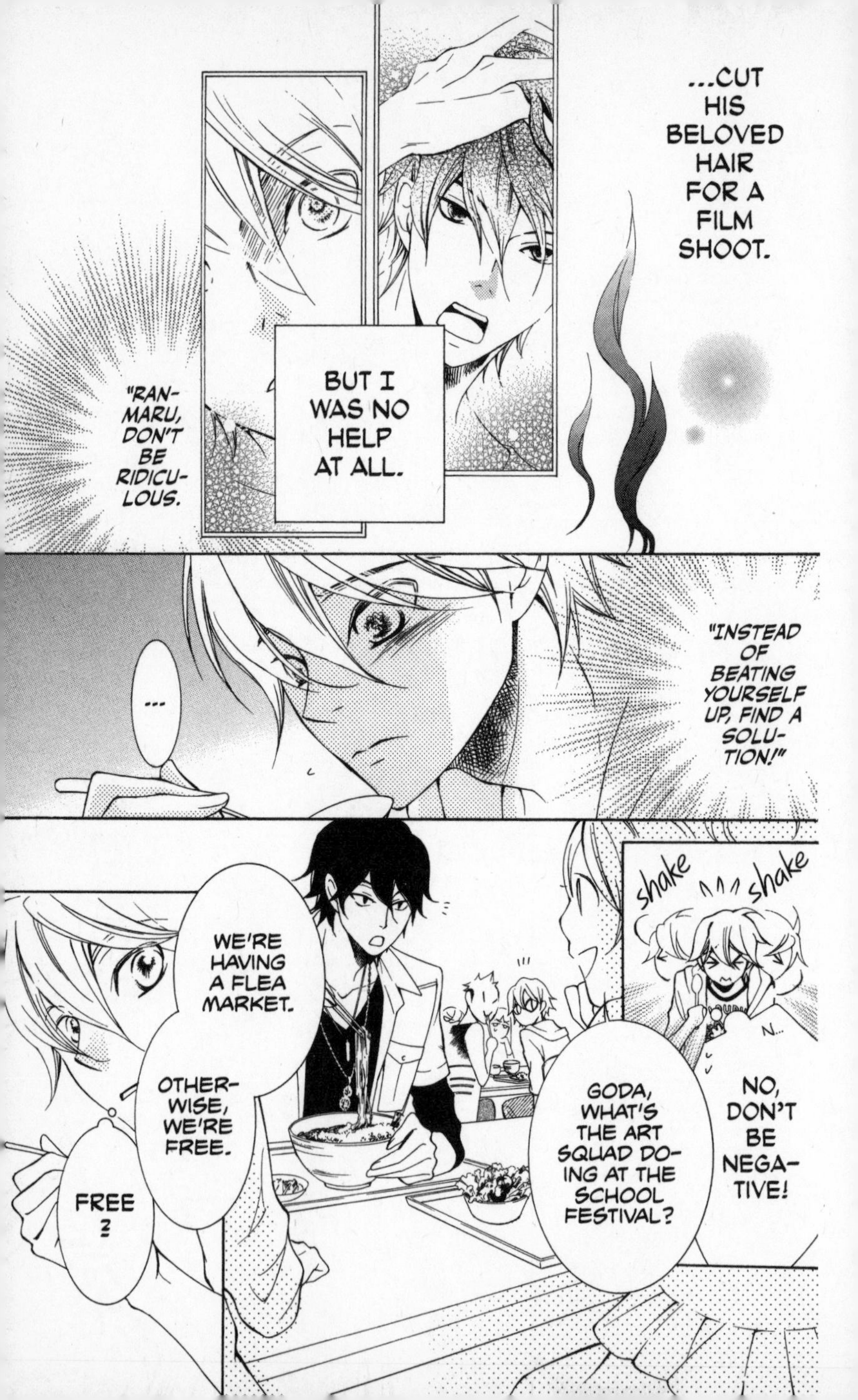
...CUT HIS BELOVED HAIR FOR A FILM SHOOT.
BUT I WAS NO HELP AT ALL.
"RANMARU, DON'T BE RIDICULOUS.
"INSTEAD OF BEATING YOURSELF UP, FIND A SOLUTION!"
...
shake shake
N...
NO, DON'T BE NEGATIVE!
GODA, WHAT'S THE ART SQUAD DOING AT THE SCHOOL FESTIVAL?
WE'RE HAVING A FLEA MARKET.
OTHERWISE, WE'RE FREE.
FREE?

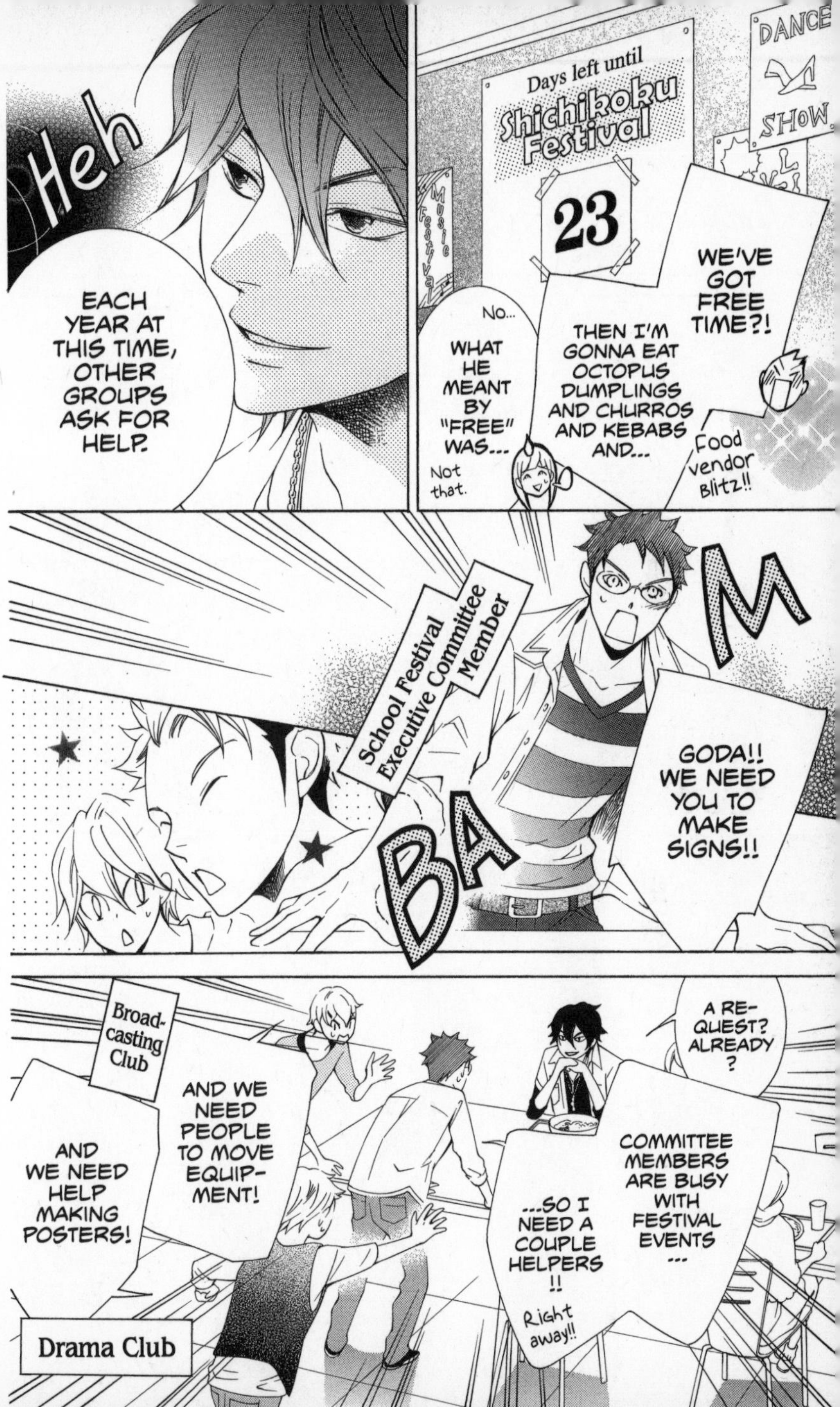
DANCE SHOW
Days left until Shichikoku Festival
23
Music Festival
WE'VE GOT FREE TIME?!
THEN I'M GONNA EAT OCTOPUS DUMPLINGS AND CHURROS AND KEBABS AND...
Food vendor Blitz!!
No...
WHAT HE MEANT BY "FREE" WAS...
Not that.
Heh
EACH YEAR AT THIS TIME, OTHER GROUPS ASK FOR HELP.
School Festival Executive Committee Member
BAM
GODA!! WE NEED YOU TO MAKE SIGNS!!
A RE-QUEST? ALREADY?
COMMITTEE MEMBERS ARE BUSY WITH FESTIVAL EVENTS...
...SO I NEED A COUPLE HELPERS!!
Right away!!
Broad-casting Club
AND WE NEED PEOPLE TO MOVE EQUIP-MENT!
Drama Club
AND WE NEED HELP MAKING POSTERS!

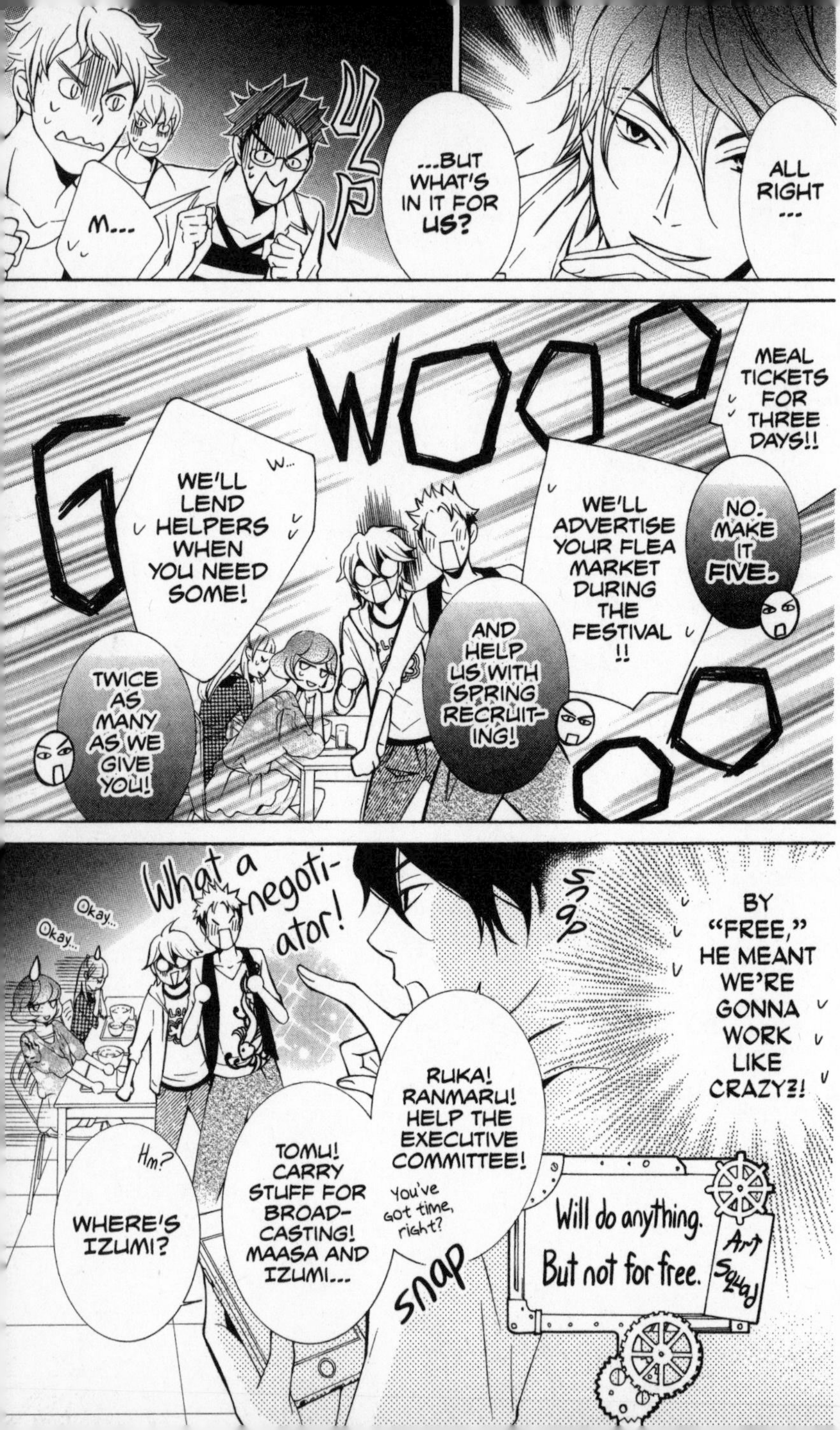
ALL RIGHT ...
...BUT WHAT'S IN IT FOR US?
M...
MEAL TICKETS FOR THREE DAYS!!
NO. MAKE IT FIVE.
WE'LL ADVERTISE YOUR FLEA MARKET DURING THE FESTIVAL!!
AND HELP US WITH SPRING RECRUIT-ING!
GWOOOOO
W...
WE'LL LEND HELPERS WHEN YOU NEED SOME!
TWICE AS MANY AS WE GIVE YOU!
BY "FREE," HE MEANT WE'RE GONNA WORK LIKE CRAZY?!
snap
What a negoti-ator!
Okay...
Okay...
Will do anything. But not for free.
Art Squad
RUKA! RANMARU! HELP THE EXECUTIVE COMMITTEE!
You've got time, right?
TOMU! CARRY STUFF FOR BROADCASTING! MAASA AND IZUMI...
snap
Hm?
WHERE'S IZUMI?

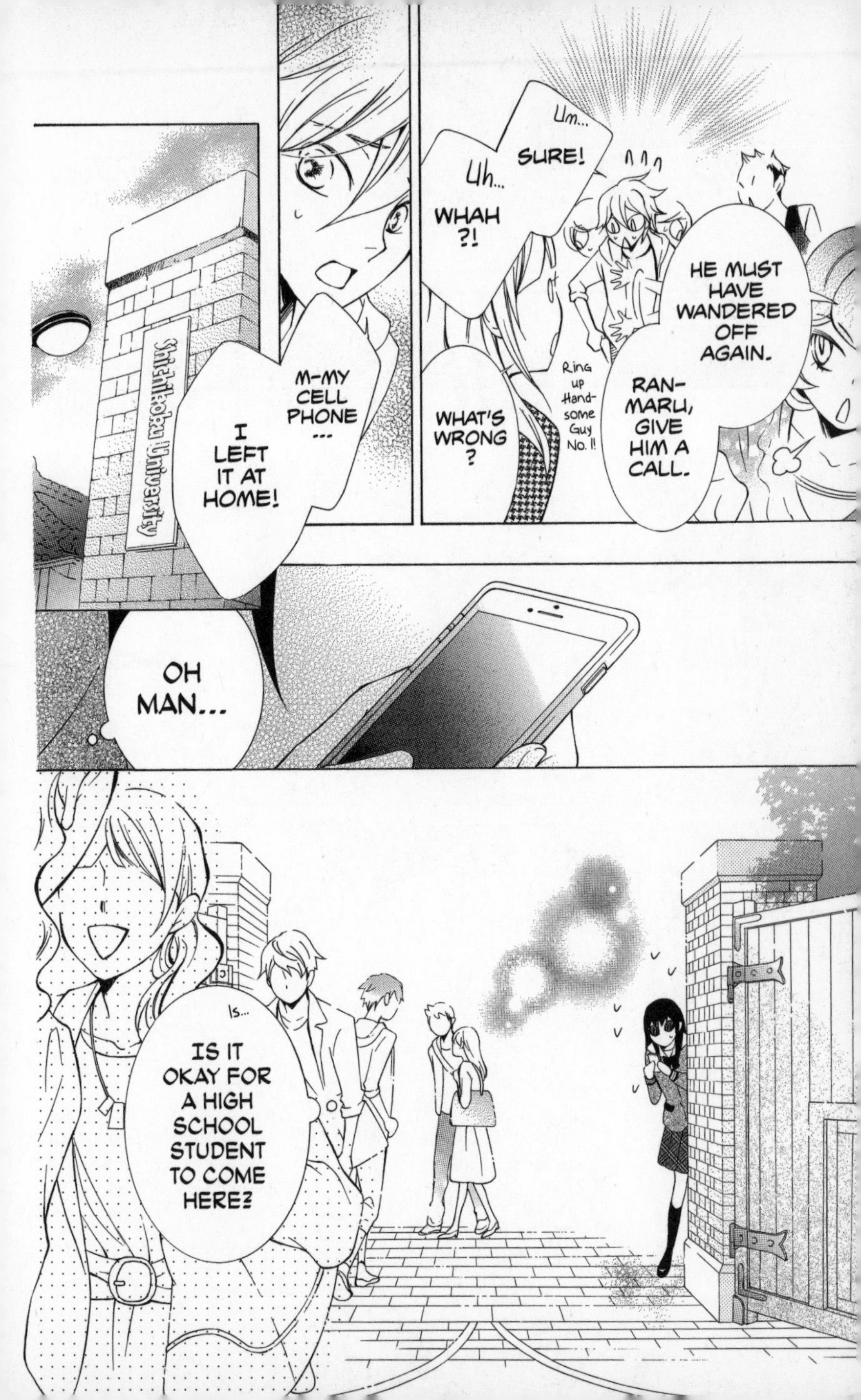
HE MUST HAVE WANDERED OFF AGAIN.
RAN-MARU, GIVE HIM A CALL.
Um... SURE!
Ring up Handsome Guy No. 1!
WHAT'S WRONG?
Uh... WHAH ?!
M-MY CELL PHONE...
I LEFT IT AT HOME!
Shichikoku University
OH MAN...
Is...
IS IT OKAY FOR A HIGH SCHOOL STUDENT TO COME HERE?

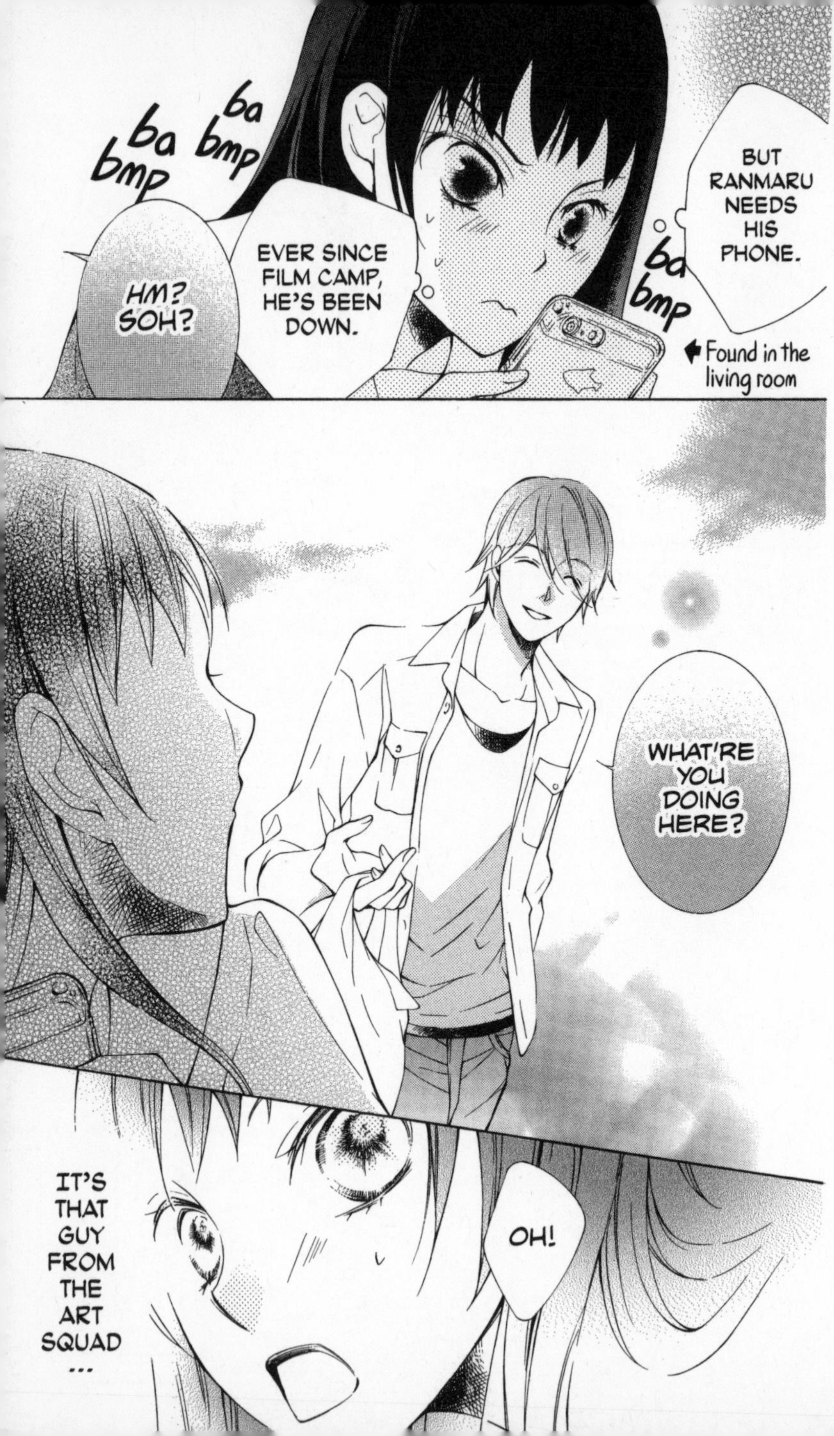
BUT RANMARU NEEDS HIS PHONE.
ba bmp
Found in the living room
EVER SINCE FILM CAMP, HE'S BEEN DOWN.
ba bmp
ba bmp
HM? SOH?
WHAT'RE YOU DOING HERE?
OH!
IT'S THAT GUY FROM THE ART SQUAD...

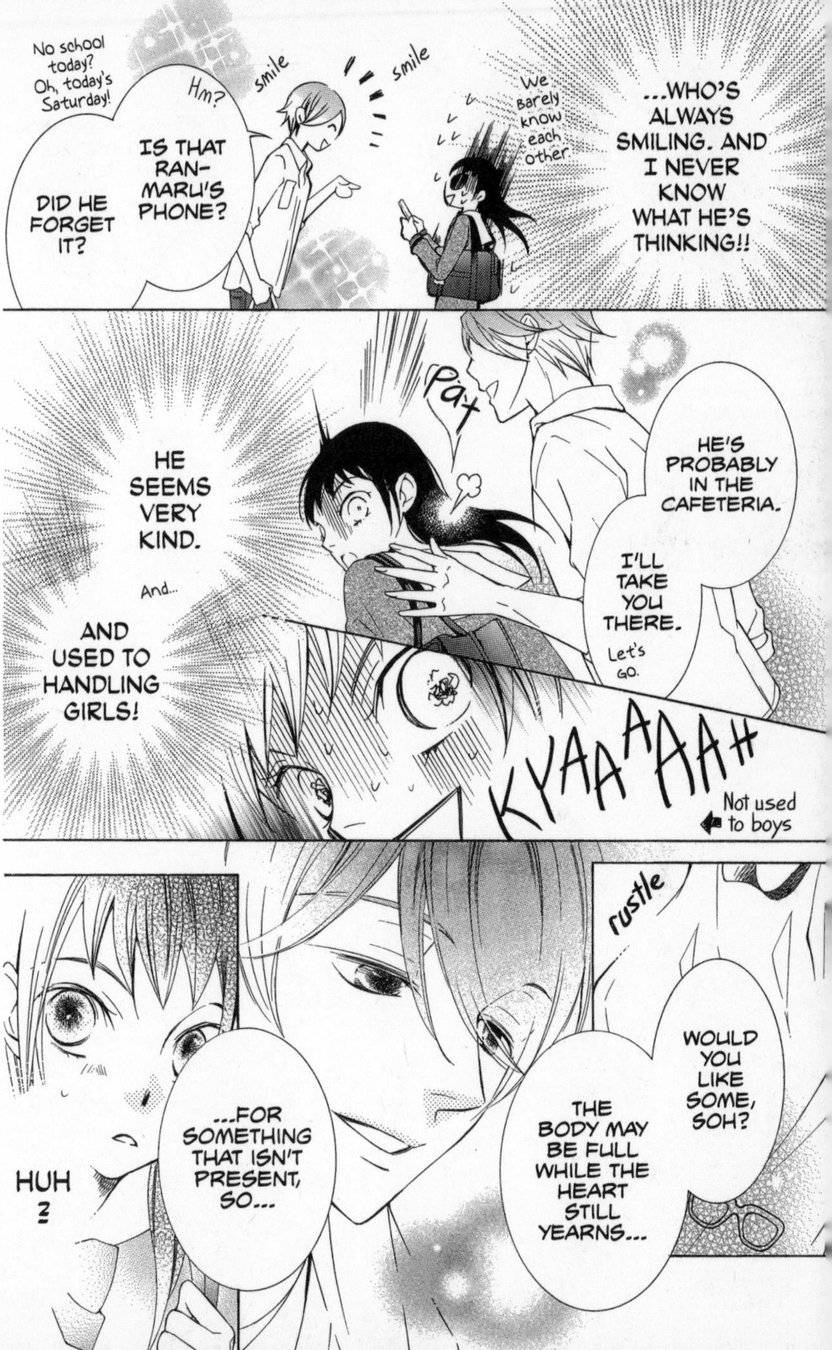
...WHO'S ALWAYS SMILING. AND I NEVER KNOW WHAT HE'S THINKING!!
We barely know each other.
smile
smile
Hm?
IS THAT RAN-MARU'S PHONE?
DID HE FORGET IT?
No school today? Oh, today's Saturday!
Pat
HE'S PROBABLY IN THE CAFETERIA.
I'LL TAKE YOU THERE.
Let's GO.
HE SEEMS VERY KIND.
And...
AND USED TO HANDLING GIRLS!
KYAAAAAH
Not used to boys
rustle
WOULD YOU LIKE SOME, SOH?
THE BODY MAY BE FULL WHILE THE HEART STILL YEARNS...
...FOR SOMETHING THAT ISN'T PRESENT, SO...
HUH

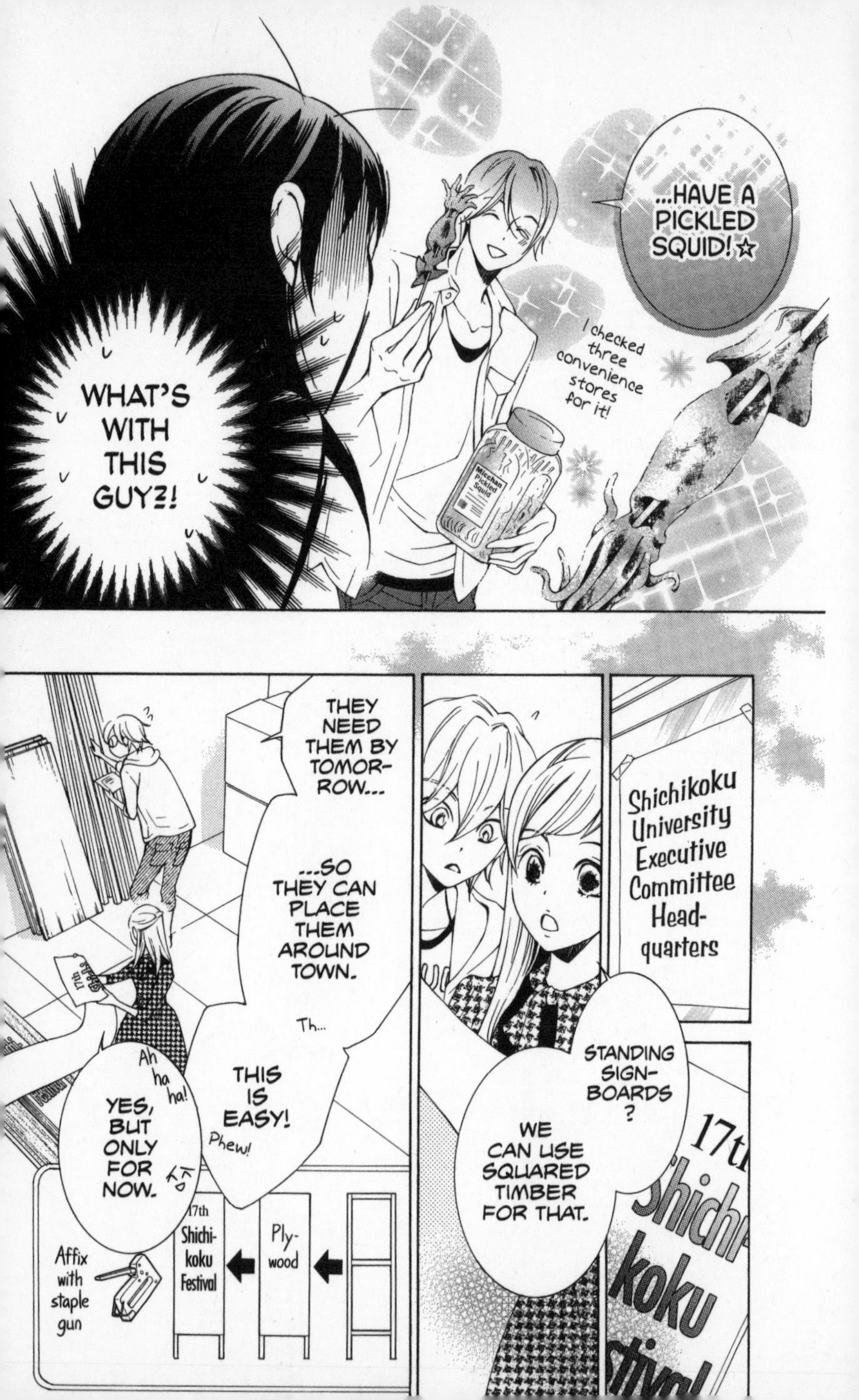
...HAVE A PICKLED SQUID! ☆
I checked three convenience stores for it!
Micchan Pickled Squid
WHAT'S WITH THIS GUY?!
Shichikoku University Executive Committee Head-quarters
STANDING SIGN-BOARDS?
WE CAN USE SQUARED TIMBER FOR THAT.
17th Shichi-koku Festival
THEY NEED THEM BY TOMOR-ROW...
...SO THEY CAN PLACE THEM AROUND TOWN.
Th...
THIS IS EASY!
Phew!
Ah ha ha!
YES, BUT ONLY FOR NOW.
17th Shichi-koku Festival
Ply-wood
Affix with staple gun

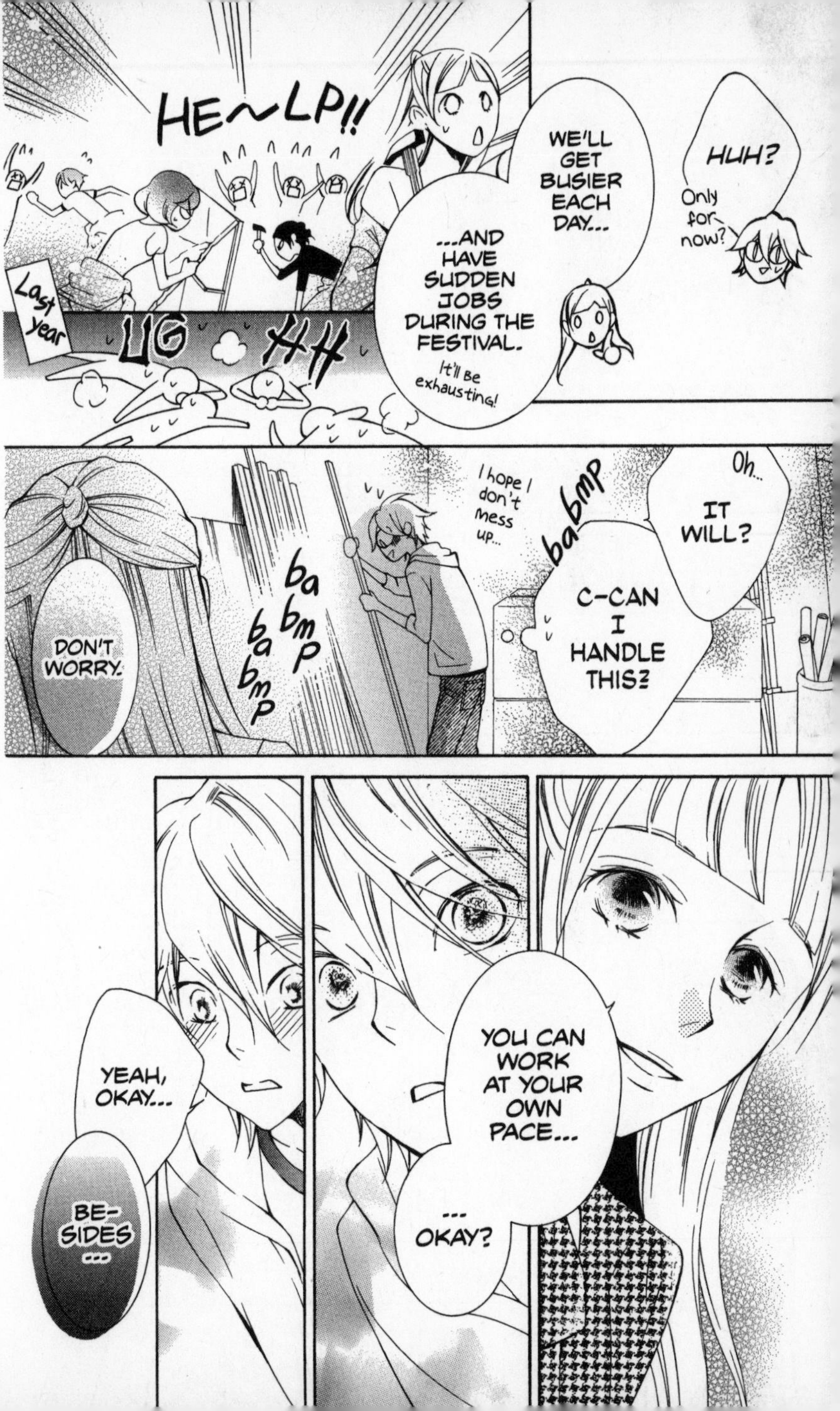
HUH?
Only for now?
WE'LL GET BUSIER EACH DAY...
...AND HAVE SUDDEN JOBS DURING THE FESTIVAL.
It'll be exhausting!
HE~LP!!
Last year
UG
XH
Oh...
IT WILL?
C-CAN I HANDLE THIS?
babmp
I hope I don't mess up...
ba bmp
ba bmp
DON'T WORRY.
YOU CAN WORK AT YOUR OWN PACE...
...OKAY?
YEAH, OKAY...
BE-SIDES...

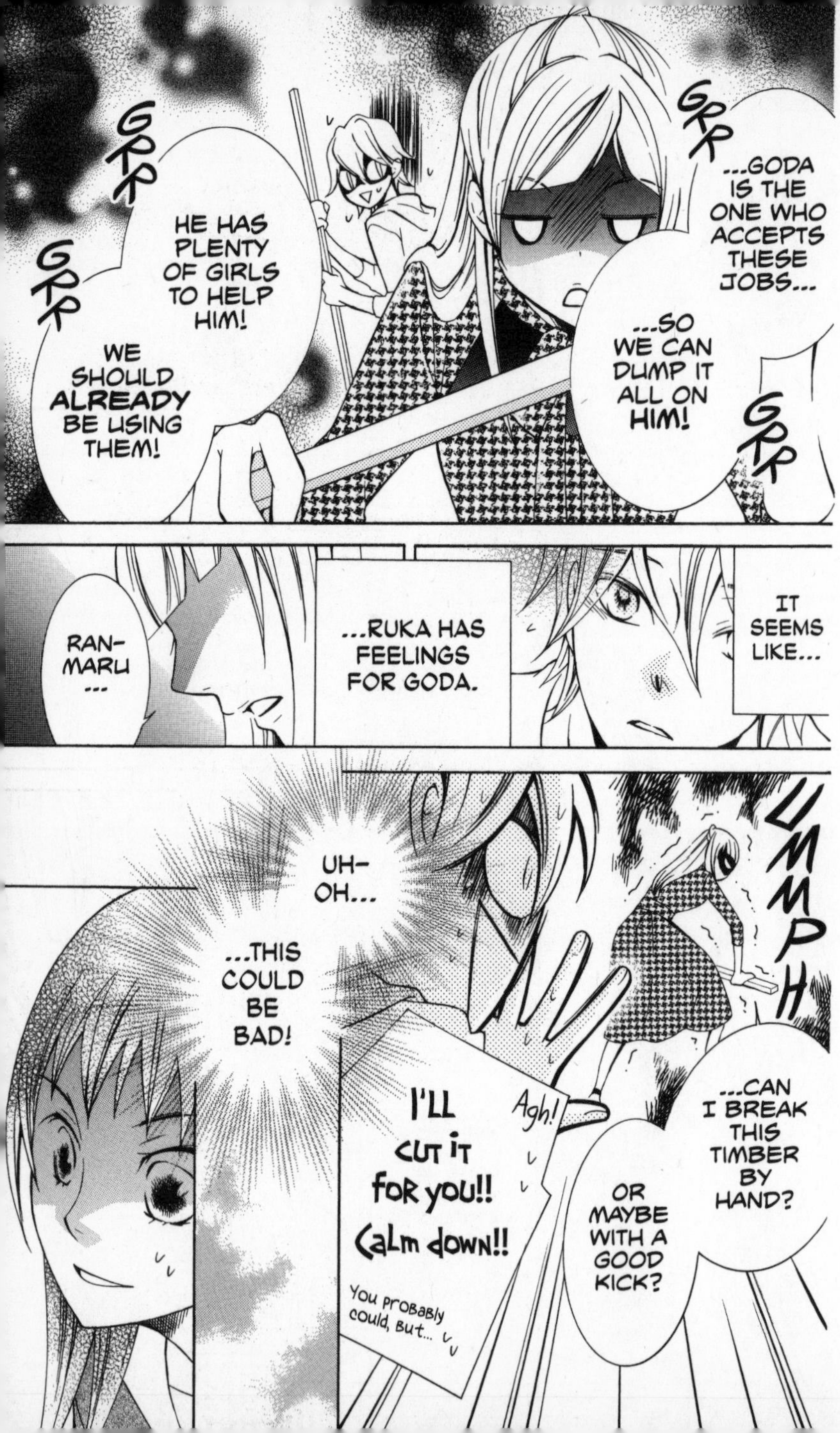
GRR
...GODA IS THE ONE WHO ACCEPTS THESE JOBS...
...SO WE CAN DUMP IT ALL ON HIM!
GRR
GRR
HE HAS PLENTY OF GIRLS TO HELP HIM!
GRR
WE SHOULD **ALREADY** BE USING THEM!
IT SEEMS LIKE...
...RUKA HAS FEELINGS FOR GODA.
RAN-MARU...
UMMPH
...CAN I BREAK THIS TIMBER BY HAND?
OR MAYBE WITH A GOOD KICK?
Agh!
I'LL CUT IT FOR YOU!! Calm down!!
You probably could, but...
UH-OH...
...THIS COULD BE BAD!

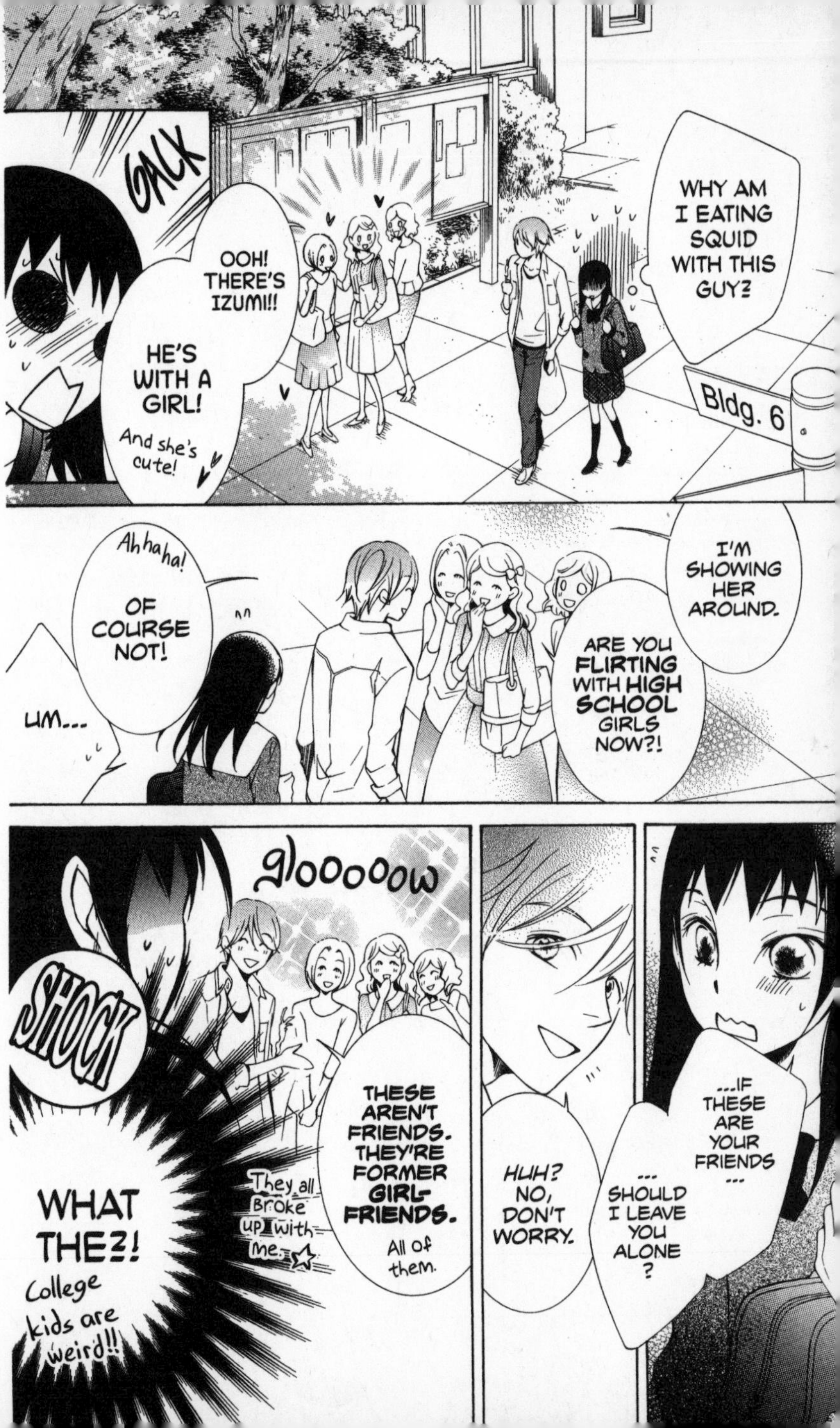

WHY AM I EATING SQUID WITH THIS GUY?
OOH! THERE'S IZUMI!!
HE'S WITH A GIRL!
And she's cute!
GACK
I'M SHOWING HER AROUND.
ARE YOU FLIRTING WITH HIGH SCHOOL GIRLS NOW?!
Ahhaha!
OF COURSE NOT!
UM...
...IF THESE ARE YOUR FRIENDS...
...SHOULD I LEAVE YOU ALONE?
HUH? NO, DON'T WORRY.
gloooooow
THESE AREN'T FRIENDS. THEY'RE FORMER GIRL-FRIENDS.
All of them.
They all broke up with me. ☆
SHOCK
WHAT THE?!
College kids are weird!!

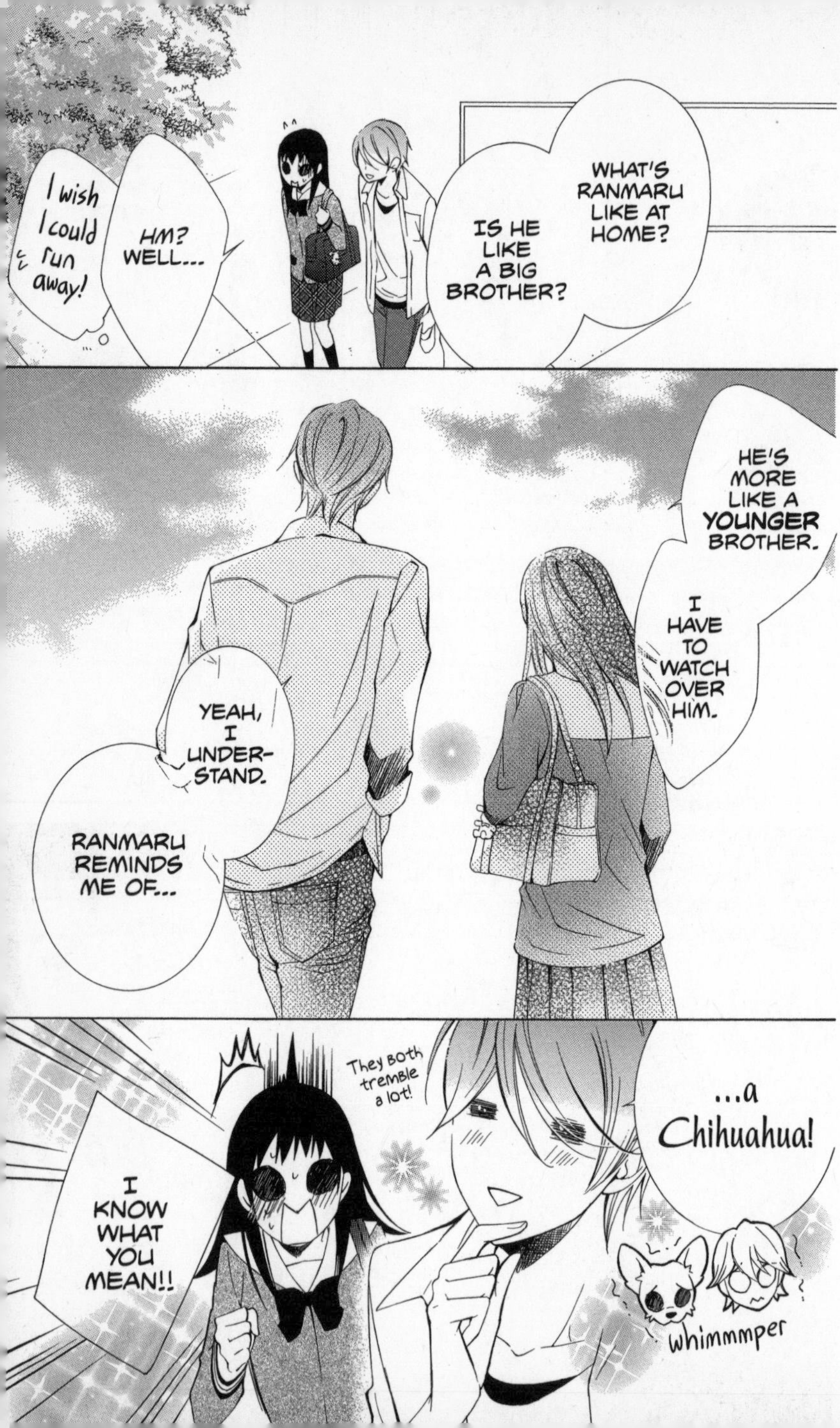
WHAT'S RANMARU LIKE AT HOME?
IS HE LIKE A BIG BROTHER?
HM? WELL...
I wish I could run away!
HE'S MORE LIKE A YOUNGER BROTHER.
I HAVE TO WATCH OVER HIM.
YEAH, I UNDER-STAND.
RANMARU REMINDS ME OF...
...a Chihuahua!
They both tremble a lot!
whimmmper
I KNOW WHAT YOU MEAN!!

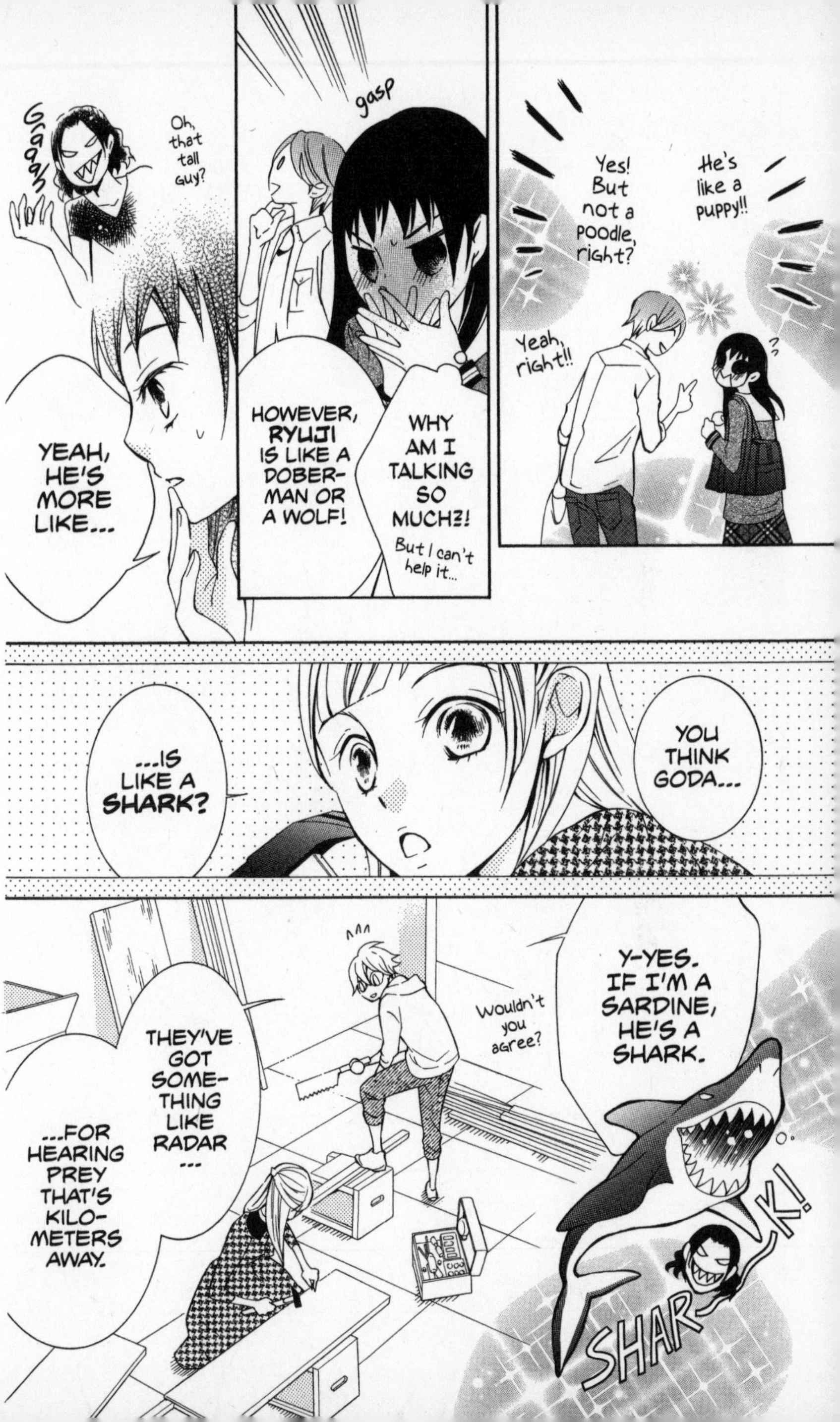
He's like a puppy!!
Yes! But not a poodle, right?
Yeah, right!!
gasp
WHY AM I TALKING SO MUCH?!
But I can't help it...
HOWEVER, RYUJI IS LIKE A DOBERMAN OR A WOLF!
Oh, that tall guy?
Graagh
YEAH, HE'S MORE LIKE...
YOU THINK GODA...
...IS LIKE A SHARK?
Y-YES. IF I'M A SARDINE, HE'S A SHARK.
Wouldn't you agree?
SHARK!
THEY'VE GOT SOMETHING LIKE RADAR...
...FOR HEARING PREY THAT'S KILOMETERS AWAY.

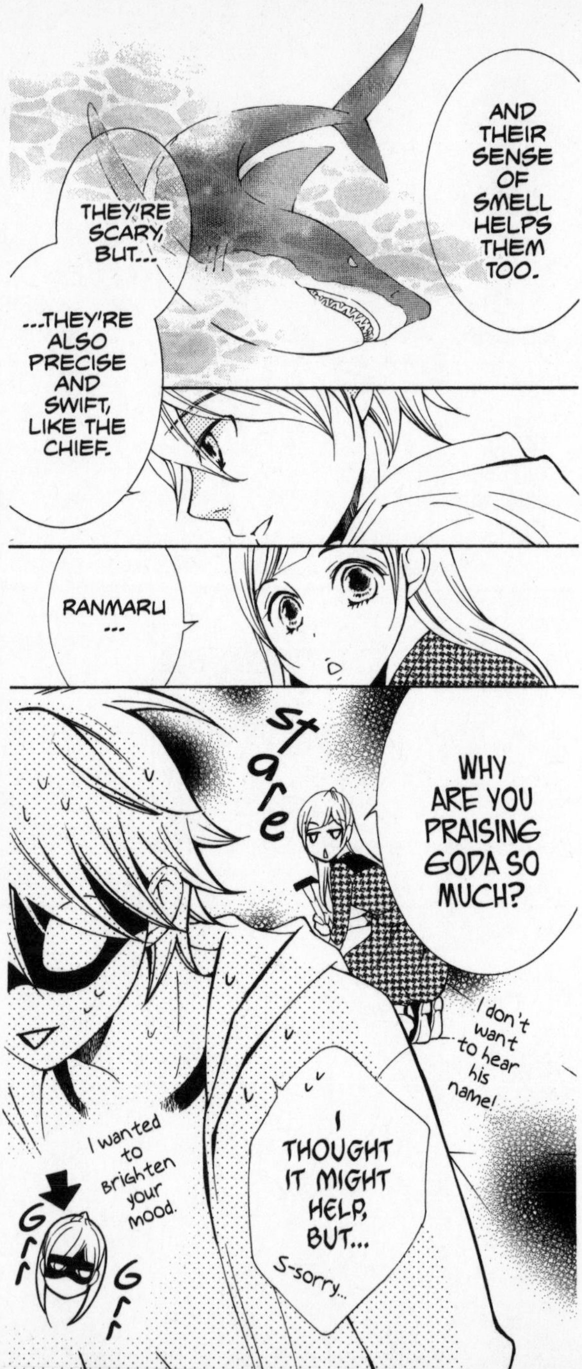
AND THEIR SENSE OF SMELL HELPS THEM TOO.
THEY'RE SCARY, BUT...
...THEY'RE ALSO PRECISE AND SWIFT, LIKE THE CHIEF.
RANMARU...
stare
WHY ARE YOU PRAISING GODA SO MUCH?
I don't want to hear his name!
I THOUGHT IT MIGHT HELP, BUT...
S-sorry...
I wanted to brighten your mood.
Grr
Grr

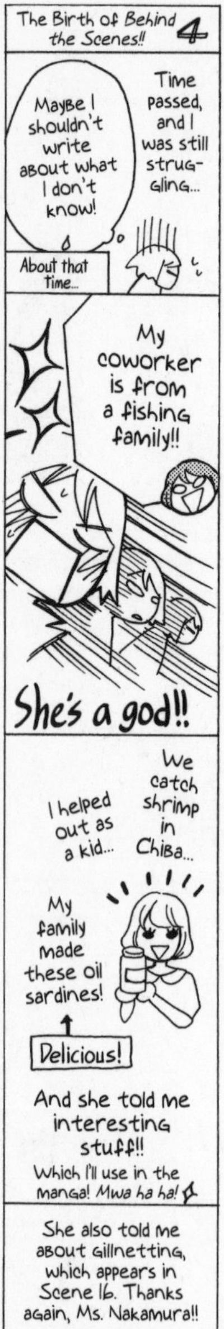
The Birth of Behind the Scenes!! 4
Time passed, and I was still strug-gling...
Maybe I shouldn't write about what I don't know!
About that time...
My coworker is from a fishing family!!
She's a god!!
We catch shrimp in Chiba...
I helped out as a kid...
My family made these oil sardines!
Delicious!
And she told me interesting stuff!!
Which I'll use in the manga! Mwa ha ha!
She also told me about gillnetting, which appears in Scene 16. Thanks again, Ms. Nakamura!!

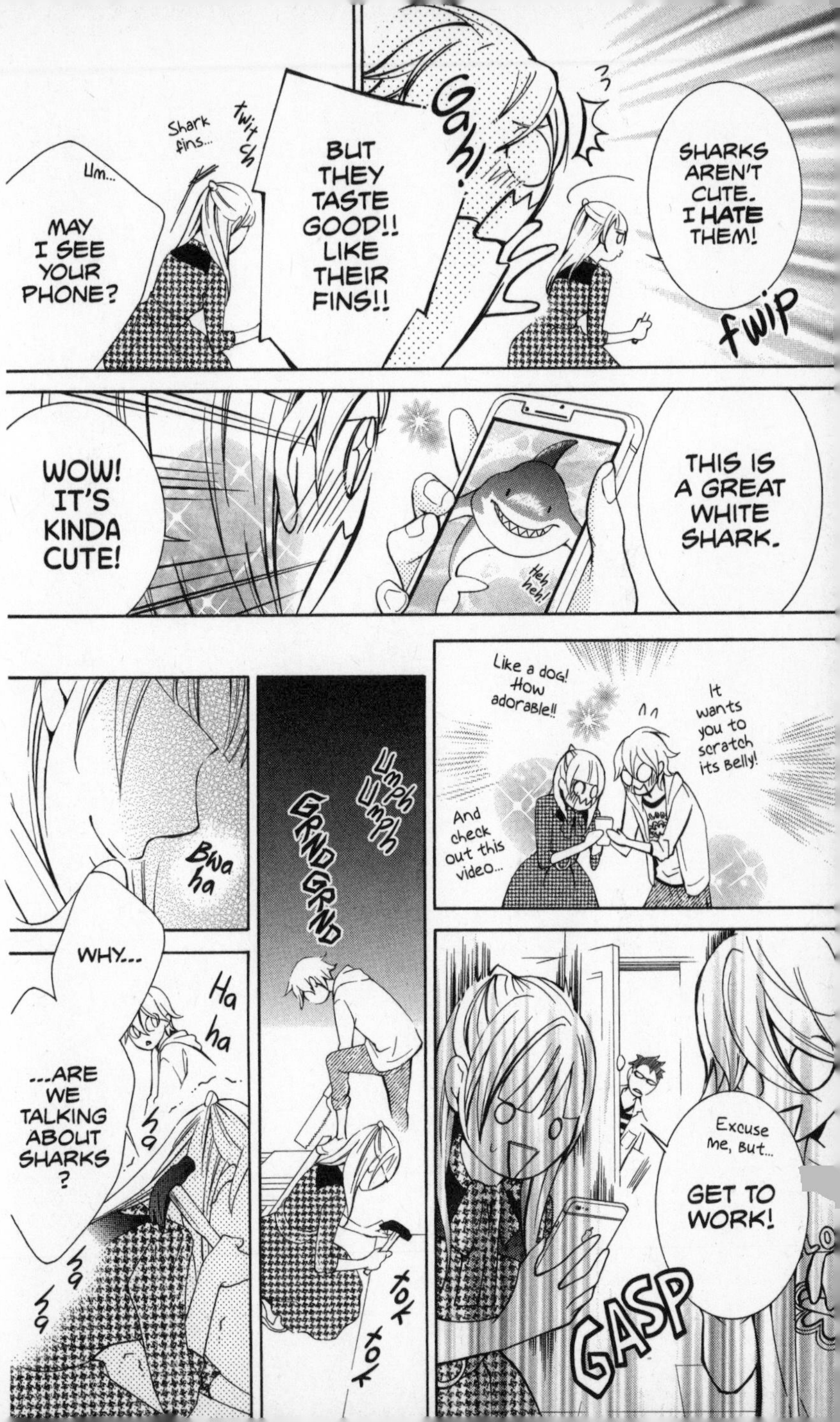
SHARKS AREN'T CUTE. I HATE THEM!
fwip
Gah!
BUT THEY TASTE GOOD!! LIKE THEIR FINS!!
twitch
Shark fins...
Um...
MAY I SEE YOUR PHONE?
THIS IS A GREAT WHITE SHARK.
Heh heh!
WOW! IT'S KINDA CUTE!
It wants you to scratch its belly!
Like a dog! How adorable!!
And check out this video...
Excuse me, but...
GET TO WORK!
GASP
Umph Umph
GRNDGRND
tok tok
Bwa ha
WHY...
Ha ha
...ARE WE TALKING ABOUT SHARKS?
ha ha ha

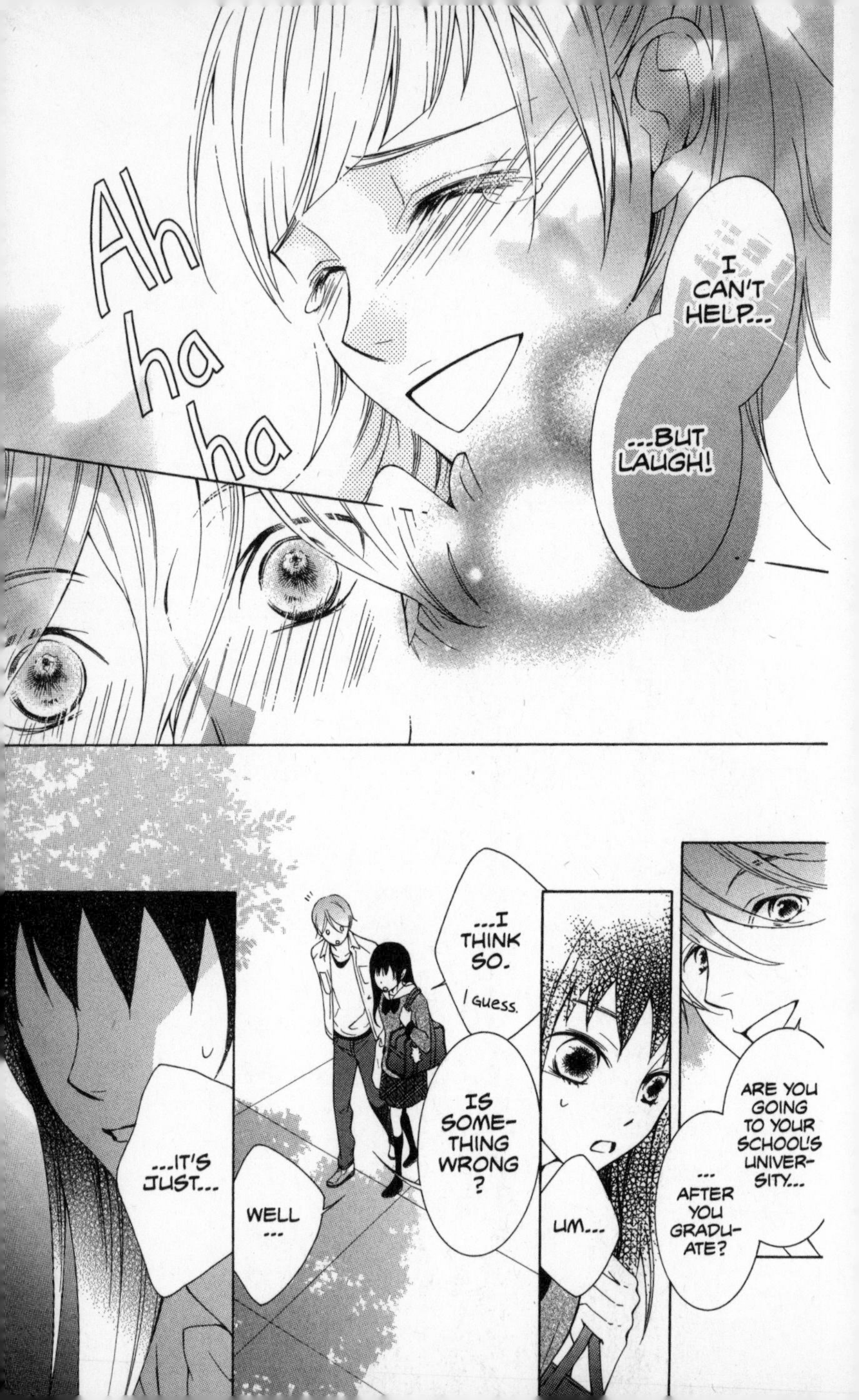
Ah ha ha
I CAN'T HELP...
...BUT LAUGH!
ARE YOU GOING TO YOUR SCHOOL'S UNIVERSITY...
...AFTER YOU GRADUATE?
UM...
...I THINK SO.
I guess.
IS SOMETHING WRONG?
WELL...
...IT'S JUST...

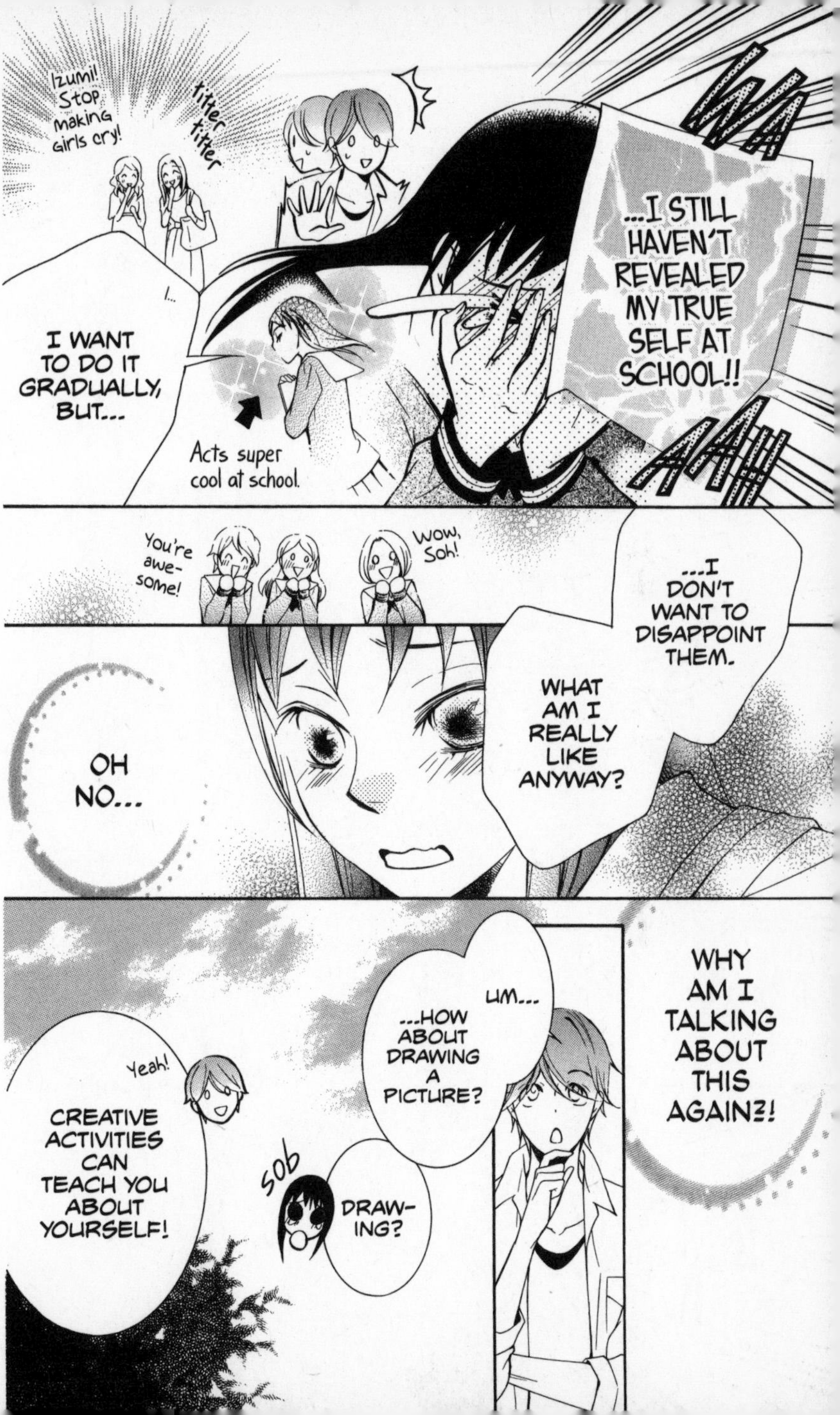
WA
...I STILL HAVEN'T REVEALED MY TRUE SELF AT SCHOOL!!
AAH!!
titter titter
Izumi! Stop making girls cry!
I...
I WANT TO DO IT GRADUALLY, BUT...
Acts super cool at school.
...I DON'T WANT TO DISAPPOINT THEM.
Wow, Soh!
You're awe-some!
WHAT AM I REALLY LIKE ANYWAY?
OH NO...
WHY AM I TALKING ABOUT THIS AGAIN?!
UM...
...HOW ABOUT DRAWING A PICTURE?
DRAW-ING?
sob
Yeah!
CREATIVE ACTIVITIES CAN TEACH YOU ABOUT YOURSELF!

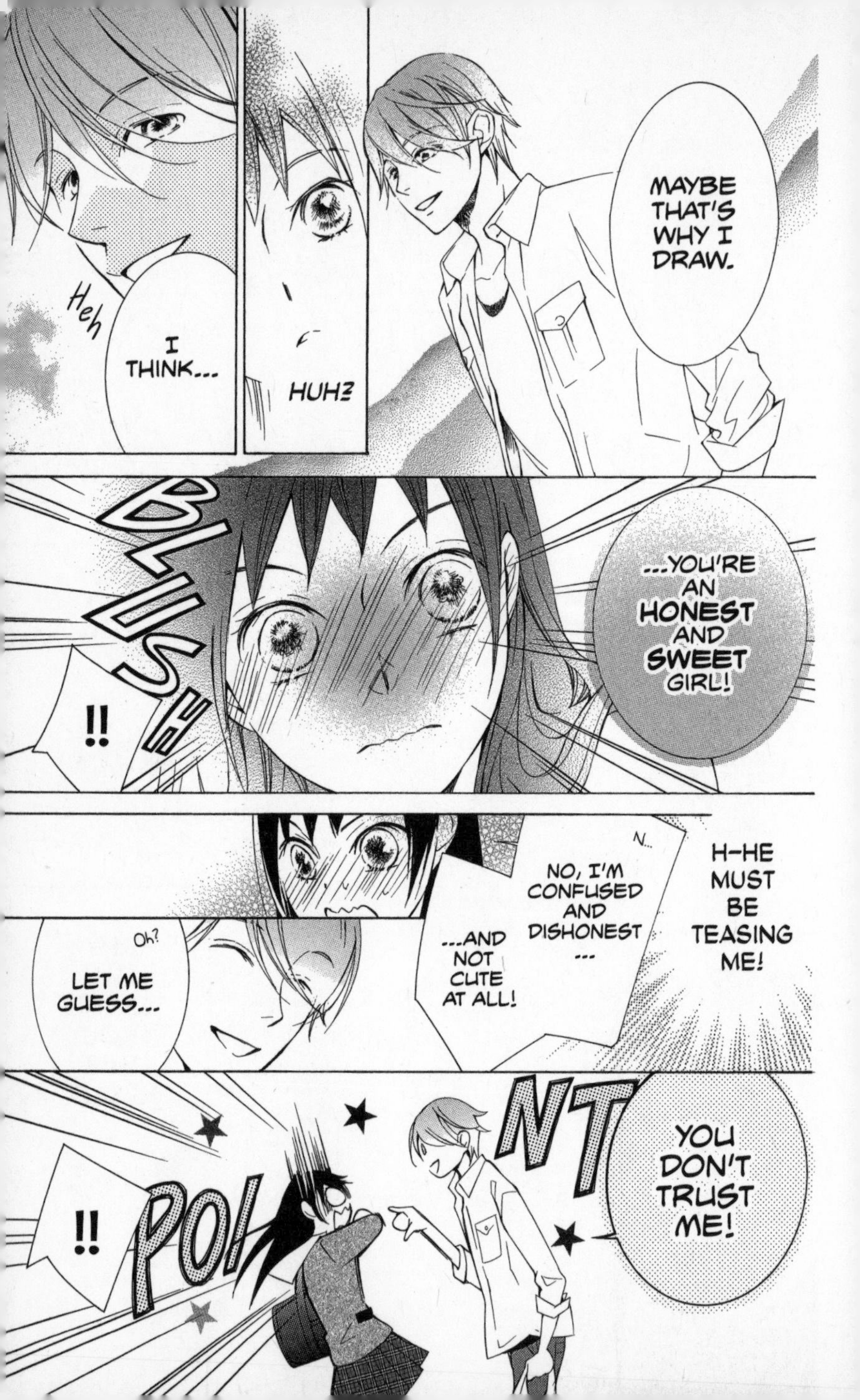
MAYBE THAT'S WHY I DRAW.
HUH?
I THINK...
Heh
...YOU'RE AN HONEST AND SWEET GIRL!
BLUSH
!!
H-HE MUST BE TEASING ME!
N...
NO, I'M CONFUSED AND DISHONEST ...
...AND NOT CUTE AT ALL!
Oh?
LET ME GUESS...
YOU DON'T TRUST ME!
POINT
!!

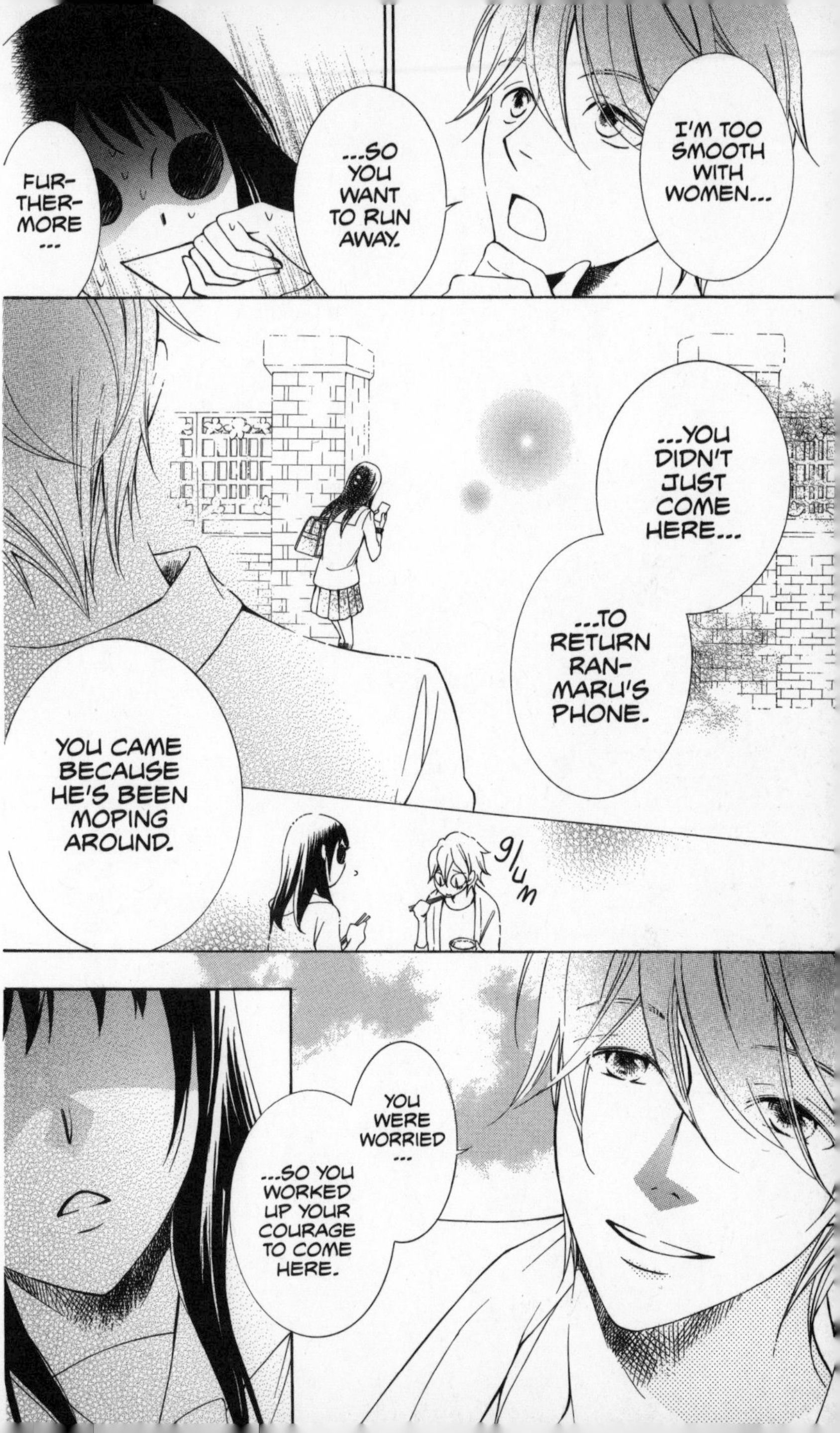
I'M TOO SMOOTH WITH WOMEN...
...SO YOU WANT TO RUN AWAY.
FUR-THER-MORE...
...YOU DIDN'T JUST COME HERE...
...TO RETURN RAN-MARU'S PHONE.
YOU CAME BECAUSE HE'S BEEN MOPING AROUND.
glum
YOU WERE WORRIED...
...SO YOU WORKED UP YOUR COURAGE TO COME HERE.

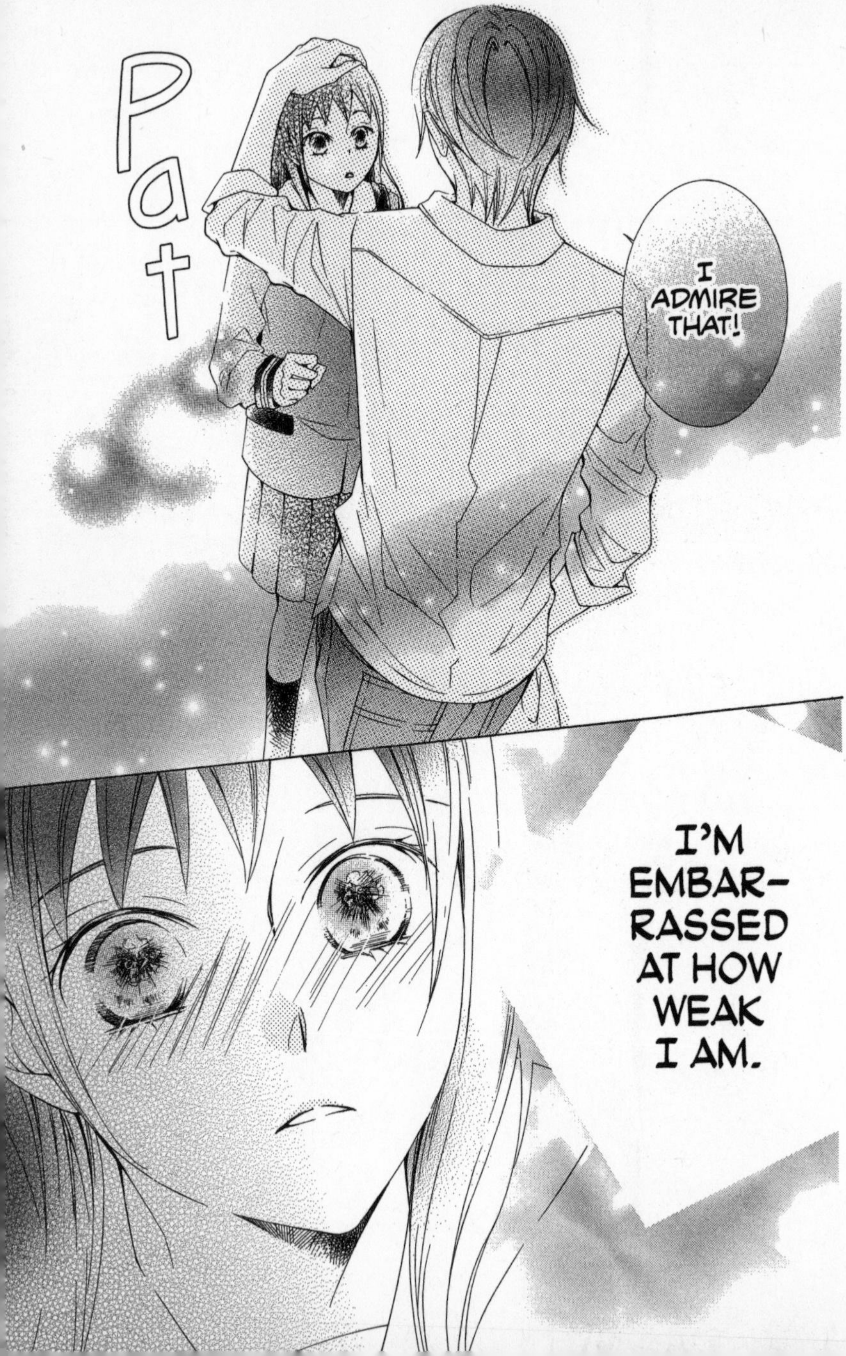
I ADMIRE THAT!
Pat
I'M EMBARRASSED AT HOW WEAK I AM.

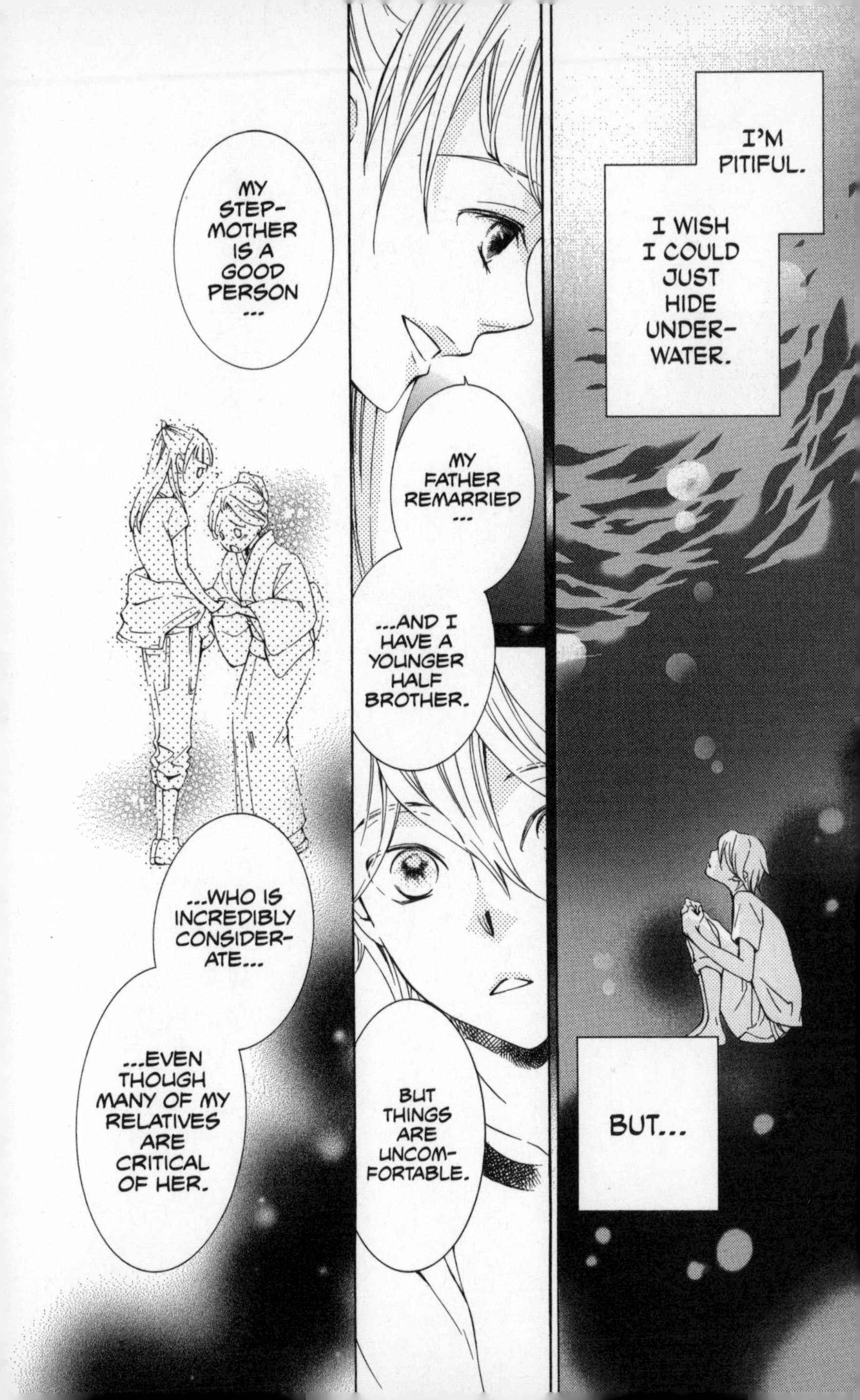
I'M PITIFUL.
I WISH I COULD JUST HIDE UNDERWATER.
BUT...
MY FATHER REMARRIED...
...AND I HAVE A YOUNGER HALF BROTHER.
BUT THINGS ARE UNCOMFORTABLE.
MY STEPMOTHER IS A GOOD PERSON...
...WHO IS INCREDIBLY CONSIDERATE...
...EVEN THOUGH MANY OF MY RELATIVES ARE CRITICAL OF HER.

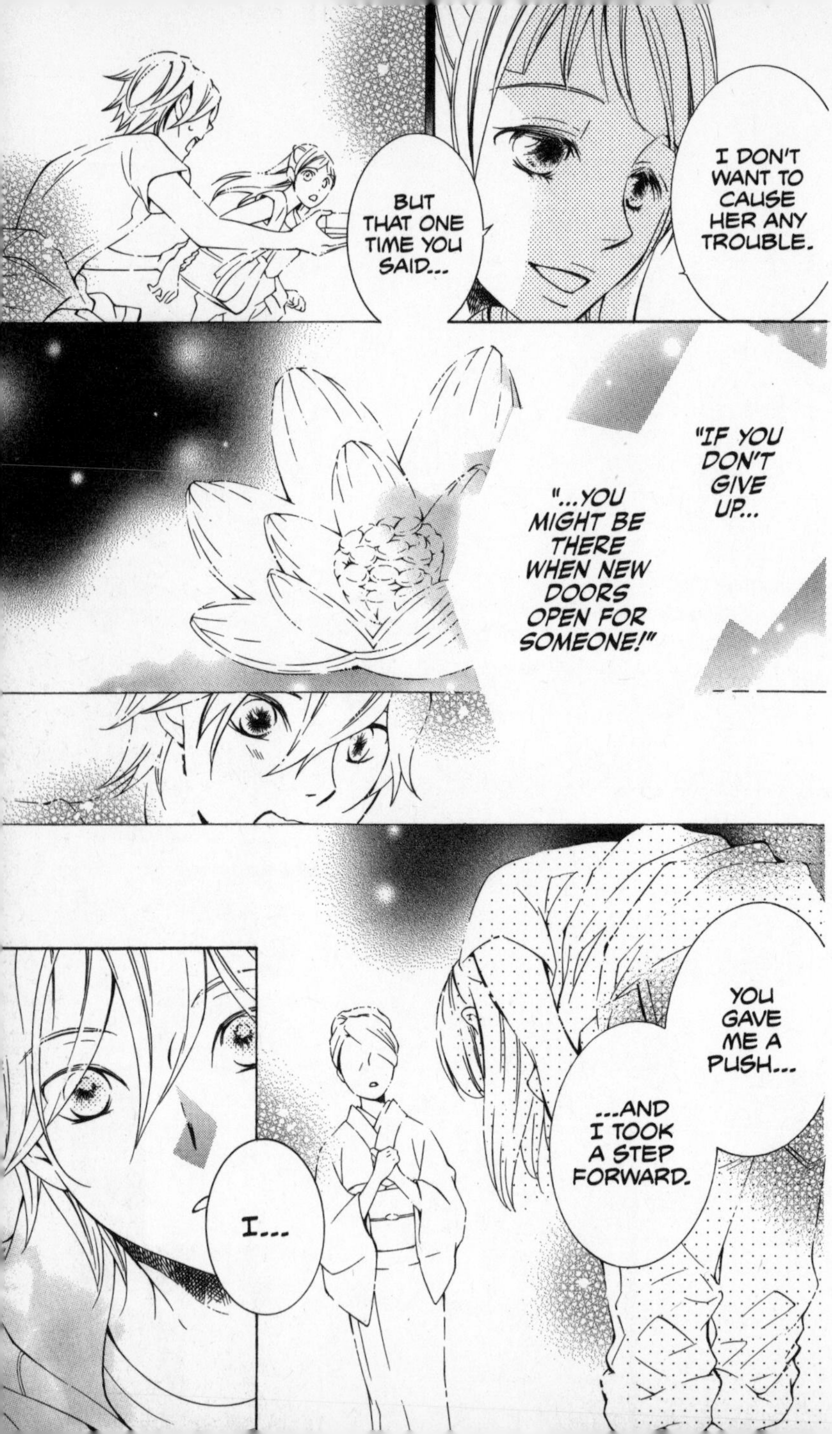
I DON'T WANT TO CAUSE HER ANY TROUBLE.
BUT THAT ONE TIME YOU SAID...
"IF YOU DON'T GIVE UP...
"...YOU MIGHT BE THERE WHEN NEW DOORS OPEN FOR SOMEONE!"
YOU GAVE ME A PUSH...
...AND I TOOK A STEP FORWARD.
I...

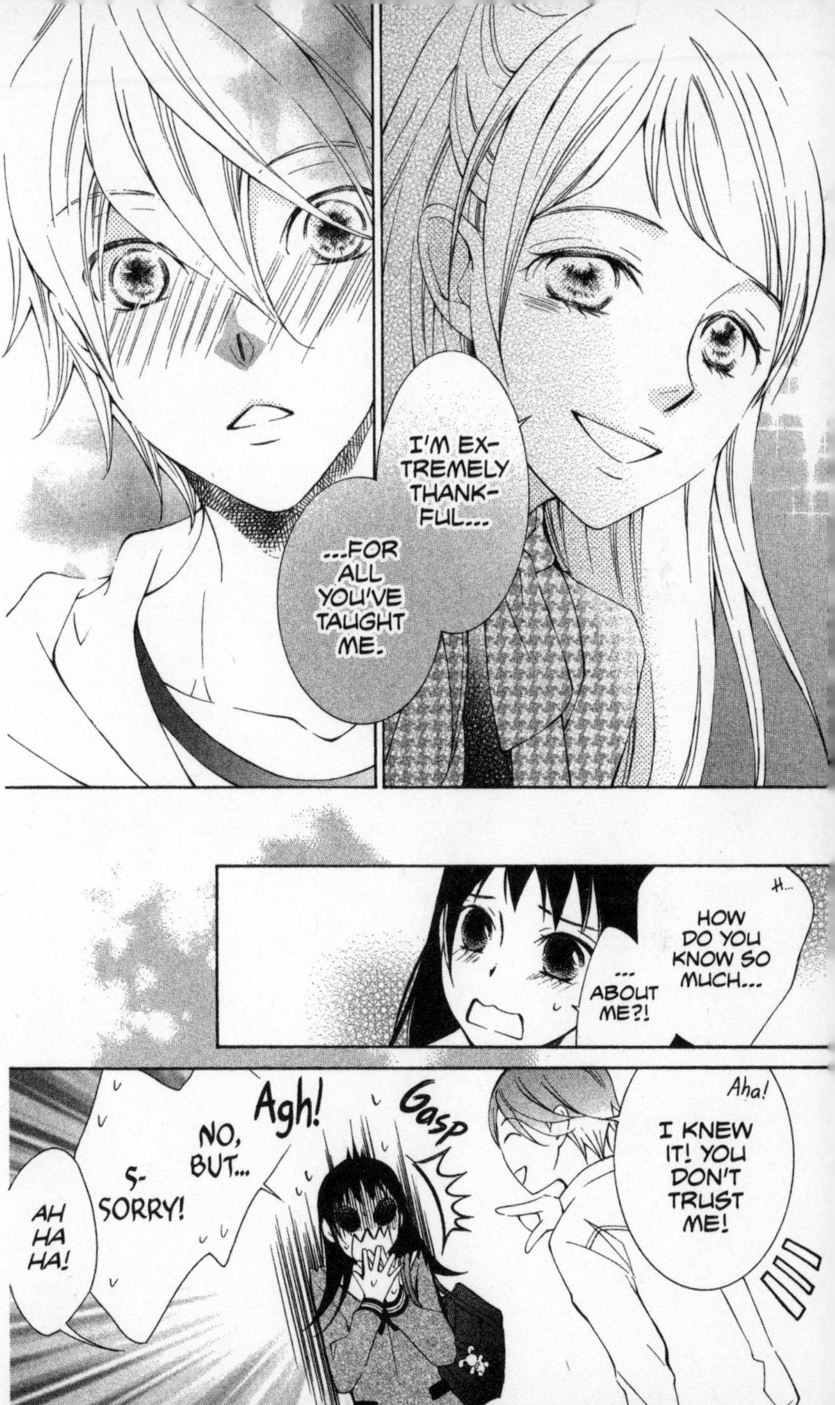
I'M EXTREMELY THANKFUL...
...FOR ALL YOU'VE TAUGHT ME.
H...
HOW DO YOU KNOW SO MUCH...
...ABOUT ME?!
Aha!
I KNEW IT! YOU DON'T TRUST ME!
Gasp
Agh!
NO, BUT...
S-SORRY!
AH HA HA!

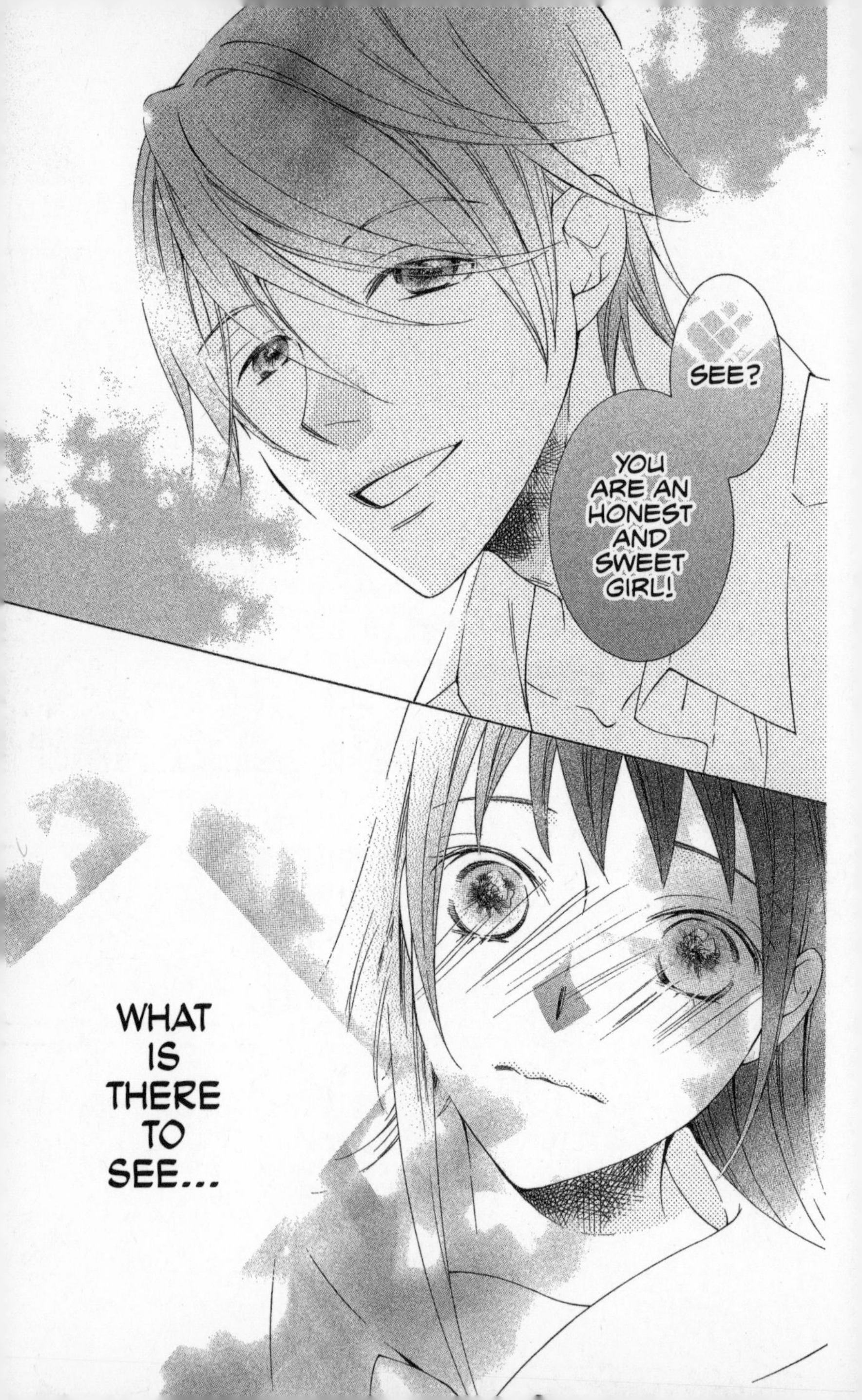
SEE?
YOU ARE AN HONEST AND SWEET GIRL!
WHAT IS THERE TO SEE...

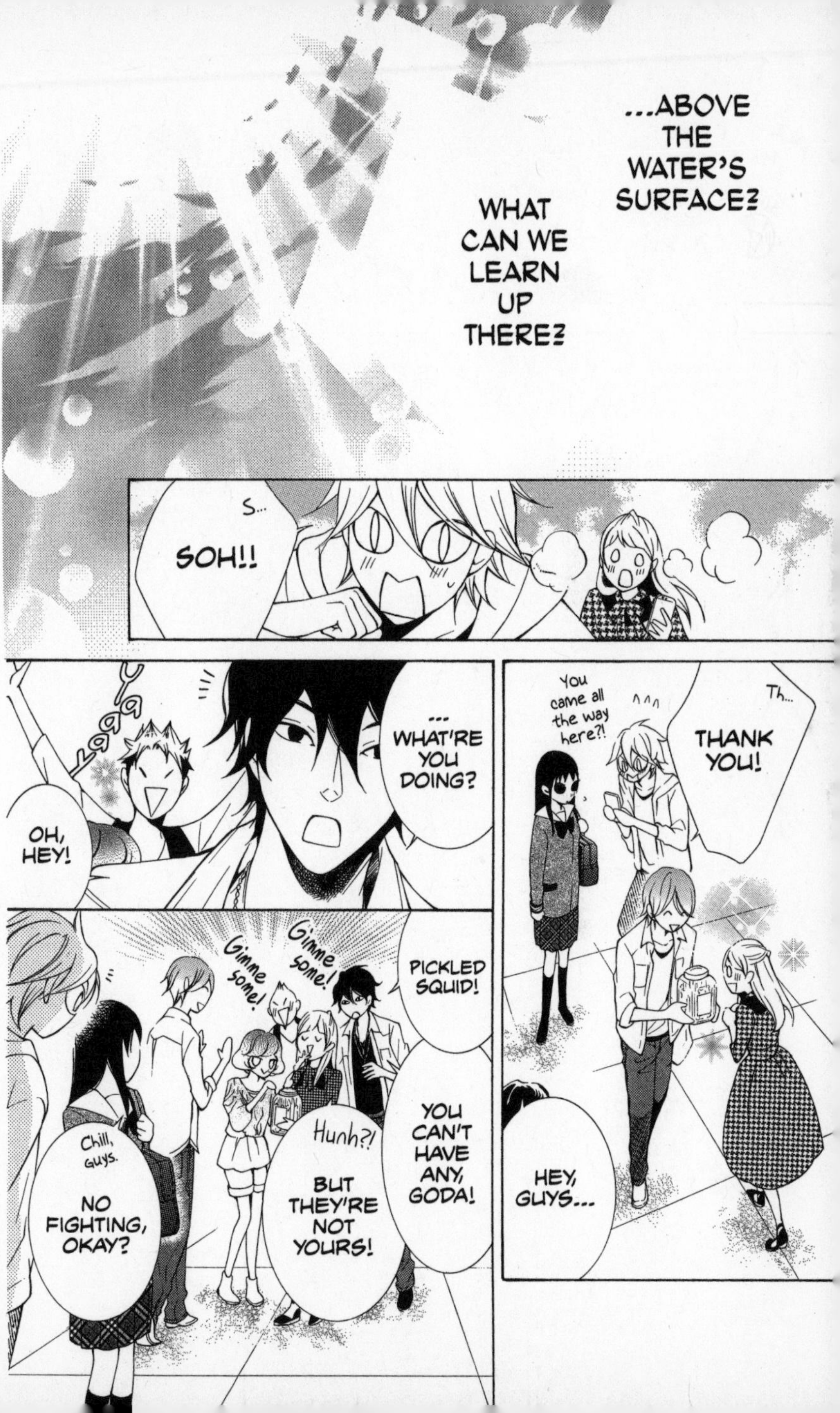
...ABOVE THE WATER'S SURFACE?
WHAT CAN WE LEARN UP THERE?
S...
SOH!!
Th...
THANK YOU!
You came all the way here?!
HEY, GUYS...
...WHAT'RE YOU DOING?
OH, HEY!
PICKLED SQUID!
Gimme some!
Gimme some!
YOU CAN'T HAVE ANY, GODA!
Hunh?!
BUT THEY'RE NOT YOURS!
Chill, guys.
NO FIGHTING, OKAY?

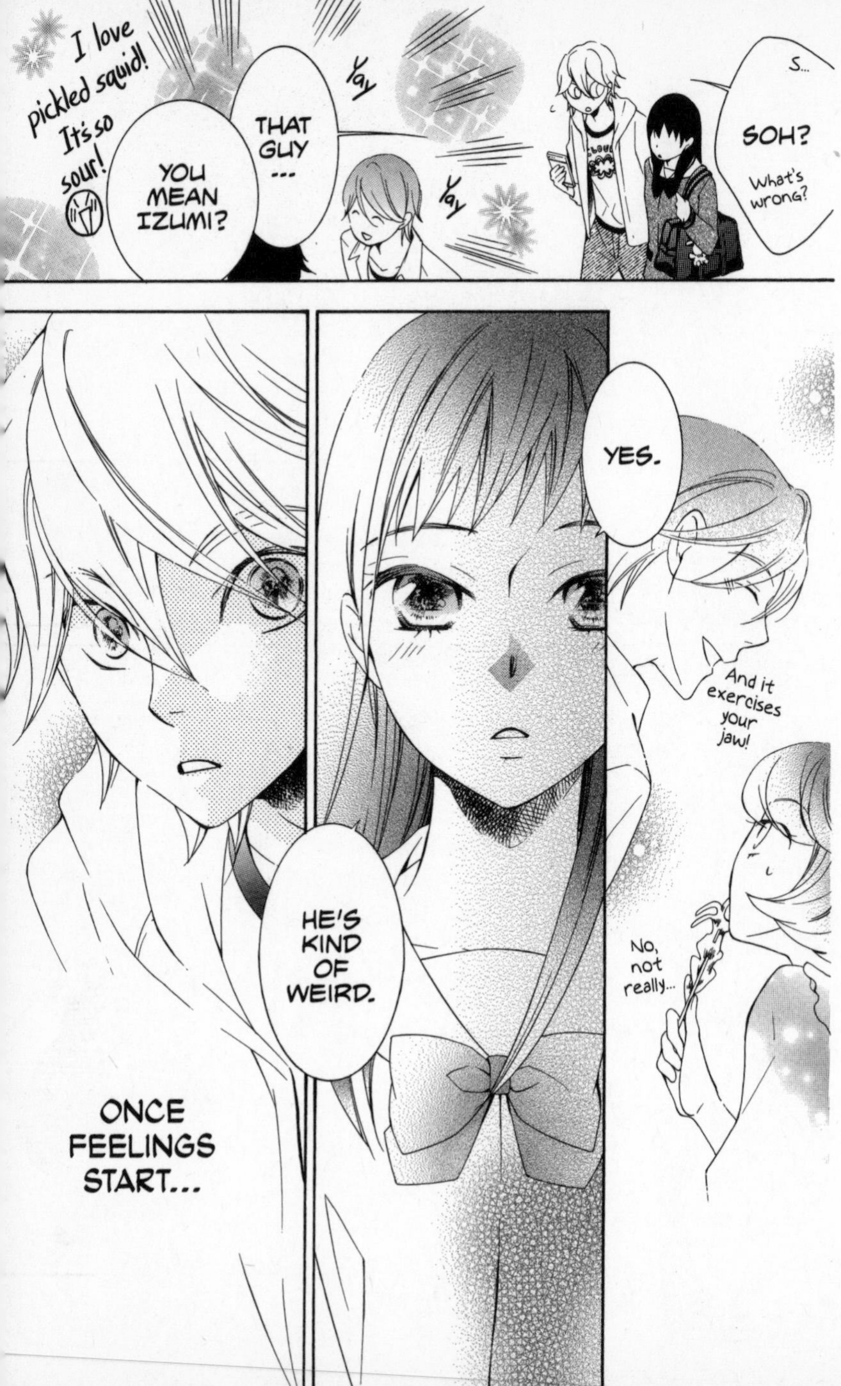
S...
SOH?
What's wrong?
Yay
Yay
THAT GUY...
YOU MEAN IZUMI?
I love pickled squid! It's so sour!
YES.
And it exercises your jaw!
No, not really...
HE'S KIND OF WEIRD.
ONCE FEELINGS START...

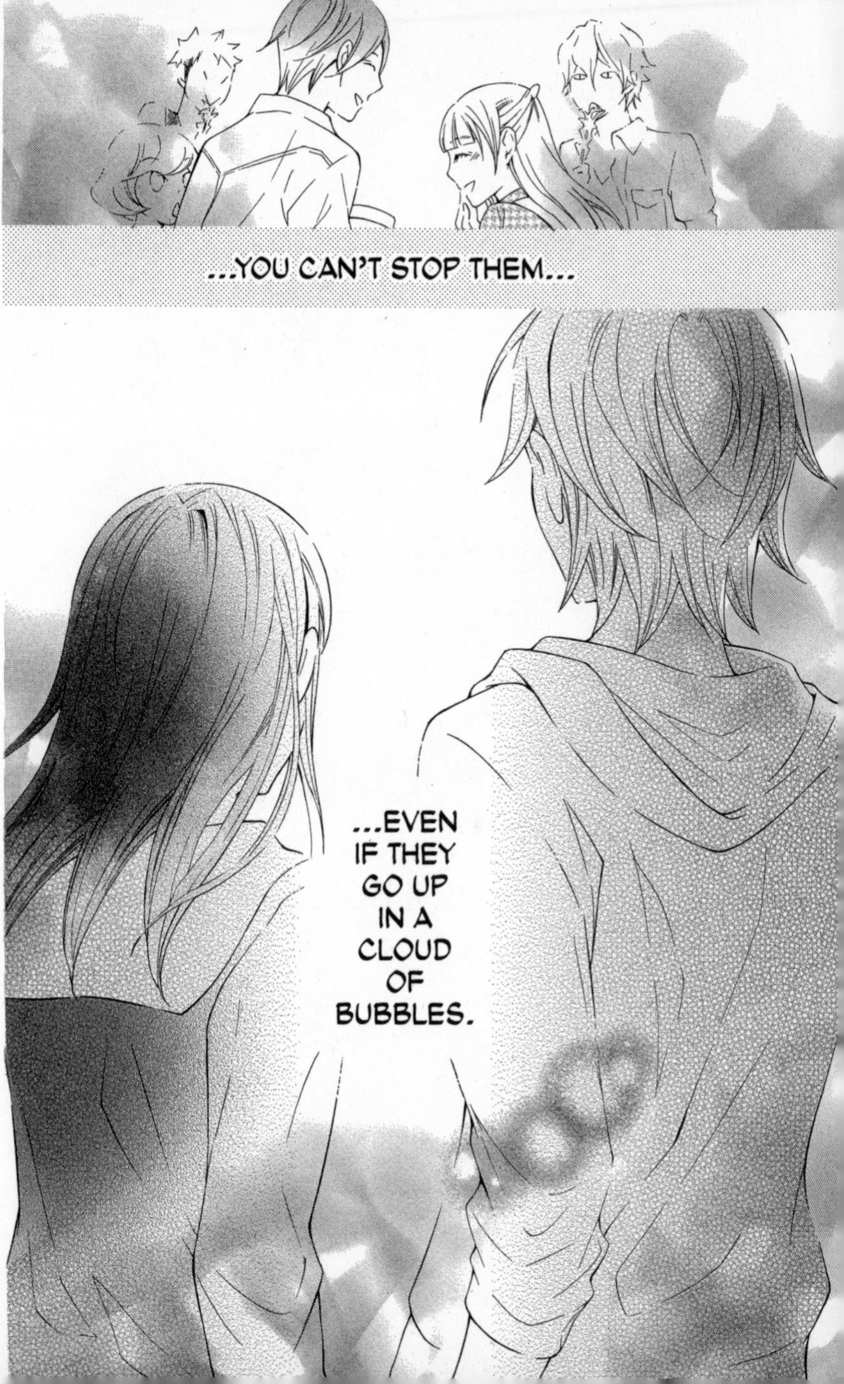
...YOU CAN'T STOP THEM...
...EVEN IF THEY GO UP IN A CLOUD OF BUBBLES.

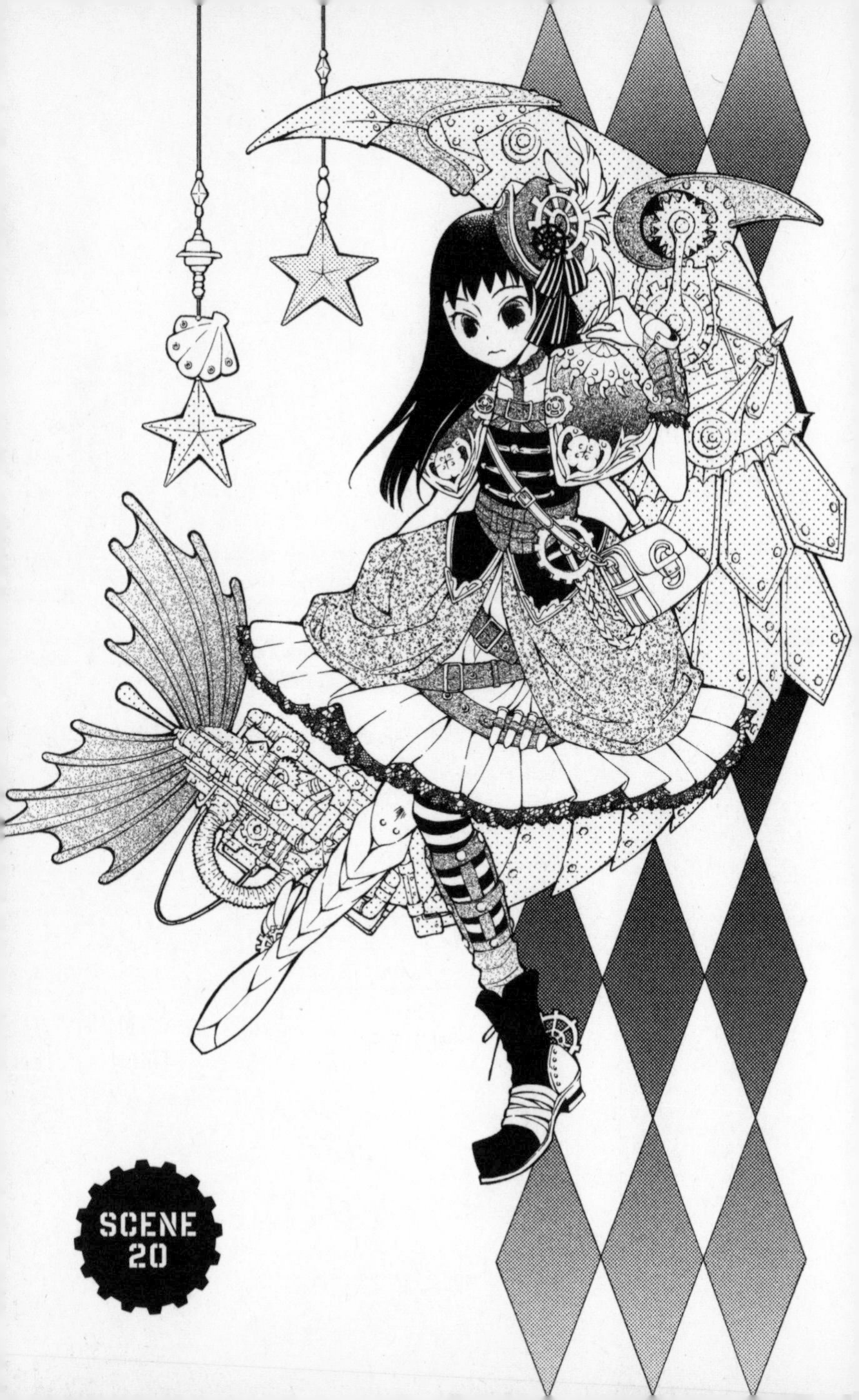
SCENE 20

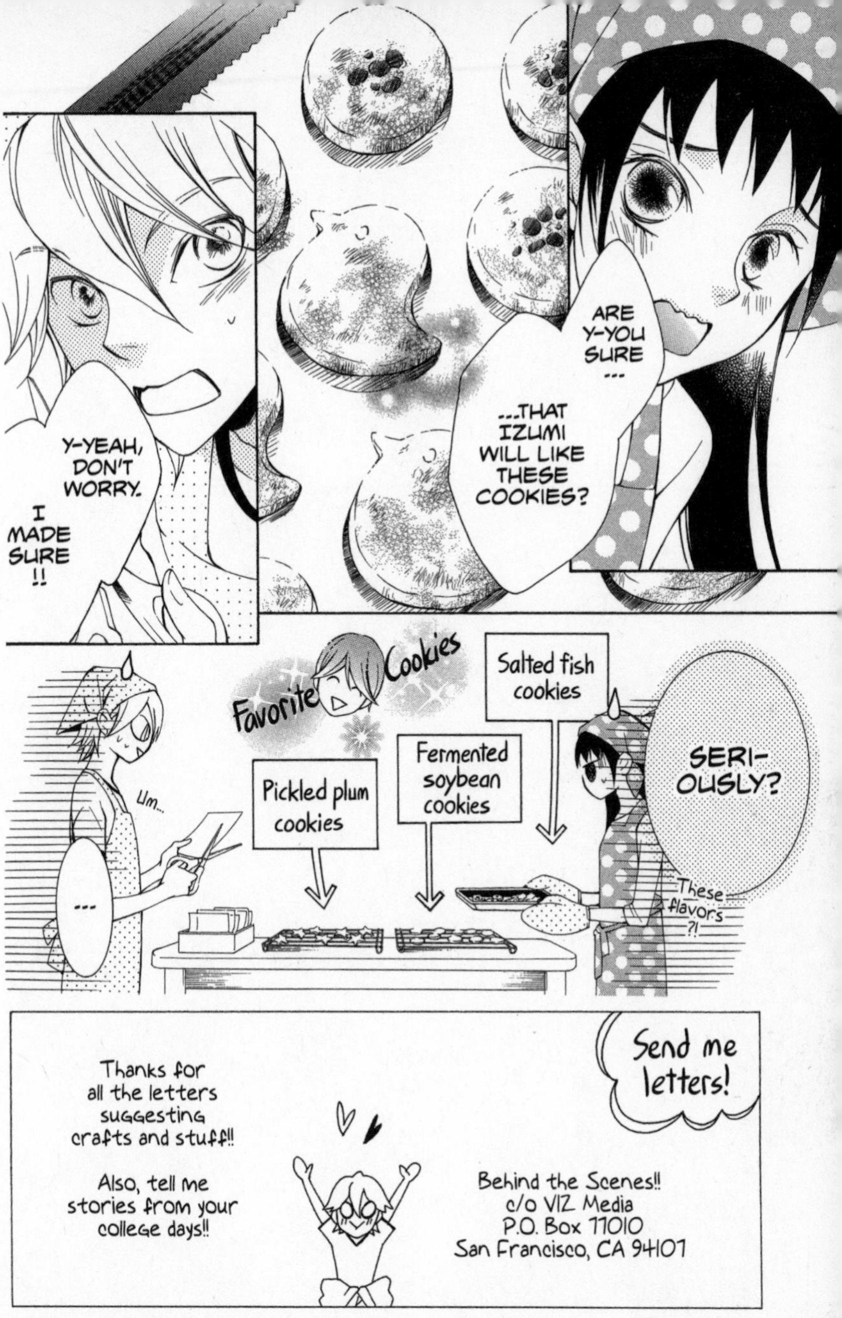
ARE Y-YOU SURE ---
...THAT IZUMI WILL LIKE THESE COOKIES?
Y-YEAH, DON'T WORRY.
I MADE SURE !!
SERI-OUSLY?
These flavors ?!
Salted fish cookies
Fermented soybean cookies
Pickled plum cookies
Favorite Cookies
Um...

Send me letters!
Behind the Scenes!!
c/o VIZ Media
P.O. Box 77010
San Francisco, CA 94107
Thanks for all the letters suggesting crafts and stuff!!
Also, tell me stories from your college days!!

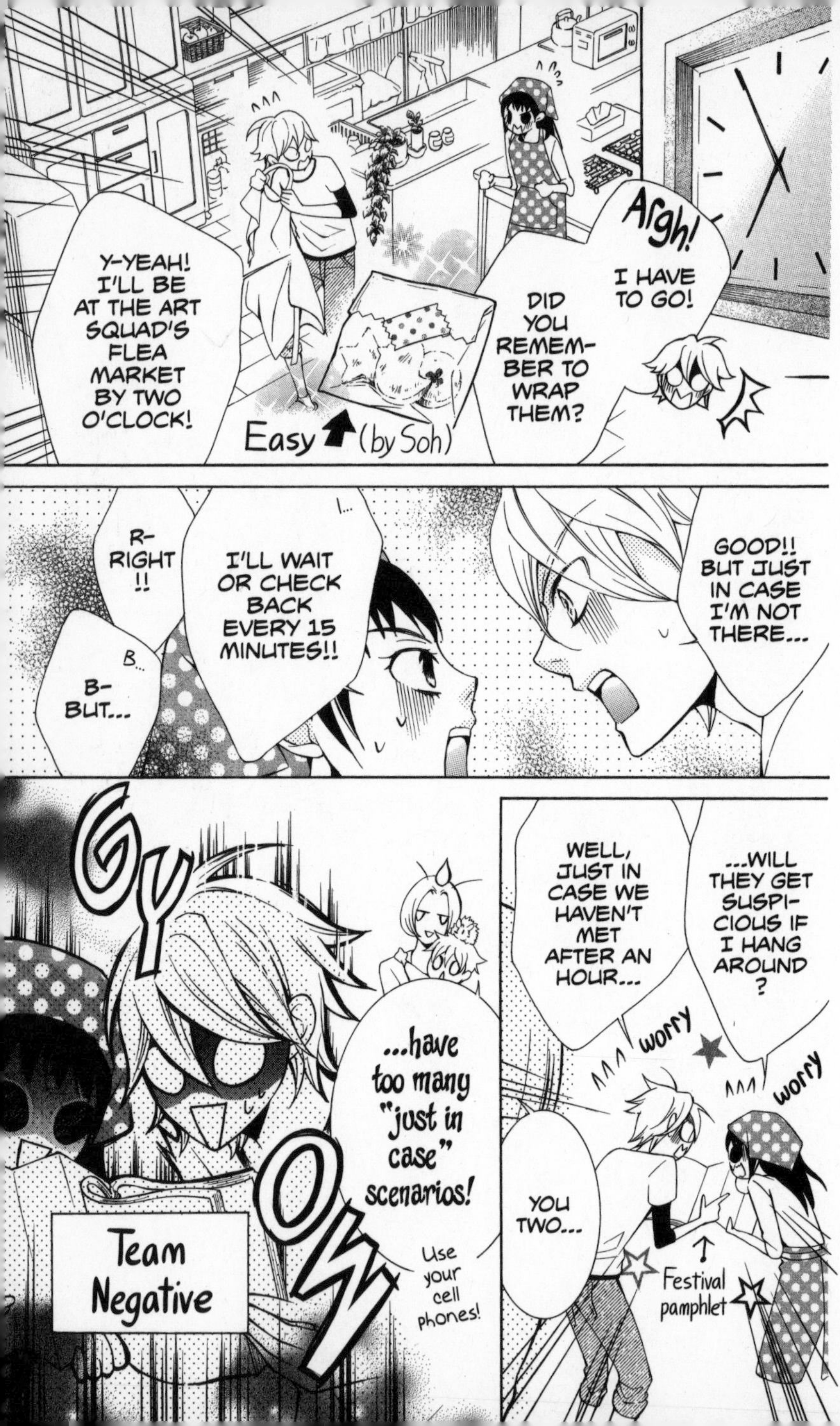
Argh!
I HAVE TO GO!
DID YOU REMEMBER TO WRAP THEM?
Easy ↑ (by Soh)
Y-YEAH! I'LL BE AT THE ART SQUAD'S FLEA MARKET BY TWO O'CLOCK!
GOOD!! BUT JUST IN CASE I'M NOT THERE...
I...
I'LL WAIT OR CHECK BACK EVERY 15 MINUTES!!
R-RIGHT!!
B...
B-BUT...
...WILL THEY GET SUSPICIOUS IF I HANG AROUND?
WELL, JUST IN CASE WE HAVEN'T MET AFTER AN HOUR...
worry
worry
YOU TWO...
Festival pamphlet
...have too many "just in case" scenarios!
Use your cell phones!
GYOW
Team Negative

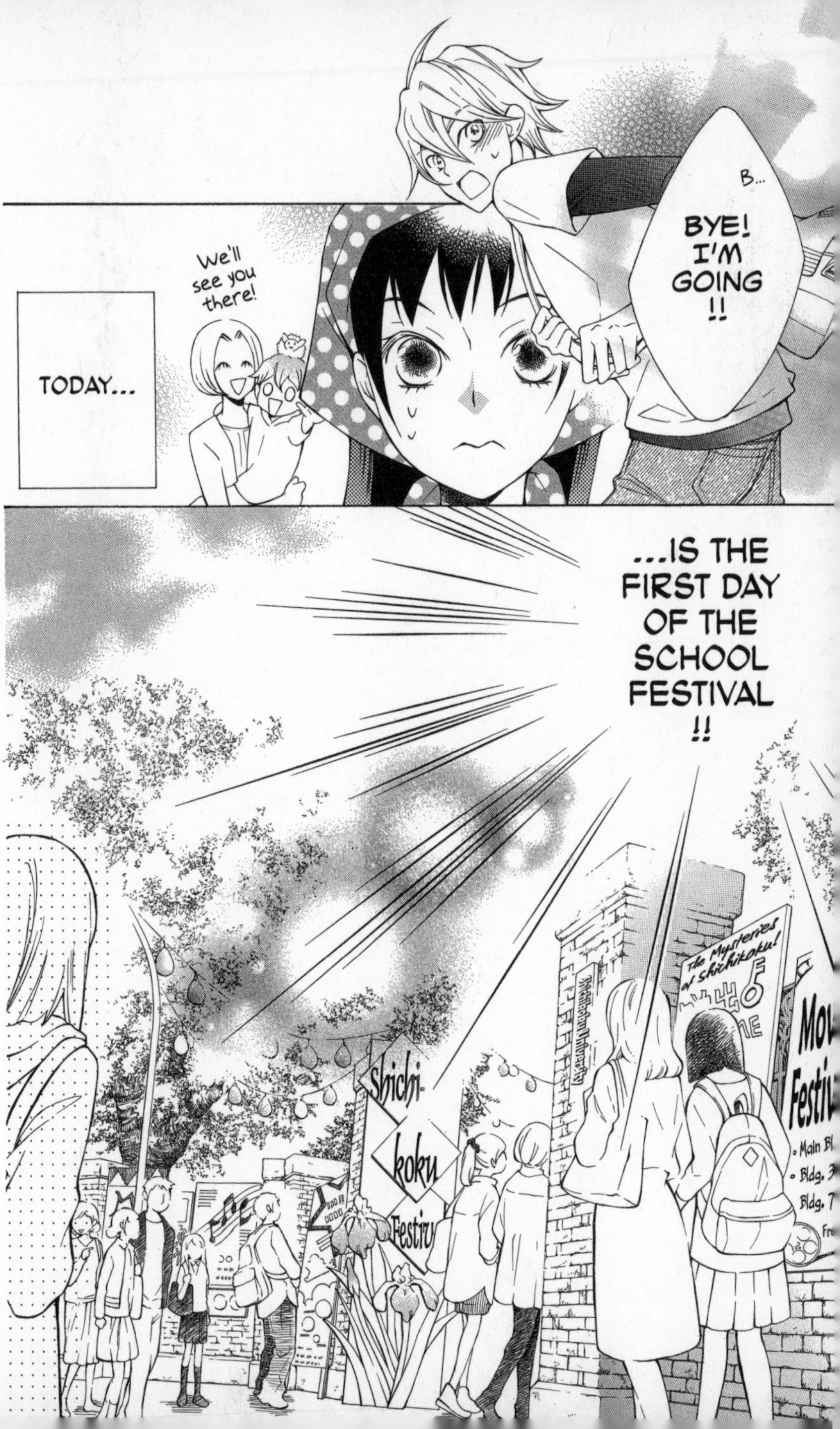
B...
BYE! I'M GOING!!
We'll see you there!
TODAY...
...IS THE FIRST DAY OF THE SCHOOL FESTIVAL!!
The Mysteries of Shichikoku!
Shichi-koku

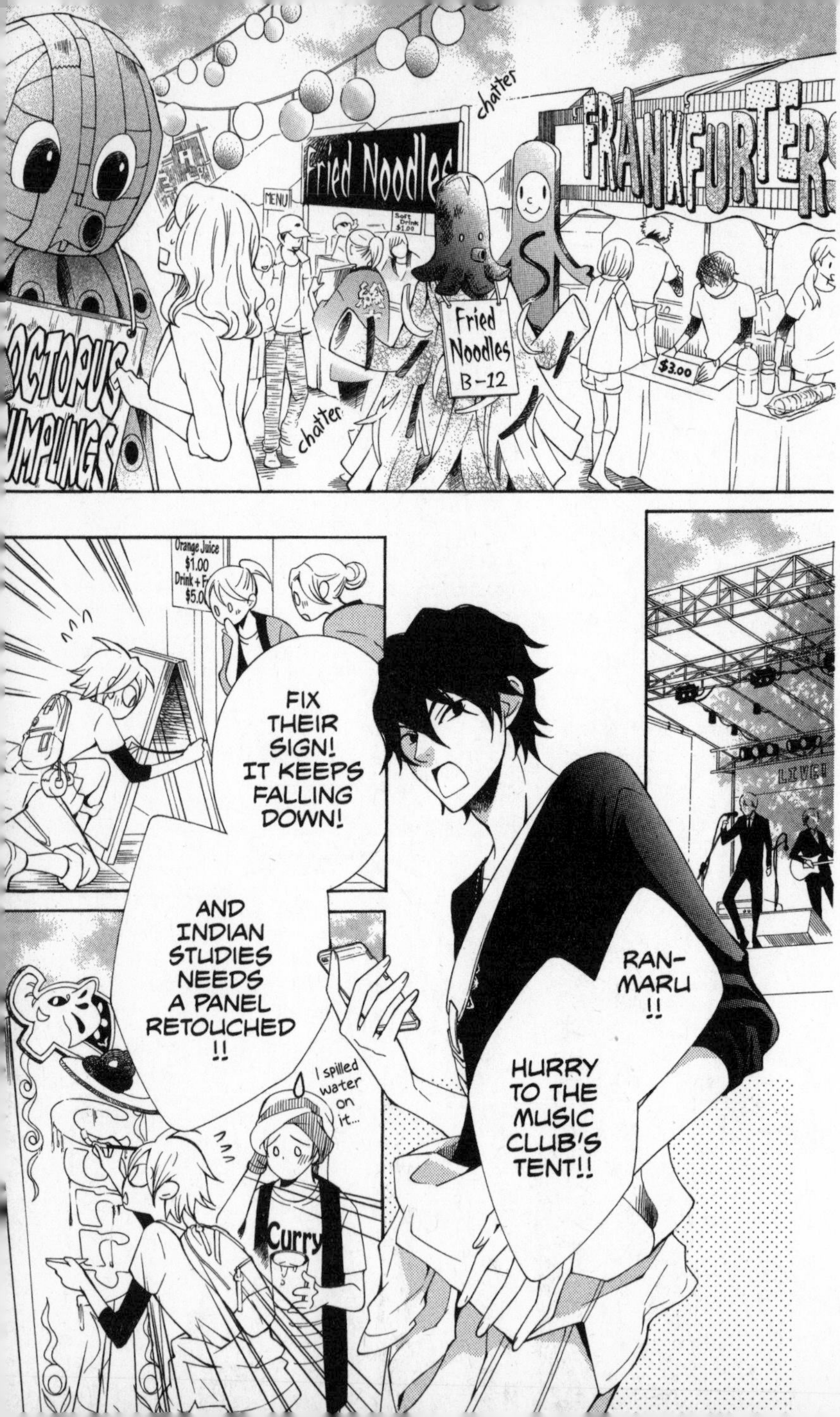
FRANKFURTERS
$3.00
chatter
Fried Noodles
Soft Drink $1.00
Fried Noodles B-12
MENU
chatter
OCTOPUS
UMPLINGS
LIVE!
RAN-MARU!!
HURRY TO THE MUSIC CLUB'S TENT!!
FIX THEIR SIGN! IT KEEPS FALLING DOWN!
AND INDIAN STUDIES NEEDS A PANEL RETOUCHED!!
Orange Juice $1.00
I spilled water on it...
Curry

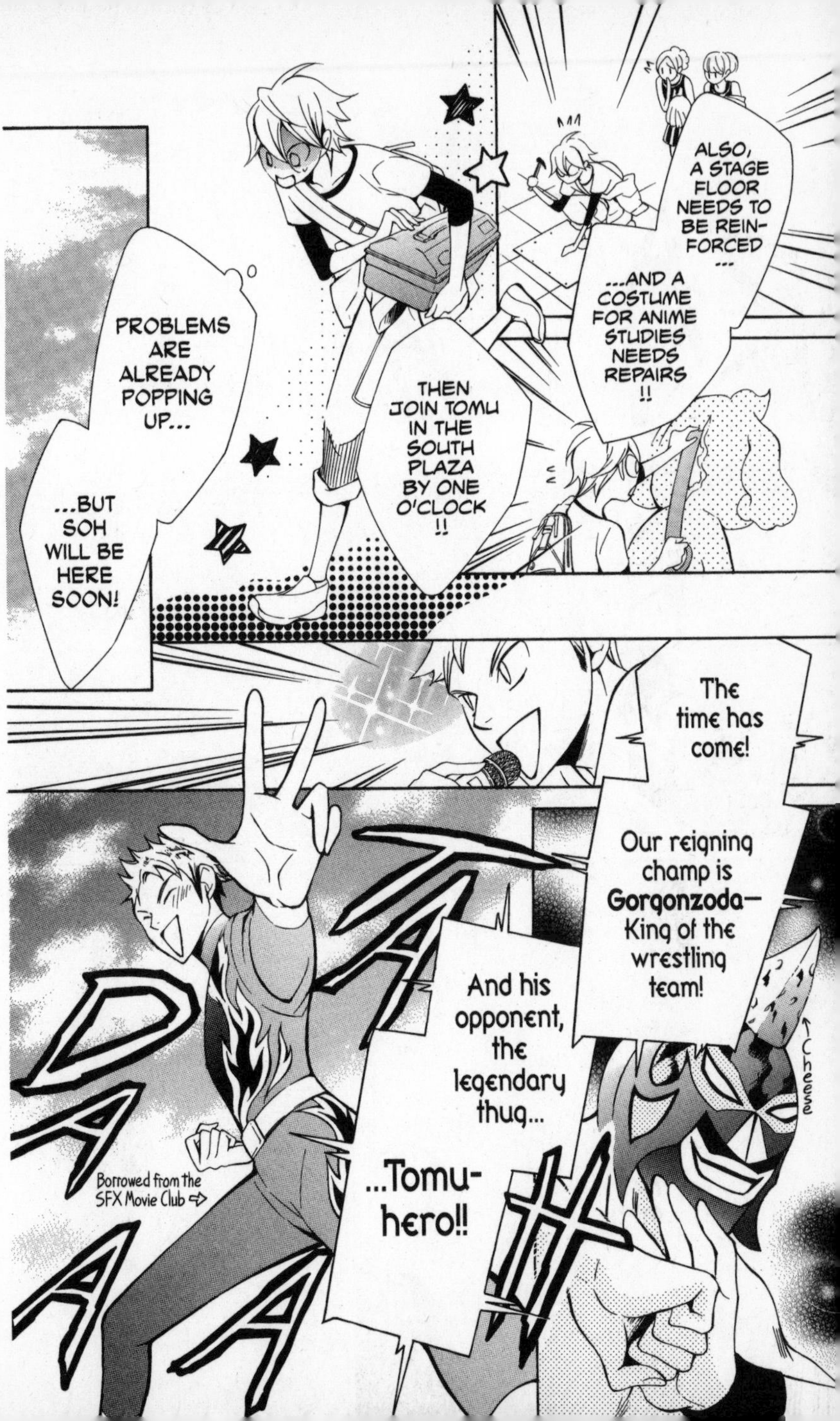
ALSO, A STAGE FLOOR NEEDS TO BE REIN-FORCED ...
...AND A COSTUME FOR ANIME STUDIES NEEDS REPAIRS!!
THEN JOIN TOMU IN THE SOUTH PLAZA BY ONE O'CLOCK!!
PROBLEMS ARE ALREADY POPPING UP...
...BUT SOH WILL BE HERE SOON!
The time has come!
Our reigning champ is Gorgonzoda—King of the wrestling team!
Cheese
And his opponent, the legendary thug...
...Tomu-hero!!
Borrowed from the SFX Movie Club

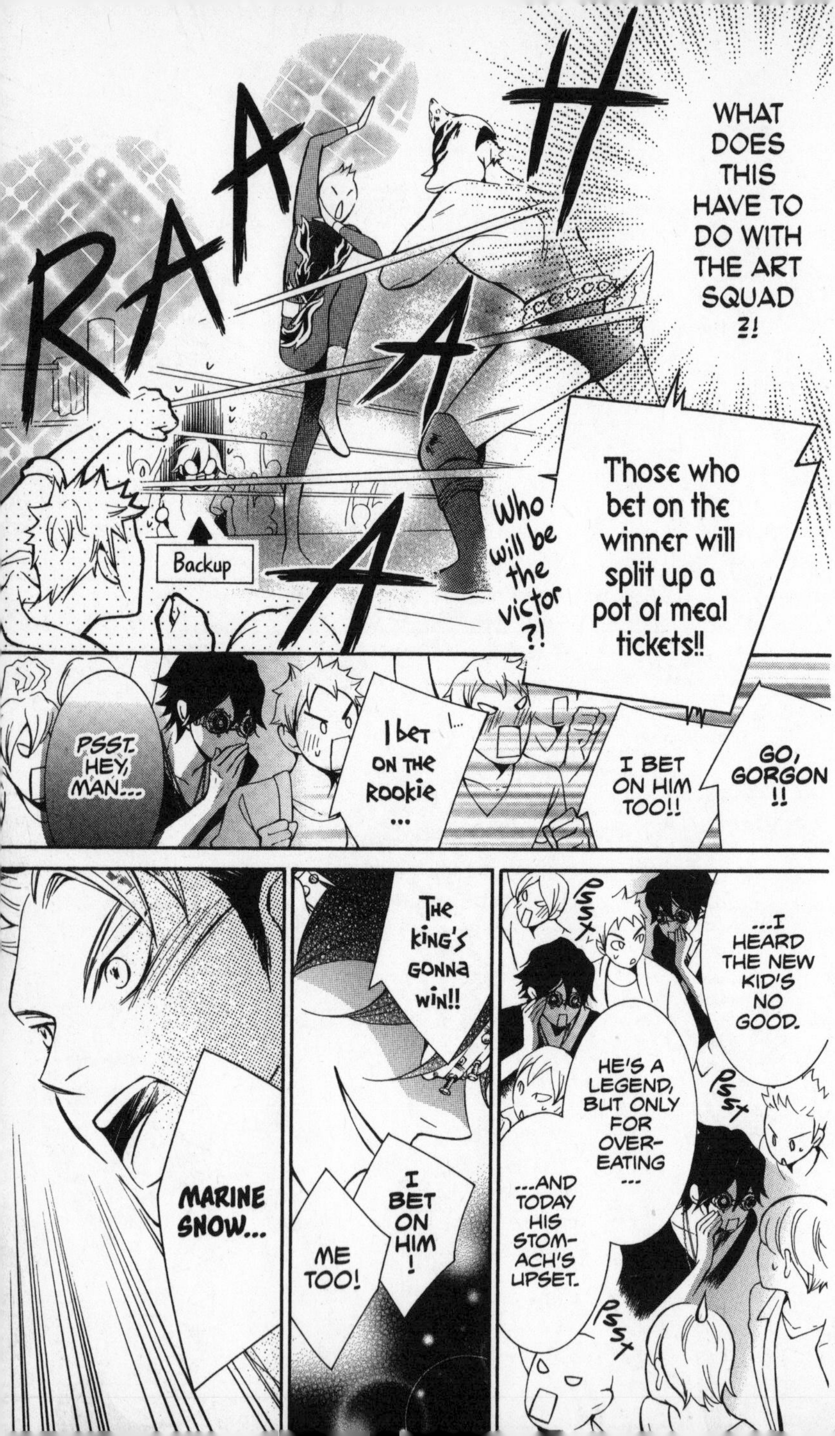
WHAT DOES THIS HAVE TO DO WITH THE ART SQUAD?!
RAAAAH
Those who bet on the winner will split up a pot of meal tickets!!
Who will be the victor?!
Backup
GO, GORGON!!
I BET ON HIM TOO!!
I bet on the rookie...
PSST. HEY, MAN...
...I HEARD THE NEW KID'S NO GOOD.
Psst
HE'S A LEGEND, BUT ONLY FOR OVER-EATING...
Psst
...AND TODAY HIS STOMACH-ACH'S UPSET.
Psst
The king's gonna win!!
I BET ON HIM!
ME TOO!
MARINE SNOW...

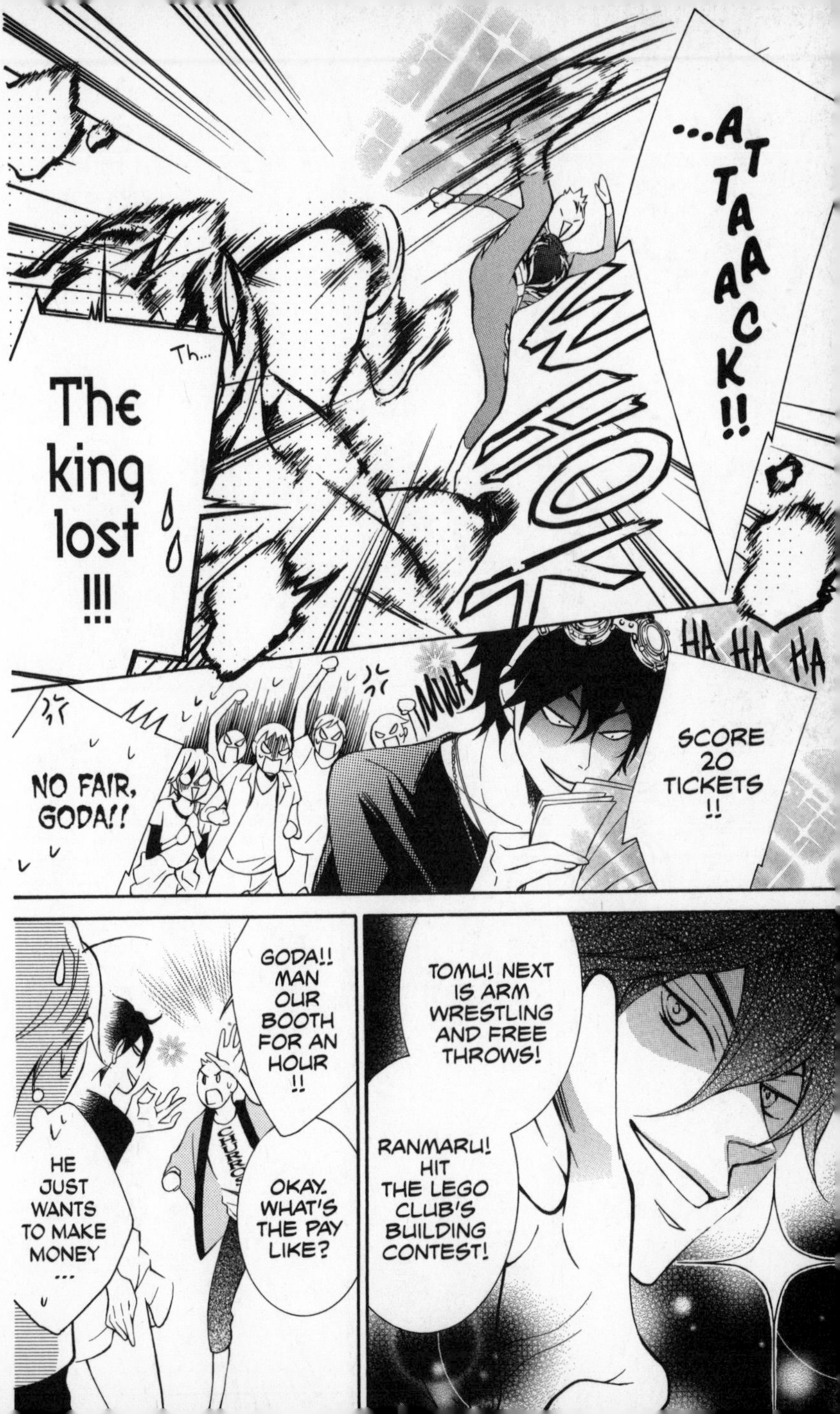
...ATTAAACK!!
Th...
The king lost !!!
HA HA HA
SCORE 20 TICKETS !!
MWA
NO FAIR, GODA!!
TOMU! NEXT IS ARM WRESTLING AND FREE THROWS!
RANMARU! HIT THE LEGO CLUB'S BUILDING CONTEST!
GODA!! MAN OUR BOOTH FOR AN HOUR !!
OKAY. WHAT'S THE PAY LIKE?
HE JUST WANTS TO MAKE MONEY ...

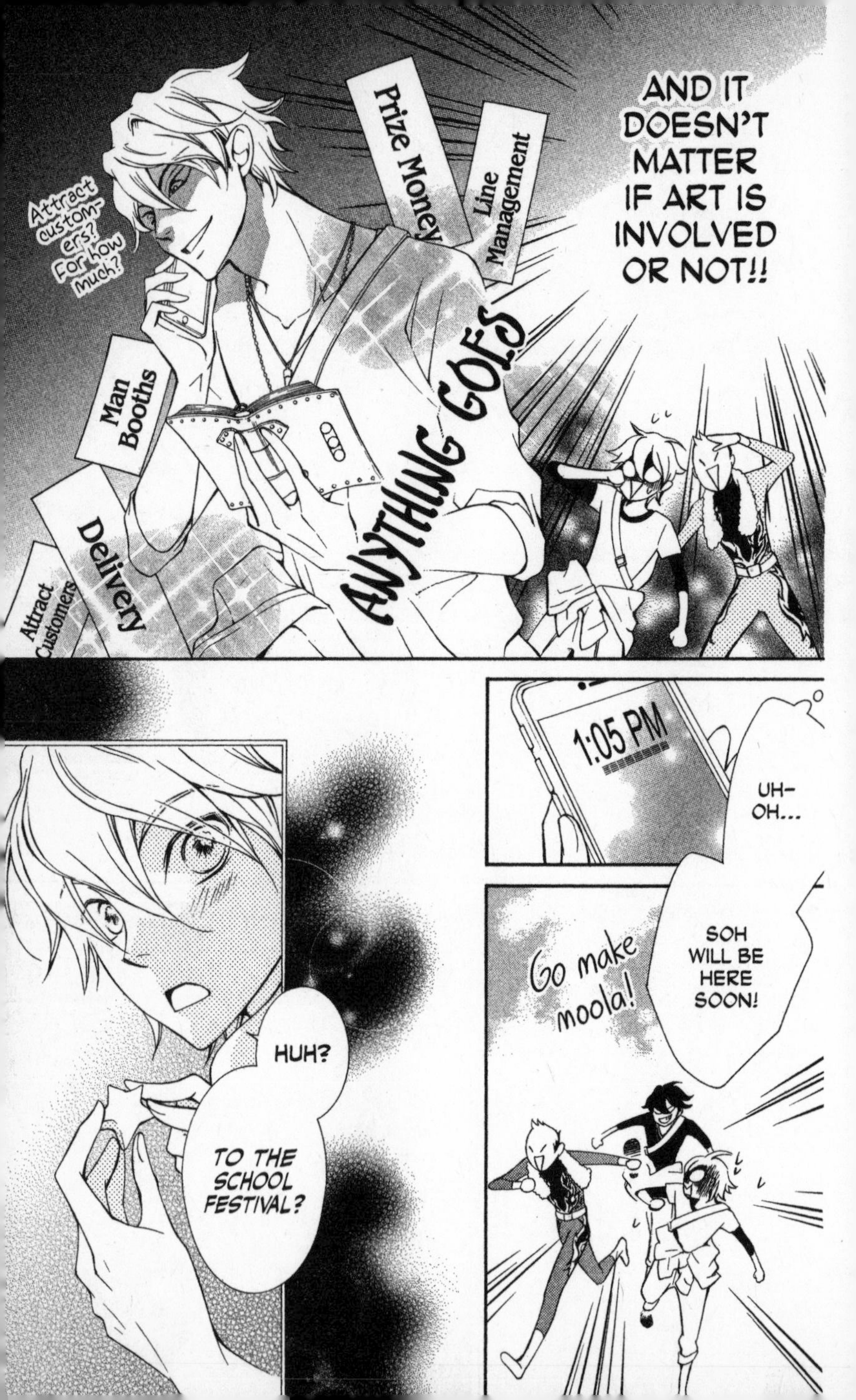
AND IT DOESN'T MATTER IF ART IS INVOLVED OR NOT!!
Line Management
Prize Money
ANYTHING GOES
Attract custom-ers? For how much?
Man Booths
Delivery
Attract Customers
1:05 PM
UH-OH...
SOH WILL BE HERE SOON!
Go make moola!
HUH?
TO THE SCHOOL FESTIVAL?

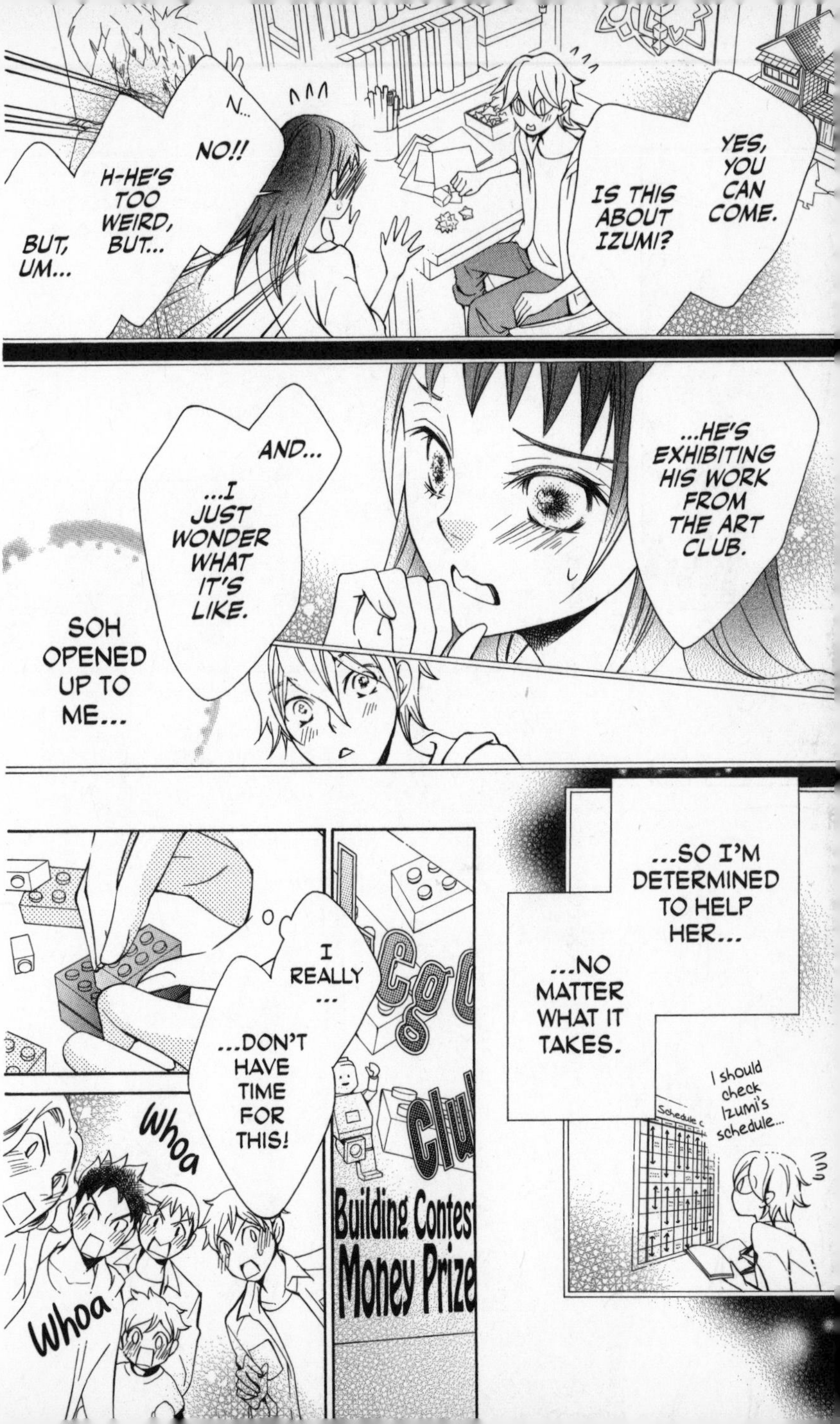
YES, YOU CAN COME.
IS THIS ABOUT IZUMI?
N...
NO!!
H-HE'S TOO WEIRD, BUT...
BUT, UM...
...HE'S EXHIBITING HIS WORK FROM THE ART CLUB.
AND...
...I JUST WONDER WHAT IT'S LIKE.
SOH OPENED UP TO ME...
...SO I'M DETERMINED TO HELP HER...
...NO MATTER WHAT IT TAKES.
I should check Izumi's schedule...
I REALLY...
...DON'T HAVE TIME FOR THIS!
Building Contest
Money Prize
Whoa
Whoa

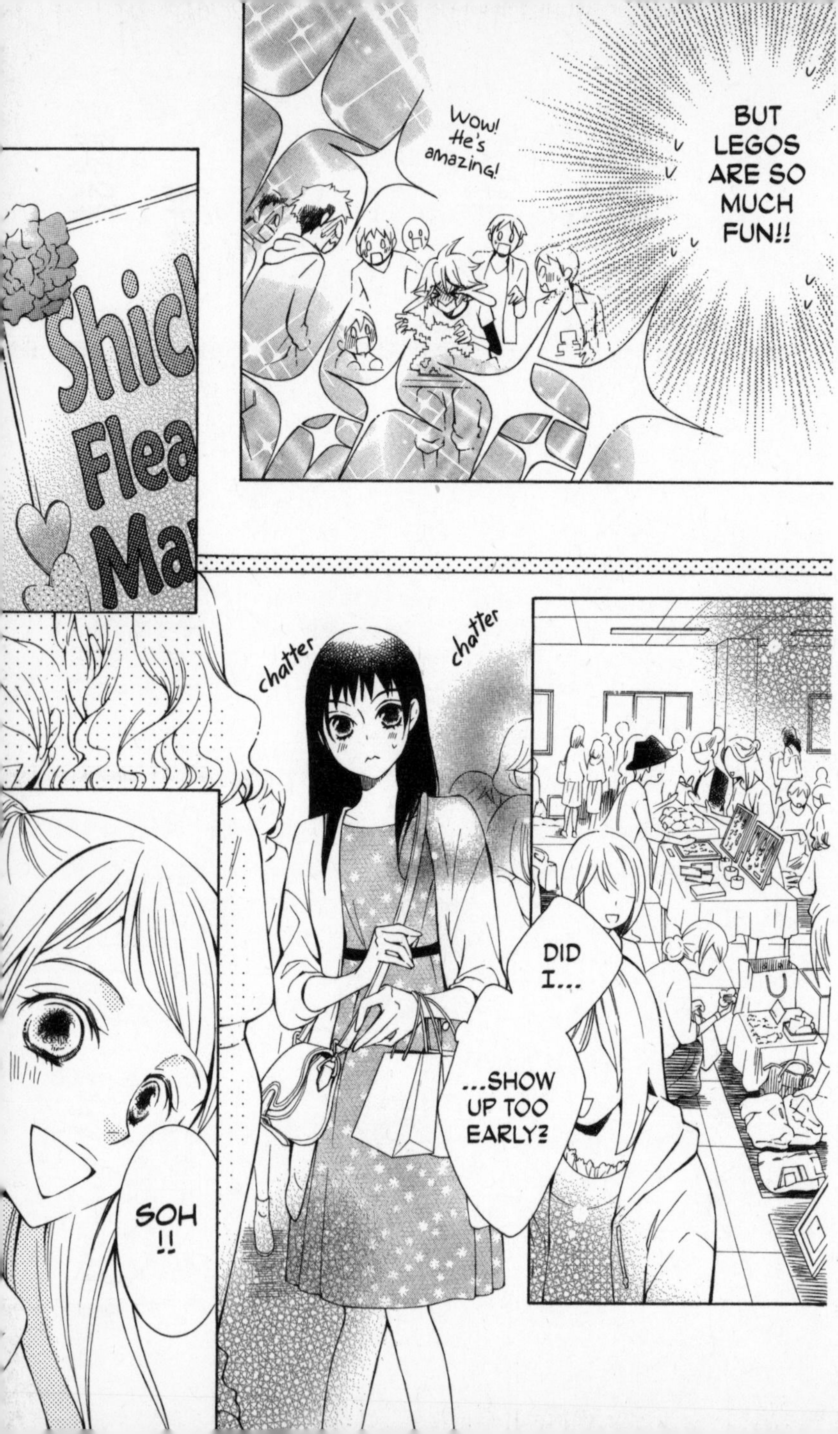
BUT LEGOS ARE SO MUCH FUN!!
Wow! He's amazing!
chatter
chatter
DID I...
...SHOW UP TOO EARLY?
SOH !!

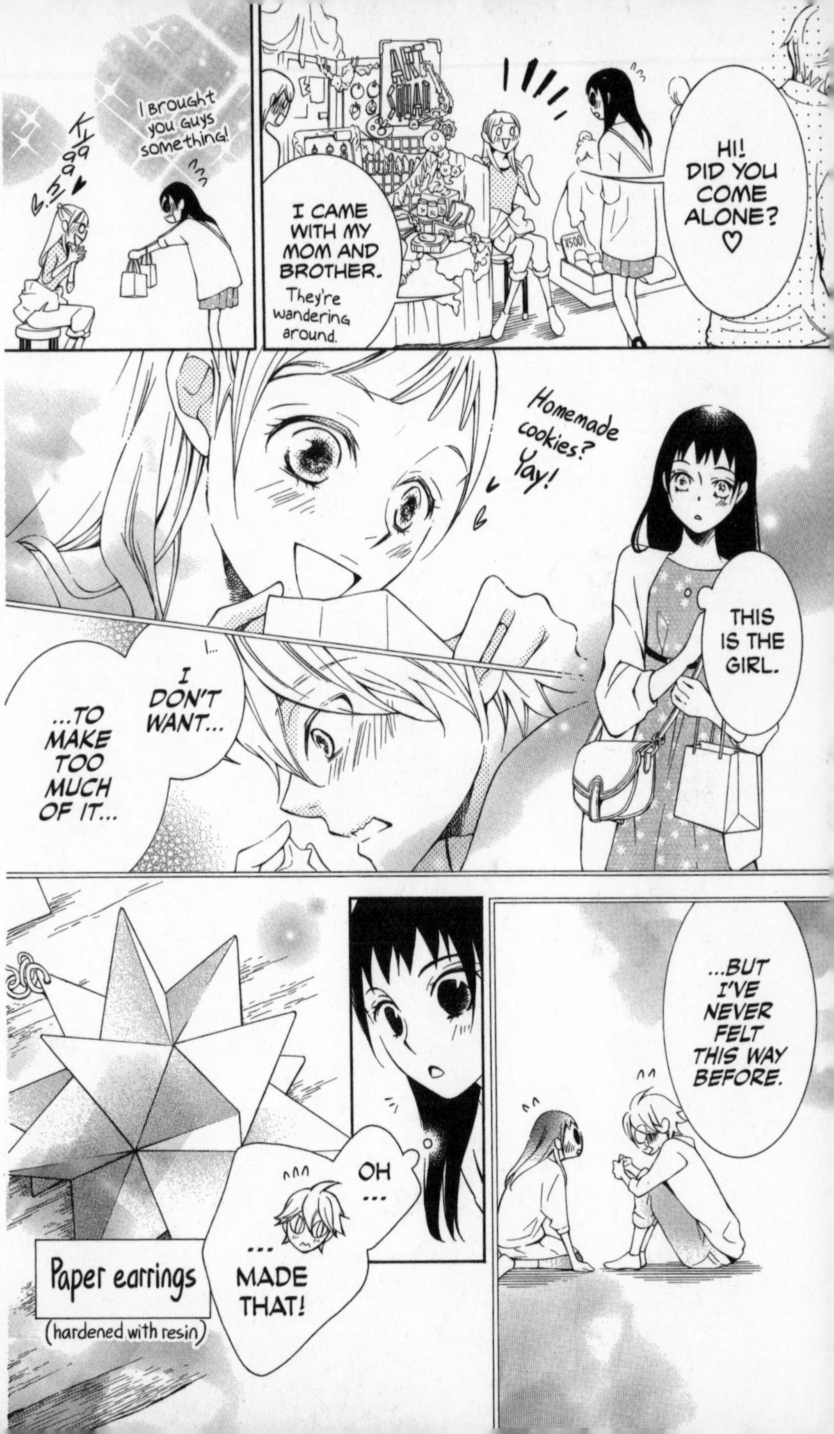
HI! DID YOU COME ALONE? ♡
I CAME WITH MY MOM AND BROTHER.
They're wandering around.
I brought you guys something!
Kyaaah!! ♥
Homemade cookies? Yay!
THIS IS THE GIRL.
I... I DON'T WANT...
...TO MAKE TOO MUCH OF IT...
...BUT I'VE NEVER FELT THIS WAY BEFORE.
OH...
...MADE THAT!
Paper earrings
(hardened with resin)

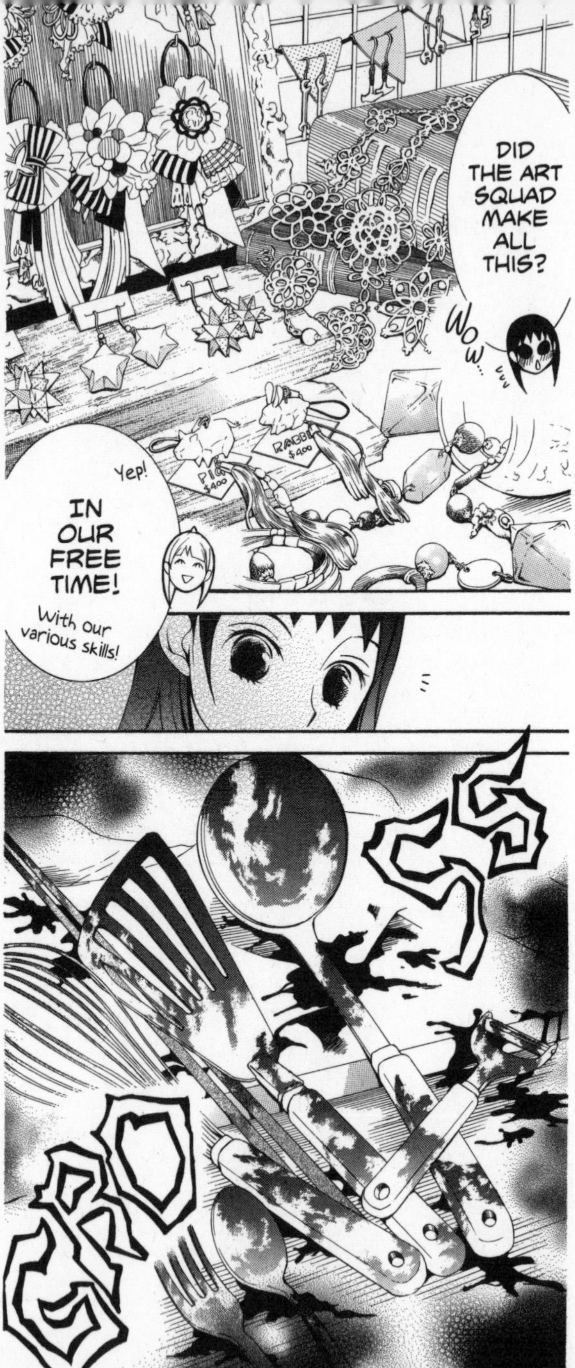
DID THE ART SQUAD MAKE ALL THIS?
WOW...
RABBIT $400
PIG $400
Yep!
IN OUR FREE TIME!
With our various skills!

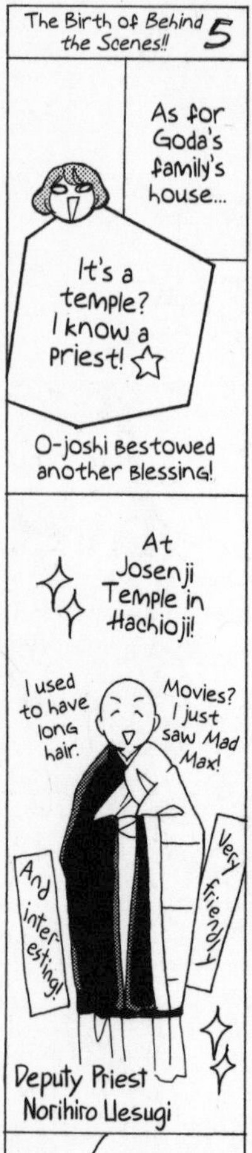
The Birth of Behind the Scenes!! 5
As for Goda's family's house...
It's a temple? I know a priest! ☆
O-joshi bestowed another blessing!
At Josenji Temple in Hachioji!
I used to have long hair.
Movies? I just saw Mad Max!
Very friendly
And interesting!
Deputy Priest Norihiro Uesugi
Have you seen the movie Fancy Dance? That featured a Buddhist dialogue too!
Yes, a long time ago!! Hmm... Hmm...
Thanks, Deputy Priest!!

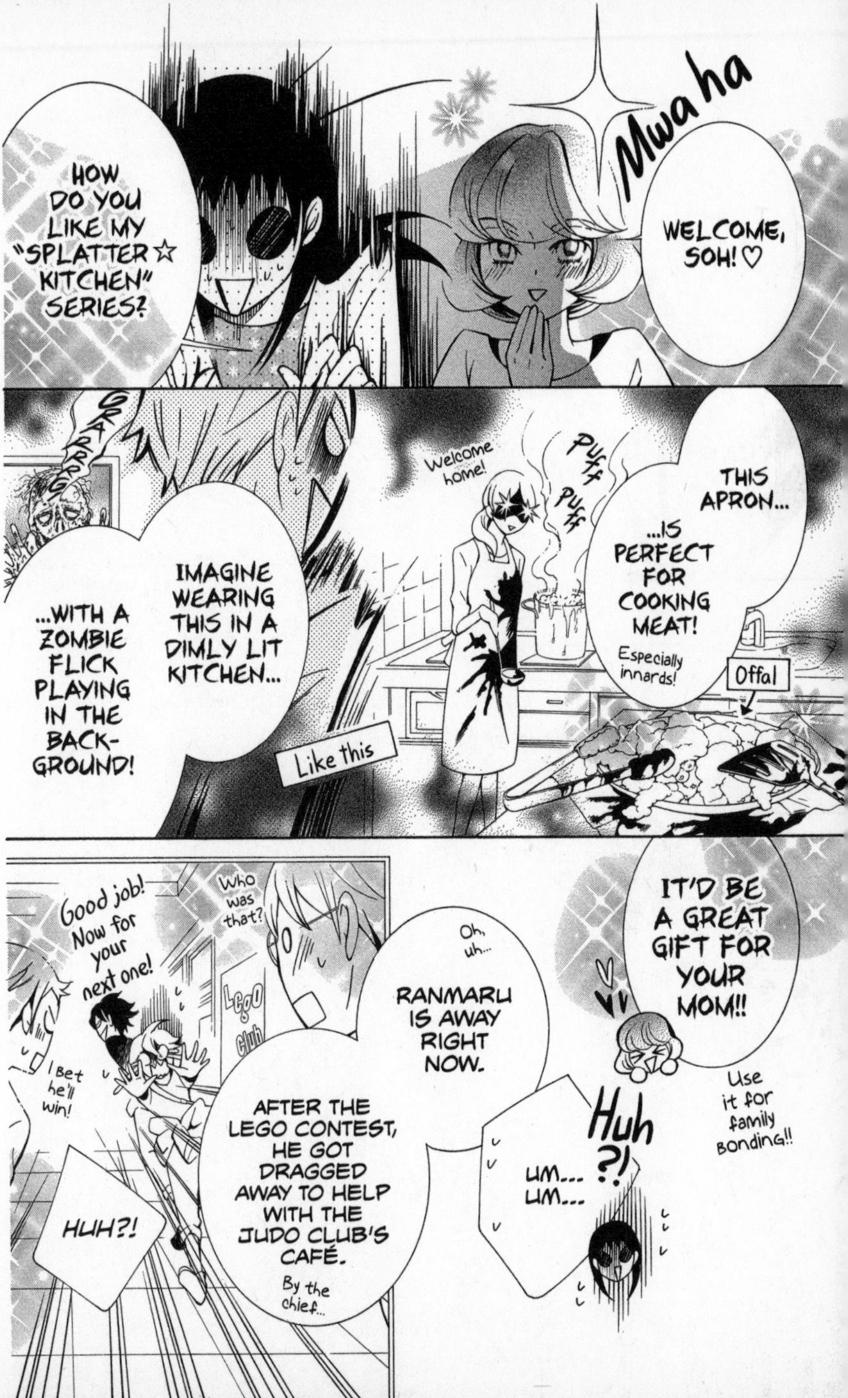
Mwa ha
WELCOME, SOH! ♡
HOW DO YOU LIKE MY "SPLATTER☆KITCHEN" SERIES?
THIS APRON...
...IS PERFECT FOR COOKING MEAT!
Especially innards!
Offal
Puff Puff
Welcome home!
IMAGINE WEARING THIS IN A DIMLY LIT KITCHEN...
Like this
...WITH A ZOMBIE FLICK PLAYING IN THE BACK-GROUND!
GRARRRG
IT'D BE A GREAT GIFT FOR YOUR MOM!!
Use it for family bonding!!
Huh ?!
UM... UM...
Oh, uh...
RANMARU IS AWAY RIGHT NOW.
AFTER THE LEGO CONTEST, HE GOT DRAGGED AWAY TO HELP WITH THE JUDO CLUB'S CAFÉ.
By the chief...
Who was that?
Good job! Now for your next one!
I bet he'll win!
HUH?!

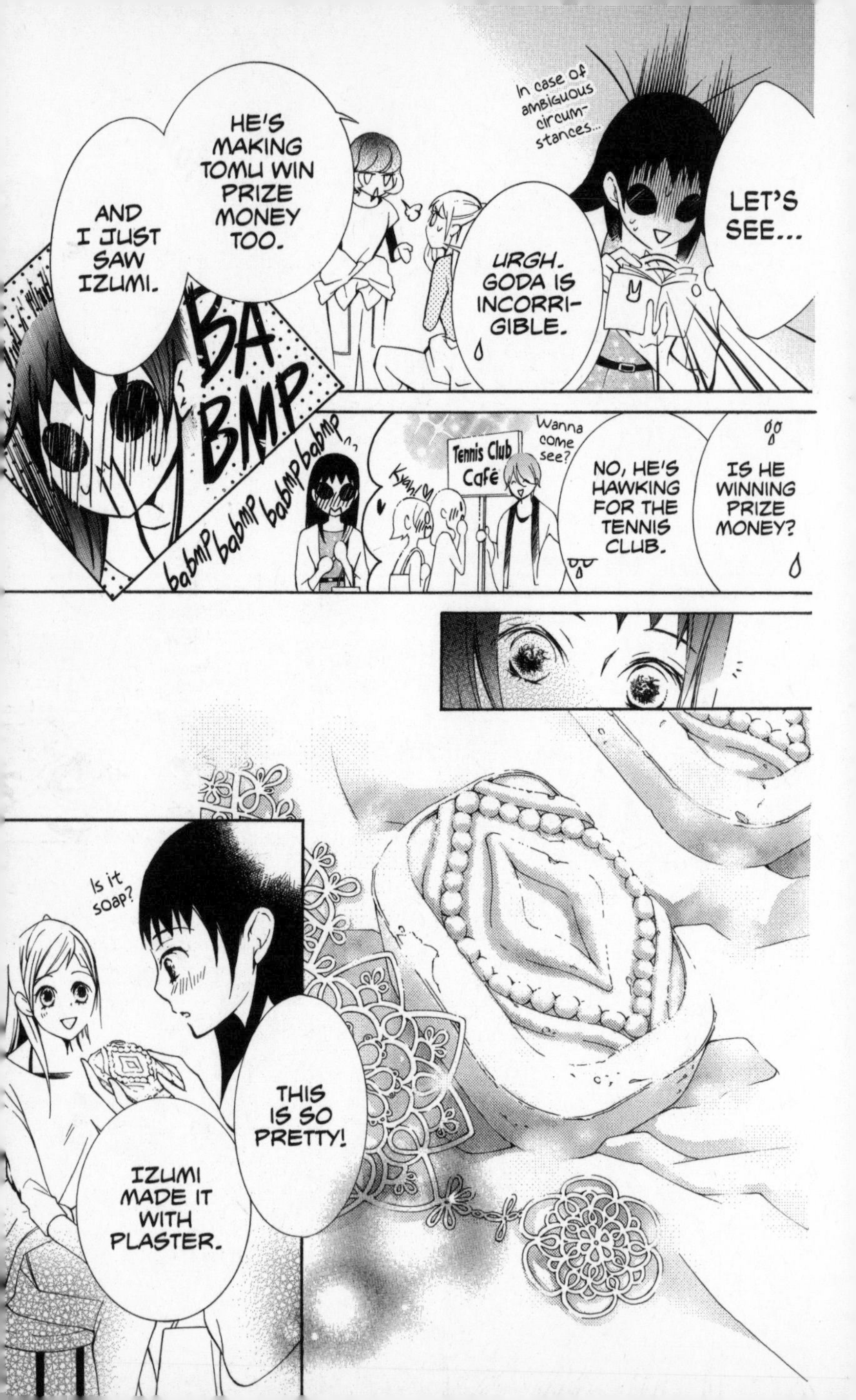

LET'S SEE...
In case of ambiguous circumstances...
URGH. GODA IS INCORRIGIBLE.
HE'S MAKING TOMU WIN PRIZE MONEY TOO.
IS HE WINNING PRIZE MONEY?
NO, HE'S HAWKING FOR THE TENNIS CLUB.
Wanna come see?
Tennis Club Café
Kyan!
babmp babmp babmp babmp
AND I JUST SAW IZUMI.
BA BMP
Is it soap?
THIS IS SO PRETTY!
IZUMI MADE IT WITH PLASTER.

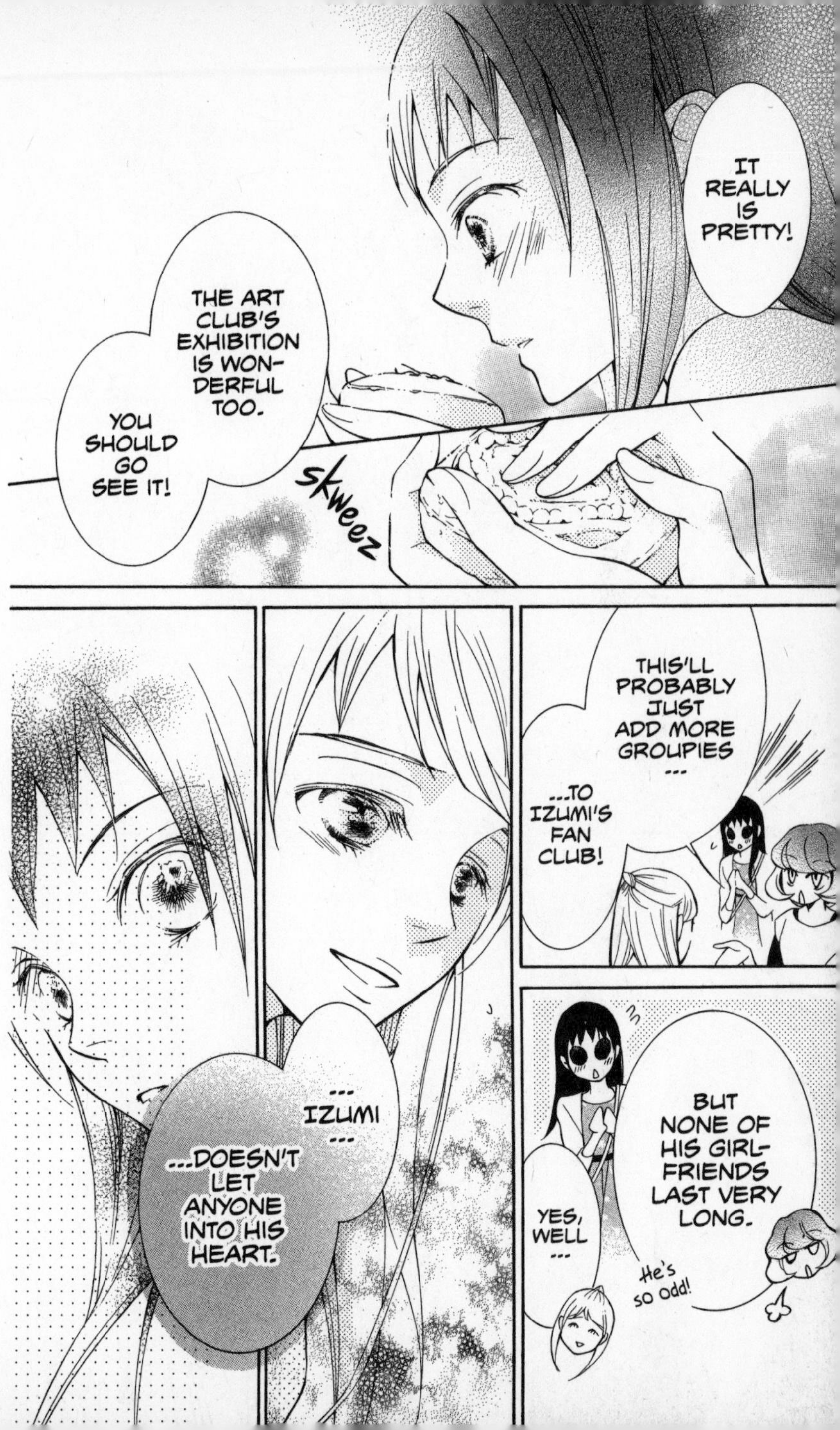
IT REALLY IS PRETTY!
THE ART CLUB'S EXHIBITION IS WONDERFUL TOO.
YOU SHOULD GO SEE IT!
SKWEEZ
THIS'LL PROBABLY JUST ADD MORE GROUPIES...
...TO IZUMI'S FAN CLUB!
BUT NONE OF HIS GIRLFRIENDS LAST VERY LONG.
He's so odd!
YES, WELL...
...IZUMI...
...DOESN'T LET ANYONE INTO HIS HEART.

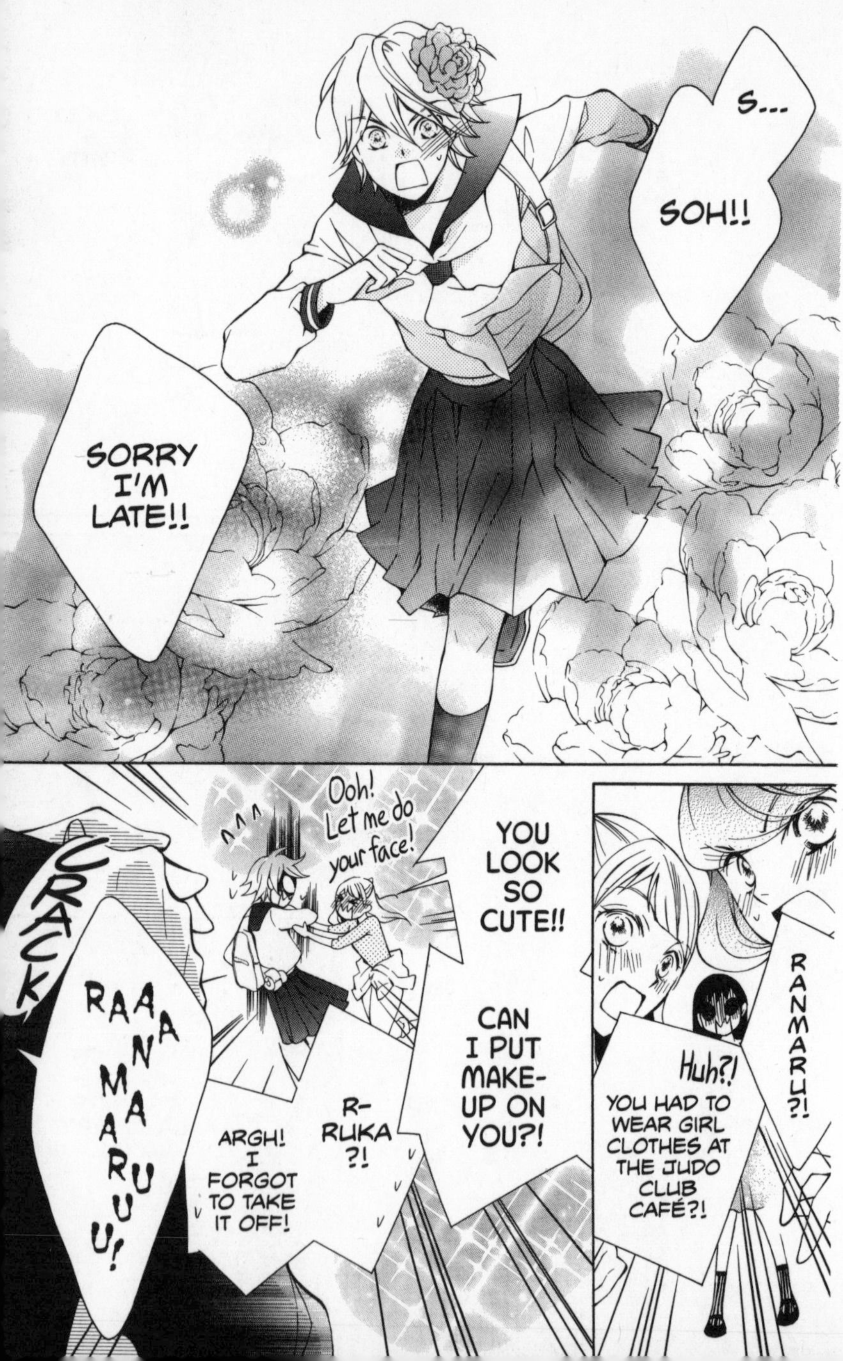
S...
SOH!!
SORRY I'M LATE!!
RANMARU?!
Huh?!
YOU HAD TO WEAR GIRL CLOTHES AT THE JUDO CLUB CAFÉ?!
YOU LOOK SO CUTE!!
CAN I PUT MAKE-UP ON YOU?!
Ooh! Let me do your face!
R-RUKA?!
ARGH! I FORGOT TO TAKE IT OFF!
CRACK
RAAANMAARUUU!

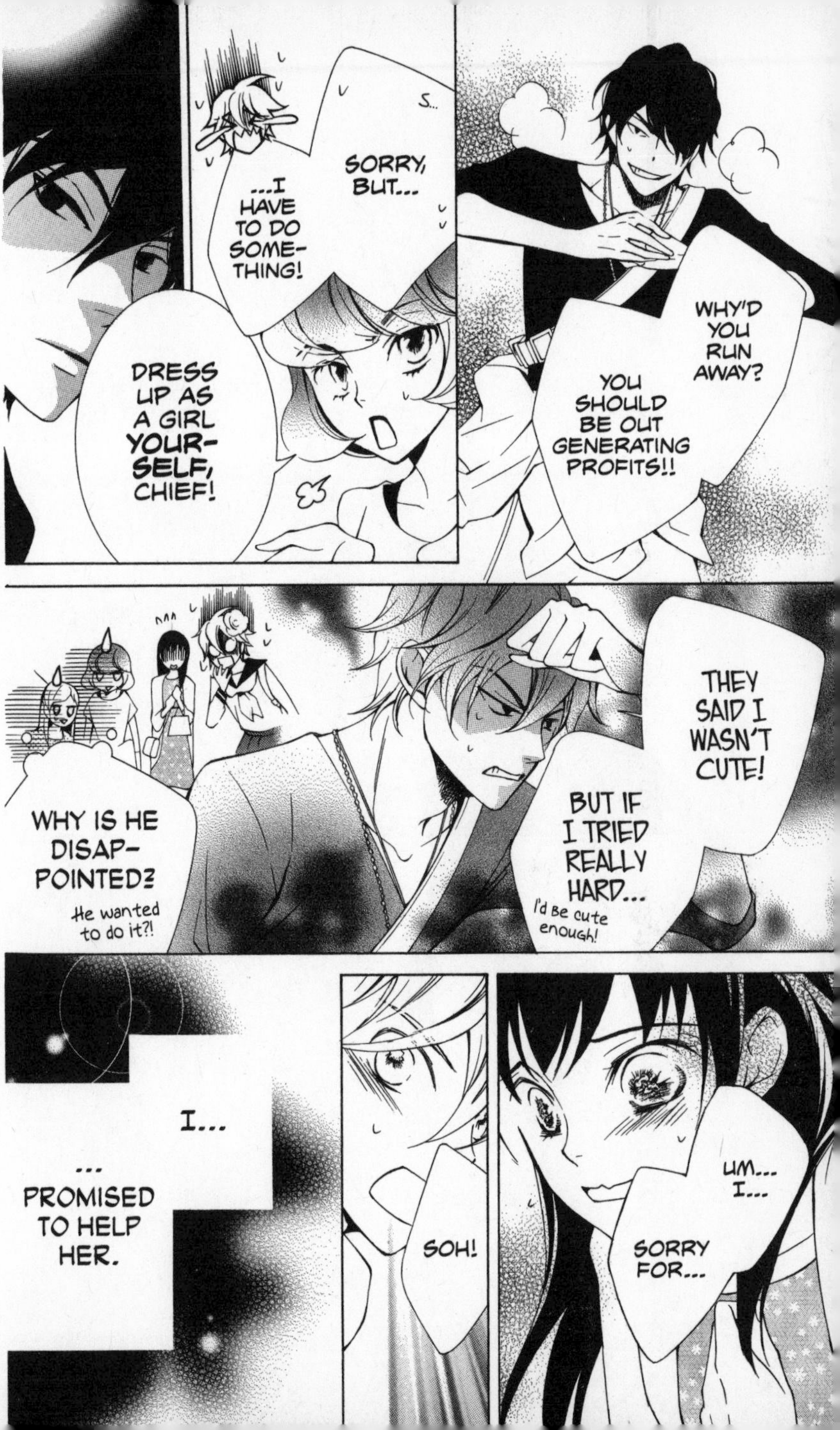
WHY'D YOU RUN AWAY?
YOU SHOULD BE OUT GENERATING PROFITS!!
S...
SORRY, BUT...
...I HAVE TO DO SOMETHING!
DRESS UP AS A GIRL YOURSELF, CHIEF!
THEY SAID I WASN'T CUTE!
BUT IF I TRIED REALLY HARD...
I'd be cute enough!
WHY IS HE DISAPPOINTED?
He wanted to do it?!
UM... I...
SORRY FOR...
SOH!
I...
...PROMISED TO HELP HER.

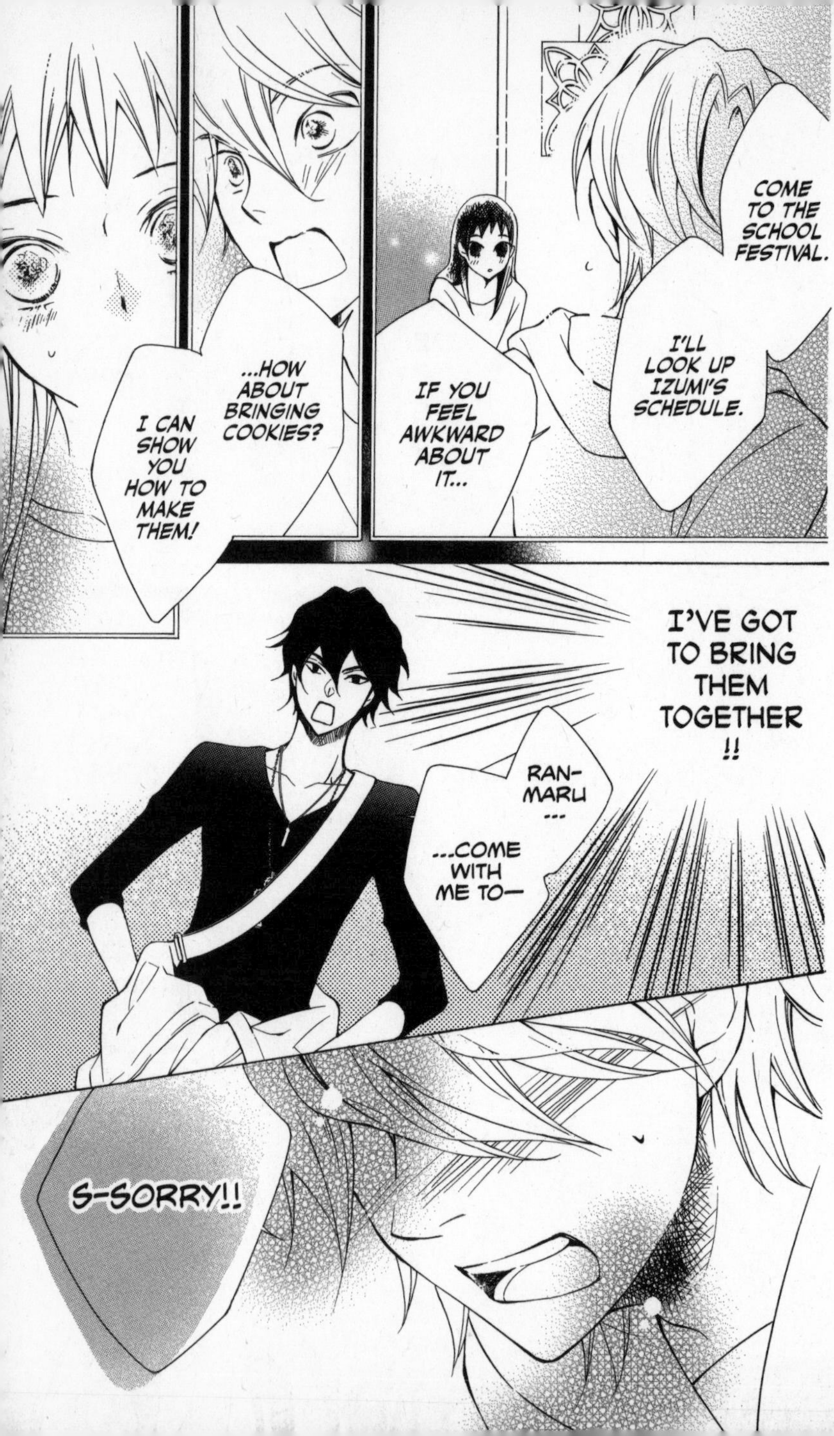
COME TO THE SCHOOL FESTIVAL.
I'LL LOOK UP IZUMI'S SCHEDULE.
IF YOU FEEL AWKWARD ABOUT IT...
...HOW ABOUT BRINGING COOKIES?
I CAN SHOW YOU HOW TO MAKE THEM!
I'VE GOT TO BRING THEM TOGETHER!!
RAN-MARU...
...COME WITH ME TO—
S-SORRY!!

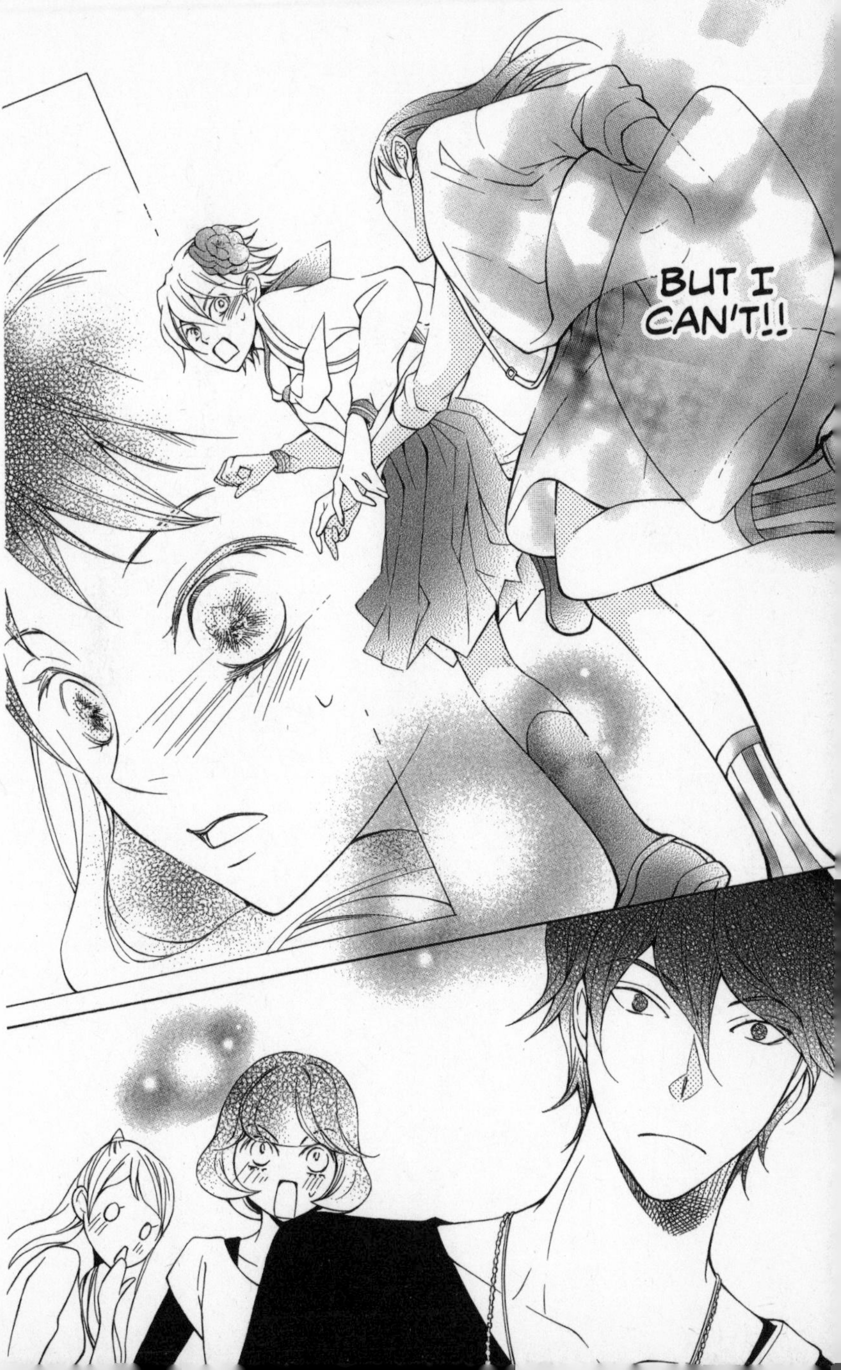
BUT I CAN'T!!

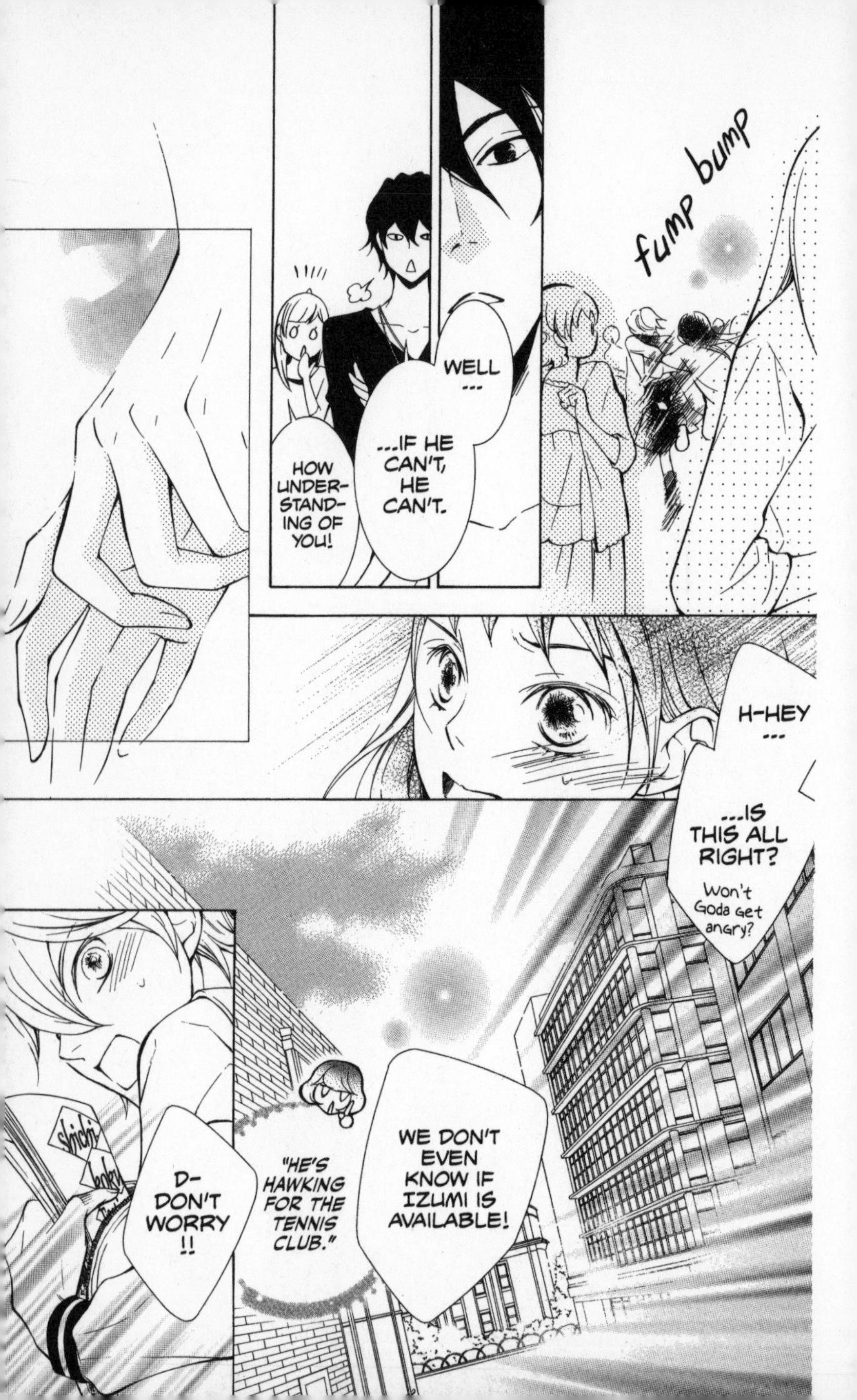
fump bump
WELL ...
...IF HE CAN'T, HE CAN'T.
HOW UNDER-STAND-ING OF YOU!
H-HEY ...
...IS THIS ALL RIGHT?
Won't Goda get angry?
WE DON'T EVEN KNOW IF IZUMI IS AVAILABLE!
"HE'S HAWKING FOR THE TENNIS CLUB."
D-DON'T WORRY !!

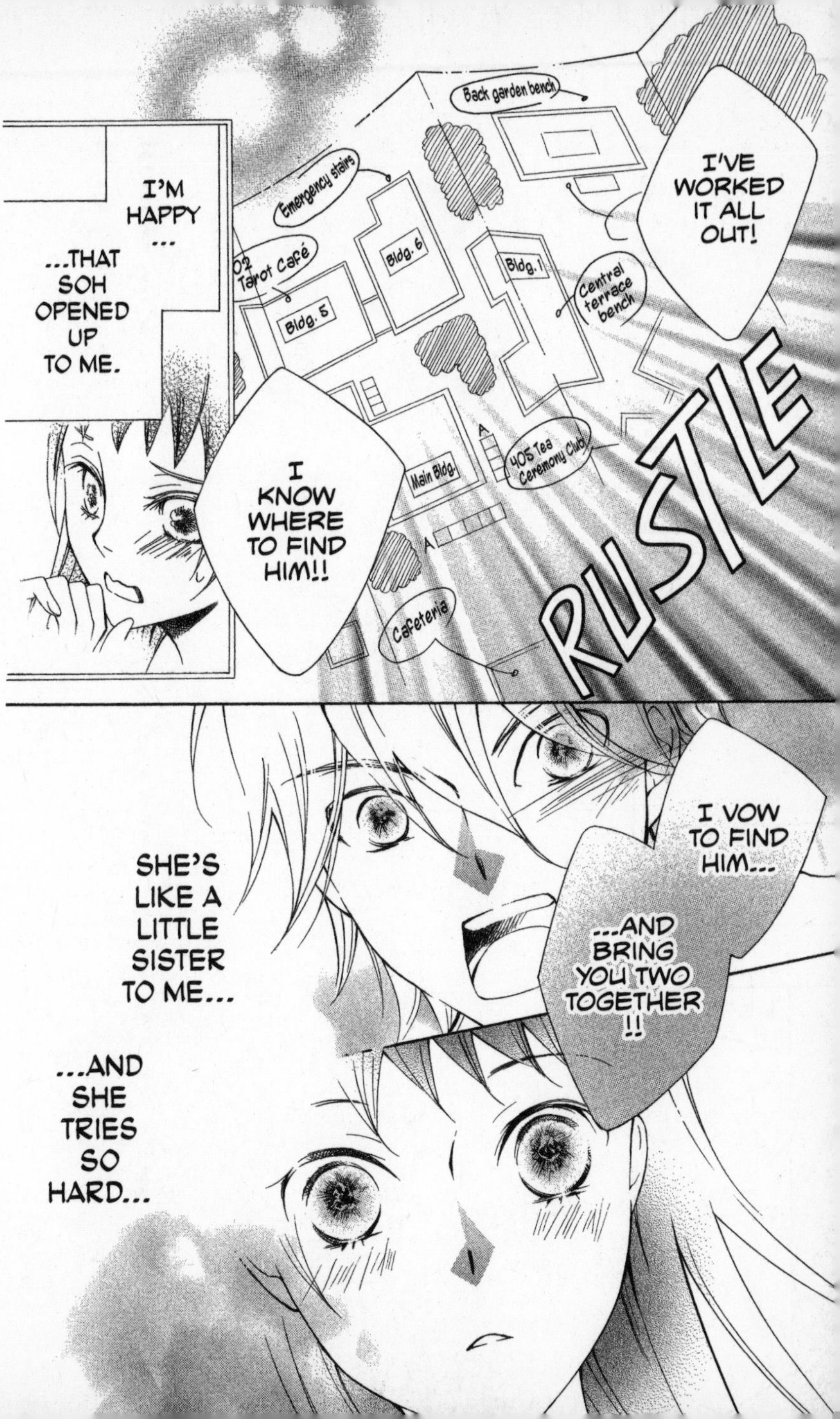
I'VE WORKED IT ALL OUT!
RUSTLE
Back garden bench
Emergency stairs
Bldg. 6
Bldg. 1
Central terrace bench
02 Tarot Café
Bldg. 5
Main Bldg.
405 Tea Ceremony Club
Cafeteria
I KNOW WHERE TO FIND HIM!!
I'M HAPPY...
...THAT SOH OPENED UP TO ME.
I VOW TO FIND HIM...
...AND BRING YOU TWO TOGETHER!!
SHE'S LIKE A LITTLE SISTER TO ME...
...AND SHE TRIES SO HARD...

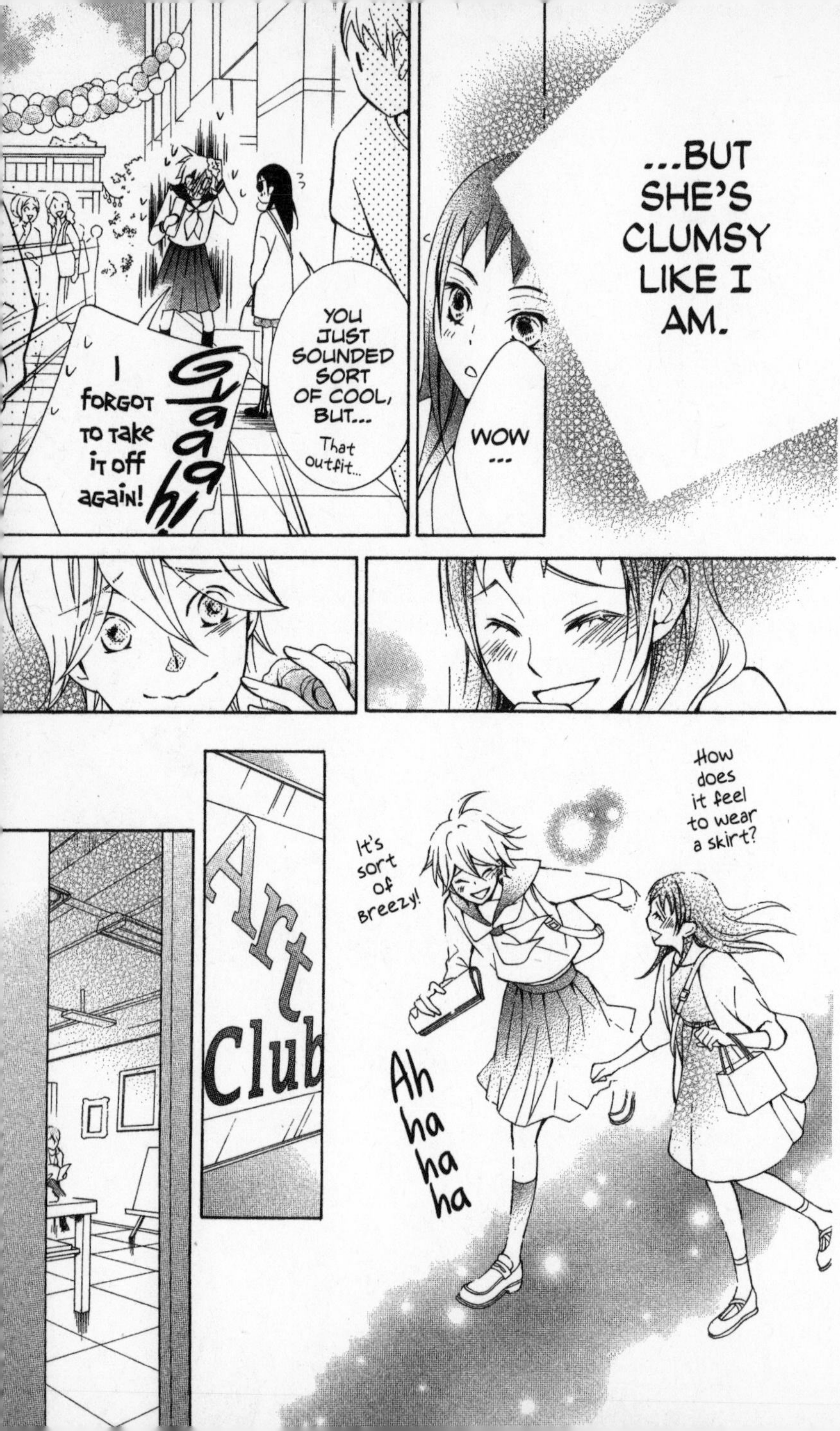
...BUT SHE'S CLUMSY LIKE I AM.
WOW...
YOU JUST SOUNDED SORT OF COOL, BUT...
That outfit...
Gyaaah!
I FORGOT TO TAKE IT OFF AGAIN!
How does it feel to wear a skirt?
It's sort of Breezy!
Ah ha ha ha ha
Art Club

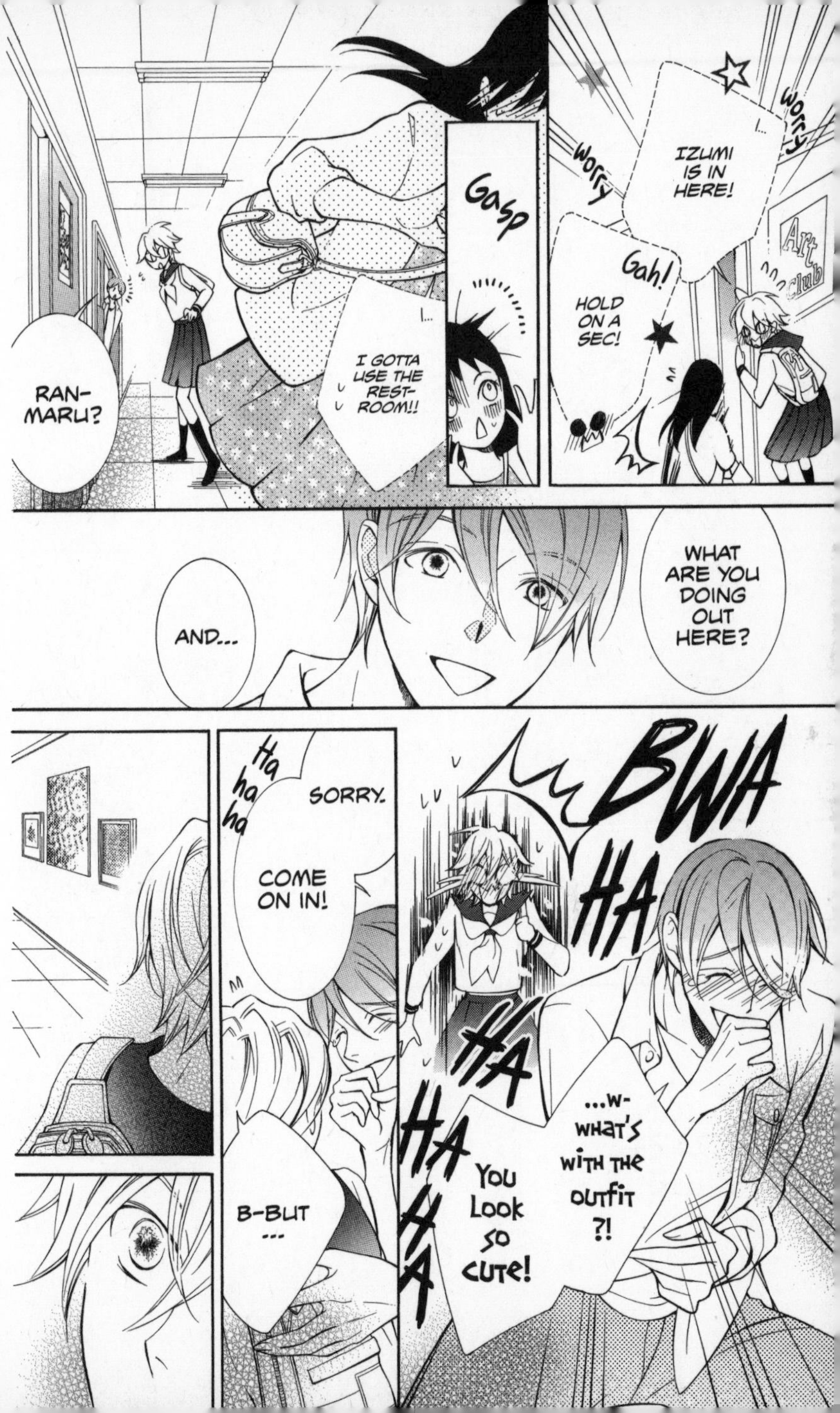
worry
worry
I...
IZUMI IS IN HERE!
Gah!
HOLD ON A SEC!
Art club
Gasp
I...
I GOTTA USE THE REST-ROOM!!
RAN-MARU?
WHAT ARE YOU DOING OUT HERE?
AND...
BWA HA HA HA HA HA HA
...W-WHAT'S WITH THE OUTFIT?!
YOU LOOK SO CUTE!
Ha ha ha
SORRY.
COME ON IN!
B-BUT ...

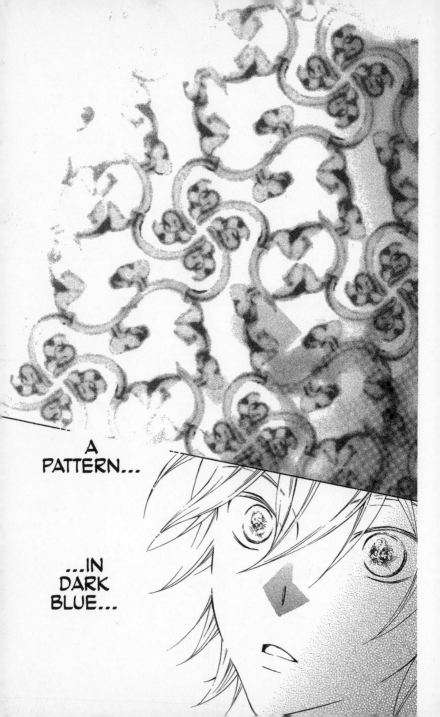

A PATTERN...

...IN DARK BLUE...

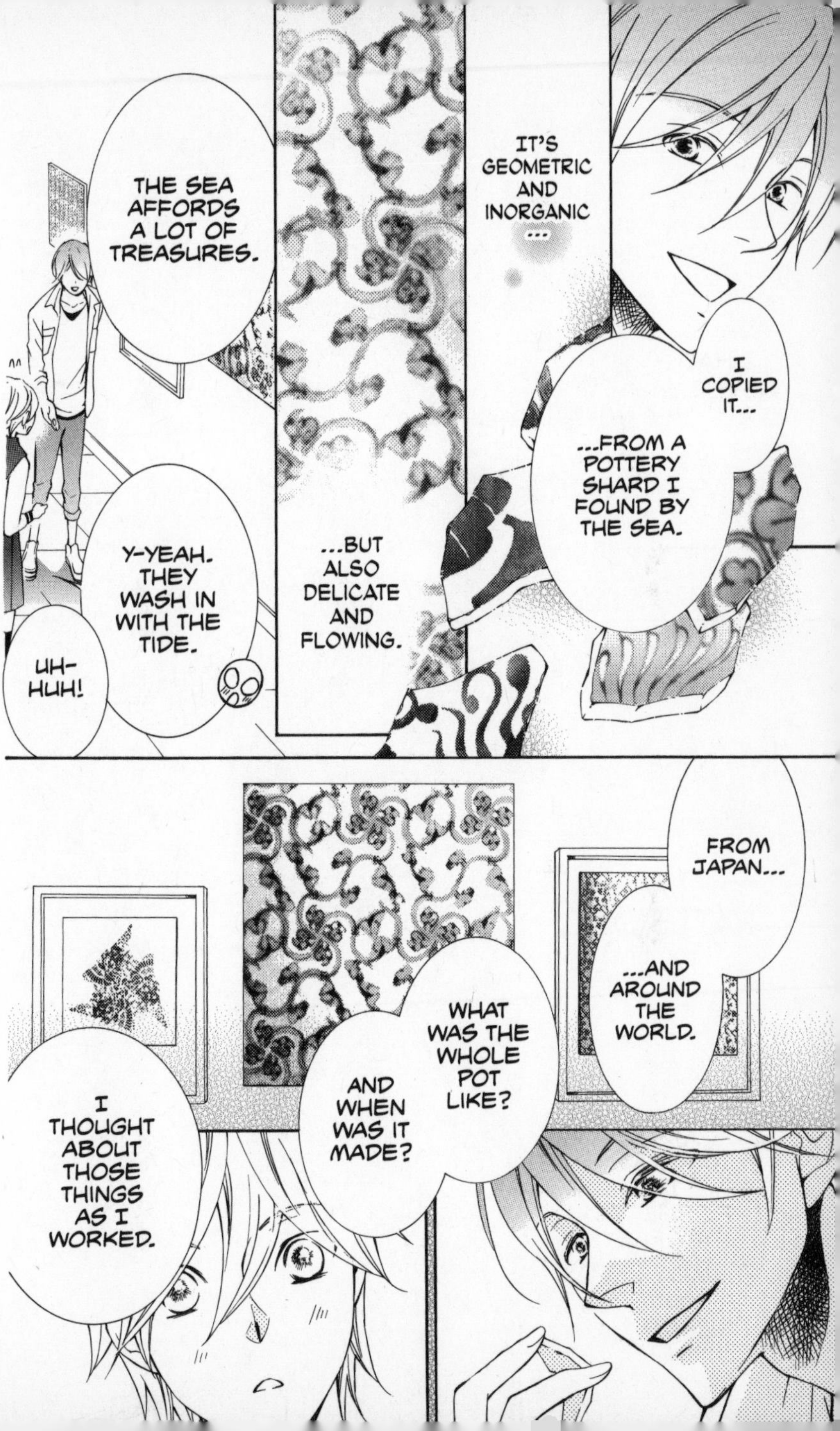
IT'S GEOMETRIC AND INORGANIC...
I COPIED IT...
...FROM A POTTERY SHARD I FOUND BY THE SEA.
...BUT ALSO DELICATE AND FLOWING.
THE SEA AFFORDS A LOT OF TREASURES.
Y-YEAH. THEY WASH IN WITH THE TIDE.
UH-HUH!
FROM JAPAN...
...AND AROUND THE WORLD.
WHAT WAS THE WHOLE POT LIKE?
AND WHEN WAS IT MADE?
I THOUGHT ABOUT THOSE THINGS AS I WORKED.

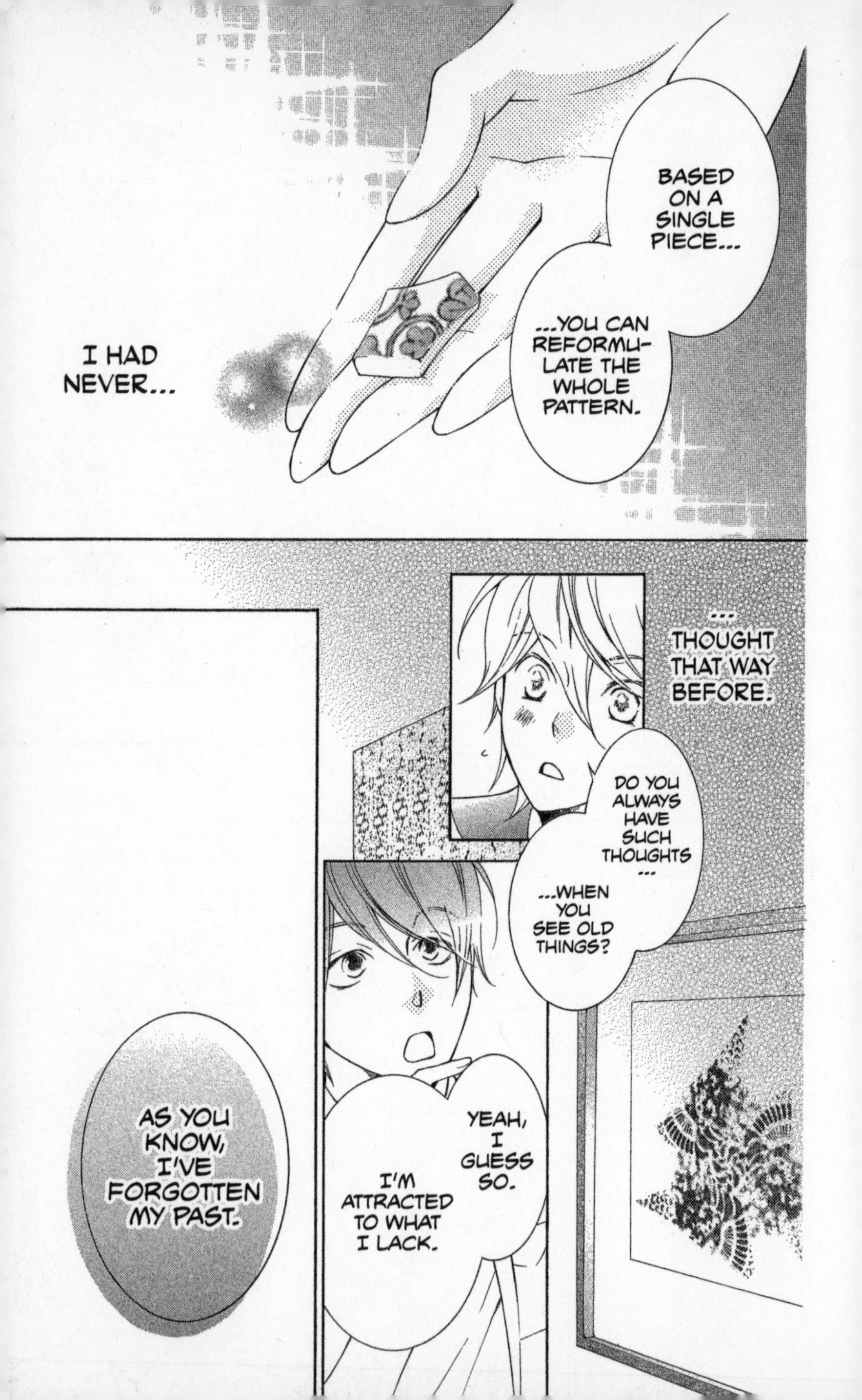
BASED ON A SINGLE PIECE...
...YOU CAN REFORMU-LATE THE WHOLE PATTERN.
I HAD NEVER...
...THOUGHT THAT WAY BEFORE.
DO YOU ALWAYS HAVE SUCH THOUGHTS...
...WHEN YOU SEE OLD THINGS?
YEAH, I GUESS SO.
I'M ATTRACTED TO WHAT I LACK.
AS YOU KNOW, I'VE FORGOTTEN MY PAST.

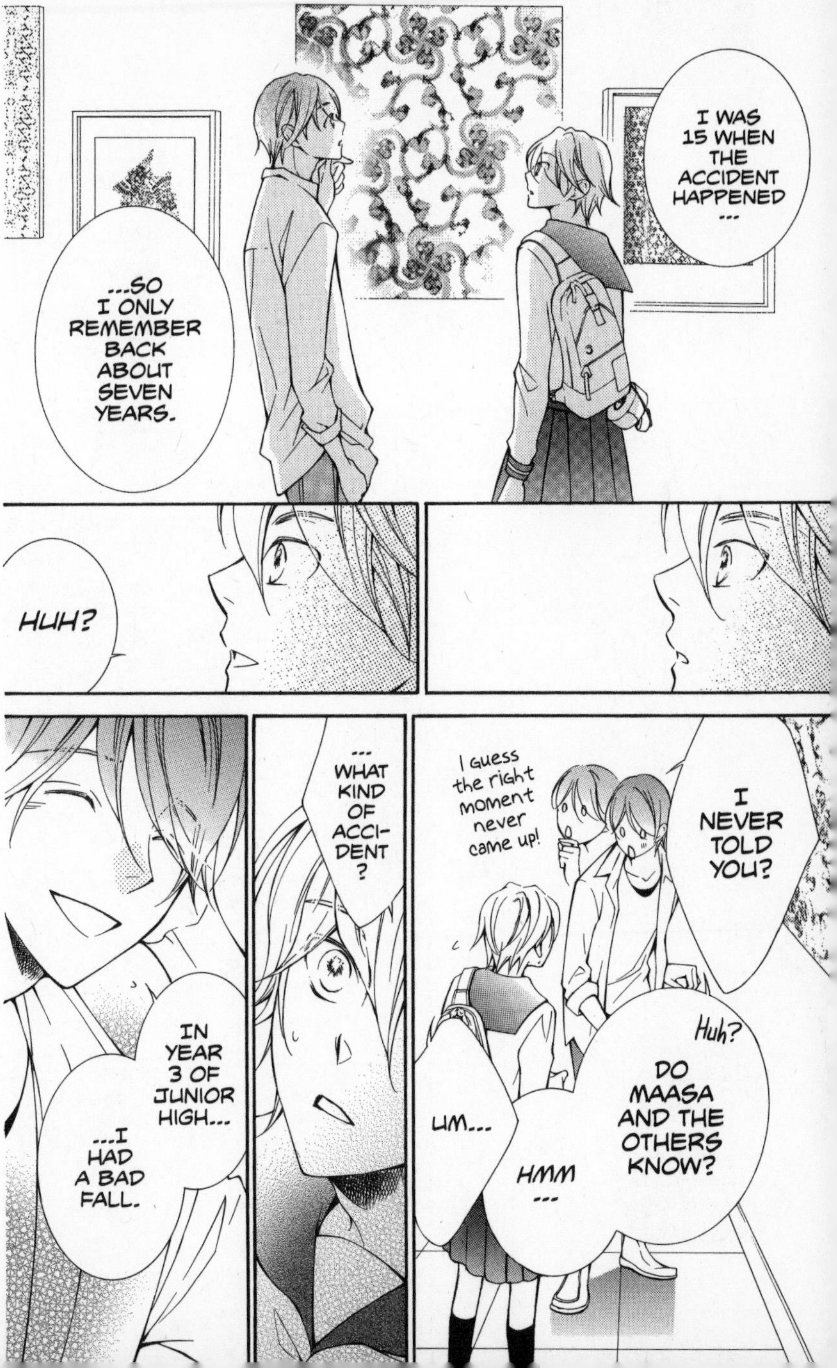
I WAS 15 WHEN THE ACCIDENT HAPPENED...
...SO I ONLY REMEMBER BACK ABOUT SEVEN YEARS.
HUH?
I NEVER TOLD YOU?
I guess the right moment never came up!
Huh?
DO MAASA AND THE OTHERS KNOW?
HMM...
UM...
...WHAT KIND OF ACCIDENT?
IN YEAR 3 OF JUNIOR HIGH...
...I HAD A BAD FALL.

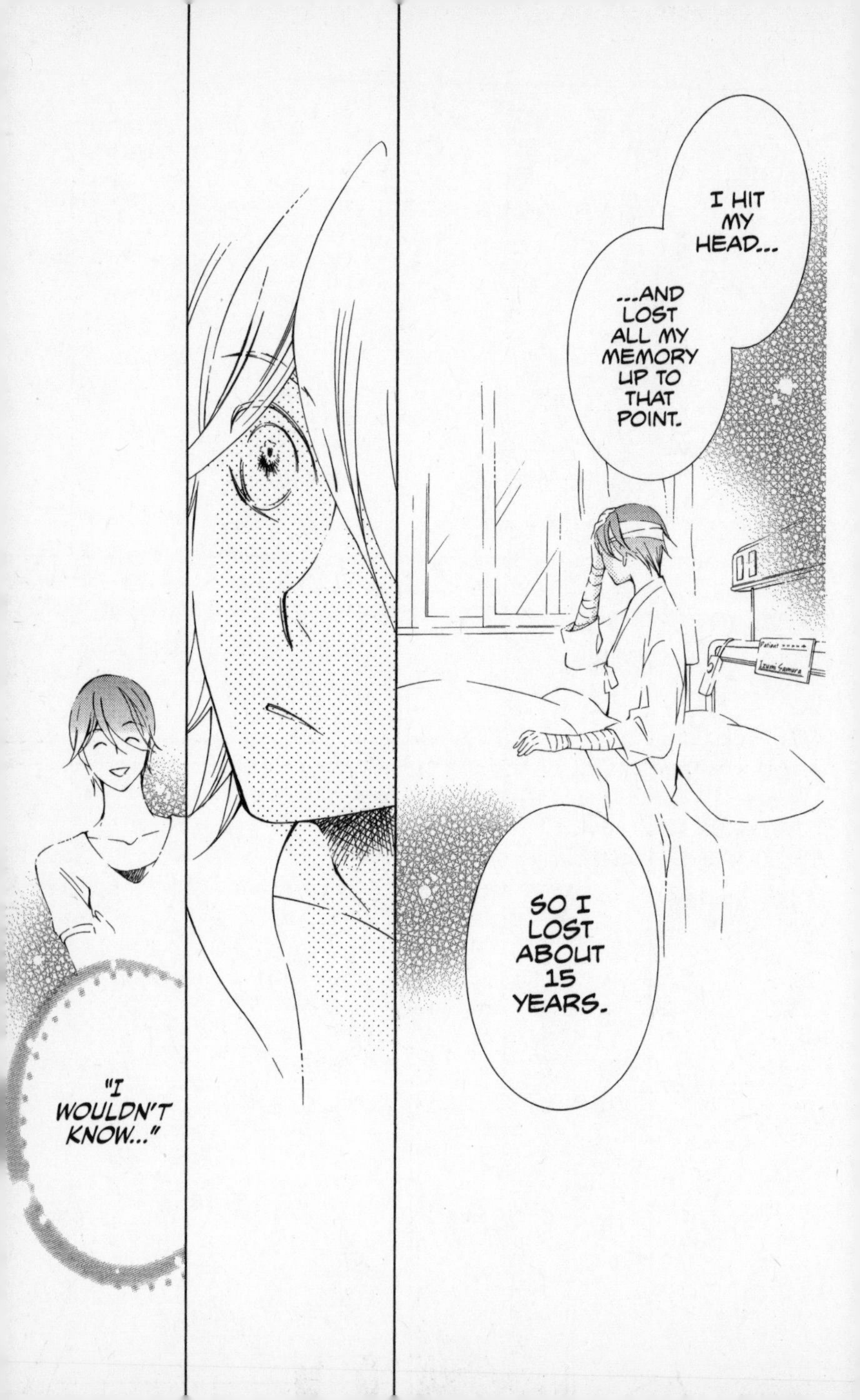
I HIT MY HEAD...
...AND LOST ALL MY MEMORY UP TO THAT POINT.
Izumi Samura
SO I LOST ABOUT 15 YEARS.
"I WOULDN'T KNOW..."

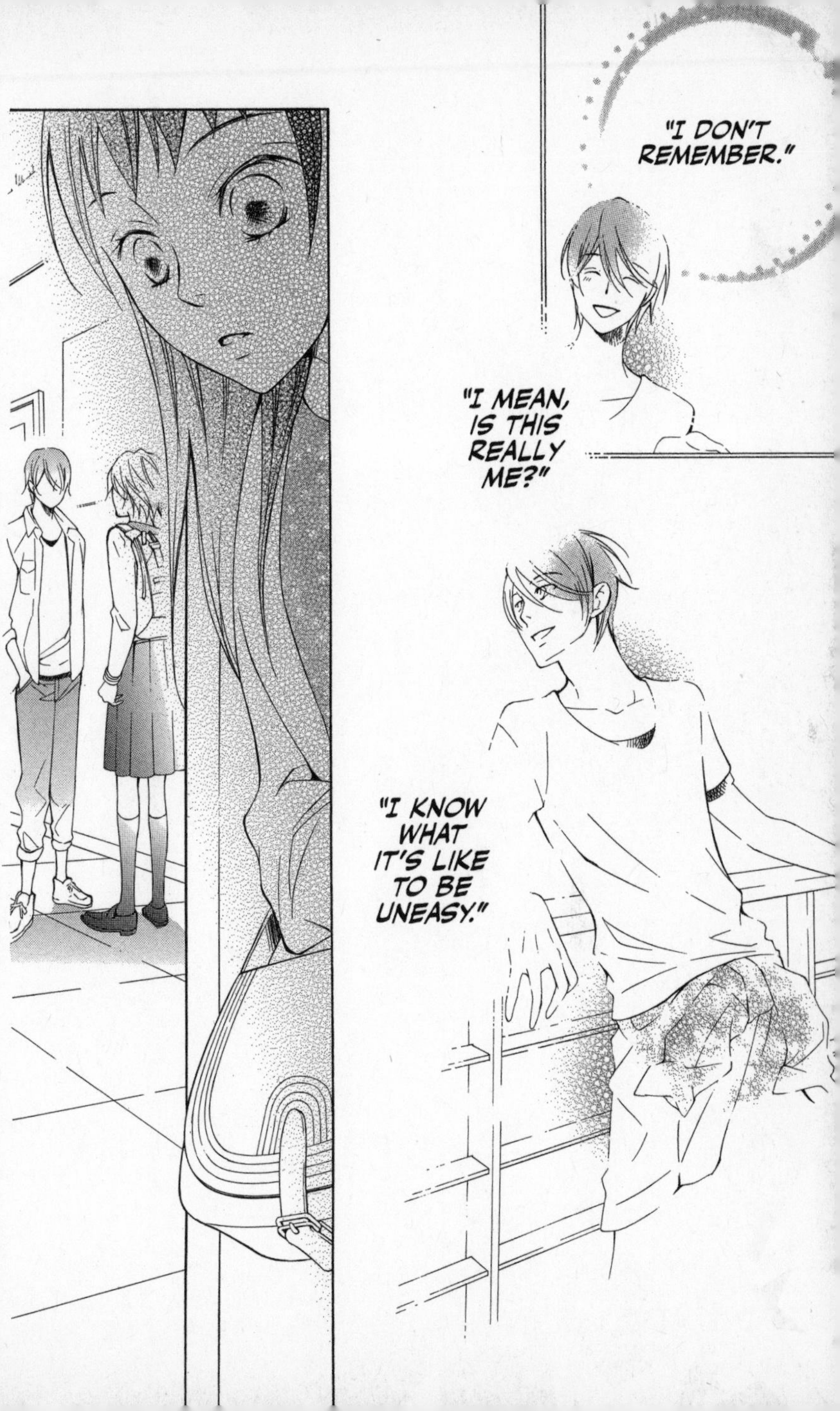
"I DON'T REMEMBER."
"I MEAN, IS THIS REALLY ME?"
"I KNOW WHAT IT'S LIKE TO BE UNEASY."

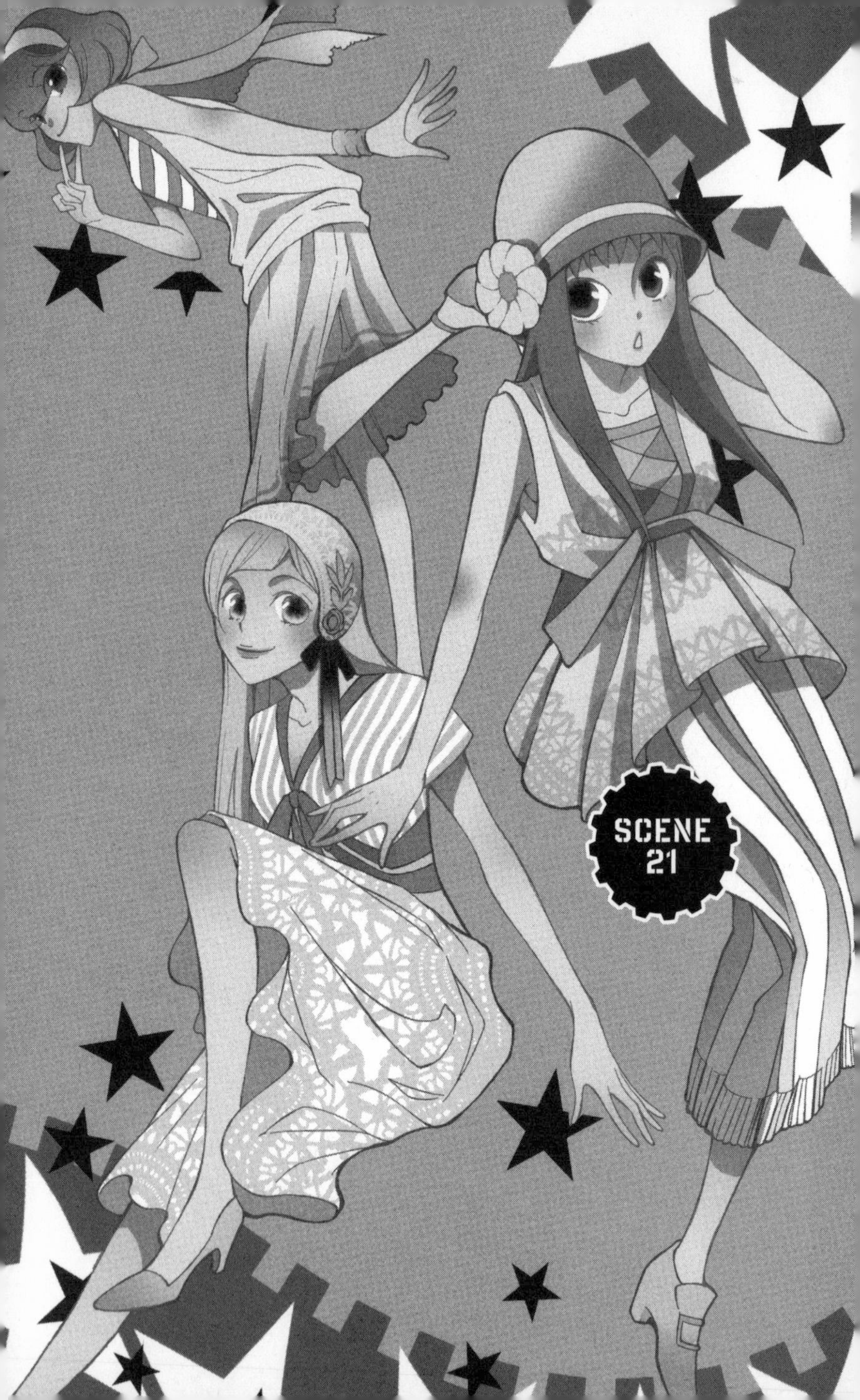
SCENE
21

Special Thanks!!

Ms. O
Nakamura-sama

Everyone involved in
publishing this book

Namiko Yokota-sama
Waseda Film Society
Norihiro Uesugi
Takashi Iwabuchi
guse ars-sama
Rodemu-sama
Forêt-sama

★Staff:
Yui Natsuki, Aya Aomura,
Keiko, Umeko, Shizuru
Onda, Miki Namiki,
Shii Tsunokawa, Meiji

And everyone who reads this BOOK!!

Bisco H 2016.Sep.

"I HAD A BAD FALL."

ONE DAY I WOKE UP IN THE HOSPITAL ...

...SUR-ROUNDED BY STRANGE FACES.

"I...LOST ALL MY MEMORY UP TO THAT POINT.

"SO I LOST ABOUT 15 YEARS."

guse ars

Thanks for letting me use your work for the manga!

sai no tsuno

A pair of artists that I love. I modeled the pattern Izumi drew on something they made.

facebook : https://www.facebook.com/gusears/
HP   : http://guse-ars.com/

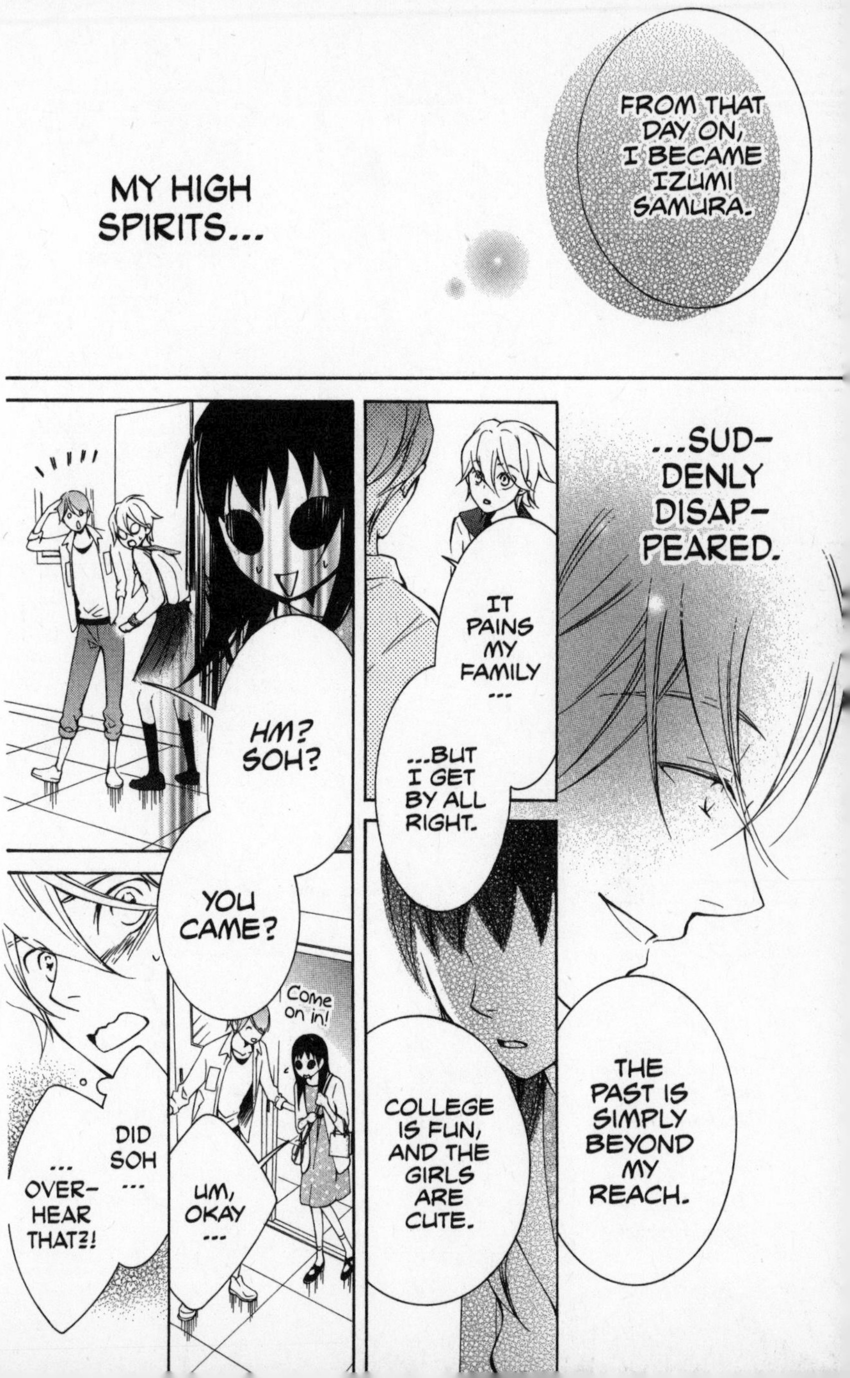
FROM THAT DAY ON, I BECAME IZUMI SAMURA.
MY HIGH SPIRITS...
...SUD-DENLY DISAP-PEARED.
THE PAST IS SIMPLY BEYOND MY REACH.
IT PAINS MY FAMILY...
...BUT I GET BY ALL RIGHT.
COLLEGE IS FUN, AND THE GIRLS ARE CUTE.
HM? SOH?
YOU CAME?
Come on in!
UM, OKAY...
DID SOH...
...OVER-HEAR THAT?!

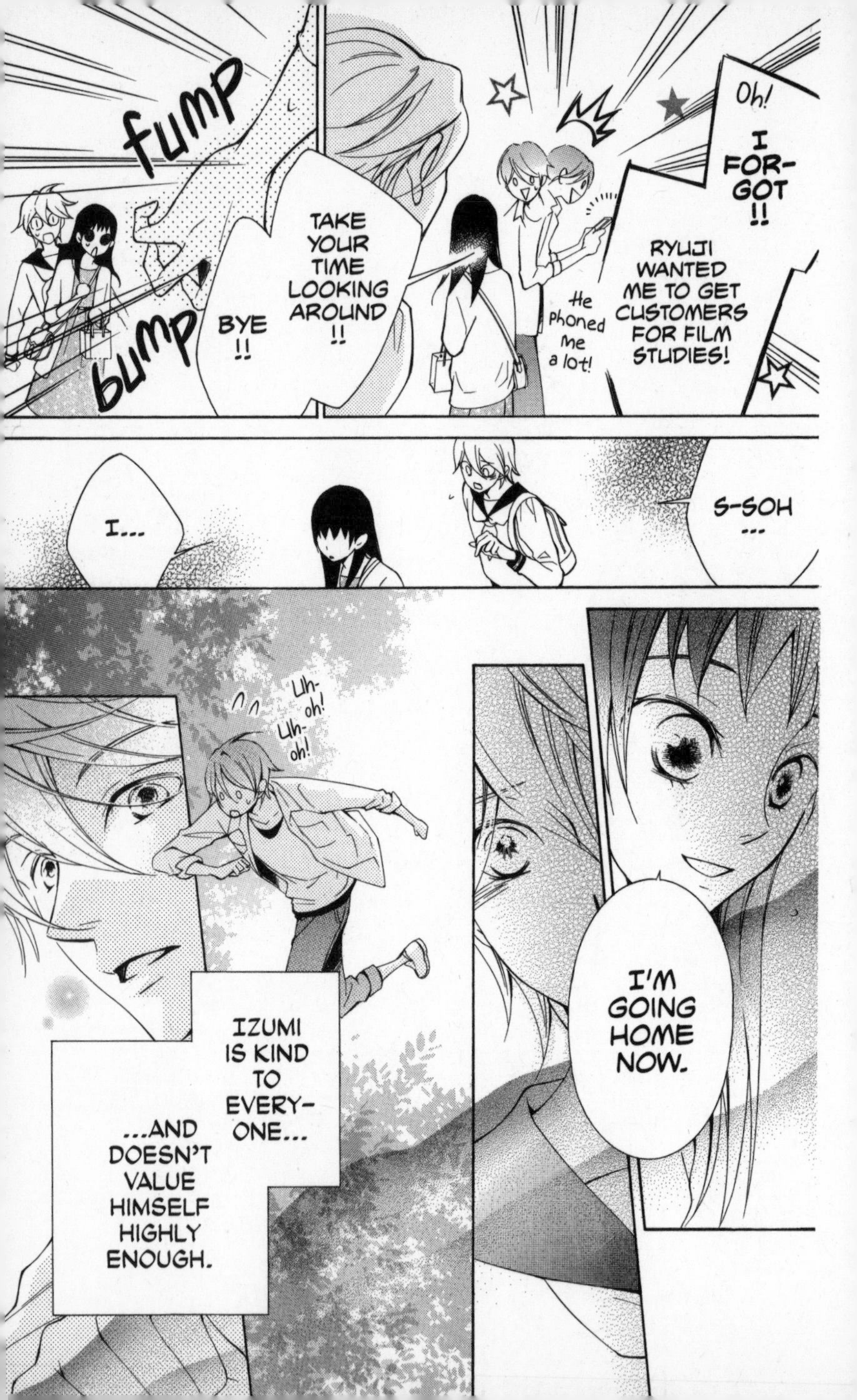
Oh!
I FORGOT!!
RYUJI WANTED ME TO GET CUSTOMERS FOR FILM STUDIES!
He phoned me a lot!
TAKE YOUR TIME LOOKING AROUND!!
BYE!!
fump
bump
S-SOH...
I...
I'M GOING HOME NOW.
Uh-oh! Uh-oh!
IZUMI IS KIND TO EVERYONE...
...AND DOESN'T VALUE HIMSELF HIGHLY ENOUGH.

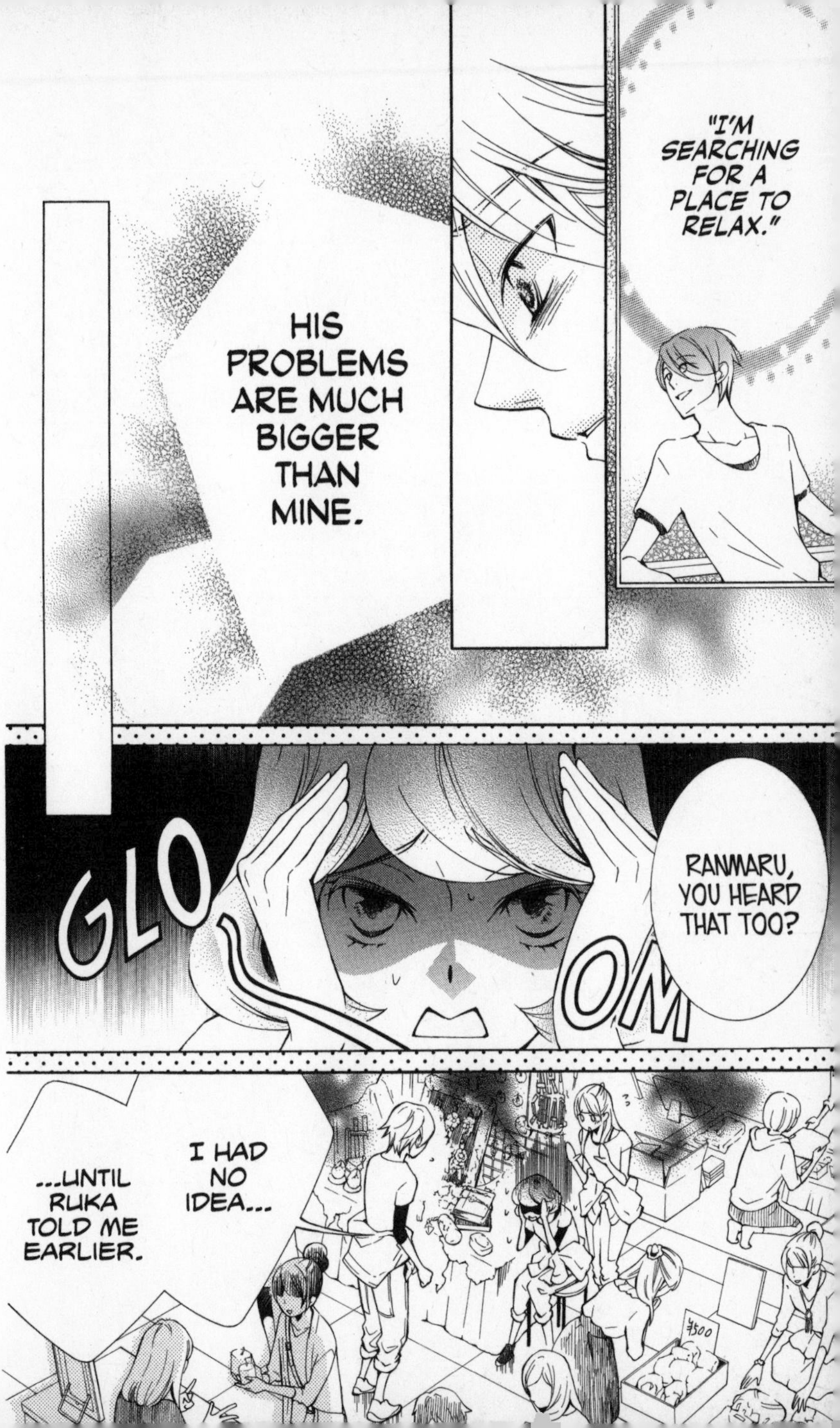
"I'M SEARCHING FOR A PLACE TO RELAX."
HIS PROBLEMS ARE MUCH BIGGER THAN MINE.
RANMARU, YOU HEARD THAT TOO?
GLOOM
I HAD NO IDEA...
...UNTIL RUKA TOLD ME EARLIER.

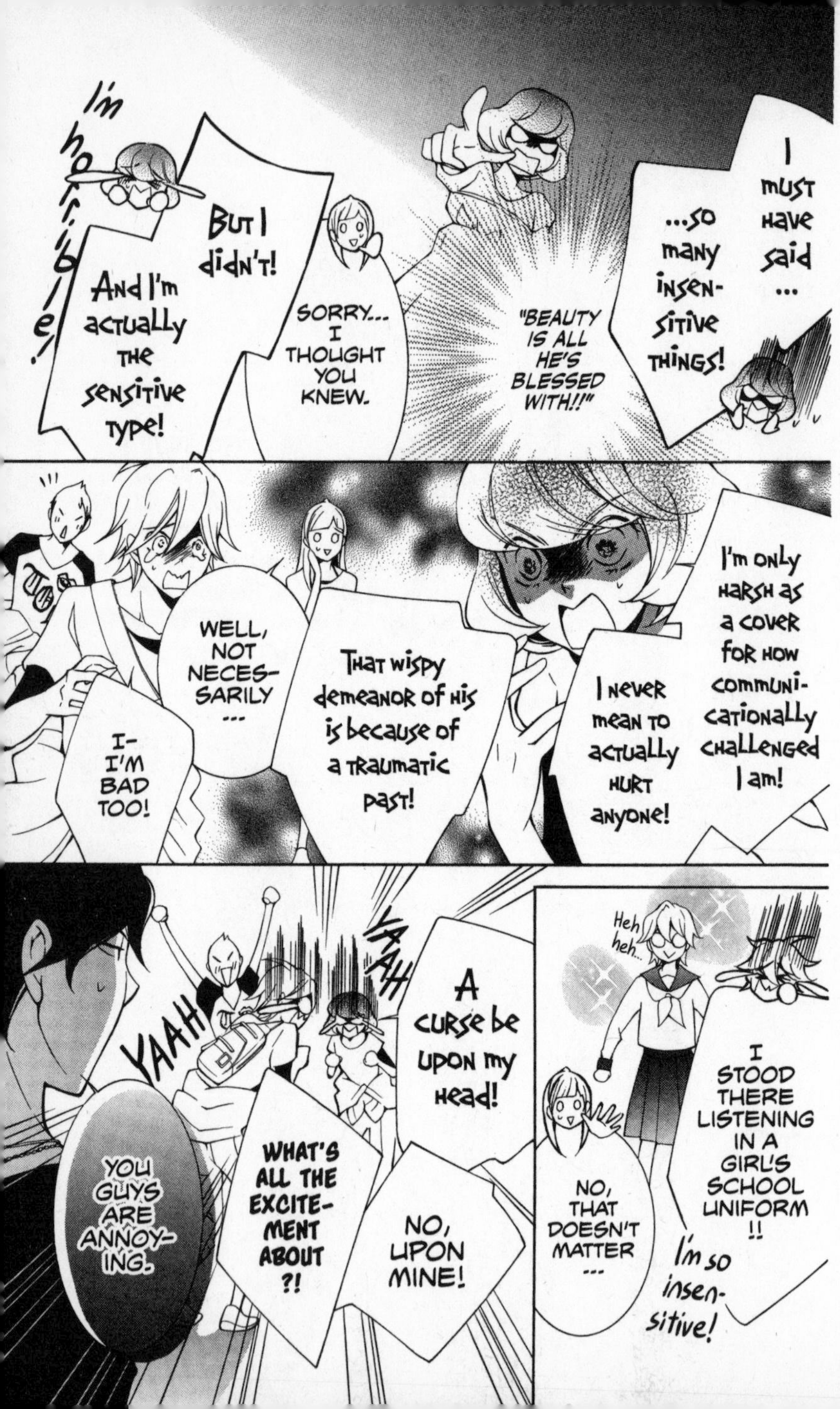
I must have said...
...so many insensitive things!
"Beauty is all he's blessed with!!"
Sorry... I thought you knew.
But I didn't!
And I'm actually the sensitive type!
I'm horrible!
I'm only harsh as a cover for how communicationally challenged I am!
I never mean to actually hurt anyone!
That wispy demeanor of his is because of a traumatic past!
Well, not necessarily...
I-I'm bad too!
Heh heh...
I stood there listening in a girl's school uniform!!
I'm so insensitive!
No, that doesn't matter...
A curse be upon my head!
YAAH
No, upon mine!
What's all the excitement about?!
YAAH
You guys are annoying.

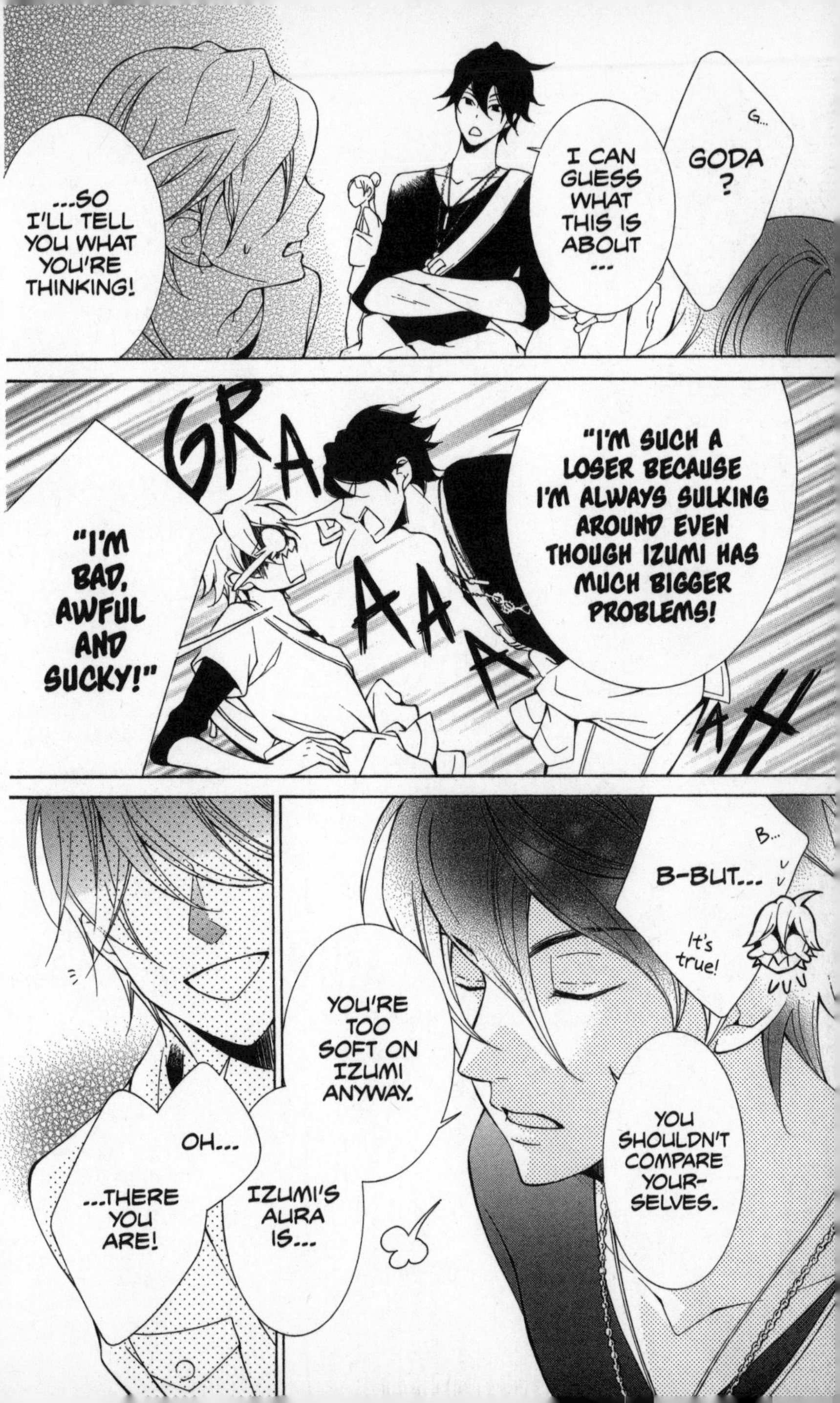
G...
GODA?
I CAN GUESS WHAT THIS IS ABOUT...
...SO I'LL TELL YOU WHAT YOU'RE THINKING!
"I'M SUCH A LOSER BECAUSE I'M ALWAYS SULKING AROUND EVEN THOUGH IZUMI HAS MUCH BIGGER PROBLEMS!
GRAAAAAH
"I'M BAD, AWFUL AND SUCKY!"
B...
B-BUT...
It's true!
YOU SHOULDN'T COMPARE YOUR-SELVES.
YOU'RE TOO SOFT ON IZUMI ANYWAY.
IZUMI'S AURA IS...
OH...
...THERE YOU ARE!

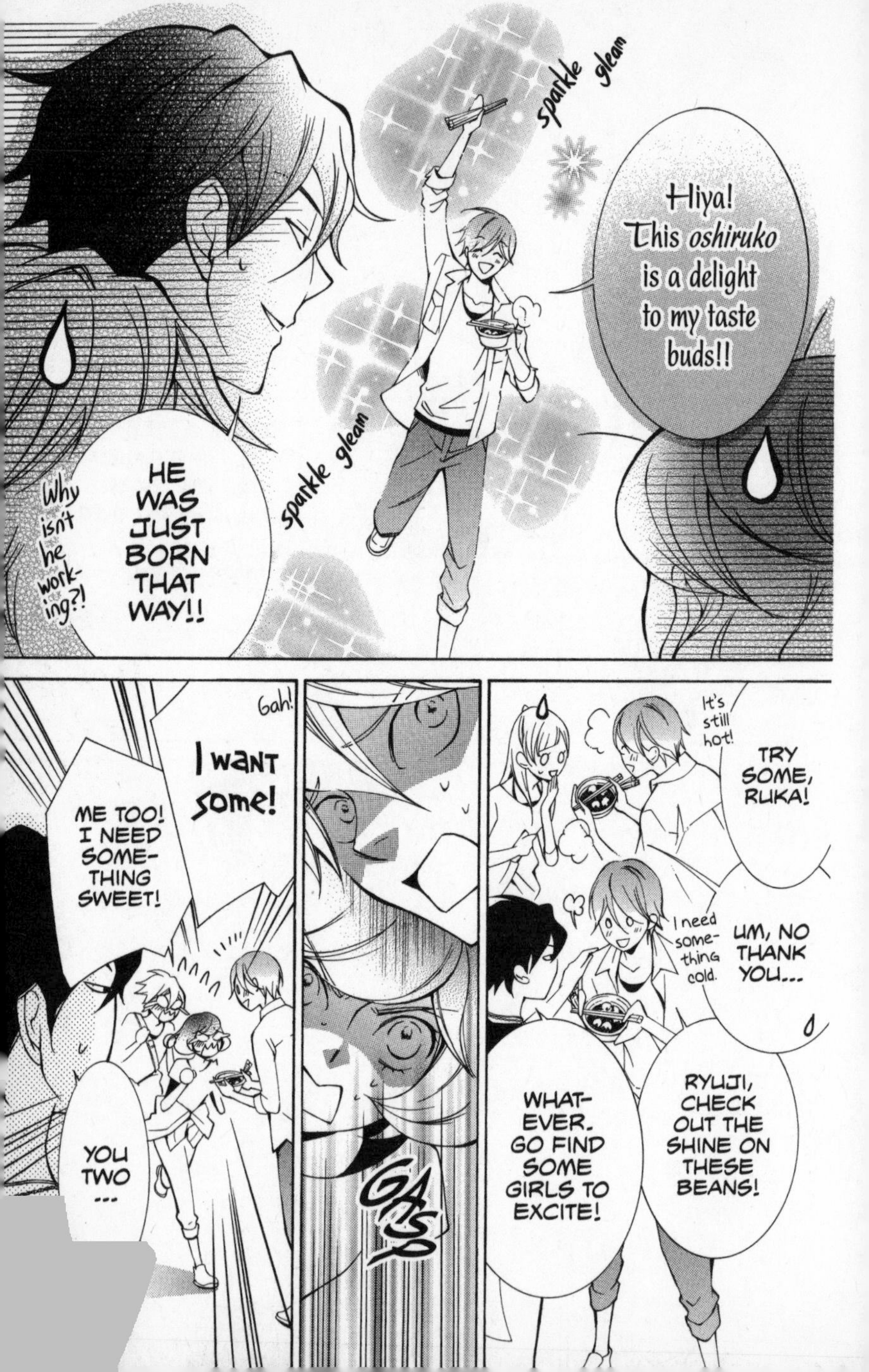
sparkle gleam
Hiya! This oshiruko is a delight to my taste buds!!
sparkle gleam
HE WAS JUST BORN THAT WAY!!
Why isn't he working?!
It's still hot!
TRY SOME, RUKA!
UM, NO THANK YOU...
I need something cold.
RYUJI, CHECK OUT THE SHINE ON THESE BEANS!
WHATEVER. GO FIND SOME GIRLS TO EXCITE!
GASP
Gah!
I want some!
ME TOO! I NEED SOMETHING SWEET!
YOU TWO ...

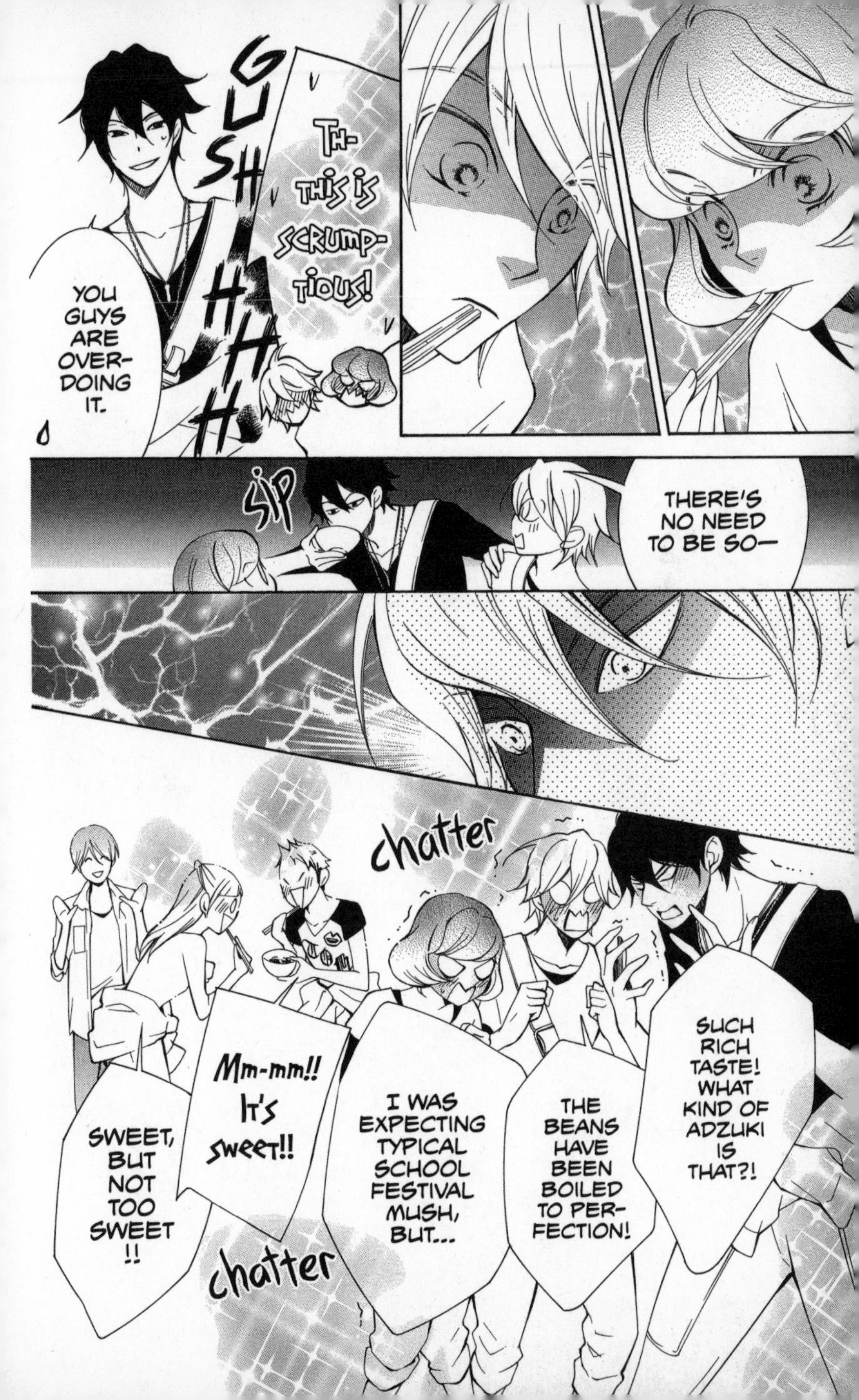
TH- THIS IS SCRUMP- TIOUS!
GUSHHHHH
YOU GUYS ARE OVER- DOING IT.
THERE'S NO NEED TO BE SO—
SIP
chatter
SUCH RICH TASTE! WHAT KIND OF ADZUKI IS THAT?!
THE BEANS HAVE BEEN BOILED TO PER- FECTION!
I WAS EXPECTING TYPICAL SCHOOL FESTIVAL MUSH, BUT...
Mm-mm!! It's sweet!!
SWEET, BUT NOT TOO SWEET !!
chatter

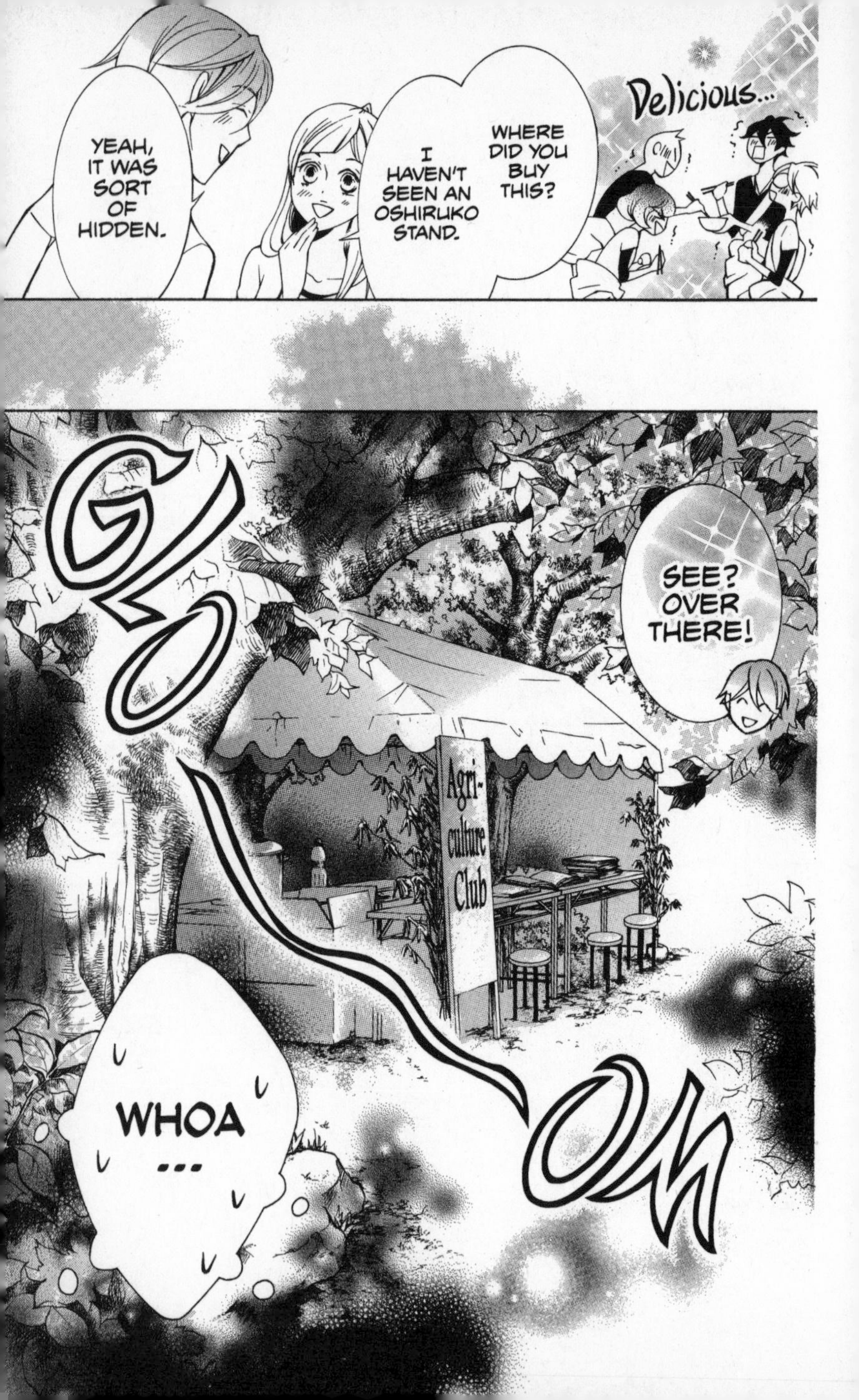
Delicious...
WHERE DID YOU BUY THIS?
I HAVEN'T SEEN AN OSHIRUKO STAND.
YEAH, IT WAS SORT OF HIDDEN.
SEE? OVER THERE!
Agri-culture Club
GLOOM
WHOA ...

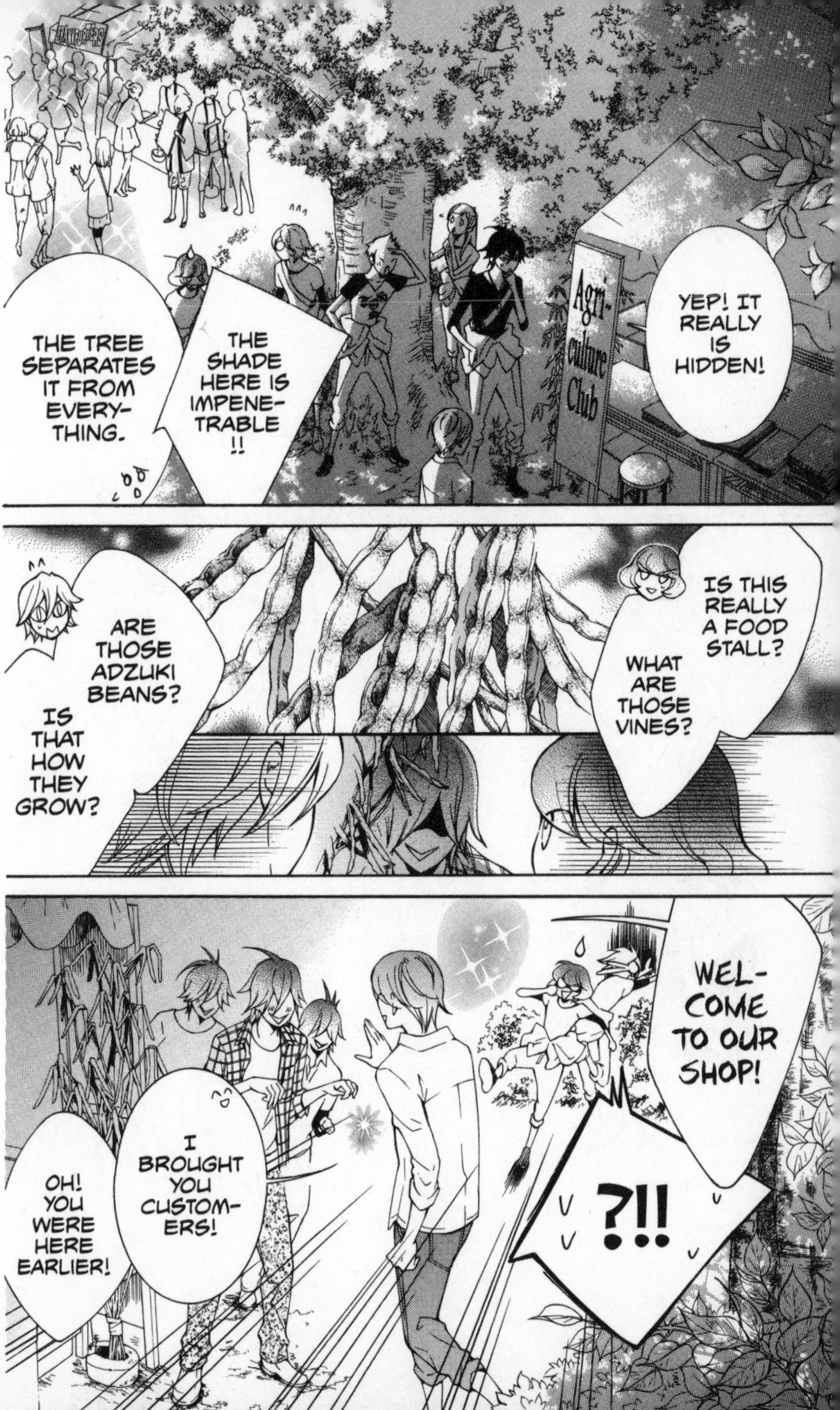
YEP! IT REALLY IS HIDDEN!
Agri-culture Club
THE SHADE HERE IS IMPENE-TRABLE!!
THE TREE SEPARATES IT FROM EVERY-THING.
IS THIS REALLY A FOOD STALL?
WHAT ARE THOSE VINES?
ARE THOSE ADZUKI BEANS?
IS THAT HOW THEY GROW?
WEL-COME TO OUR SHOP!
?!!
I BROUGHT YOU CUSTOM-ERS!
OH! YOU WERE HERE EARLIER!

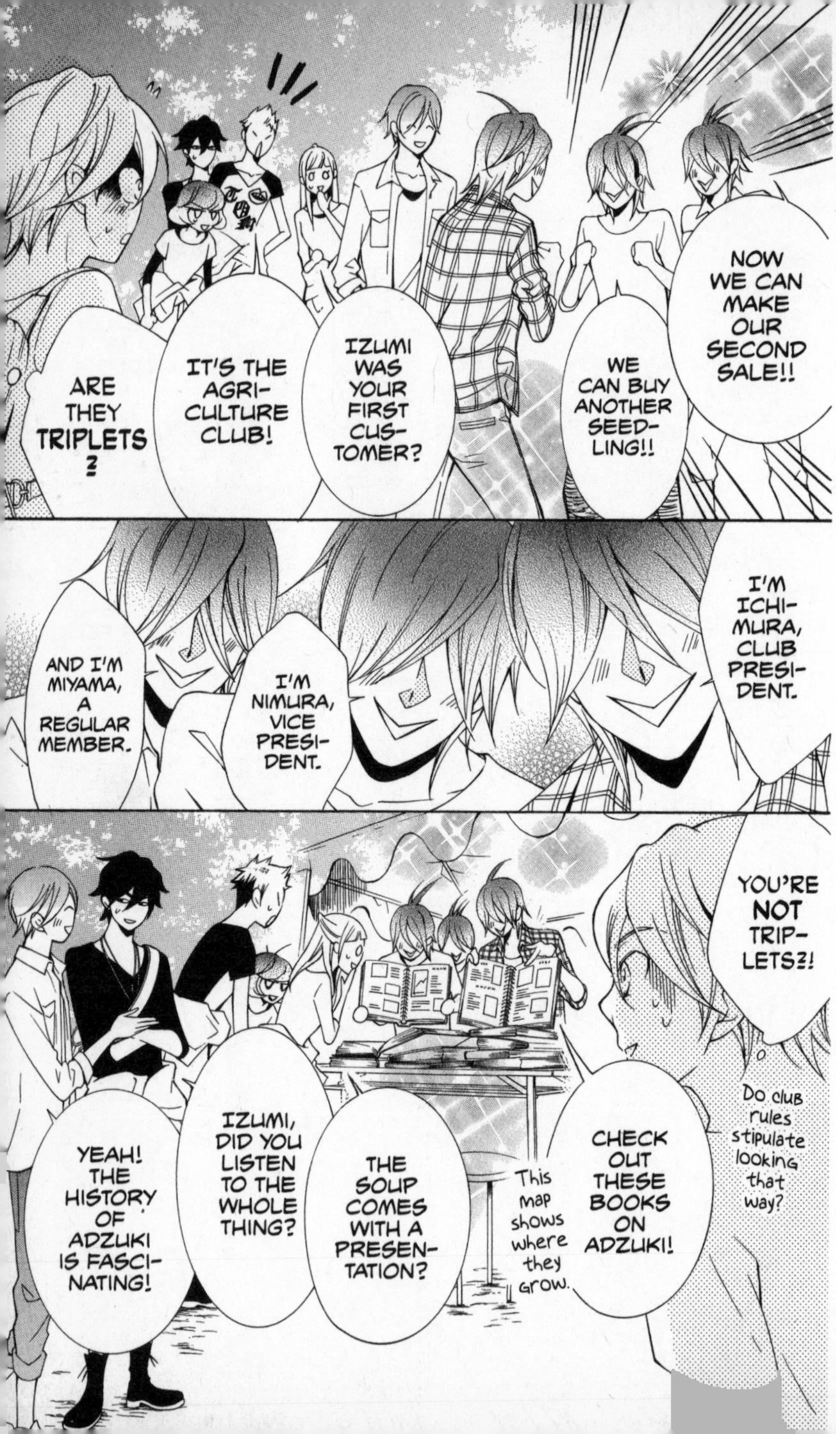
NOW WE CAN MAKE OUR SECOND SALE!!
WE CAN BUY ANOTHER SEEDLING!!
IZUMI WAS YOUR FIRST CUSTOMER?
IT'S THE AGRICULTURE CLUB!
ARE THEY **TRIPLETS**?
I'M ICHIMURA, CLUB PRESIDENT.
I'M NIMURA, VICE PRESIDENT.
AND I'M MIYAMA, A REGULAR MEMBER.
YOU'RE **NOT** TRIPLETS?!
Do club rules stipulate looking that way?
CHECK OUT THESE BOOKS ON ADZUKI!
This map shows where they grow.
THE SOUP COMES WITH A PRESENTATION?
IZUMI, DID YOU LISTEN TO THE WHOLE THING?
YEAH! THE HISTORY OF ADZUKI IS FASCINATING!

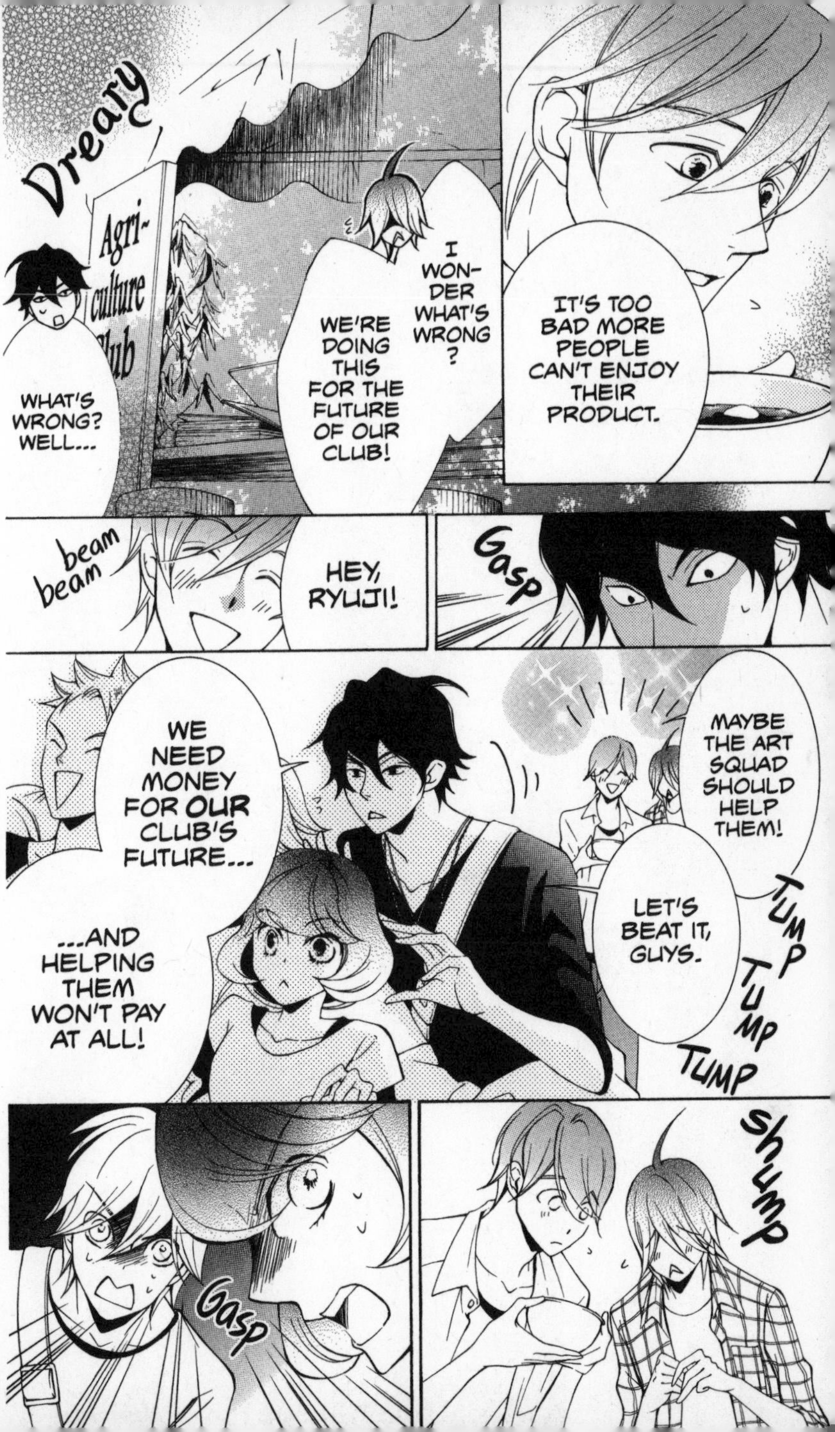
IT'S TOO BAD MORE PEOPLE CAN'T ENJOY THEIR PRODUCT.
I WONDER WHAT'S WRONG?
WE'RE DOING THIS FOR THE FUTURE OF OUR CLUB!
Dreary
Agri-culture Club
WHAT'S WRONG? WELL...
Gasp
HEY, RYUJI!
beam beam
MAYBE THE ART SQUAD SHOULD HELP THEM!
TUMP TUMP TUMP
LET'S BEAT IT, GUYS.
WE NEED MONEY FOR OUR CLUB'S FUTURE...
...AND HELPING THEM WON'T PAY AT ALL!
Shlump
Gasp

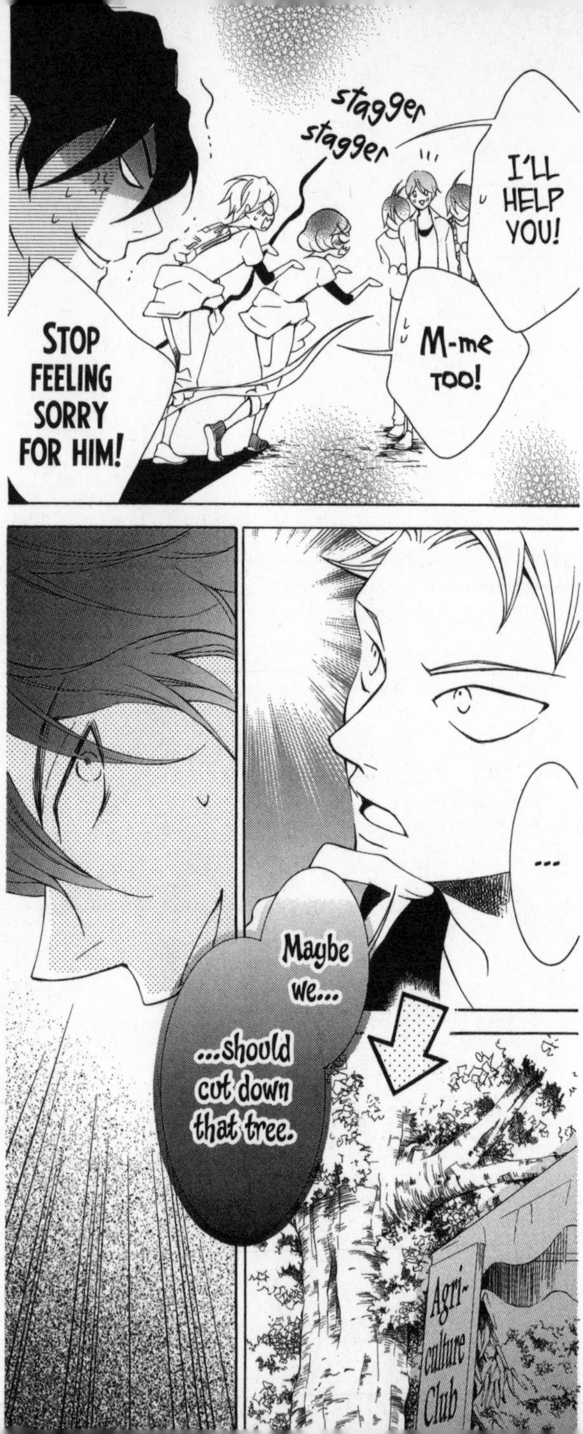
I'LL HELP YOU!
stagger stagger
M-me TOO!
STOP FEELING SORRY FOR HIM!
...
Maybe we...
...should cut down that tree.
Agri-culture Club

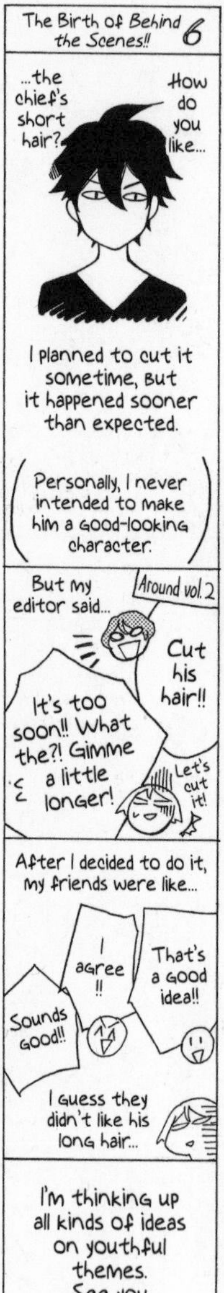
The Birth of Behind the Scenes!! 6
How do you like...
...the chief's short hair?
I planned to cut it sometime, but it happened sooner than expected.
(Personally, I never intended to make him a good-looking character.)
But my editor said...
Around vol. 2
Cut his hair!!
It's too soon!! What the?! Gimme a little longer!
Let's cut it!
After I decided to do it, my friends were like...
That's a good idea!!
I agree!!
Sounds good!!
I guess they didn't like his long hair...
I'm thinking up all kinds of ideas on youthful themes.
See you next time!!

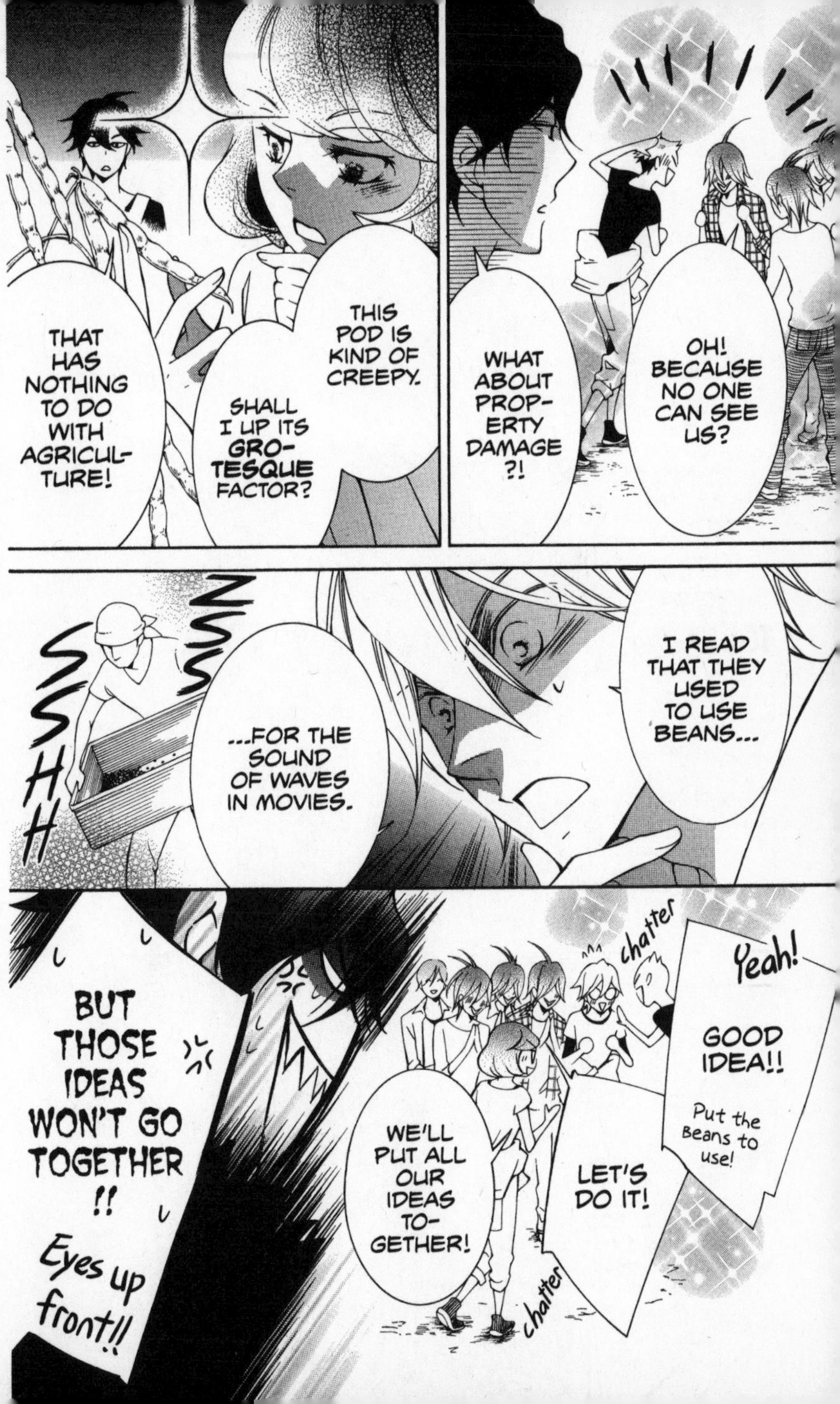
OH! BECAUSE NO ONE CAN SEE US?
WHAT ABOUT PROPERTY DAMAGE?!
THIS POD IS KIND OF CREEPY.
SHALL I UP ITS GROTESQUE FACTOR?
THAT HAS NOTHING TO DO WITH AGRICULTURE!
I READ THAT THEY USED TO USE BEANS...
...FOR THE SOUND OF WAVES IN MOVIES.
ZSSS
SSHH
Yeah!
GOOD IDEA!!
Put the Beans to use!
chatter
LET'S DO IT!
WE'LL PUT ALL OUR IDEAS TOGETHER!
chatter
BUT THOSE IDEAS WON'T GO TOGETHER!!
Eyes up front!!

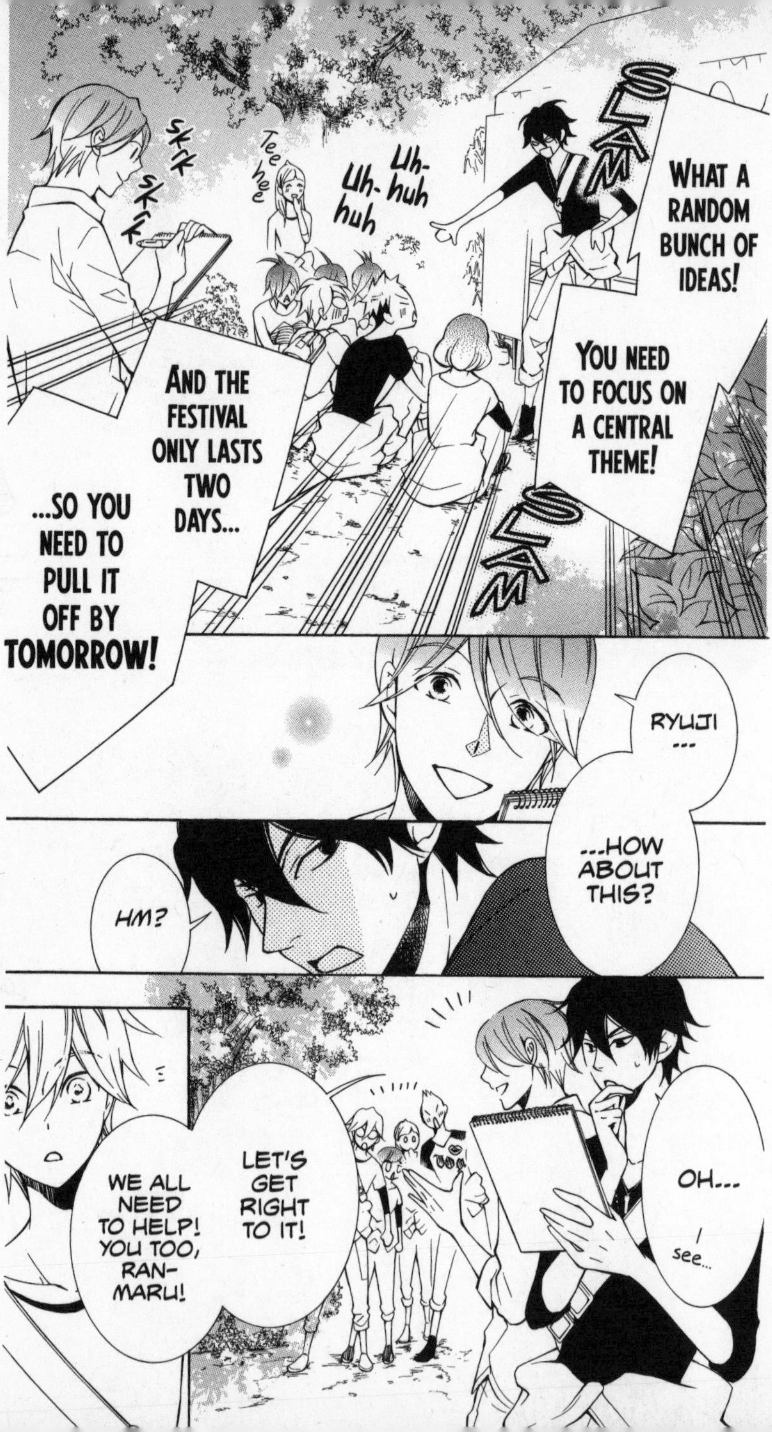
SLAM
WHAT A RANDOM BUNCH OF IDEAS!
YOU NEED TO FOCUS ON A CENTRAL THEME!
SLAM
Uh-huh Uh-huh huh
Tee hee
SKRK SKRK
AND THE FESTIVAL ONLY LASTS TWO DAYS...
...SO YOU NEED TO PULL IT OFF BY TOMORROW!
RYUJI...
...HOW ABOUT THIS?
HM?
OH...
I see...
LET'S GET RIGHT TO IT!
WE ALL NEED TO HELP! YOU TOO, RAN-MARU!

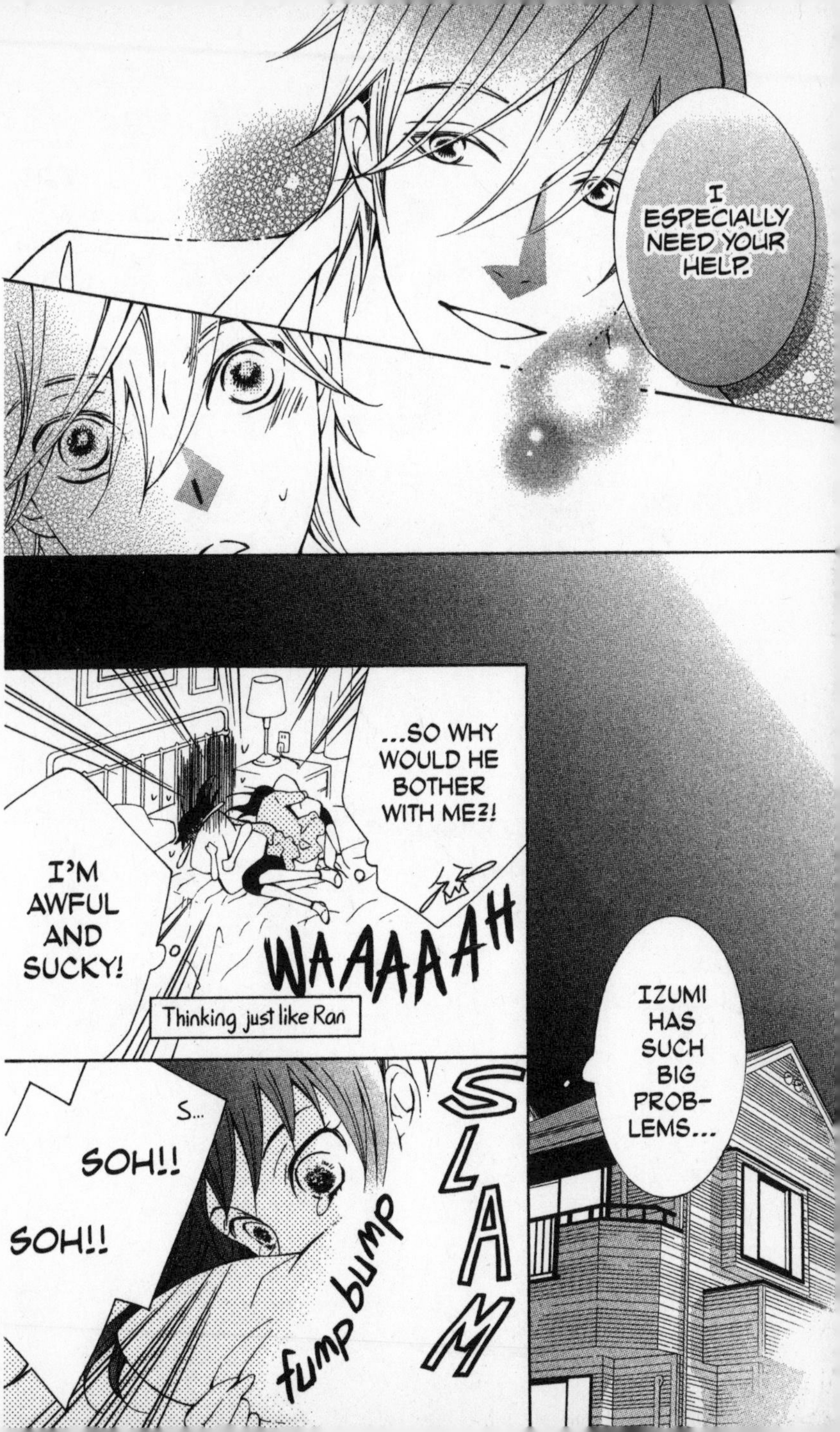
I ESPECIALLY NEED YOUR HELP.
IZUMI HAS SUCH BIG PROBLEMS...
...SO WHY WOULD HE BOTHER WITH ME?!
I'M AWFUL AND SUCKY!
WAAAAAH
Thinking just like Ran
SLAM
fump bump
S...
SOH!!
SOH!!

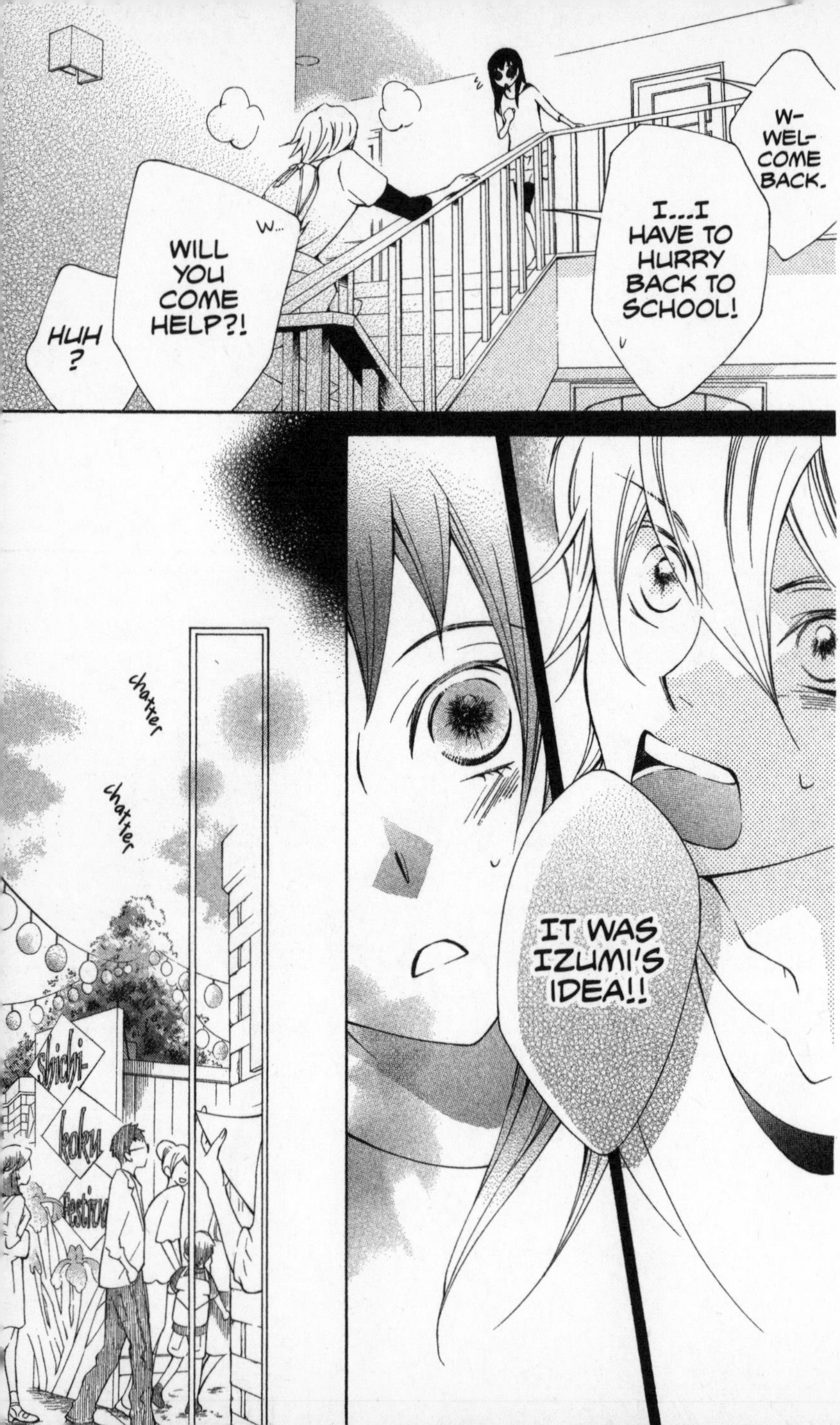
W-WEL-COME BACK.
I...I HAVE TO HURRY BACK TO SCHOOL!
W...
WILL YOU COME HELP?!
HUH?
IT WAS IZUMI'S IDEA!!
chatter
chatter
shichi-
koku

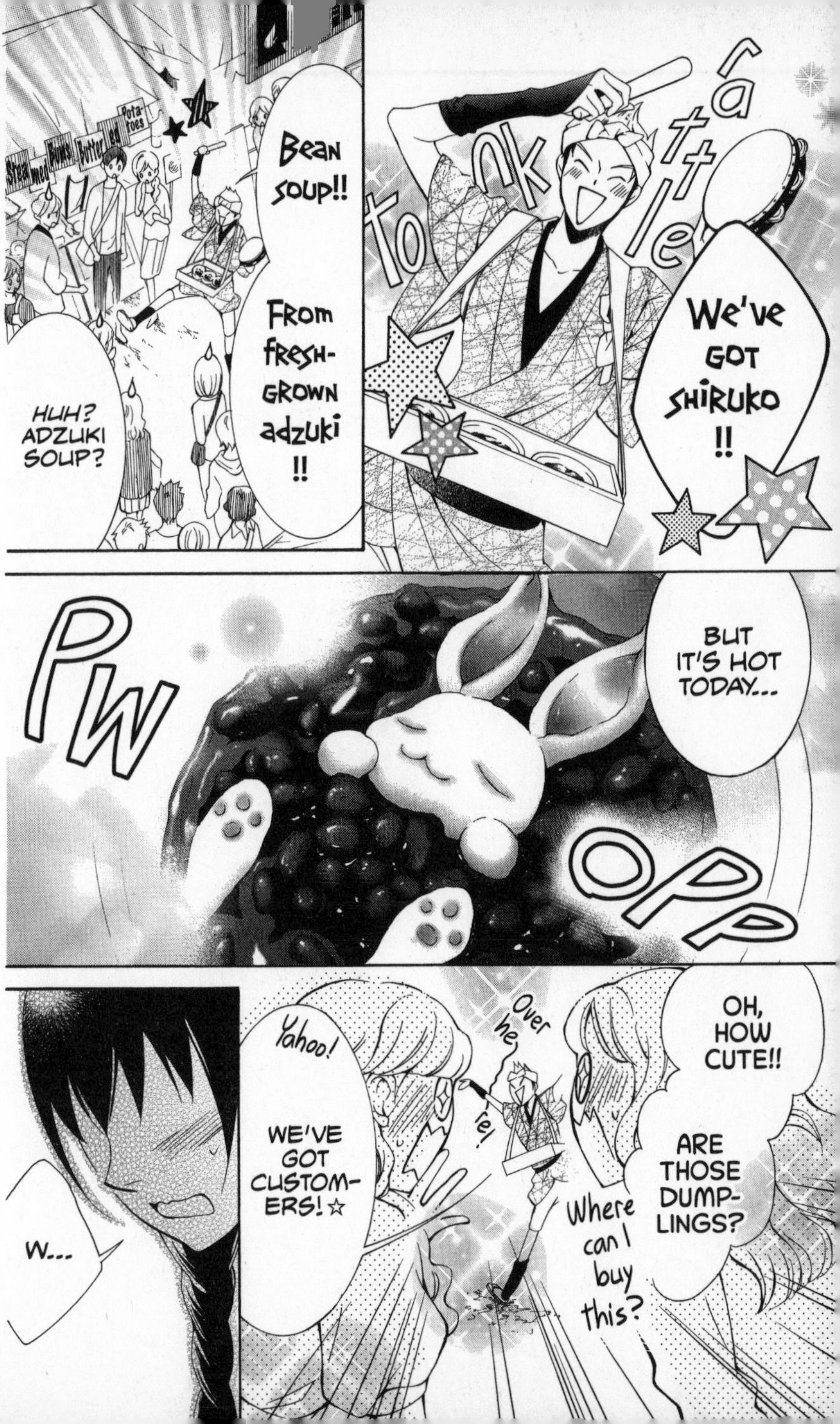
ráttle
tonk
We've got shiruko!!
Bean soup!!
From fresh-grown adzuki!!
Steamed Buns
Butter
egg
Potatoes
Huh? Adzuki soup?
But it's hot today...
Pw
opp
Oh, how cute!!
Are those dumplings?
Where can I buy this?
Over here!
Yahoo!
We've got customers! ☆
W...

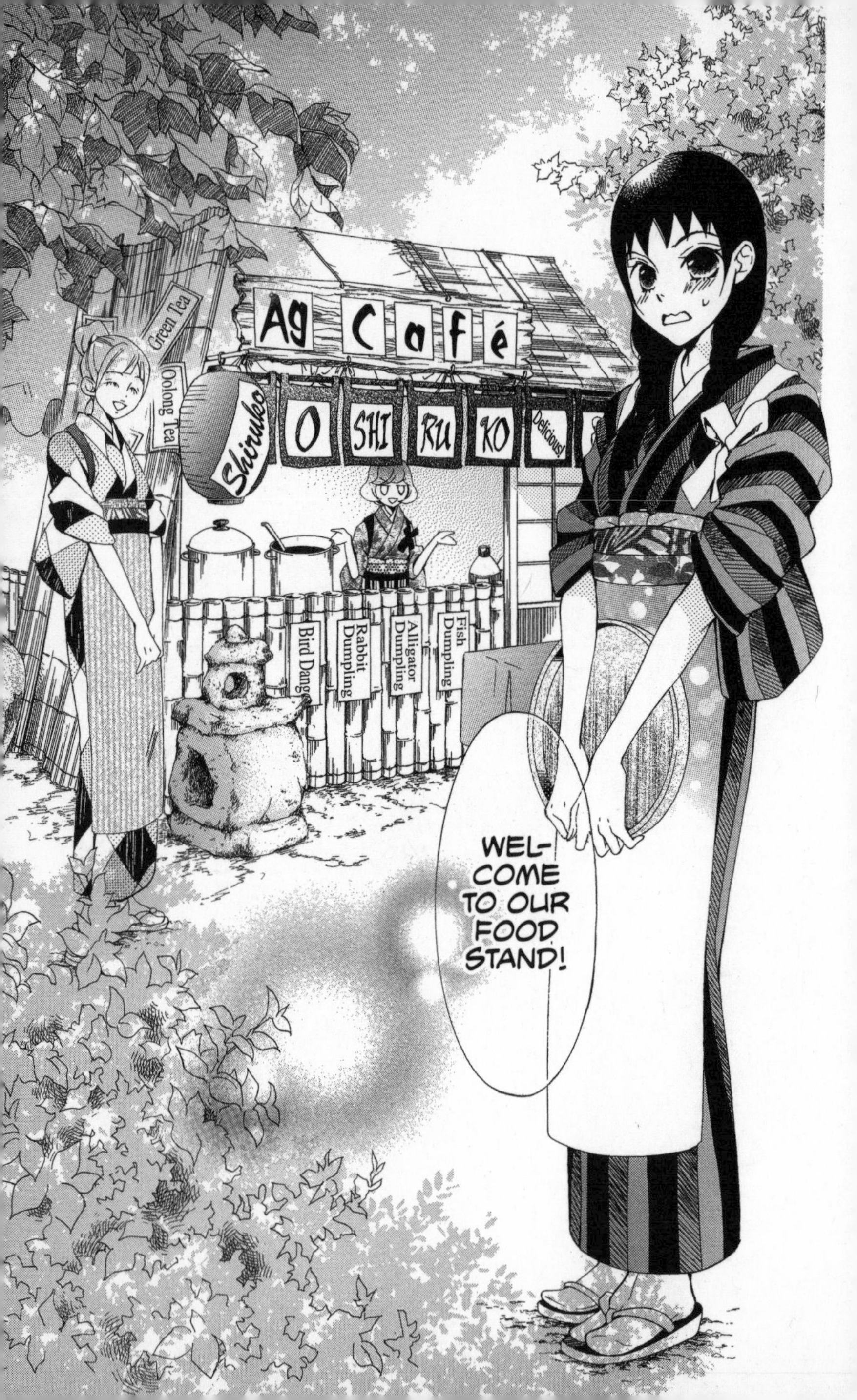
WEL-
COME
TO OUR
FOOD
STAND!
Ag Café
O SHI RU KO
Delicious!
Shiruko
Green Tea
Oolong Tea
Fish Dumpling
Alligator Dumpling
Rabbit Dumpling
Bird Dang

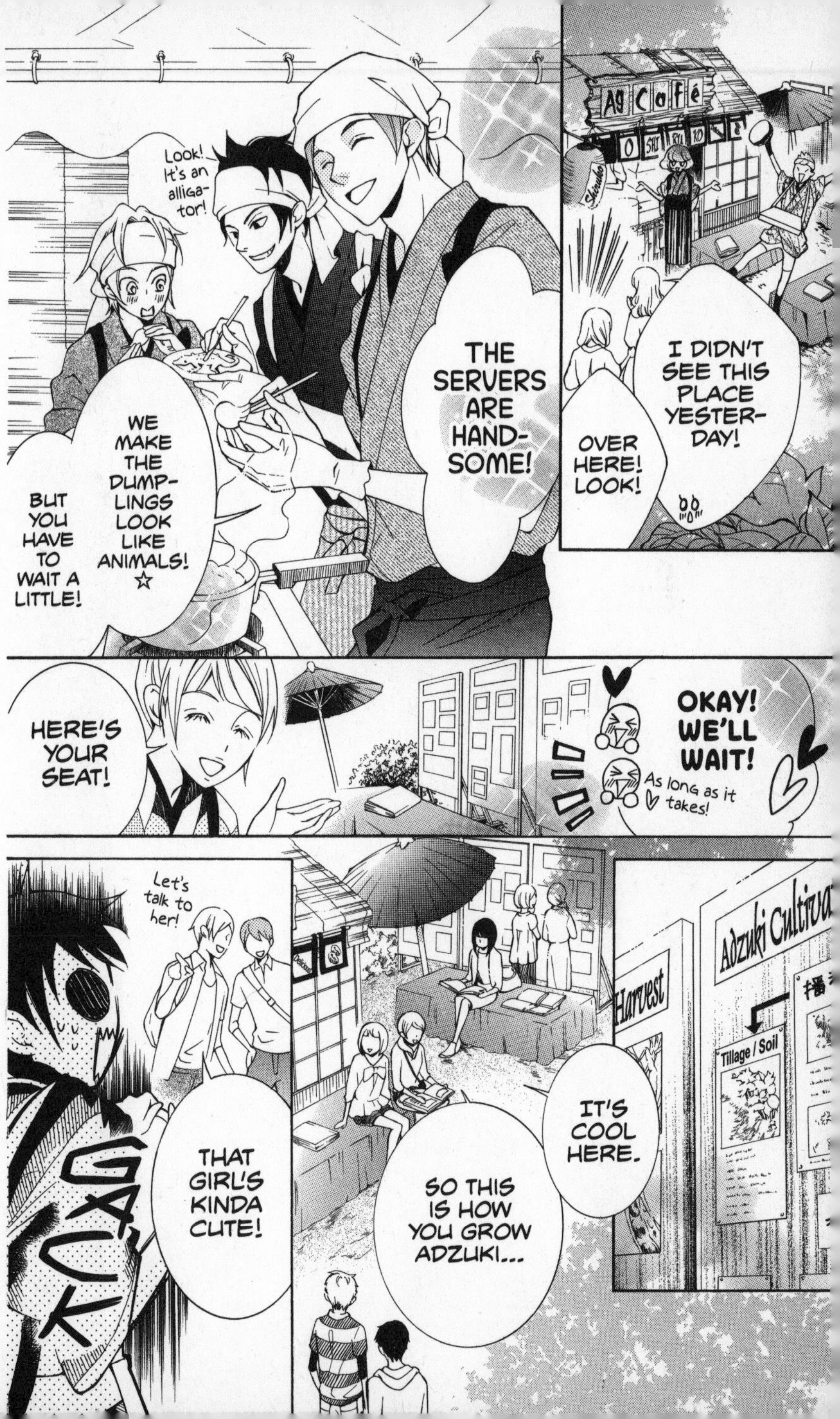
Ag Café
I DIDN'T SEE THIS PLACE YESTER-DAY!
OVER HERE! LOOK!
THE SERVERS ARE HAND-SOME!
Look! It's an alliga-tor!
WE MAKE THE DUMP-LINGS LOOK LIKE ANIMALS! ☆
BUT YOU HAVE TO WAIT A LITTLE!
OKAY! WE'LL WAIT!
As long as it takes!
HERE'S YOUR SEAT!
Harvest
Tillage / Soil
IT'S COOL HERE.
SO THIS IS HOW YOU GROW ADZUKI...
Let's talk to her!
THAT GIRL'S KINDA CUTE!
GACK

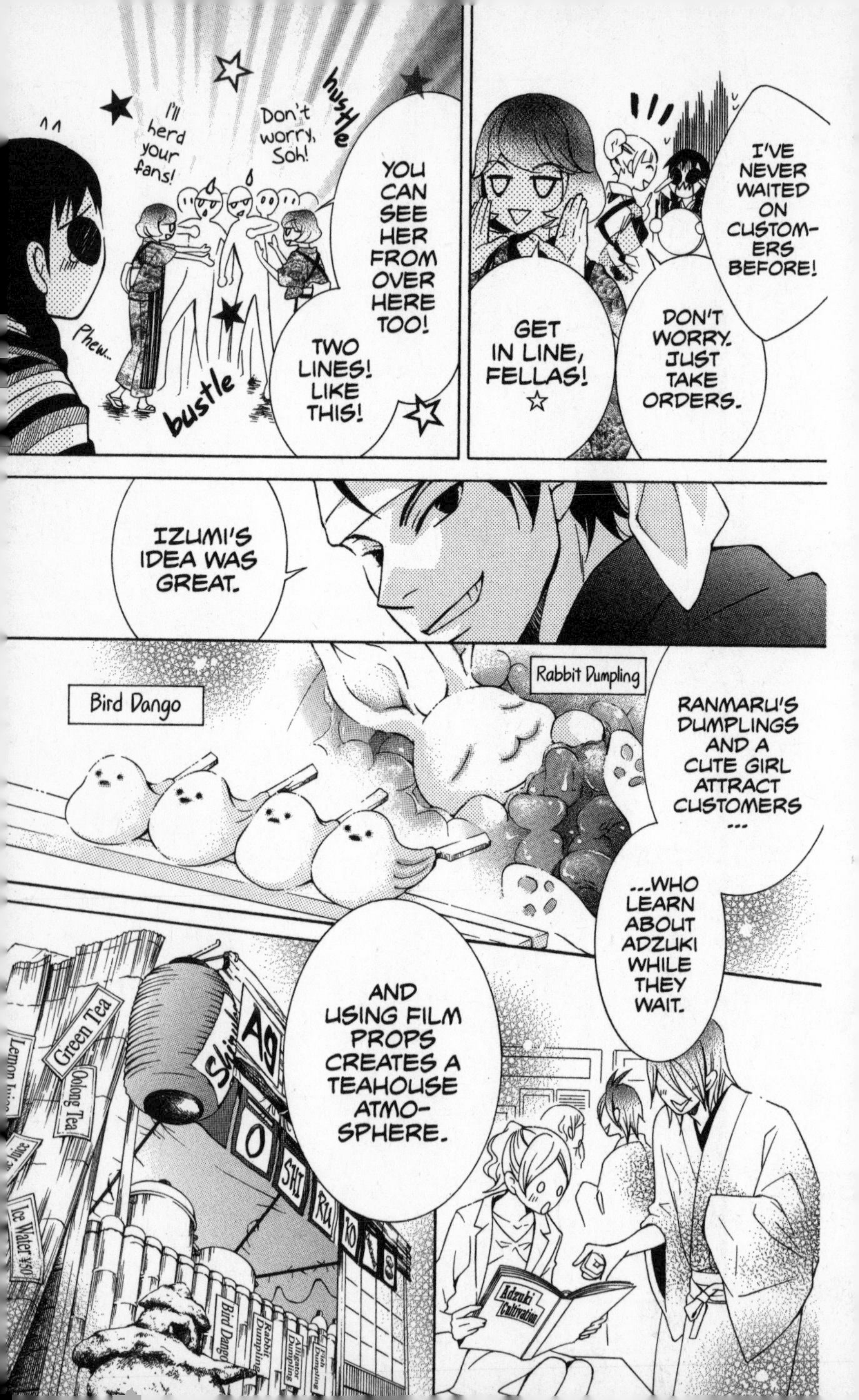

I'VE NEVER WAITED ON CUSTOM-ERS BEFORE!
DON'T WORRY. JUST TAKE ORDERS.
GET IN LINE, FELLAS! ☆
hustle
YOU CAN SEE HER FROM OVER HERE TOO!
TWO LINES! LIKE THIS!
Don't worry, Soh!
I'll herd your fans!
bustle
Phew...
IZUMI'S IDEA WAS GREAT.
Rabbit Dumpling
Bird Dango
RANMARU'S DUMPLINGS AND A CUTE GIRL ATTRACT CUSTOMERS ...
...WHO LEARN ABOUT ADZUKI WHILE THEY WAIT.
AND USING FILM PROPS CREATES A TEAHOUSE ATMO-SPHERE.
Green Tea
Oolong Tea
Ice Water ¥50
Bird Dango
Rabbit Dumpling
Alligator Dumpling
Fish Dumpling
Adzuki Cultivation

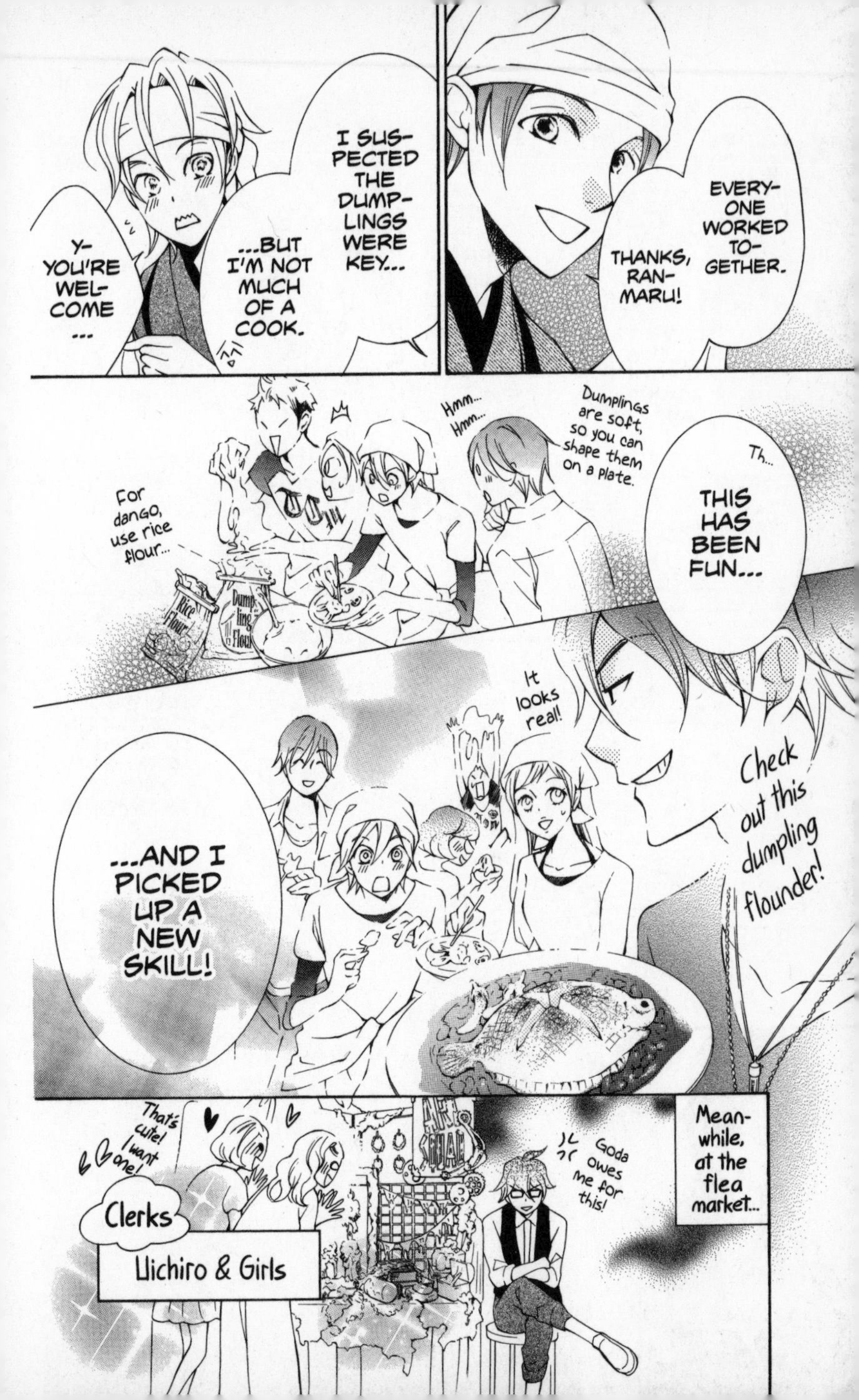
EVERYONE WORKED TOGETHER.
THANKS, RANMARU!
I SUSPECTED THE DUMPLINGS WERE KEY...
...BUT I'M NOT MUCH OF A COOK.
Y-YOU'RE WELCOME...
Th...
THIS HAS BEEN FUN...
Dumplings are soft, so you can shape them on a plate.
Hmm... Hmm...
For dango, use rice flour...
Rice Flour
Dumpling Flour
Check out this dumpling flounder!
It looks real!
...AND I PICKED UP A NEW SKILL!
Meanwhile, at the flea market...
Goda owes me for this!
That's cute! I want one!
Clerks
Iichiro & Girls

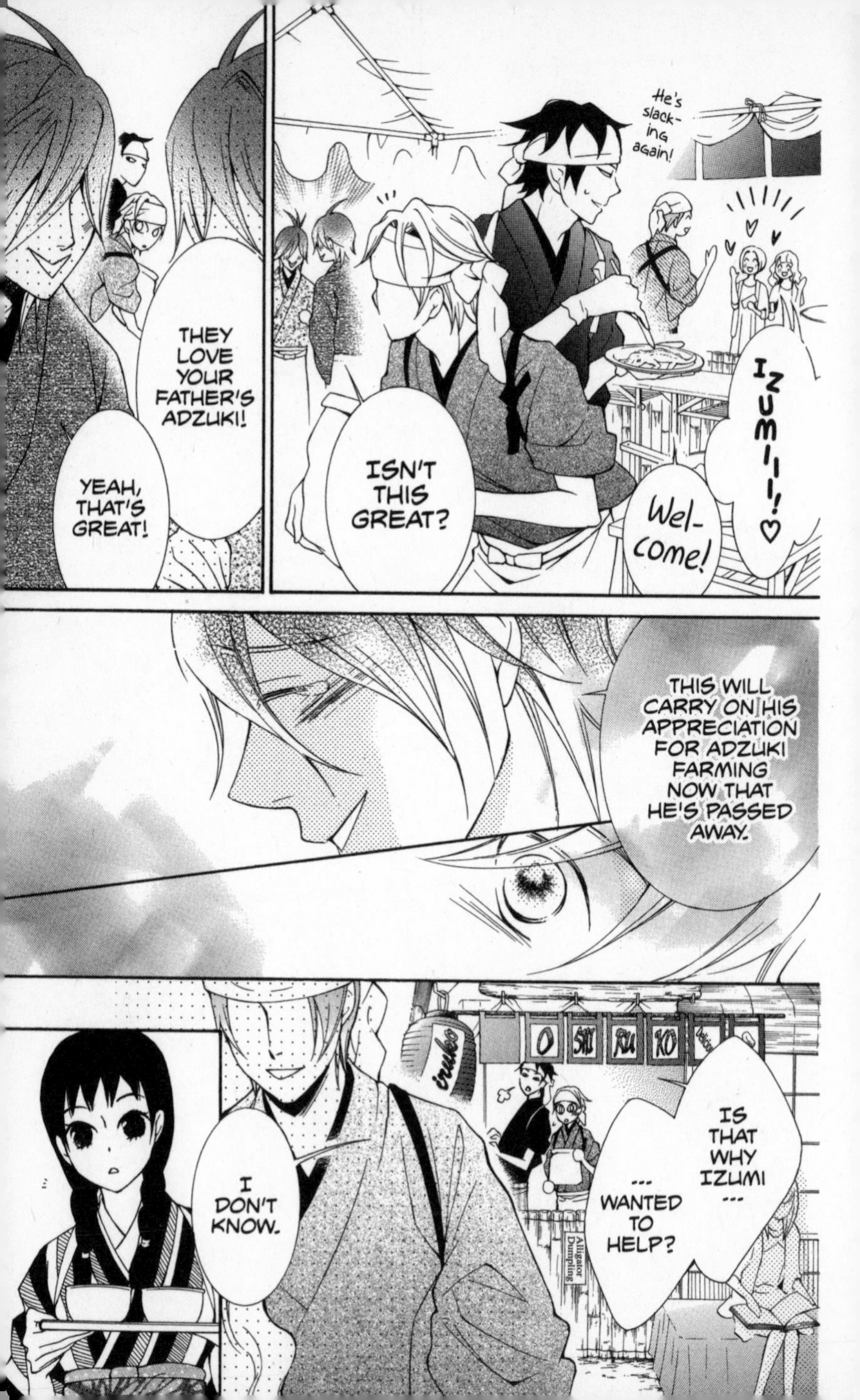
He's slack-ing again!
IZUMIII!♡
Wel-come!
ISN'T THIS GREAT?
THEY LOVE YOUR FATHER'S ADZUKI!
YEAH, THAT'S GREAT!
THIS WILL CARRY ON HIS APPRECIATION FOR ADZUKI FARMING NOW THAT HE'S PASSED AWAY.
O SHI RU KO
IS THAT WHY IZUMI ...
... WANTED TO HELP?
Alligator Dumpling
I DON'T KNOW.

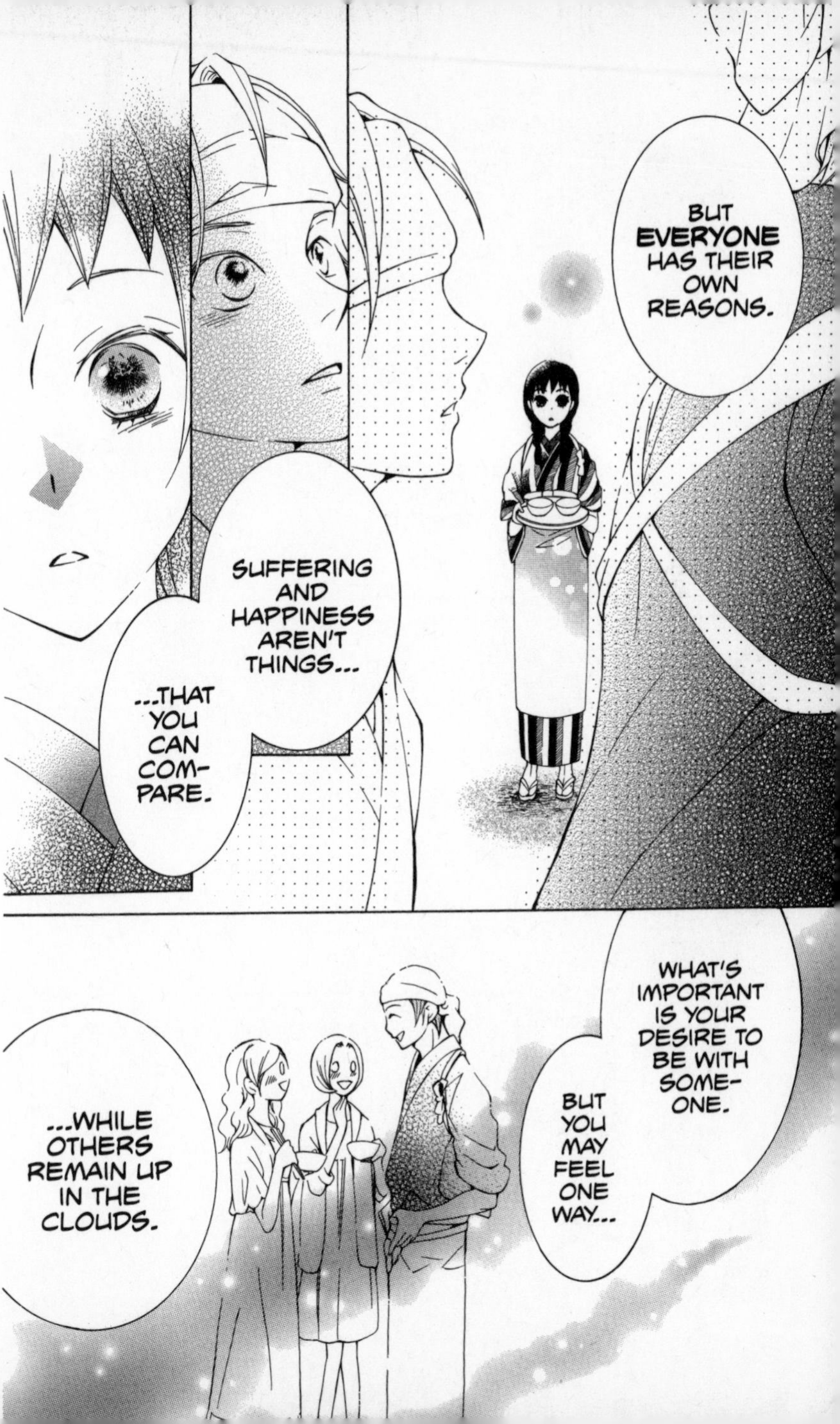
BUT EVERYONE HAS THEIR OWN REASONS.
SUFFERING AND HAPPINESS AREN'T THINGS...
...THAT YOU CAN COM-PARE.
WHAT'S IMPORTANT IS YOUR DESIRE TO BE WITH SOME-ONE.
BUT YOU MAY FEEL ONE WAY...
...WHILE OTHERS REMAIN UP IN THE CLOUDS.

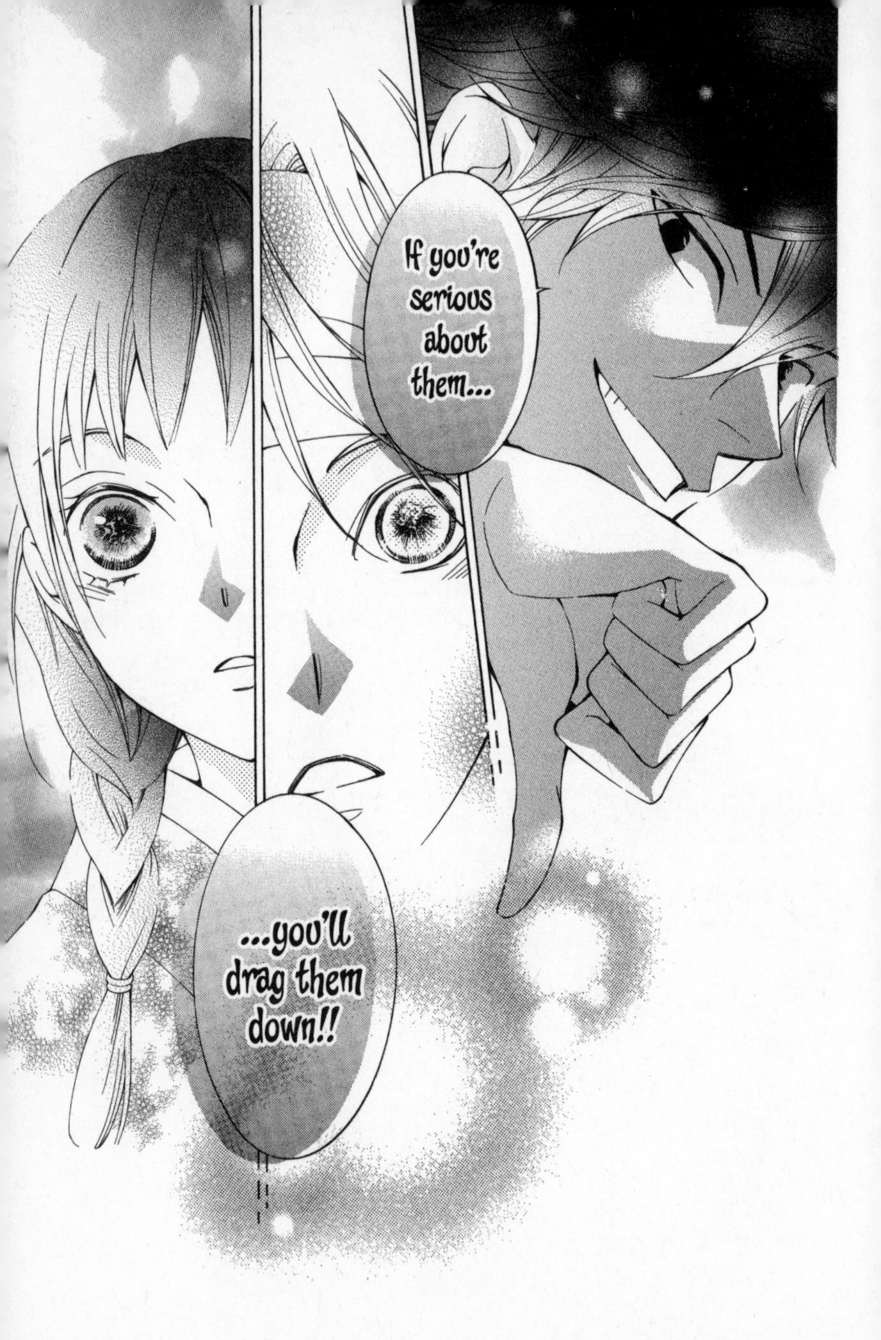
If you're serious about them...
...you'll drag them down!!

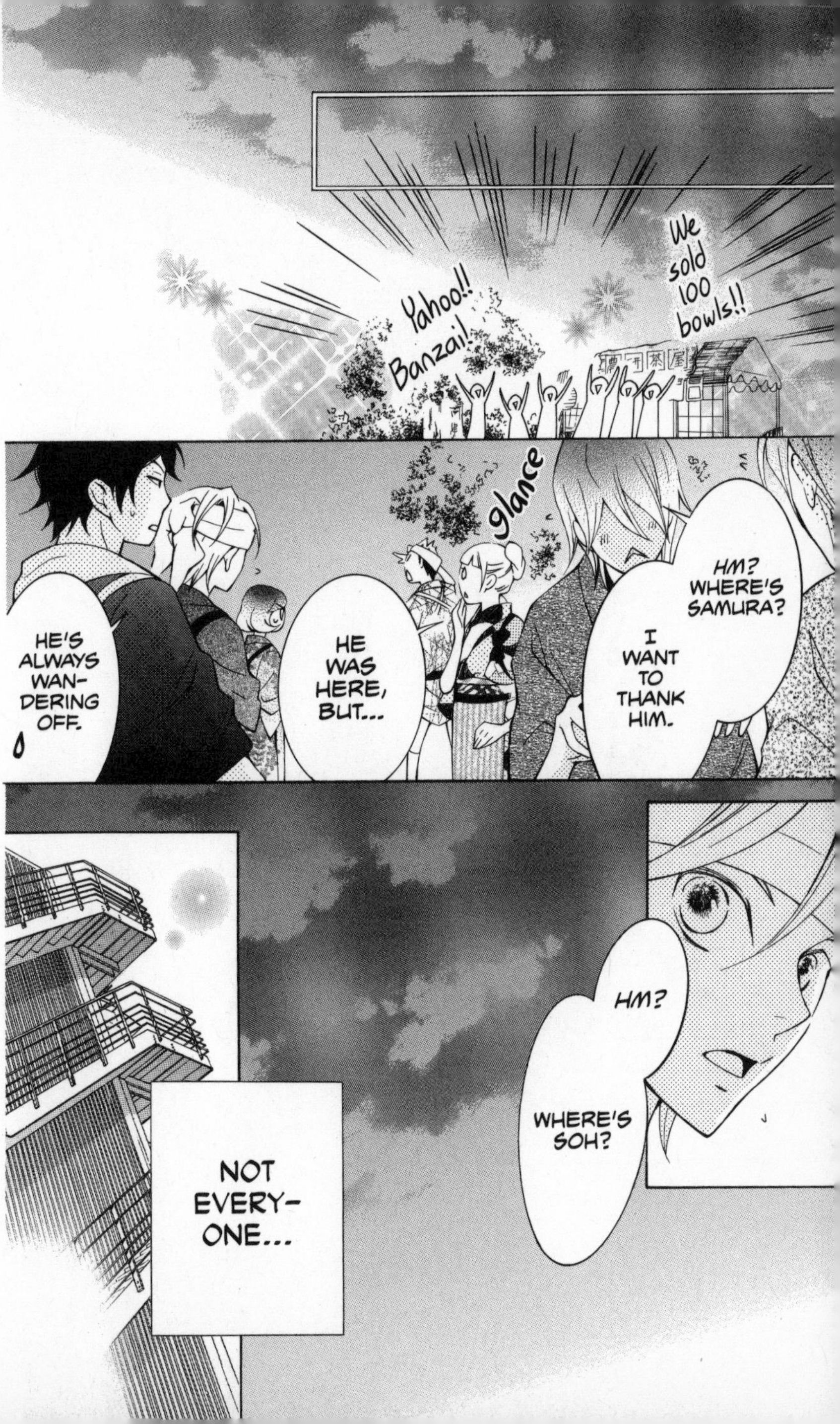
We sold 100 bowls!!
Yahoo!!
Banzai!
HM? WHERE'S SAMURA?
I WANT TO THANK HIM.
glance
HE WAS HERE, BUT...
HE'S ALWAYS WAN-DERING OFF.
HM?
WHERE'S SOH?
NOT EVERY-ONE...

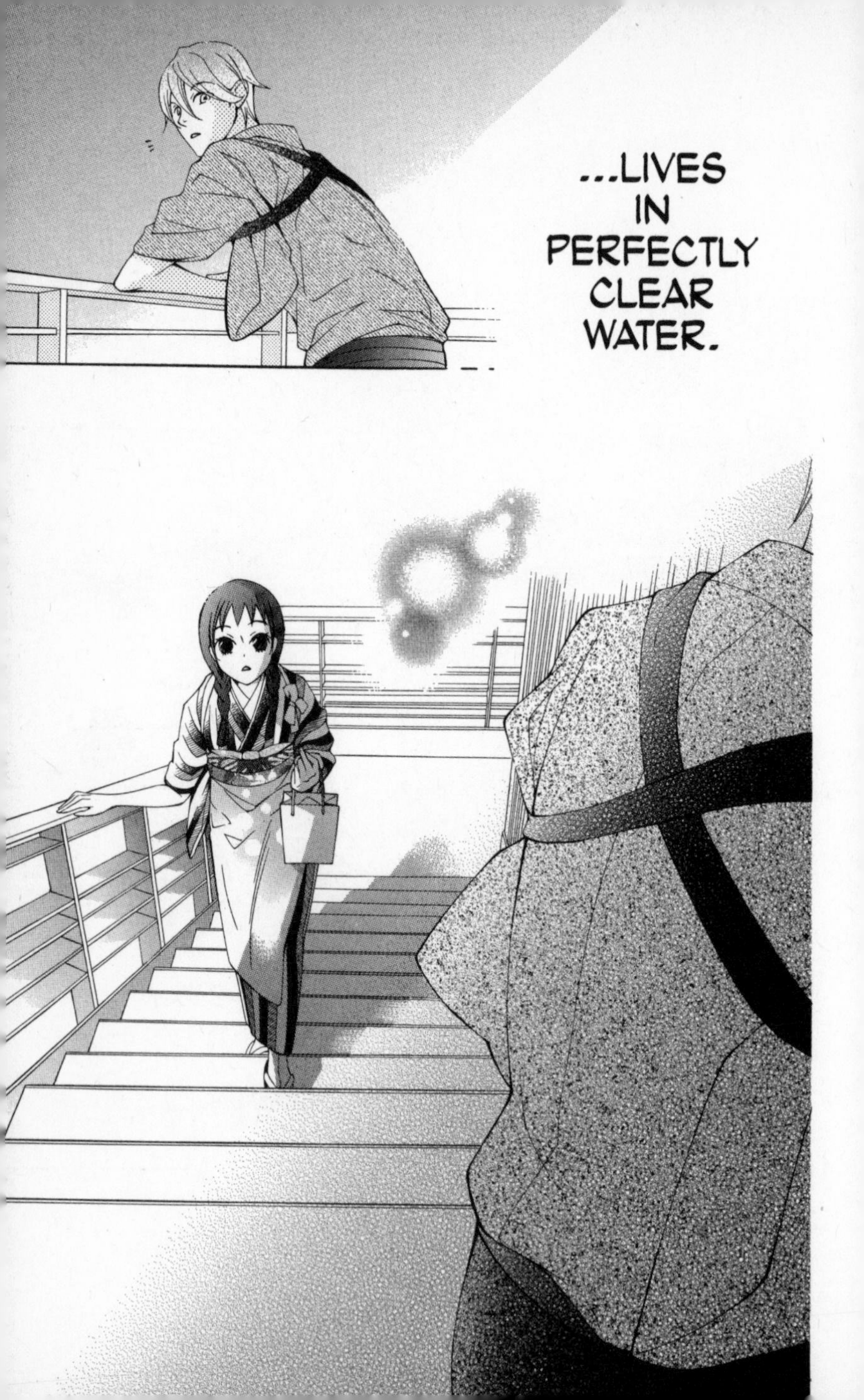
...LIVES
IN
PERFECTLY
CLEAR
WATER.

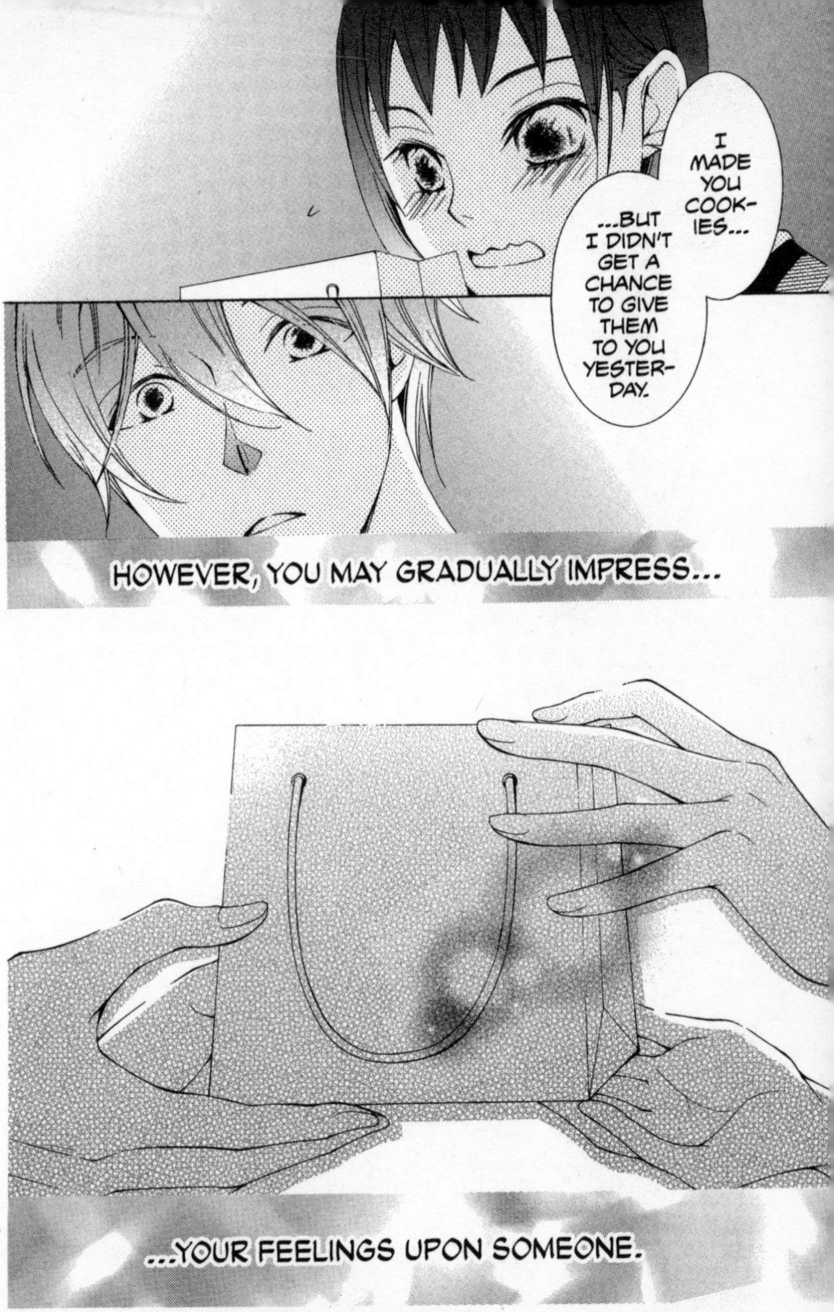
I MADE YOU COOKIES...
...BUT I DIDN'T GET A CHANCE TO GIVE THEM TO YOU YESTERDAY.
HOWEVER, YOU MAY GRADUALLY IMPRESS...
...YOUR FEELINGS UPON SOMEONE.

BEHIND THE SCENES!! VOLUME 4 – THE END

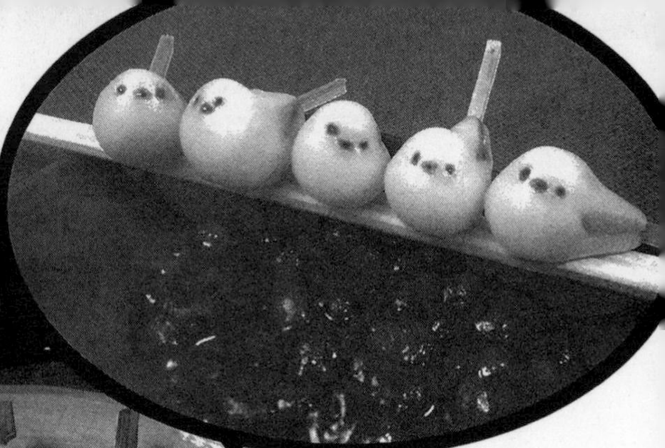

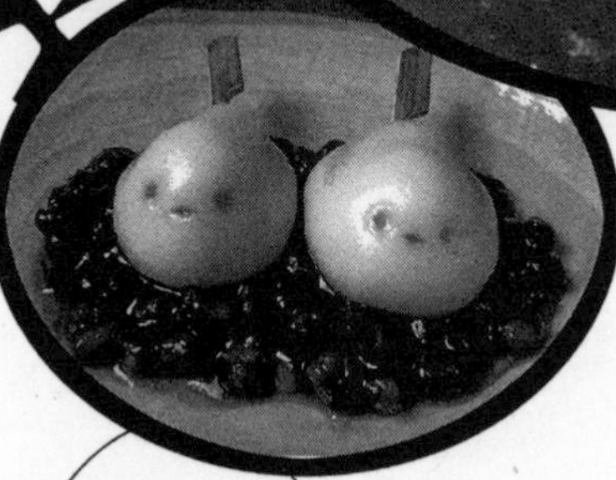

Bird Dango by Rodemu-san

The rabbit dumplings and other dumplings that appeared in scene 21 were all designed by Rodemu-san, who appeared in volume 3. They're so cute that I'm including some photos here and with my author note...

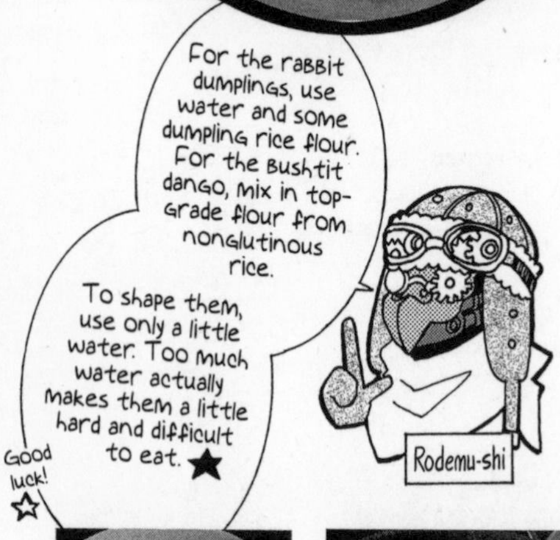
For the rabbit dumplings, use water and some dumpling rice flour. For the bushtit dango, mix in top-grade flour from nonglutinous rice.
To shape them, use only a little water. Too much water actually makes them a little hard and difficult to eat. ★
Good luck! ☆
Rodemu-shi

☆Ray dumpling☆

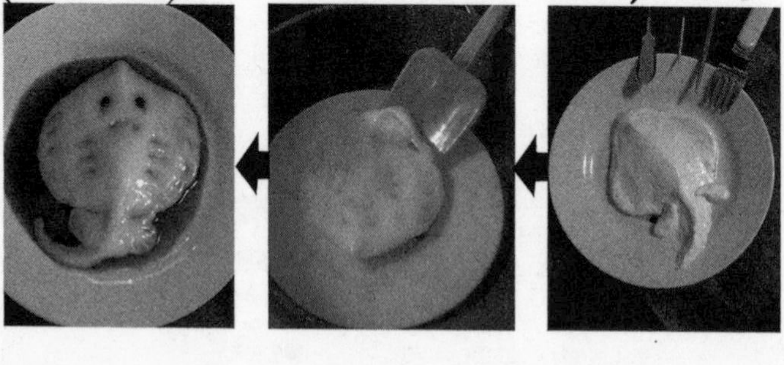

GLOSSARY

Page 70, panel 4: Kon Ichikawa
A Japanese film director.

Page 126, panel 4: Fermented soybeans, pickled plums
Natto is a type of fermented soybean considered to be an acquired taste due to its strong smell and slimy texture. *Umeboshi* are unripe ume (a fruit similar to plums or apricots) pickled in salt.

Page 137, sidebar: Fancy Dance
Fancy Dance is a manga that was made into a movie.

Page 163, panel 1: Oshiruko
A hot, sweet red bean soup that sometimes has mochi (rice-flour dumplings) in it.

Page 164, panel 6: Adzuki
Red mung beans. Often used in sweets like oshiruko.

Page 175, panel 1: Dango
Rice-flour dumplings threaded onto a skewer and frequently topped with sweet syrups or pastes.

Page 178, panel 3: Dumpling flour
Called *shiratamako* in Japanese, it is refined rice flour made especially for dumplings.